Paul Gauguin

Nancy Mowll Mathews

# Paul Gauguin An Erotic Life

Yale University Press *New Haven and London*

Designed by Daphne Geismar.
Set in Scala and ScalaSans type by Amy Storm.
Printed in Hong Kong through World Print

Library of Congress Cataloging-in-Publication Data
Mathews, Nancy Mowll.
Paul Gauguin : an erotic life / Nancy Mowll Mathews.
     p.    cm.
Includes bibliographical references and index.
ISBN 0–300–09109–5 (alk. paper)
1. Gauguin, Paul, 1848–1903. 2. Gauguin, Paul, 1848–1903 — Psychology.
3. Gauguin, Paul, 1848–1903—Sexual behavior. 4. Painters—France—
Biography. I. Title.
ND553.G27  M378  2001
759.4—dc21

2001001878

A catalogue record for this book is available from the British Library.

The paper in this book meets the guidelines for permanence and
durability of the Committee on Production Guidelines for Book Longevity
of the Council on Library Resources.

10 9 8 7 6 5 4 3 2 1

Contents

**Preface** vii

**Introduction** 1
1   **Ancestry: The Moscosos and the Gauguins** 5
2   **Young Man in Paris** 18
3   **Impressionism** 34
4   **The Crash** 48
5   **PGo Emerges** 63
6   **The Lost Continent of Atlantis** 78
7   **The Sun God** 91
8   **Theo and Vincent: Flying Too Close to the Sun** 106
9   **The Martyr** 126
10   **Desperate Measures** 145
11   **Tahitian Tourist** 168
12   **Return to Paris** 190
13   **Tahitian Resident** 211
14   **Final Retreat** 235

**Appendix: Mette Gauguin Letters** 259
**Notes** 271
**Acknowledgments** 309
**Index** 311

# Preface

This is not a book.
—Paul Gauguin, "Avant et après," 1903

This is not a biography. That is, it is not a narrow enterprise isolating Gauguin the person from the social and economic forces surrounding him.[1] Rather, this is the study of an artist who was extraordinarily aware of his social context and created art in direct response to it. It is also a study of the "biography" that Gauguin created for himself through his letters and auto-biographical writings (and, to a certain extent, through his visual art) and how that differs from the picture painted by other documentary sources. My life of Gauguin, consequently, has required me to employ not just traditional biographical methods but psychological, social, and philosophical methods as well. To grapple with the considerable impact Gauguin's personality had on his art and rise to prominence in the art world, I could not avoid psychoanalytical or social-psychological interpretations. To put Gauguin into a social context, I had to confront the structures of power, including class and gender, that affected his behavior. To understand the metaphysical implications of his work, if any, I had to investigate the philosophical framework in which he operated and apply recent theories of verbal and visual language to interpret his unique forms of communication. In this preface, I will outline my approach and how it relates to other recent literature on Gauguin.

Paul Gauguin was living in the French colonial capital Papeete, on the island of Tahiti, when Sigmund Freud published his first major psychoanalytic treatise, *The Interpretation of Dreams*, in 1899.[2] Though three thousand miles apart, it is hard to imagine two cultural figures more evocative of the symbolist milieu at the end of the nineteenth century, particularly the contemporary fascination with the role of sexuality in human creative acts. To account for Gauguin's erotic life, therefore, it would be folly to ignore the stunning parallels between Gauguin's behavior and beliefs and the psychoanalytic theories expounded by Freud that have shaped notions of personality to this day. In fact, psychoanalytic interpretations of Gauguin's life and art abound in the art historical literature of recent years.[3] Gauguin's life offers exceptional opportunities for Freudian interpretation—from the loss of his father before his second birthday, to his frequent depiction of such phallic symbols as snakes and birds, to his insistence on the health benefits of sexual freedom, to his untimely death from syphilis in 1903, at the age of fifty-four.

Most important, I have found that Freudian theories of the roles sexuality and aggression play in creativity are extraordinarily useful in understanding Gauguin.[4] What I confronted time and again in going over the verbal and visual evidence was how central sex and violence were to

Gauguin—separately and, very often, in combination. Rather than dismiss this evidence as irrelevant to Gauguin's art[5] or downplay Gauguin as an artist because of it,[6] I propose that Gauguin made excellent use of these twin drives in developing his greatest works. When dealing with the less fundamental complexities of his life events, I point out possible Freudian interpretations even when they do not, to me, seem the most compelling lens through which to see the artist. Perhaps because of the historical coincidence of a psychologist and an artist espousing similar cultural beliefs, or perhaps because Gauguin happens to offer a textbook illustration of psychoanalytic theory, it is impossible not to take Freud's ideas seriously in interpreting Gauguin's personality.[7]

Having said this, I must confess that I have not used a strict Freudian methodology in my interpretation of Gauguin's life. I think it is more accurate to say that my method is a mixture of pre-Freudian vernacular psychology and postmodern pluralism. Freud himself credited poets and writers (to whom I will add art historians) with arriving at many important psychological conclusions through creative empathy.[8] Those who know my work on Mary Cassatt and Maurice Prendergast will recognize that I have taken the same commonsense approach to Gauguin. Like the nineteenth-century empiricists (including Freud), I gather as much evidence in a case study as possible and then draw conclusions that I believe are revealing and plausible.

At the same time, my approach is inevitably colored by the time in which I live. I put my subjectivity on constant view. In fact, to borrow a postmodern understanding of clinical psychoanalytic practice, my purpose is not to arrive at absolute truth but to enter into a dialogue with my "patient" in order that together we might forge a new understanding of his behavior.[9] Another way such an interactive approach yields important new results is in helping us understand Gauguin in dialogue with his own audience of friends, critics, and collectors. In psychoanalysis, this construction of culture is called an enactment,[10] whereby the artist and the work of art are part of a dynamic interplay that includes the internal and external realities of the artist.[11] The quality of performance that this model recognizes is particularly apt for an artist like Gauguin, who was theatrical in dress, speech, and the presentation of his art to the public. This adaptation of classical psychoanalysis to include lessons learned from semiotics and social and feminist history seems to me to give a rich new framework for understanding visual culture.

In the spirit of pluralism, I do not hesitate to bring in other recent psychological writings to help interpret Gauguin's behavior. His overt presentation of sexuality and aggression in his creative productions, such as *Manao Tupapau (Spirit of the Dead Watching)* (1891) and its related explanatory text in the pseudo-autobiographical *Noa Noa* (1893), for example, begs for interpretation in light of recent studies of male codes of honor, wife beating, and "artificial horror"[12] that have been carried out by a range of social psychologists, in addition to Freudian theorists.

The multifaceted psychological method I employed led me to an understanding of Gauguin that differs from that of many (but not all) of my colleagues in one essential point. From the evidence I was able to weigh, I found Gauguin to be intelligent, witty, and productive—but not spiritual or scholarly. Whereas his writings on religion, myth, and social issues are often emotional, they tend to be derivative in content and vengeful in spirit. I find the religious, mythological, and socially radical content of his art to be similarly shallow, albeit aesthetically intriguing. Therefore, as much as I admire the voluminous recent literature that explores Gauguin's connections to either Western or Polynesian religions and social movements and interprets his art in that light, I have been unable to expand on it.[13]

As a feminist and a social liberal, I cannot apply these methods to my Gauguin studies without finding Gauguin on the winning side of the classic social power struggles. He portrayed himself as the helpless victim of a domineering wife and a callous art establishment, but in fact he used his privileged status as a well-born European male to seduce and intimidate those around him in order to achieve personal and professional goals. While this does not make him less interesting as an artist and a person, it does make me doubt the efficacy of interpreting him as a Marxist or feminist cultural hero.[14]

Those familiar with the Gauguin bibliography will see that my combination of empirical and postmodern interactive methodologies does not allow me to build easily on the writings about Gauguin by my predecessors and contemporaries. This should in no way be interpreted as disrespect for the contributions made by those scholars, nor do I mean to suggest that my approach yields complete interpretations of works of art. Rather, my interpretations primarily relate to the artist's *intention* and his interaction with audiences that were known to him.[15] My conclusions are meant to enrich our understanding of his works of art—not reduce them to one narrow meaning. I look forward to a productive dialogue with those colleagues who disagree with my methods.

There is yet another difficulty. In revisiting all the documentary evidence I could gather on Gauguin, I was struck by how many factual inaccuracies had been handed down to today's scholars. Rereading of the correspondence to, from, and about Gauguin, as well as ferreting out other archival documents, allowed me to make slight but important alterations in the accepted chronology and understanding of his actions. In aid of clarity, I have pointed out the instances where my documentary evidence corrects or contradicts previous assumptions.

Another outcome of my close reading of documentary evidence was to discover discrepancies between the circumstances of Gauguin's life (for example, the state of his health, finances, and employment) and the way he portrayed them to his many correspondents. In some cases we see him telling different versions of events to the different recipients of his letters according to the favors he hopes to elicit from them. The correspondent who received the most exaggerated version of his life was his wife, Mette, toward whom he felt guilt and anger, yet from whom he harbored an almost childish desire for sympathy. Unfortunately the letters most often used by scholars to interpret Gauguin's life have been the letters that the conscientious Mette saved and their son Pola donated to the Bibliothèque d'Art et d'Archéologie Fondation Jacques Doucet, Paris. These letters were badly transcribed and lightly edited by Maurice Malingue (in 1947) to eliminate passages unbecoming to Gauguin—especially in regard to his wife. Reading the original, unedited letters does a great deal to diminish the sincerity, not to mention the heroism, of the artist. In surveying all the existing letters, it became clear to me that Gauguin was more manipulative and calculating in his dealings with his wife, influential friends, dealers, and patrons than many people recognized.[16] Some scholars will be distressed at my interpretation, but the result, I feel, is a much more plausible construction of a man using all the skills at his command to succeed in an incredibly competitive profession.

We can now see how preoccupied Gauguin was with marketing his work. Although all artists must pay more attention to dealers and patrons than we like to acknowledge, the letters reveal that the art market was far more than a necessary evil for Gauguin.[17] With his background in the stock market, he entered the art world with a deeper sense of sales techniques than most artists had, and began his association with the Impressionists acting not only as a fellow artist but also as a conduit to buyers in the financial district. Gauguin's arrangements with dealers, agents, friends—as well as his wife—to sell his works were never-ending, and his reporting on his financial situation varied from correspondent to correspondent.

If one of my goals in writing this book was to understand how the related concepts of eroticism, sexuality, and aggression functioned in the life of Gauguin, another was to see how Gauguin constructed an erotic identity for himself even when his actual day-to-day existence was far from erotic. His ability to tell powerful stories about his experiences provides us with what anthropologists have termed thick description.[18] How participants in a culture describe as their experience of a game or spectacle, say, is quite different from what an anthropologist observes about the same event. The participant's testimony, when studied in the context of other sources of information and the outside witness's observations, can lead to a multifaceted understanding of that individual and the cultural environment.[19] It is this outcome that I seek in *Paul Gauguin: An Erotic Life*.

My interest in the power of language, both verbal and visual, to shape ideas coincides with a century-long investigation into the philosophy of perception, from Edmund Husserl's concept of phenomenology, through semiotics, to Michel Foucault's more recent writings on power. Philosophers like to see themselves as purveyors of insights into the higher reaches of the mind, in agreement with the person who wrote, "Psychoanalysis can safely be left to rummage about in the dark basement of the mind, but the mind's sunlit upper stories, where reason and morality reside, are the residences of philosophy."[20] Gauguin, in his writings, echoes many of the social critics and philosophers of his time, such as Georg Brandès and Friedrich Nietzsche, to whom he would have been introduced through his Danish wife's intellectual circles as well as through his Parisian friends. Gauguin's desire to use language to shape the world's understanding of him warrants cross-references to historical and current philosophical theory.

No one reading this book will miss my personal disapproval of Gauguin's abusive behavior toward his wife and others who were close to him. Equally, no reader will doubt that I admire most of what this artist produced, both his art objects and the inspirational message that subsequent generations have gleaned from them. My purpose in making such value judgments is neither to diminish nor to aggrandize Gauguin's contribution to world culture, but to give a personal dimension to a historical interpretation. Reasoned consideration and even personal judgment will, I hope, enrich our understanding of the man and his art so that they may continue to intrigue and inspire the generations to come.

# Introduction

It may have been an accident of nature that eroticism became a touchstone of Gauguin's life and art. Paul Gauguin (1848–1903) was physically attractive — not classically handsome, but exuding a heavy-lidded sensuality that others, particularly men, found intriguing (fig. 1). Few artists inspired so many descriptions of their physical appearance. Reminiscences of Gauguin record how he stood out in a crowd, how his expression was hypnotically inscrutable, and how his body had a menacing power that seemed just barely held in check. Recognizing his own appeal, Gauguin came to expect as his due the influence he exerted over others by sheer physicality.

Alternately seductive and bullying in his manner, he capitalized on the powers of his body not simply to reap physical pleasure (sexually and athletically) but also to carry out his wishes in the larger professional arenas of his life. His method of dealing with most people and situations was first to cajole and persuade, then, if not successful, to threaten and menace. His unceasing quest for power over others ultimately destroyed most of his personal relationships, but can be credited with his eventual success in the competitive international art world of his day. The inborn power and talent of his body — which he honed to a fine degree both in his art and in such avocations as fencing — led him also to travel alone around the world, to face the unknown and the strange without fear, and to define foreign cultures in physical terms, such as race and sexuality.

Paradoxically, Gauguin's pride in the masterful power of his body was accompanied by a fascination with the pleasures of weakness and yielding, most often described as feminine but not necessarily referring to women. Androgyny as a concept was embraced by the avant-garde circles that Gauguin frequented, and he courted the attention of younger men with his theatrical costumes, his pleas for monetary and other practical assistance, and his martyr's mien. Although he did not hesitate to physically abuse both men and women and evidently was titillated by their submission, he also imagined the pleasurable sensation of receiving such abuse.[1] His many paintings of Eve frightened by the snake attest to his belief in the eroticism of both rape and submission.

Another paradox revealed in examining the documentary evidence of Gauguin's erotic life is how little actual love he experienced. Although there can be little doubt that he formed sexual relationships with women (he is known to have fathered at least ten children), only his wife, Mette, can be said to have been an object of his love. Few details exist of relationships with the women whose names are known to us, such as Juliette Huet, Annah the

Javanese, the three Tahitians—Titi, Tehamana, and Pahura a Tai—and the Marquesan Vaeoho (also called Marie-Rose), aside from slight mentions in letters. Even their participation in his life as models is difficult to verify. Still, Gauguin disclosed, in his few mentions of these Polynesian liaisons, the young ages of his *vahines*, indicating his titillation with the subject of sex with adolescents.

His close male friends, on the other hand, were clearly dear to him, and those relationships had a patent homoerotic element. Although he took up residence with five male friends at one time or another, however, it cannot be shown conclusively that the liaisons were fully sexual or romantic. Firsthand accounts of Gauguin's social behavior give the impression of a detached observer of the erotic adventures of others, rather than the impression of an actively engaged amorous artist. His pose as a daringly erotic man, willing to actively challenge taboos regarding marriage, homosexuality, and sex with children cannot be backed up with significant evidence.

Instead, the erotica of his imagination most often flowed into his conversation, his writings, and his art. He decorated his homes with pornographic objects—many of his own making, including a collection of carved wooden phalluses—and held social gatherings of friends and neighbors there. This crude use of erotica in a public forum was significantly refined when he created the paintings and sculpture intended for exhibitions in

Paris, Brussels, and elsewhere in Europe that he hoped would establish him as one of the great artists of his day. Into these carefully produced works he poured all his sophistication and skill in manipulating color, form, and subject matter, along with hints of his daring, transgressive eroticism. He knew his audience well. The works were and are appreciated openly for their beauty and subliminally for their erotic content.

In the end, it is the art that makes Gauguin's erotic life worth investigating. His struggle for prominence in the art world of his day is thus the subtext of any biography. Because of his background in the investment world, Gauguin was perhaps more acutely aware of the business of art than most artists. But he was also aware of the personal ingredient in obtaining success; he was not above courting, and politicking among, powerful people to gain an introduction to an important dealer or to secure a key review from an influential art critic. In this arena he once again employed his seductive charms and appealed whenever possible to the erotic interests of those he needed to impress. At times, as when he lived with Vincent van Gogh, he traded his time and attention for money in an arrangement that was dangerously close to prostitution. If, in his writings, he portrayed marriage and other "normal" social relationships in terms of prostitution, we can safely say that he knew the subject from both sides.

Gauguin's use of his powers of seduction to manipulate his wife and friends and to achieve his professional goals is a key to understanding his life, that of a complex man and gifted artist. His discovery of the sexual and socially tolerant climate of Tahiti, which encouraged the flowering of his erotic imagination, unfortunately also coincided with early signs of the onset of syphilis. This multisymptom disease gradually attacked Gauguin's body, crippling his legs and causing internal hemorrhaging. By 1900 the source of his magnetic power over others was seriously eroded, although Gauguin continued to use his voice, his writings, and his art to dominate those around him. Finally, in 1903, his body gave out, and he died in his new house in the Marquesas. But thanks to the memoir he had completed some months before, and with the complicity of new friends in Atuona and old friends in Paris, he managed to disseminate his thoughts and adventures and to create a provocative self-portrait for the annals of history. If we now, a hundred years later, prefer to modify the myth with a more human and believable narrative, we do so with a genuine appreciation of this artist's imagination and the mythic persona with which he reinvented himself.

3

Gauguin was born to a family with a history of sexual violence and piquant cruelty. Because his father died when he was an infant, the young Eugène Henri Paul Gauguin naturally gravitated to his mother's side of the family, which was dominated by the Spanish-Peruvian Moscosos. In this branch were colorful figures whose passions led them to form irregular liaisons, to carry on feuds across two continents, and to threaten each other with physical and psychological violence. Not only may we assume that Gauguin inherited some of his ancestors' personality traits, but we may also deduce that this extraordinary family had a practical impact on his life.[1]

Gauguin was one-eighth Peruvian. His great-grandfather Don Mariano de Tristan Moscoso was the scion of an old Spanish family that had been established in Arequipa, south of Lima, since the seventeenth century. Like many other Spanish-Peruvian upper-class children, Don Mariano was sent to Paris to be educated. He pursued a military career in Peru and, in the 1790s, was sent to Spain to command Peruvian troops there (Peru was still under Spanish rule). While in Spain he met and married a French woman, Anne-Pierre Laisnay, whose family had fled across the border during the Reign of Terror. The young couple had settled in Paris by 1800; there they led a fashionable life in the wealthy South American community, which included such figures as the future South American liberator, Simón Bolívar.

Because they had not filed the proper civil marriage forms, the union of Moscoso and Laisnay was deemed invalid in the eyes of both the French government and the Tristan Moscoso family in Peru, and upon the premature death of Don Mariano in 1807, the young widow and her two children were cut off from his considerable holdings in France and in South America. Laisnay spent the rest of her life in court trying to overturn this ruling.[2]

When their daughter, Flora Célestine (Gauguin's grandmother), came of age, she took up the battle, journeying to Peru in 1833–34 to appeal to the family (fig. 2). This strategy was modestly successful in financial terms in spite of the resistance of her father's brother, the charming but wily Don Pio de Tristan Moscoso. The trip was even more fruitful socially: a connection was formed with the Peruvian relatives, many of whom had spent time in Paris as students, pleasure seekers, or merchants and investors. Flora brought up her daughter, Aline (Gauguin's mother), in these social circles in Paris, and Aline continued the connection while raising her own children, Paul and Marie. This fashionable group of wealthy and powerful South American expatriates was much like the better-known colony of international businessmen and pleasure seekers from the United States and Canada.

Paul Gauguin's entrée into these rarefied circles bolstered his early successes on the stock exchange and in the art world. As important as Gauguin's Peruvian bloodline was, his later romantic claim to be descended from the Incas cannot be substantiated.[3] The Spanish roots of the Tristan Moscosos could be traced back to the Borgias, and in Peru the family intermarried only with other Spanish ("Criole") families. Some prominent Peruvians did indeed have Inca ancestry, because the Inca nobility occasionally married Spanish colonists in the early days after the conquest; but these members of Peruvian society were known to be of mixed blood and were not related to Gauguin.[4] An anecdote that Gauguin told about his mother playing a practical joke on an army officer of Indian descent, a guest in Lima, demonstrates that even as a child Gauguin was aware of the distinction.

Inca or not, Gauguin drew on his Peruvian blood to fashion an exotic identity for himself, which had an impact in artistic circles. In this he imitated his grandmother, who had obtained special permission to use her Peruvian father's name rather than her French married name and thus achieved fame under the name Flora Tristan. The book she published about her voyage to Peru in 1833–34, *Peregrinations of a Pariah* (1838), gave her a start in the French literary world and gained her friends like George Sand.[5] She went on to publish other observations of life in England and France and had become one of France's best-known advocates for poor and working-class people by the time of her death in 1844. Fifty years later, in 1894, Flora Tristan's fame as a writer and social reformer had diminished but not disappeared; during her grandson's struggle for artistic recognition, it not only opened many doors for him but gave him something to live up to.[6] He knew her books well and kept copies with him throughout his life. His use of the title "Avant et après" (Before and After)[7] for his memoir curiously echoes that of her own unpublished manuscript, "Past and Future."[8]

Flora Tristan's husband (Paul Gauguin's grandfather) was the artist and printmaker André Chazal.[9] Tristan met him when she was apprenticed in his lithography shop in Paris around 1819, and showed artistic ability herself. Although Gauguin may not have known this grandfather personally, he certainly was aware of the artistic legacy of the Chazal family. The print shop had been founded by André Chazal's mother. André's brother, Antoine, and Antoine's son Charles Camille Chazal both had modestly successful careers as painters, forming a minor artistic dynasty that lasted in Paris until 1875. Even after the marriage between André Chazal and Flora Tristan ended, Tristan's interest in art continued, and in addition to publishing some articles on art topics, she was active in a Parisian art circle that included avant-garde painters like Eugène Delacroix.[10] When Paul Gauguin was born in 1848, his family lived only two doors from Delacroix on rue Notre-Dame-de-Lorette.

Such an exotic and artistic ancestry shaped Gauguin's view of himself and eased his entry into the Parisian artistic and intellectual world of the late nineteenth century. It is also possible to detect in Gauguin some of the personality traits of his flamboyant forebears. Flora Tristan is often held up as the source of Gauguin's wanderlust and creativity, and there are indeed parallels between the passionate, crusading temperaments of grandmother

and grandson.[11] Both wrote and published in a highly personal manner that allows us to measure the pulse of their intense feelings and beliefs. But reading the diatribes of Tristan and Gauguin side by side reveals great differences in their approach to life and society. Tristan's writings show a profound empathy for the poor and the disadvantaged, particularly women. Her evocations of the degradation of prostitutes in London and the cruel working conditions of laundresses in Nîmes are vivid and moving. Her grandson's writings, in contrast, tend to be short-tempered and sarcastic rather than philanthropic, even when he assumes the guise of a social reformer, as he later did in regard to the treatment of the Marquesan natives.[12] His carping criticisms of women also contrast strongly with the gentle feminism of his grandmother.[13]

Gauguin's personality may actually have been closer to his grandfather's. The artist André Chazal and his beautiful young assistant Flora Tristan were passionately in love when they married, but Chazal's hot temper soon eclipsed his love for her, and his bullying caused Tristan to leave him after only four years of marriage. She took her son and daughter along and gave birth to their third child at the home of her mother, with whom she sought refuge. Because French law recognized only the father's rights to children, Chazal fought Tristan for custody of all of them, eventually taking their older son, Ernest, from her. He was also awarded custody of their daughter Aline (the younger died in infancy). When Tristan discovered that he had abused Aline sexually, she brought charges of incest and was able to resume custody.[14] At this point Chazal's anger toward Tristan became obsessive. For several years he harassed and stalked her until he finally shot her in 1838 in a murderous rage. She survived the attack; he received a life sentence in prison.[15]

The public nature of the struggle between the angry husband and the wife who worked to support her children alone prefigures Gauguin's later marital situation, about which he spoke and wrote at length. Although as far

as we know he did not try to kill his wife, Gauguin physically and often verbally abused her with shocking hostility.[16] He took one of their children from her and threatened to take them all. It is also well known that, like his grandfather, he was sexually attracted to girls in their early teens and possibly even to his own daughter.[17]

Paul Gauguin was not the only one to inherit the Chazal temperament. Both his mother and his sister were capable of sharp remarks and cruel practical jokes (fig. 3). In later life, Gauguin still chuckled over the joke his mother had played on the army officer of Indian descent who was part of their circle in Lima. Knowing the officer loved a dish made of peppers, she served him a specially prepared plateful of hot peppers; everyone else at the table was served sweet peppers. Playing the role of solicitous hostess, she forced the polite man to down the whole portion of the inedible dish.[18] Gauguin would always think of the practical joke as the highest form of humor.

Paul's sister, Marie, only a year older, was his childhood companion (fig. 4). As they grew up, Marie maintained ties to the Spanish-American community in Paris, and, a beauty in the dark, Latin style of both her mother and her grandmother, she was courted by many of the young men in this group. After their mother died and until their respective marriages, Paul and Marie shared an apartment on the rue de la Bruyère in the same fashionable neighborhood where they were born. The mocking humor of both brother and sister shocked those who did not know them well, and in later years they never hesitated to turn their verbal knives on each other.[19] As the only son and the youngest child in a close-knit but combative household, Gauguin developed a high opinion of himself; and his wife later claimed that he had not been sufficiently disciplined as a child.[20] Since hot

tempers ran in his family, an orderly, disciplined household must have been hard to achieve.

Gauguin's willful personality was not improved by living, until he was six, with his mother and sister amid the huge extended family of the Tristan Moscosos in Lima. In 1846, Aline Chazal had married Clovis Gauguin, a man associated with Republican politics and the newspaper *Le National* in Paris. Three years and two children later, the family set off for Lima, perhaps at the urging of the Moscosos, who may have persuaded Clovis to start a Republican newspaper there. The political power of the Moscosos had recently been strengthened, and, in 1851, the husband of one of Aline's cousins, Don José Rufino Echenique, was elected president of Peru. Sadly, Clovis Gauguin died of a stroke during the sea voyage, leaving his family to continue on to Lima alone.

They were welcomed warmly by Aline's great-uncle Don Pio de Tristan Moscoso, who was still head of the extended family; Aline and the children lived with the Moscosos in Lima for the next four years. Since her mother had died in 1844 and her father was still in prison, Aline had no closer relatives. She did not record her experiences there, but judging from the prickly relationships between factions of the family, described by her mother in *Peregrinations of a Pariah,* the situation was probably not entirely comfortable. Political, social, and sexual intrigue abounded in the city and country homes where the many branches of the family congregated. When the Gauguins were in Lima, they lived at the center of the intrigue: in the presidential palace, where, according to Gauguin's account, the displaced Parisians had been assigned quarters.[21]

Thus it happened that Paul Gauguin's earliest memories were of the exotic city of Lima, where his family received all the privileges of being

9

cousins by marriage to the president of the Republic, including living in the most luxurious setting in a wildly extravagant city. For centuries, wealth in Peru had been concentrated in the hands of those, like the Moscosos, who controlled the silver mines. The conspicuous display of wealth was a tradition in Lima, whose residents' stylish clothes and fine palaces were the envy of all South Americans. In the 1840s a new source of wealth had opened up with the systematic marketing of guano, the ancient deposits of bird droppings found on islands off the coast of Peru.[22] This rich fertilizer was suddenly in demand all over the world. Peruvians with money, including Gauguin's family, invested in guano futures and prospered greatly from the 1840s to the 1860s. It was in this extraordinary environment that the young Paul Gauguin spent the early years of life.

The stories of Lima that Gauguin recounts in his memoirs include the many-hued servants of Asian and African descent, walls covered with portraits of ancestors that shook ominously during earthquakes, and lunatics chained to the rooftops who occasionally got free and wandered into children's rooms in the dark of night.[23] He also wrote of the distinctive costume of Lima women, which was associated with the remarkable sexual freedom they claimed for themselves, when he described his mother dressed in the traditional Lima veil, which eerily revealed only one of her soft, beautiful eyes.[24] The whole costume, which consisted of the *saya,* a long, tight, pleated skirt, and the *manto,* a veil with one eyehole cut into it, had been written about by visitors to Lima for more than a hundred years.

Gauguin's grandmother Flora Tristan had been especially taken by the sensuousness of the skirt and the freedom that the women gained by hiding their features under the veil. She wrote of the amorous adventures that perfectly respectable women could pursue in this disguise: "Her husband doesn't ask where she has been for he knows perfectly well that if she wants to hide the truth, she will lie, and since there is no way to keep her from it, he takes the wisest course of not asking her. Thus these ladies go alone to the theater, to bull fights, to public meetings, balls, promenades, churches, go visiting, and are much seen everywhere . . . [unlike] their European sisters who from childhood are slaves to laws, values, customs, prejudices, styles, and everything else."[25] When Paul Gauguin wrote his own reminiscence of the Lima costume in 1903, he may have had vague memories of the sexual freedom of his own mother, a beautiful young widow.[26] The boy, in Latin fashion, would have been spoiled by his relatives (if not by his mother) and encouraged by the amused adults to develop a precocious interest in sexual matters.

Despite the exclusive lifestyle of the Moscosos in Lima, when an opportunity arose to return home to France in 1854, Aline seized it. Aware that her presidential cousin Echenique was losing political power and that Don Pio's promises to leave her a comfortable legacy might not materialize, Aline decided that her best chances for an independent life lay in Europe. She had received word that her husband's father was near death and that he wanted to make Paul and Marie, his only grandchildren, his heirs. It was time for her Peruvian children to become French once again.

Up to this point, the six-year-old Paul had not attached much importance to his last name. He had always been surrounded by the more powerful Tristan Moscosos, Echeniques, and other Peruvian relatives. But when he arrived at his grandfather's home in Orléans, he quickly learned that being a Gauguin was very useful indeed. They were not a socially prominent or powerful family in Orléans, but in the quarter of Saint-Marceau, they were numerous and influential. Saint-Marceau, across the Loire River from downtown Orléans, was famous for its small-scale gardening. For generations the Gauguins and their neighbors had raised produce and flowers, which were exported by river and by road (and later railroad) to Paris, about one hundred miles to the north.

Paul Gauguin's grandparents Guillaume Gauguin and Elizabeth Juranville had started an *épicerie*, a general store that specialized in imported goods. They gradually relocated closer to the river, eventually obtaining property on the Quai Neuf (now Quai de Prague), a prime spot above the commercial boat landings of the Loire and very near the crossing of the new railroad.[27] Trade in that section of Saint-Marceau was brisk. In a typical week in February 1844, the number of boats that docked there was 197, unloading cargo at an estimated value of 12 to 13 million francs.[28] By that time, however, the Gauguin-Juranvilles had retired from the épicerie and were able to live off their investments.[29] Other Gauguin and Juranville cousins also bought property along the Quai, and they formed a powerful family compound. Trade by riverboat succumbed to the quickly encroaching railroads after midcentury, but the family had invested well in land and stocks and remained in their fine houses overlooking the river for generations.

The successful Guillaume and Elizabeth Gauguin-Juranville had two sons, Clovis (born in 1814) and Isidore (born in 1819). Although the boys' education is not on record, they were apparently given good starts in their chosen careers, both of them leaving the more mundane family pursuits of gardening and shopkeeping behind. By the 1840s, Clovis had made his way into newspaper publishing in Paris.[30] He frequented literary and artistic circles, where he met his future wife, Aline Chazal. They married when he was thirty-two and she was twenty-three. Clovis's younger brother, Isidore, established himself as a fine jeweler—an *orfèvre joaillier,* or specialist in gold jewelry. He lived with his parents and commuted across the river to his shop downtown on the old commercial rue de Petits-Souliers.

The families of Saint-Marceau were traditionally republican (antiroyalist and anti-Napoleon), and the two Gauguin sons proved to be no exception when revolution broke out in France in 1848. In Paris, Clovis and *Le National* were at the center of the new republican government that was set up and then taken over by Louis-Napoléon in less than a year. The rise of Napoléon (soon to call himself Napoléon III) and the start of the Second Empire sealed Clovis and Aline's decision to move to Peru. In Orléans, Isidore was also active in the local rebellion, which was quashed rather violently, leaving many young men wounded and at least one fellow jeweler dead.[31] Isidore was arrested at a demonstration in front of the town hall and sentenced to be deported to Africa. After spending some time in prison,

however, he was allowed to return to Saint-Marceau, where he quietly spent the rest of his life, surrounded by his family and old friends.[32]

When Paul Gauguin arrived at his grandfather's house at the end of 1854, he began a new life as a comfortable middle-class French boy with republican sentiments. His grandfather died a few months after seeing his "Peruvian" grandchildren once more. Enough of Guillaume Gauguin's estate was left to Isidore that he would never have to work again, and the property on Quai Neuf and the remainder of the assets were left to Clovis's children under the guardianship of their mother and uncle until they came of age. The Gauguin property had two houses back to back, one facing on Quai Neuf and the other facing the next street, rue Tudelle, with a large shared garden in between. Aline and her two children moved into the house looking out over the river, while Isidore continued to live in the smaller house, on rue Tudelle. For the next five years they enjoyed the peace and plenty of French small town life. Gentle Uncle Isidore, who remained unmarried and childless, adopted the two fatherless children in his heart.[33]

By the time Paul Gauguin lived on the Quai Neuf, it had lost much of the commercial bustle of only ten years before. The natural beauty of the wide river interrupted at intervals by grassy islands and sandbars was enhanced by the view of old Orléans across the heavy, arched bridge (fig. 5). As Paul and Marie grew up, they had their carefully tended garden to play in, and, in the summer, could race around in their rowboats and try their luck in the many fishing holes formed in the shifting recesses of the islands. The children were healthy and athletic and would have had no trouble fitting in with their many Gauguin cousins from the neighborhood once their native tongue changed from Spanish to French. While Paul and Marie were still young, Aline sent them to local boarding schools as day students so that they could remain at home with her as long as possible.[34]

Gauguin's memories of Orléans, where he spent the formative years of his life (from six to sixteen), were not nearly as colorful as his memories of Lima. He was an aloof and indifferent student who frustrated teachers into making remarks like "That child will be either an idiot or a man of genius."[35] In general he felt that he received an excellent French classical education and was indeed so typical a student that none of his classmates came forward in later years to tell of any early indications of artistic greatness. A few incidents occurred to Gauguin when he wrote his memoirs: being inspired to run away from home by a picture of a pilgrim with his belongings slung across his back; a neighbor complimenting him on a cane that he had carved with a knife. Given the artistic leanings of his mother and his uncle, these would not be unusual experiences for an imaginative boy.

Some other incidents are more curious: Paul's uncle finds him in the garden stamping his feet and flinging sand in a self-destructive tantrum. Why, asks his uncle? "Baby is naughty," he declared. Gauguin says: "As a child I was already judging myself and feeling the need of making it known."[36] He also remembers an incident with a cousin, "a child of about my own age, whom it appears I tried to violate; at the time I was six years old."[37] Although both masochistic behavior and sexual experimentation are common among children, it is significant that these episodes were among the few that Gauguin recorded.[38]

When Paul was eleven, Aline sent him to the prestigious boarding school at La Chapelle-Saint-Mesmin, just a few miles outside Orléans. It had been founded in 1816 to provide an alternative to the cathedral school of Sainte-Croix in the center of town. Attached to the ancient Chapelle-Saint-Mesmin, which dates back to 530 A.D., the new "Petit Séminaire" gave the sons of local upper-class and professional-class citizens of Orléans a healthy rural spot by the river at which to gain an education. But after 1849, the new bishop of Orléans, Monsignor Félix-Antoine-Philibert Dupanloup, took an interest in the school and, through his own reputation as a scholar, catapulted it into national prominence. For the three years that Paul Gauguin was in residence, it was at the height of its fame and drew students from all over France. No records have survived to shed light on his performance as a student, but later he believed that he emerged a well-educated man, and felt free to drop the name of the school whenever it was useful.[39]

With her younger child in boarding school, Aline decided it was time to leave the protective but provincial Gauguin family home in Orléans and return to her hometown of Paris. In 1861 she opened a dressmaking business on the rue de la Chaussée in the heart of the fashionable shopping district. Thanks to her mother's crusading ideals about the nobility of labor, Aline had been apprenticed to and had subsequently practiced as a dressmaker in Paris in her late teens and early twenties.[40] It is unlikely that she could have returned to this employment on such a scale if she had not practiced it in some small way since her marriage in 1846, and it is probable that she kept her hand in by working for private clients during the years she spent in Lima and Orléans. Both Paul and Marie both seem to have acquired their lifelong interest in clothes, fabrics, and decorative design at their mother's knee. Paul's experience of his mother as a businesswoman and single mother no doubt affected his ready acceptance of his own wife's ability to do the same.

When Aline returned to Paris, she also renewed old friendships and once again took her place in the art circles where she had grown up. Her ties to the South American community were now doubly strong because many of her relatives from Lima also came to Paris in the wake of Echenique's loss of the presidency, including the family of the ousted president himself.[41]

Paul, at age thirteen, was increasingly drawn to Paris, and within a year he left La Chapelle-Saint-Mesmin to enter a naval preparatory school located on the rue d'Enfer, on the left bank of the Seine. Called the Loriol Institute after its founder, this school offered coursework in military and navigational subjects that would allow students to pass the entrance exam for the naval academy. Paul studied there for two years and then returned to Orléans to take his final year at the Lycée Jeanne d'Arc.[42]

In spite of all the time and money to prepare Paul for the all-important exam, he, by his own admission, squandered his opportunity. When the time came, he knew that it would be futile to take the exam; and the next year he would be too old. His mother was furious. In the will she drew up that year she advised him "to get on with his career, since he has made himself so unliked by all [her] friends that he will one day find himself alone."[43] Like many a parent who has been disappointed by a teenage child, Aline was infuriated by Paul's cavalier behavior. Indeed, all his life it was Gauguin's tendency, when pressed, to disregard family and social obligations.

A career in the French navy was considered one of the most lucrative that a young man could choose. Because naval officers received handsome bonuses for their operations around the world, enlisting provided a splendid opportunity for the son of a good family to improve his financial future or help out back home. The romantic travel writer Pierre Loti, a contemporary of Gauguin's and a man whose career Gauguin envied all his life, was encouraged to go into the navy for just these reasons. Loti struggled with algebra and trigonometry in his *cours de la marine* and finally passed the entrance exam for the Naval College in 1866.[44] Loti became a successful officer, saving his family from losing all their property. Gauguin might have done as much for his mother and sister if he had properly applied himself.

Instead, still determined to go to sea, Paul settled for the less prestigious career of a merchant seaman. An educated young man of good family could do well in the commercial shipping industry, but the financial and social rewards were not as great as in the navy. Because no prior training was required (a merchant seaman learned by apprenticeship), young men of Gauguin's class who ended up on these ships tended to do so after academic failure or out of a spirit of adventure, rather than as a part of a serious career plan.[45]

These young men still needed some kind of recommendation to get the apprenticeships that would lead to officer status and avoid being trapped in the lower ranks. In Gauguin's case, this influence may have come from a rather shadowy figure in his life—his uncle, Aline's brother, Ernest Chazal. Ernest had been raised by his father, André Chazal, and had gone into a career at sea probably at the time his father was put into prison. It is not known how much contact Aline had with her brother over the years, and he was already deceased by the mid-1860s, but he may have been the inspiration for Paul's pursuit of a career at sea, and his contacts may have helped his nephew get established.[46]

In 1865, at the age of seventeen, Paul Gauguin reported for duty on the ship *Luzitano* docked at Le Havre.[47] He was five foot four and thin, but he carried himself upright, and the glance from his heavy-lidded eyes projected adolescent disdain mixed with uncertainty. In spite of the exoticism of his early childhood in Lima (which he had already largely forgotten), he was a typical French schoolboy. He had frittered away his time reading Balzac and Hugo and dreaming about adventures in foreign lands. He tended to be sullen with adults and sarcastic with his peers. He looked upon the girls in his life—his sister and her friends—with suspicion and longing. He did not love the sea the way other boys did, but he wanted to get far away from school and family, and seafaring would serve the purpose.

What Gauguin remembered most about going to sea was that it was the start of his sexual life. His many tales of life at sea make it clear that his first goal after arriving in Le Havre was to lose his virginity, and for his next five years as a sailor he sought sexual adventure in the ports and aboard ship. He found that he was well suited to the sexual life of seamen, particularly the transitory nature of alliances so unlike the seriousness of male-female relationships of his social class. He had a fear of being caught by a marriage-minded woman. He told the story of one German passenger he met on his first voyage from Le Havre to Rio de Janeiro:

> On the return voyage, we had several passengers, among others, a fine fat Prussian woman. It was the captain's turn to be smitten, but fiercely as he burned he burned in vain. The Prussian dame and I had found a charming nest in the room where the sails were stored, the door of which opened into the cabin near the companionway.
>
> An astonishing liar, I told her all manner of absurdities, and the Prussian lady, who was deeply smitten, wanted to see me again in Paris. I gave her as my address "La Farcy [name of a famous prostitute], rue Joubert."
>
> It was very bad of me and I felt remorse for some time afterwards, but I could not send her to my mother's house.[48]

The story is probably largely adolescent boasting, but it shows how delighted he was to be able to engage in sexual activity without having to answer to the strictures of his social group.

The sexual life of a sailor also appealed to Gauguin in that the men around him played as important a role as the women he pursued. By taking him to brothels and giving him addresses of "loose" women in foreign ports, they were his sexual guides. Paul also fit in with those for whom amorous adventures were a kind of competition.[49] In Gauguin's anecdotes he invariably wins the woman away from another man—usually richer or more powerful—as in this story about the singer Aimée who was a legend in Rio de Janeiro.

This charming Aimée, in spite of her thirty years, was extremely pretty; she was the leading actress in Offenbach's operas. I can still see her, in her splendid clothes, setting out in her carriage, drawn by a spirited mule.

Everyone paid court to her, but at this moment her acknowledged lover was a son of the Czar of Russia, who was a midshipman on the training-ship. . . .

Aimée overthrew my virtue. "Let me take a good look at you, my dear. How handsome you are!" At this time I was quite small; although I was seventeen and a half, I looked fifteen. The soil was propitious, I dare say, for I became a great rascal.[50]

Not only did Gauguin triumph over the Czar's son, but he had what he considered the exquisite pleasure of being seduced. But Aimée was so famous among visitors to Rio of all nationalities that it seems highly unlikely that this seduction actually occurred.[51] The story should be read instead as a wishful memory including the most piquant ingredients—competitiveness and seduction—of Gauguin's fantasy life.

Aboard ship Paul quickly learned how to be a favorite among the men. He honed his storytelling skills, he learned to play the popular musical instruments, including the concertina, and he was an avid participant in the physically competitive games on deck. He had learned fencing and wrestling in school. and as his body developed a sailor's strength, he became a formidable opponent. especially if he felt slighted in any way. He was thin-skinned and not by nature a jovial man, but the social skills he learned in the all-male environment of a ship served him well in years to come.

Young Paul Gauguin sailed to Rio twice on the *Luzitano,* each voyage taking almost four months. In the fall of 1866 he shipped out on the *Chili* for an around-the-world trip that lasted over a year. The itinerary took him around the tip of South America (for the first time since he was six) and back up the western coast, with a stop in Iquique, in southern Peru, before heading across the Pacific to the Far East. This time Paul was serving as second lieutenant, or second mate, an awkward position between the common seamen and the captain. His role was to lead half the crew during the alternate watches that were the work shifts. He had an air of command, and he might have made a good leader, but his competitiveness and willingness to fight made it obvious that he would not have a brilliant career as an officer.

In fact he seems to have been demoted. When the *Chili* docked again at Le Havre in 1867, Gauguin was at the age of compulsory military service, so he enlisted in the navy as a third-class sailor. This time he was assigned to a large yacht built for the use of Napoléon III's cousin, Prince Jérôme Napoléon. Although at first he was a stoker (steam was gradually replacing sail power, although most ships used a combination at this time), he was soon reassigned to the quartermaster's department.[52]

The ship sailed at the pleasure of Prince Jérôme, who not only conducted some official government business but carried out scientific studies of the lands around the North Pole. For almost two years, Gauguin sailed on the *Jérôme-Napoléon* in the company of 150 crewmen and a small number of distinguished passengers, including both the imperial family and such well-known scientists as Ernst Renan. Gauguin saw a large part of the European coastline from the Arctic Circle to the Mediterranean. Although this experience was educational, and he whiled away the time making drawings and carvings, it did not have the appeal to Gauguin that his earlier voyages on long-range commercial vessels had had, and he acquired a reputation for being insubordinate. He did not take well to the discipline of the navy, nor to his lowered status, especially since he knew he had once had the opportunity to become a naval officer. Early on, he got into a fight with the quartermaster and was nearly court-martialed for dunking the officer's head into a bucket of water.[53]

Soon after the Franco-Prussian War broke out in July of 1870, Napoléon III was overthrown, and the *Jérôme-Napoléon* was recommissioned as a warship and renamed the *Desaix*. The *Desaix* captured four German boats in the North Sea. Gauguin was among the crew that boarded and took control of one of the captured ships. Gauguin remained on the *Desaix* until a few months after the end of the war, when he became eligible for a long shore leave.

On April 23, 1871, when he was almost twenty-three years old, Gauguin went home to resume civilian life. Although he was feeling bitter about his recent military experience at sea, he still fondly remembered the heady freedom of his earlier voyages.[54] Gauguin never returned to the sea as a profession, but all his life he kept the air and swagger of a seaman and often gravitated toward men who sailed. In those five years aboard ship, travel to unknown lands and freedom—primarily sexual freedom—had become integral to his identity.

Until Gauguin was twenty-three years old, he lived in one cocoon or another. In Lima and Orléans it was a huge extended family, then boarding school, and finally it was the navy. Gauguin wanted freedom, but he also wanted the safety of a privileged group that would protect and support him. When he left the navy and faced being on his own for the first time, he immediately pulled the comforting mantle of old friends and family around him and quickly established himself as a "man" as defined by society: he launched a career, married, and had children — all by the age of twenty-six (fig. 6).[1] He was proud of his easy assumption of this role, and the excitement he discovered both in his marriage and in his career in high finance soon overshadowed his previous sexual restlessness. The power that society accorded him as a young man on his way up was thrilling in and of itself, and he added to that thrill his discovery that art held for him a surprisingly sensual fascination.

He began his new life by accommodating the changes in his immediate family. His mother, Aline, her health worsening, had had to give up her dressmaking business in 1865. She moved out of Paris to the suburban town of Saint-Cloud, where she died less than two years later, at the age of forty-two. During the last years of her life, she was attended by her daughter, Marie, while Paul was away on his lengthy ocean voyages. Mother and son corresponded as best they could over long distances, but Paul did not learn of his mother's death until several months afterward, when a letter from Marie caught up to him. Without her mother, Marie was alone, and she returned for a year to Orléans to be close to the larger Gauguin family and to settle the estate that would now be held in trust until she and Paul reached their majority. In 1868, Marie returned to Paris, where she lived with close family friends, Gustave and Zoé-Françoise Arosa and their daughters.

Aline had been a diligent guardian of the funds left equally to her children by their paternal grandfather in Orléans so many years before. When she died, each child received approximately 20,000 francs, including the sum from the sale of the property on the Quai Neuf, which took place in 1870.[2] The inheritance would not make Paul and Marie wealthy, but it could provide a dowry for Marie and investment capital for Paul; and, in a pinch, it would generate a small income.

A blow to both of them was the destruction by fire of their mother's house in Saint-Cloud in 1871, during the Franco-Prussian War. The Germans had invaded Saint-Cloud, burning Napoléon III's summer palace and the town where he had signed his declaration of war. The Gauguins didn't lose much of substantial monetary value, but they each lost the possessions

that had been left to them in their mother's will. Marie lost the furnishings, laces, and other fine materials that her mother had prized; Paul lost the books, pictures, and family keepsakes that interested him. Also destroyed was a large portion of the books, documents, and other memorabilia left to them by their grandmother, Flora Tristan, and the collection of Inca silver and pottery that Aline had acquired while in Peru.[3]

When Paul left the navy, Marie moved from the Arosas' home on the place Gustave-Toudouze to share an apartment with him around the corner on the rue la Bruyère.[4] The Arosas had been appointed Paul's guardians upon Aline's death, but because he had been at sea, this was the first time they were able to show their benevolence to the son of their close friend. Thus, with his sister by his side and the Arosas only a few steps away, Paul changed his sailor's uniform for a dress coat and started his adult life.

After a sullen adolescence and five years of escape on the high seas, it is astonishing to see how quickly Paul Gauguin took on the role of the bourgeois gentleman. Although he still had some rough edges, he gamely accepted the entry-level position on the stock exchange arranged for him by Gustave Arosa, and he even entered enthusiastically into the social circle of young people around his sister and the Arosa daughters, who were also in their early twenties. He was still, however, horrified by the thought of being a good catch: "One day I was treacherously taken to call on a respectable family (my sister was with me) where they talked about nothing but family duties and household virtues. It was like a flash of lightning for me; *unmistakably* I saw it was a marriage-trap. There is nothing so terrible as virtue."[5] But when he was not being pursued by the marriage-minded, he was intrigued by the conversations of the people who now surrounded him—which were full of ideas about art, literature, and politics. He missed the casual sexuality of his old life at sea, but the ideas being debated in Paris in the early 1870s stimulated in him an intellectual curiosity that he had not known could be so compelling.

Seemingly everyone Gauguin knew wanted to be an artist. The Arosas' younger daughter, Marguerite, who was only sixteen or seventeen, had already begun to study painting.[6] A colleague of Gauguin's at the investment firm, Claude-Emile Schuffenecker, had also studied drawing and painting before taking an office job and was continuing his studies on his own.[7] The young crowd around the Bourse, including the Spanish who gathered at the Arosas, were interested in art: they went to the exhibitions and read the latest art news. Gustave and Zoé-Françoise Arosa were collectors of modern painting and fine ceramics who, along with Gustave's brother Achille, amassed an important collection and associated with the prominent artists of their day. From the older generation of artists, they owned works by Flora Tristan's friend Eugène Delacroix, as well as Corot, Courbet, Jongkind, Daumier, Diaz, Harpignies, and other members of the Barbizon school of landscape painting. They had recently discovered the work of a younger artist, Camille Pissarro.[8]

Paul Gauguin, who had been making pencil drawings and wood carvings all his life, was intrigued by the art craze and began painting side by side with Marguerite and dropping in on art classes with his friend Schuffenecker. The paintings most favored by the Arosas were idyllic landscapes where nymphs play. When Gauguin looked at the nymphs in their silvery setting, he was drawn to the freedom they represented, "with their vigilant love of life and the flesh, beside the ivy of Ville-d'Avray that entwines the oaks of Corot."[9]

Ever since childhood, visual images, such as the portraits shaking on the walls of the presidential palace in Peru or the folk print of the pilgrim that made him run away from his home in Orléans, had had a strong impact on him. Now that he was in his twenties, he was undoubtedly familiar with the pornography typical of the sailor's locker, but found that an even more powerful eroticism could be found in an object of fine art. The sensuously painted nude body, incongruously exposed to the outdoors yet veiled in a cloak of respectability, was titillating to a man who was used to seeing sex as furtive and crude. This new view of sexuality was liberating, not only because of the imagined freedom of the unclothed nymphs but also because such images could be enjoyed in polite society—either in public exhibitions or on parlor walls. Since the commonly accepted difference between erotica and pornography hinged on the presence or absence of "violent, degrading, or nonconsensual sexual activity," it would seem that Gauguin's assumption of the role of the socially acceptable man was complete.[10] He could enjoy sexual fantasies without the overt aggression that marked a less-than-powerful man. As contemporary manuals of etiquette cautioned, politesse came from knowing how "not to give offense, nor humiliate, nor importune, nor intimidate."[11]

The idea of painting similar scenes was irresistible to him. The very act of putting paint onto canvas, of making pictures that seduced and surprised, was exciting. He could make the sensual content as open or as hidden as he liked, as blatant as a nude body or as suggestive as the softness of clouds in the sky. In either case, it could arouse in the perceptive viewer a state of awakened senses, even an almost physical desire.[12] And as Gauguin took up the brush, he found that he liked working with the materials and the images—and loved the attention his amateur paintings brought him.

As much as he enjoyed his artistic dalliances, he derived even greater pleasure from the competitiveness in his new profession. Within a year after returning to Paris, Gustave Arosa had found Gauguin a position in the firm of the stockbroker Paul Bertin, a company in which Arosa was a major investor.[13] Gauguin was hired as one of the many clerks who worked for the forty official brokers on the Paris Bourse. His job was one of the higher paying ones among the clerks, albeit one of the most restrictive. He was a "liquidator," a position unfamiliar to Americans but common in the accounting system of European stock markets. In the Paris Bourse, brokers did not keep track of each investor's running total from day to day, but waited to total up their accounts once a month (either at the middle or the end, depending on the type of stocks). Not surprisingly, this "liquidation" was a massive process that took clerks away from their homes for five days at the end and four days at the middle of the month to do around-the-clock bookkeeping.[14]

What specific qualifications Gauguin might have brought to this job is hard to see, for his job training had been in engineering and navigation. But perhaps his position on the quartermaster's staff of the *Jérôme-Napoléon* was as a bookkeeper, and after some on-the-job training in the broker's office, the rest was up to his common sense and intuition. Gauguin's work on the exchange was extremely detail oriented. For the five years he worked as a liquidator for Bertin, the young, insubordinate ex-sailor kept strict business hours and routinely gave up several days and nights every month to business. He earned his living making endless lists of names, stocks, buys, sells, and totals. The patience that this sort of occupation requires is not consistent with the image of an impetuous, spontaneous artist, which Gauguin did his utmost to create in later years. But it does explain the dogged determination that he had in later life as he pursued a lonely career: Gauguin's bookkeeping mentality gave him the steadiness to practice his art day after day even in the most primitive and remote locations. It also explains the extraordinary feats of patience we see in Gauguin—such as copying and recopying his writings and those of others and his penchant for lists—as well as his remarkably legible handwriting.

Although the everyday work might have been relatively prosaic, the larger world of the stock market suited his need for excitement and self-importance. He felt he had an appropriate occupation for a man of his privileged background in that both the Gauguins and the Moscosos were rentiers—they lived off their investments rather than pursued any business or profession.[15] From his Latin background and from his years aboard a ship he understood the ways of a hierarchical society and learned how to identify the people of influence who could help him. His competitive personality and the formal manners learned from his mother were further assets in the clamor of the stock exchange. Now that he was a man of the world, he was determined not to alienate his friends as he had done as a teenager.

The most important friend he had was Gustave Arosa. Arosa, born in 1818 of a Spanish father and French mother, grew up in Paris in the Spanish and South American community.[16] Although his association with Aline Gauguin can be traced only to 1861, when she returned to Paris from Orléans, it is likely that they knew each other while they were growing up. Arosa and his brother had a share in a brokerage house and were speculators on the exchange. Gustave Arosa's older daughter, Victorine, was also married to a financier, Adolphe Calzado, who eventually opened his own investment bank. Calzado's cousin, José Sanjurjo (called Pepito) was also in the investment and banking business. These were the intimate friends of Paul and Marie Gauguin. Marie met and married Juan Uribe, a wealthy young South American merchant from Bogotá, Colombia, through her association with this group.[17] Paul made the most of these connections to advance in the world of high finance.

Such a fortuitous beginning in his profession added worldly stature to the physical attractiveness of the new man about town. The many Parisian mothers who tempted Paul with their marriageable daughters were justified in believing he was a good catch despite his arrogant dismissal of their efforts to engage him. In the postwar period, when large numbers of young men were returning from military service, the atmosphere was charged with the heat of courtship as young couples made up for lost time and began families. Paul's objections notwithstanding, he was eager to share in this wave of respectable sexuality, which in many ways was akin to the sexuality of Corot's nymphs.

In the fall of 1872, not long after Paul had been given his start on the stock exchange, he met a young Danish woman who was visiting Paris with a friend. The Danish visitors were boarding with Pauline Fouignet, a friend of the Arosas, who introduced them into the Arosas' circle. The two friendly and attractive Danes charmed this group, and they were included in all future social activities. The women in the local group—Paul's sister Marie, Marguerite and Victorine Arosa, and Pauline Fouignet's daughter Marie—welcomed them warmly.[18] One of the visitors, Marie Heegaard, caught the eye of Pepito Sanjurjo, and the other, Mette Gad, made an instant impression on Paul Gauguin (fig. 7). For the next six months the young people were inseparable.[19]

Marie openly encouraged Pepito. She wrote to her family, "I like very much a young Spaniard named Pepito Sanjurljo." But, Marie went on, Mette ignored Paul: "There is a young Monsieur Goguain who pines in secret for Mette, who in turn plays the role of a beauty with a heart of stone."[20] Mette could not have chosen a more effective way to get Paul's attention. Given his sensitivity to the marriage-trap, he would have been scornful of a more encouraging response. Overcoming a woman's objections, however, inflamed

him. His courtship of Mette Gad was so ardent that within a month he had overcome her initial hesitation and convinced her to marry him.

What was the appeal of this woman? As Gauguin explained to Marie Heegaard's mother soon after announcing their engagement, it was the "originality of her character and the honesty of her feelings."[21] Mette Gad at twenty-two was an independent thinker, and her high level of education enriched her ideas beyond the commonplace. Though not wealthy herself, she had moved in the highest Danish political circles and had a broader understanding of the world than most young people her age.

Mette was the eldest of five children of a provincial Danish judge and his well-born wife. When Mette's father died, her mother took the children back to their grandmother's home in Copenhagen, where the two widows raised them in a comfortable manner befitting the children of a judge and the grandchildren of a military officer. In 1867, through family connections, Mette became a governess for the children of the celebrated Danish prime minister Jacob B. S. Estrup.[22] In 1872 she traveled to Paris as a companion to her friend Marie Heegaard, the daughter of a Danish industrialist.

Despite her strength of character, Mette was as susceptible to amorous pursuit as anyone her age. For the past five years, as governess, she had become accustomed to shouldering responsibility and taking care of those around her. By the persistence of Paul Gauguin's advances, she was no doubt persuaded that the forceful fellow was the one who would finally take care of *her*. Furthermore, like Paul, she had a passionate nature and was willing to take risks. She was probably attracted to the sexuality lurking just beneath his recently civilized demeanor. In later years the Danish writer Otto Rung described Mette as a woman whose daring and salty language captivated men used to more sedate manners in the women of their class. "Everyone loved Mette Gauguin for her indomitable courage and her never-broken, often drastic high spirits. . . . The gentlemen not only forgave, but delighted in the fact that she would sit at social gatherings in the usually exclusive circle of the smoking-room and entertain everyone with her gay remarks. . . . Mette would come sweeping in with a *bon mot* in French or in the Copenhagen slang—often a touch on the bold or provocative side."[23]

During their courtship, when costume parties were in vogue, the two chose outfits that suggested the wide range of their personas. In the first costumes that Marie Heegaard describes to her family, Mette and Marie dress up as men—Mette in ordinary men's clothes and Marie as a soldier.[24] The sight of the tall, blond, broad-shouldered Mette in men's clothes must have been both shocking and titillating to Paul, who was still rather new to sophisticated society. For the second costume party, Mette goes to the other extreme and appears in a short dress as a baby with her nurse; Paul counters by posing as a soldier.[25]

For the third party that Marie describes, Paul and Mette, now engaged, go as eighteenth-century fashion plates—Paul as an "*Incroyable*" (a fop, or dandy) and Mette as his female counterpart, a "*Merveilleuse*."[26] Evidently both of them reveled in the sumptuousness of fashion and the thrill of shocking their friends by appearing in public in an unexpected pose or costume. Nor was either Paul or Mette afraid of crossing gender lines in their appearance. In later years Paul grew his hair long and wore flowing capes; Mette cut hers short and smoked cigars.[27]

Given Paul's fear of conventional women, it is possible that a strong, androgynous woman like Mette was the only type to whom Paul would have been sufficiently attracted to marry. By his own account, his adolescent sexual and romantic experiences were with prostitutes or other unsuitable women, from whom he fled as soon as possible. Women of his own class held no appeal until he met Mette. His ardent feelings for her must have been as much a relief as they were a surprise. In his early twenties he may already have feared that his misogyny could direct his life into less acceptable social channels, such as homosexuality or sexual practices only with prostitutes or others with whom conventional marriage and family life was impossible. Gauguin's desire for social acceptability within his upper-middle-class community at this time made his discovery of a woman like Mette, for whom he felt such overwhelming passion, a godsend.

Their courtship was curtailed about two months after they became engaged and about six months after they met. In March of 1873, Mette was compelled to return to Copenhagen, leaving a heartsick Paul and all her friends, including Marie Heegaard. Although it is usually said that she returned home to prepare for her wedding the following fall in Paris, it is hardly likely that the simple ceremony with no festivities required six months' preparation in Copenhagen.[28] Nor would it have been unseemly for her to remain in Paris after her engagement, because, as Paul complained later, the Danes had very lax customs governing the conduct of engaged couples. As he pointed out, betrothal in Denmark "has all the appearance of love, liberty, and morality. You are engaged; you can go for a walk or even a journey; the mantle of the betrothal is there to cover everything. You play with Everything-but-That."[29]

It is far more likely that Mette returned to Denmark so soon after her engagement for a reason unrelated to her upcoming marriage. Perhaps she felt compelled to honor a commitment to her employer, Prime Minister Estrup, or perhaps a death in the family called her back. At any rate, it was a blow to the relationship and may have caused serious harm to their future marriage. It certainly prevented them from going into the marriage with a deep knowledge of each other's characters. The separated lovers made the best of the situation, however, and corresponded constantly. Mette had the added contact of letters from Marie Heegaard and probably her other female friends in Paris, including Paul's sister. Mette, Marie Heegaard, and Marie Gauguin remained friends all their lives.[30]

A glimpse of Paul Gauguin left alone in Paris comes through the eyes of Marie Heegaard. Her perspective is extremely affectionate—a tribute to the closeness of the group and the optimism that lifted Gauguin's spirits in the early days of his new life in Paris. Both men and women found him charming. Interestingly, the themes that became central to his life are suggested in Marie Heegaard's descriptions. Most significantly, Paul was known as an artistic person. Not only did he spend all his free time painting,[31] but he expressed himself through his creative costumes, his portraits and sketches of all those around him,[32] and the caricatures and doodles with which he decorated his letters. He presented his dabblings with flair— sending one unsigned sketch to Marie Heegaard mysteriously through the mail,[33] competing with Marguerite Arosa to paint Marie Heegaard's portrait,[34] and in other ways using his art as a social gambit. The son of a dressmaker and the nephew of a jeweler, he respected all the ways that art could be used to make life more beautiful.

Another similarly talented person might have spent his time learning the language of the fine arts—enrolling in the Ecole des Beaux-Arts, entering competitions, and in general segregating himself and his art into the narrow and highly specialized world of professional artists. Gauguin from the first was more interested in art as a social language and followed the habits and vocabulary of flirtation, satire, and debate rather than the stylized language of high art. It was important to him to create a dynamic relationship between artist, art object, and audience, as well as between artist and art object. The art object, therefore, was part of an overall performance rather than a static and emotionally distant abstraction.[35] When Mette Gauguin wrote Paul's biographer in 1905 that "she did not know when they got married that he was planning to become an artist," she meant a professional one. She did not mean that he was not already an artist. In fact, she explained that art was ingrained in his life: "No one gave him the idea to paint. He painted because he could not do otherwise."[36]

Art aside, even in the early days Gauguin presented himself as a man without polish, offering the unexpected and the dramatic instead, as in this tale of Marie Heegaard's: "It was a miracle—the other day Paul got up to help Marie F. [Fouignet], who had picked up a chair to take to the roof [of the Arosas' house in Saint-Cloud] to watch the fireworks over the city of Paris for the Shah of Persia. Just as she picked up the chair, Paul ran toward her with as much zeal as if he were her devoted swain; the poor girl nearly fainted she was so surprised. You see he's making progress, but it is true that he still needs a bit more polish. Tell this to Mette, she'll be happy."[37] We can infer from Marie's affectionate description that Paul was usually considered to be lacking in courtesy, especially according to the accepted norms of chivalrous conduct, and that Mette and the others in their group were trying to civilize him. His parody of civilized manners suggests that he was highly conscious of the rules of politesse, but as with his art, he wanted to use the rules to provoke social dialogue, not silently embrace them. Later, when he made serious claim to be a savage, he could truthfully say that he had always been that way.

Manners, virtue, and morality were favorite topics of Gauguin's from the beginning. He presented himself as ignorant of proper behavior and engaged those around him to be his instructors.[38] All along, he claimed that the difference between virtue and vice was a mystery to him, as he wrote to Marie Heegaard's mother in 1874.[39] But rather than explore the matter in a concerned way so that he could act on a code of moral principles of his own, he placed the responsibility for such decisions in the hands of others —his wife, his friends, or "society"—and kept for himself the luxury of finding fault with their all too human solutions. This also left him free to flout manners, virtue, and morality if it suited him, while holding all others to standards that he would never consider adopting for himself. He had the double advantage of behaving badly and appearing superior to his friends.

In the normal course of events, Gauguin made an effort to pay his debts and maintain his social ties. He was keenly aware of assaults on his pride or his honor.[40] But when self-interest or bad luck interrupted the everyday pattern, he was prone to overlook accepted practices in matters of money or human kindness and act to suit himself alone. It was at these junctures that the person who reminded him of the honorable path became the object of his scorn and cynicism. His wife had at first willingly taken on the responsibility of educating him in proper manners and morals, but she discovered that his deference to her inevitably changed to contempt when her idea of virtue clashed with his desires.

But when Paul and Mette were married in a simple ceremony on November 22, 1873, they were still quite unknown to each other. Attended by their circle in Paris—Paul's sister and probably his uncle from Orléans, the Arosas and their extended family, as well as Paul's boss, Paul Bertin, and a dignitary from the Danish consulate—they said their vows at both the *mairie* of the Ninth District and the nearby Lutheran church. Once they had settled into their apartment overlooking the charming place Saint-Georges (not far from their old haunts), they found married life exhilarating as well as lonely. At last able to carry out their sensual and sexual

fantasies within a traditional European marriage, they bonded to some extent: despite the bitterness of their later separation, neither found another mate. Yet marriage had brought to an end the easy sociability of the friends among whom they had carried out their courtship. Mette, of course, missed her family and friends in Copenhagen, who were too far away for frequent visits. But they both missed being with a group in Paris. Marie Heegaard had gone back to Denmark; Marie Gauguin traveled a great deal and was now preoccupied with her fiancé, Juan Uribe; Adolphe Calzado had business in Rio de Janeiro. Paul's letters to the Heegaards complain of the inattention of their friends in Paris and the lack of frequent letters from their friends in Copenhagen.[41] The gregarious Gauguins were forced to find a substitute for the daring costume parties that no longer enlivened their social calendar.

They found their substitute naturally enough in the immediate pregnancy of Mette Gauguin. Almost nine months to the day of their wedding, the Gauguins' first child was born, on August 31, 1874. They named him Emil, probably after Mette's mother, Emilie.[42] As young parents—Paul and Mette were only twenty-six and twenty-four—they missed having parents of their own to help (three were dead, the remaining one in Copenhagen). Their situation brightened when both of their sisters married, began having their own children, and settled into apartments nearby. Paul, Mette, and Emil moved from the place Saint-Georges to the newer, more fashionable district west of the Champs Elysées in the beginning of 1875. Marie Gauguin married Juan Uribe at the end of that year and moved into the same neighborhood. Mette's sister Ingeborg had married a young Norwegian painter, Frits Thaulow, in 1874, and that couple came to Paris with their child, Nina, in 1876 (fig. 8).[43] The Gauguins had already developed a friendship with Frits, who had studied in Paris before his marriage. The couples probably no longer had costume parties, but they formed a congenial group of young professionals embarking on family life.

The makeup of the Gauguins' larger circle of friends reflected the cosmopolitan backgrounds and occupations of the three couples. Together they represented the young Spanish and Scandinavian communities of Paris, as well as the financial and artistic communities. These groups formed a base of support for Gauguin over the next fifteen years. The Spanish community was already behind him because of the influence of the Arosas and the Moscosos living in Paris and because of the respect still felt for his grandmother Flora Tristan. Now, Gauguin became acquainted with the Scandinavian artistic community through his brother-in-law, Thaulow, and the powerful business connections of the Heegaards and the Estrups and other friends of Mette. Gauguin's position in the financial world made it advantageous for the wealthier Scandinavians of his acquaintance to take an interest in him and ask his advice about investments.[44]

Gauguin's friends from the Bourse went beyond the Spanish clique to include colleagues in his own office as well as acquaintances in the larger financial community. The brokerage firms employed many young men like Paul Gauguin. Well connected but not wealthy themselves, they worked to get ahead in a field that seemed to offer limitless possibilities. For the time being they had to be satisfied with the salary of a clerk or liquidator, but they saw that the astute speculator could make enough to free himself from such drudgery. Few of these young men in their twenties felt secure enough to marry, so most of the Gauguins' friends from the Bourse were single men. Emile Schuffenecker, with whom Paul shared his artistic interests, did not marry until 1880. Paul's best friend, Charles Favre (whom he nicknamed le Marsouin [army slang for something like "Sarge"]), did not marry until 1888. Another clerk from the Bourse and a dear friend was Georges Polonini, who, along with José Sanjurjo, served as a witness on the birth certificate of Emil Gauguin.[45] All these young men were warmly welcomed by Mette and spent many evenings with the Gauguins sampling domestic life.

In the early years of his marriage Paul Gauguin used everyone around him as models for his art work. Portrait sketches of Mette, the baby Emil, Marie Heegaard, Ingeborg Thaulow, Charles Favre, Georges Polonini, and Ingel Fallstedt have survived, a token of what must have been a large group of drawings of friends and family (fig. 9). These appear to have been done at home in the evenings during family hours or during casual visits from friends. When Gauguin had a day off he would head outside with his sketchpad or paint box and canvas. Views of his neighborhood, the banks of the Seine in the city, or the nearby suburbs are the subjects of early paintings, and they were probably done during family or group outings.

Gauguin's art was part of his social interaction, and increasingly he had access to people who encouraged him. Some he had known for a while. Emile Schuffenecker, who had had some art training before he entered the firm of Paul Bertin and met Gauguin in 1872, was likewise painting in his spare time.[46] Marguerite Arosa was painting full-time and preparing for a

long Salon career, which began in 1882.[47] Frits Thaulow was shuttling back and forth between Norway and France. Through Thaulow, Gauguin met the Swedish painters Auguste and Otto Hagborg and the Danish painters Peter Kroyer and probably Theodor Philipsen, whose brother had married a cousin of Mette's.[48] Although Gauguin became acquainted with art through his Spanish friends, he entered his first circle of professional artists through Mette and the Scandinavian community.

In 1876 this largely self-taught painter achieved what art students in Paris normally devoted years to accomplish: he had a painting accepted into the Paris Salon of 1876. His friends Schuffenecker and Thaulow could not claim the same honor until 1877. His pride in being self-taught is evident in the conspicuous lack of professional lineage—teacher or school— listed after his name in the Salon catalogue. Whereas most Salon exhibitors used this opportunity to advertise their connections in the art world, Gauguin presents himself as having sprung full-blown from the head of an unknown god.

The painting was a landscape, today unidentified, but seemingly consistent with the other landscapes that Gauguin carefully signed and dated between 1873 and 1877 (fig. 10). Although these early paintings are unexceptional in comparison to the thousands of similar Barbizon-inspired landscapes submitted to the judgment of the Salon juries in the 1870s, they are extremely skillful for an artist who has received little, if any, formal art training. For Gauguin to be able to compete with artists who were engaged in full-time art studies is quite remarkable. It shows an ability to learn from

casual conversations with artists and connoisseurs and careful study of works of art with or without actually copying them.

Gauguin's avoidance of the "normal" steps of an art student is consistent with his belief that he was above, or at least outside, the rules that others conformed to. He could rely on his intuition and his intellectual quickness to leap ahead of his more conscientious colleagues. He paid a price for skipping these steps, however, for the credentials and connections that came through formal study with established masters would have proven useful to him when he finally decided to make painting his profession. He also carried with him a certain insecurity about his technique that surfaced at critical junctures in his career.[49] If he had gone through the traditional student experience of tests and validation, he would not have had to worry about technique.

Being outside the system but still wanting its rewards, Gauguin inevitably resented those who succeeded within it. In later years his bitterness toward the official Ecole des Beaux-Arts, the Salon exhibitions, and anything that smacked of the Academy cut him off from the support of those who might have helped him, and made even radical artists raise their eyebrows at his vehemence. Although he justified his scorn in the name of artistic purity, the posture he took toward officialdom in the art world may have stemmed from his self-consciousness about his origins as a self-trained artist.

After his smug triumph at the Salon of 1876, Gauguin changed his job and his residence. Marie Heegaard visited Paris in the fall of that year and reported back home that Mette was worried about the stability of Paul's income.[50] His employer, Paul Bertin, had recently retired, and a former partner, Léon Galichon, took over the brokerage.[51] The subsequent shake-up, along with Paul's success at the Salon, may have made him wonder if he shouldn't find another position. As a liquidator, he made good money, but he was always tied down; there are constant references in his early letters to Copenhagen to his inability to get away from Paris. The lengthy periods of liquidation at the middle and end of each month must also have limited his time to paint and to take painting trips in search of the landscape motifs he was interested in. So Gauguin changed jobs at some point between the end of 1876 and the beginning of 1877; his new employer, André Bourdon, was a banker rather than a stockbroker. Gauguin probably continued to serve as some sort of clerk or bookkeeper for Bourdon's investment activities, but his new hours were now set by the regular afternoon sessions of the Bourse (one o'clock to three o'clock), not by the monthly schedule demanded by liquidation.

When Paul, Mette, and Emil moved this time, they went to a part of Paris that was little known to them. The friendly circle of couples in their old neighborhood was breaking up: Ingeborg and Frits returned to Norway, where Frits began teaching and established himself as a leader of a progressive art community. Marie and Juan Uribe moved to a more fashionable neighborhood, across from the Parc Monceau and near the new mansion that the Arosas had built. The Gauguins themselves moved across the Seine to the suburban Vaugirard district, where Paul's great-grandparents, the Tristan Moscosos, had once had a villa, but the area was now the site of produce gardens and small factories.

The green, open spaces of Vaugirard can be seen in many of Paul's paintings done during the three years they lived on the rue des Fourneaux. Living there was good for the children, Emil and the new baby, Aline, who arrived on Christmas Eve of their first year there (1877). Vaugirard was not a fashionable place to live, and Mette was sorry to lose the proximity to her closest friends; but she was sociable and soon established ties to their new neighbors—most of whom were sculptors. The large buildings in the area lent themselves to becoming sculpture studios, and the Gauguins rented their apartment from Jules Bouillot, a successful creator of monumental statues. Their next-door neighbor was Jean-Paul Aubé, whose apartment was also his sculpture studio. The Gauguins became friendly with Aubé, as well as with students and assistants who worked with him, such as Charles Orsolini, who was a witness on Aline's birth certificate.[52]

This move into an artistic community that specialized in sculpture suggests a serious interest on Gauguin's part. He did indeed execute two marble busts of Mette and Emil under the guidance of Jules Bouillot. He also created wooden sculptures in relief and in the round, seemingly as a result of this immersion in three-dimensional craftwork. But oddly, most of the art he made in this setting was in oil painting or pastel, in casual disregard of what those around him were doing. He may also have discovered that his lack of academic training kept him from going far in sculpture, and so he fell back on painting, which he had already mastered. A sculptor needed to obtain commissions to subsidize the enormous cost of producing a major work, whereas a painter needed less capital to produce a work and could sell the finished product through a number of different outlets. Even though Gauguin was drawn to various three-dimensional media over the years—sculpture, ceramics, decorative objects—he always returned to paintings, drawings, and prints, in part because of their marketability.

The Gauguins were now living among full-time artists, but they were still primarily tied to the stock market for their income and their identity. Paul's new position took him to the sessions of the Bourse every day, and while he worked there he achieved substantial gains from buying and selling stocks on his own behalf. Employees of the brokerage houses and banks were usually drawn into some level of speculation following the lead of the major investors whose money they handled day in and day out. Paul had probably made some extra income in this way since 1872, when he obtained his first job; but from 1878 to 1880, his success grew conspicuous. The friends he made on the stock exchange in those years, such as Emile Bertaux and Eugène Mirtil, formed lasting impressions of Paul Gauguin as a flamboyant presence in the world of high finance. Mirtil remembered his coming to the sessions of the Bourse in a hansom cab whose driver he paid to wait for two hours to take him home again![53] According to another tale, he owned fourteen pairs of trousers.[54]

The Gauguins lived well during these years, and although Paul complained that Mette loved to shop, there is no doubt that he outspent her on luxuries for himself. Paul Gauguin's attitude toward money puzzled his friends in later years. Even when he was desperately poor, he could not resist spending money as soon as he received it. Several times in his life he was handed sums of money large enough to allow him to live well, if he were prudent, for many years. He inherited such sums from both his mother and his uncle, and he apparently made a similar amount from speculations on the stock exchange. In none of these instances did he appear to emerge with financial security.

During his spending binges he was generous to those around him. Mette grew accustomed to spending money on the same high level, and Paul encouraged her so that he could be proud of his elegantly dressed wife and children. When the money disappeared, Paul blamed Mette for overspending, claiming that "I spent nothing on myself"; but although she may have been carried away by their wave of prosperity, later evidence indicates that she was very responsible with money, and it was her husband who was the spendthrift.[55]

Gauguin may have always been like that, but his work on the stock exchange certainly didn't help him to curb his flamboyant impulses. Speculation in stocks was so similar to gambling that it could distort a weak person's grasp of money. Emile Zola, in his novel of the stock exchange, *L'Argent* (1891), described the fall of an honest businessman: "A couple of strokes, which one after the other yielded him considerable profit, made him altogether lose his head. What was the use of giving thirty years of one's life to the earning of a paltry million, when, in a single hour, by a simple transaction at the Bourse, one can put the same amount in one's pocket? . . . The worst of such a fever as this is that a man becomes disgusted with legitimate gains, and finally even loses an exact idea of money."[56] In the same way, Gauguin showed that despite all the shrewdness of his financial strategies, money had become an abstraction to him.

Gauguin's years on the stock market shaped his thinking in other ways. As Zola points out, the Bourse was at the center of many types of speculative transactions. Official stockbrokers, like Paul Bertin, had seats on the exchange or the "*corbeille*" (basket), where trading was officially sanctioned. But trading was also conducted outside the hall by the "*coulissiers*" (those in the corridors) and at the "Petite Bourse," an informal gathering of traders that took place in the evenings near the Opéra. Insurance brokers, traders in uncollected debts, and others also made a living by buying and selling money of one kind or another. But money wasn't the only commodity traded; all types of valuable goods from stamps to antiques and jewelry were of interest to the various groups around the Bourse. Naturally, works of art were part of the free-for-all, because they were collected by the newly rich speculators as a sign of success and were sold just as easily when speculation brought loss.[57]

Gauguin's patrons, the Arosa brothers, were financiers who took art seriously both as a symbol of their prosperity and as a valuable commodity. After years of careful buying, Gustave Arosa put his collection up for auction in February of 1878. He cashed in his works of art like stocks that had risen sufficiently in value. Perhaps following Arosa's example, Gauguin later used the auction himself as a method of trading his art for money in an open exchange. Gauguin also devised other schemes to involve investors in his art, plying his expertise as a trader in the art world.

Brash and reckless though Gauguin was in his twenties, he was sheltered by the indulgence that society grants to daring young men. He was able to follow his desires into all arenas of adult male life long before most cautious men would have been ready. He was launched into a profession that rewarded bold, impetuous decisions with the occasional shower of money; he made a precipitous marriage that, fortunately, reflected well on him for many years; and he fathered children as if they were badges of his potency. Even his art, which started primarily as a social amusement, earned him an unlikely success at the Salon.

Once he passed the age of thirty, in 1878, more of the responsibilities and fewer of the quick rewards of adult life were accorded him. Brashness became less attractive to his wife, his friends, and his employers. In the face of the dull realities that now stretched ahead of him, the one activity still providing the erotic thrill that had once been present in all facets of his life was—art. Rather than mature into a man who derived satisfaction from professional accomplishment and family stability, Gauguin increasingly clung to the more immediate sensual rewards of making, discussing, and marketing art.

In most artists, adult responsibility and art making are not mutually exclusive; but in Gauguin, art came to compete with his marriage and his career. In fact, Gauguin himself portrayed his art as equivalent to a lover when, years later, he self-righteously claimed that he had been a better husband than most because he spent his spare time with his art rather than with a mistress.[58] What we know about Gauguin's private life and erotic attractions during these years offers no hint of womanizing or scandal. He was remarkably untempted by affairs with women—whereas making art and interacting with artists was irresistible.

If Gauguin hoped to duplicate Gustave Arosa's success in the buying and selling of art, he would have to find artists who looked like they were on their way up but whose prices were still low.[1] Arosa had discovered the Barbizon painters in the 1850s and 1860s. By the 1870s, when Barbizon prices were high, it appeared that the Impressionists would form the next wave. Also landscape painters, they experienced a similar controversial reception, and the same dealer who promoted the Barbizon painters, Paul Durand-Ruel, was promoting them. When Gauguin made a windfall profit of 35,000 francs in 1879, the year after the Arosa auction, he began to put some of his money into paintings, turning immediately to the Impressionist painter whom Arosa had already identified as a good bet, Camille Pissarro.[2]

By the beginning of April of that year not only did Gauguin own three works by Pissarro, apparently the first paintings he had ever bought, but he saw his own name in print in the catalogue of the fourth Impressionist exhibition—as a lender.[3] Gauguin bought these paintings directly from the artist, probably after an introduction by Arosa. For Gauguin, meeting Camille Pissarro was pivotal. Most who joined the Impressionists were already full-time, professional artists. For them the encounter meant a change of style and aesthetic philosophy. But for Gauguin, the change was far more complete: the freedom that the new movement brought to art, Gauguin gradually broadened to encompass every aspect of his life.

It is not insignificant that Gauguin's introduction to Impressionism came through Camille Pissarro rather than any of the other charismatic figures in the group. Of all the members of this exhibiting "company" (*société anonyme*), Pissarro saw the Impressionist movement in the purest, most spiritual light. At forty-eight, his flowing white beard suggested not only his superior age and wisdom but a gentle flouting of convention that was rare among artists his age. He was the oldest in the Impressionist group and eighteen years older than Gauguin.

Pissarro had been born of French parents on the Danish island of Saint Thomas in the Caribbean Sea. Although Danish, French, and English were spoken by the upper classes on Saint Thomas (and Pissarro's official nationality was Danish), he also learned Spanish, which was used among the local population (the island is only fifty miles from Puerto Rico). In his early twenties, encouraged by a Danish artist, Fritz Melbye, he renounced the family business to make art his career.[4] He traveled with Melbye to Venezuela, and by the time he settled permanently in Paris in 1855, he had close ties to both the Hispanic and the Scandinavian artistic communities. Fritz Melbye's brother Anton, who had been a painter in Paris for many years, took the young Pissarro under his wing and introduced him into Danish circles. At the same time, Pissarro had many Spanish-speaking friends and was close to a young Puerto Rican artist, Francisco Oller y Cestero, who introduced him to Paul Cézanne and Armand Guillaumin in the early 1860s.[5] It may have been through the Hispanic community that Pissarro came to the attention of the Arosas, or perhaps through Corot, with whom Pissarro studied in those early years.

Although Pissarro came from a wealthy family, he was repelled by the restrictions of bourgeois life. This led him to *la vie de Bohème,* which he learned about firsthand from friends of Henry Murger, the author of the best-selling novel of that name.[6] Artistic poverty never completely lost its appeal to him, and through his example, he sold many younger artists on the concept, including Paul Gauguin. Pissarro also had a genuine love of the lower classes, which can be seen in the abstract in his socialist and anarchist political views and in practice in his marriage to his parents' young housemaid, Julie Vellay.[7] Vellay had come from a small town to find employment in Paris in 1857. She took a position with Pissarro's parents, who had moved back to France that year. The two fell in love, married, and, by 1863, had their first child, Lucien, and set up housekeeping. With contributions from both sets of parents and with Julie's income from her job at a florist's, Camille was able to paint full-time, ever hopeful of attracting some sales.

It took almost ten years for Pissarro to begin earning even a subsistence income from his art. During this time the couple lived in the countryside outside Paris; Pissarro's widowed mother gave them 1,000 francs a year, and his wife grew enough food in their garden to feed the steadily increasing brood of children.[8] Help also came from the many friends that the couple made in the art world. Camille's willingness to teach fledgling artists and Julie's to welcome all visitors made their home a pilgrimage site for Parisians of greater means and leisure who wanted to learn art's secrets at the knee of a master. Paul Cézanne was one regular visitor, but many lesser-known would-be artists came, whose gifts helped the struggling family. The picturesque poverty of the Pissarros warmed many hearts—the kindly paterfamilias working in his studio for the love of his craft, the solid earth mother providing abundant meals for all, and the happy children who grew up learning that art was the highest of all callings. Pissarro seemed to have realized every artist's dream: he could work without capitulating to a crass, commercial world.

Few visitors took into account that Pissarro had a wealthy family who could give monetary aid and help educate his children. The Pissarros' country homes were comfortable middle-class dwellings, complete with maid. Often the Pissarros kept an apartment in town so that Camille could have a presence in the art world. Furthermore, the peaceful image that Camille and Julie Pissarro presented to guests was belied by the constant bickering about money that runs through family letters and is an important part of the children's recollections.[9] Camille Pissarro was pragmatic enough to warn his disciples not to give up their jobs and steady incomes, but his own example sometimes proved to be more compelling than his words. And he could not resist trying to make an artist out of his own son, Lucien, in spite of his wife's objections and his own better judgment.[10]

This was the man whom Gauguin met in 1879. At first he saw only Pissarro's apartment in Paris, where he went to pick out a few works.[11] But even this glimpse was enough to intrigue him. Soon he was invited to come to the informal gatherings at the café Nouvelle Athènes on the place Pigalle in the heart of the Parisian avant-garde. There he met the regulars: Degas, Manet, Renoir, Caillebotte, and the critic Duranty. The conversation was combative, but it was not intolerant. Establishment views were the only ones *not* defended; everything else was proposed and debated with a freedom that Gauguin had never before encountered.[12]

What did the Impressionists see in Gauguin? A new patron certainly. But money did not entitle just anyone to sit down with this outspoken crowd. Gauguin had nerve. In those days he was riding the crest of his recent successful speculations, and the same cab that waited for him for hours outside the Bourse probably drove him across Paris from his home in Vaugirard to the Clichy section of the Right Bank and waited while he sat in the smoke-filled café. He was elaborately deferential, as befitted his Latin upbringing. His Saint-Mesmin boarding school education gave him the necessary academic credentials for this largely upper-middle-class group. But as he gradually entered into the conversations, it was probably his skill as a storyteller and his love of puns and paradoxes that entertained the group and won his acceptance.

Underlying the intellectual dynamism of the Impressionist group was an unconventional sexual dimension that Gauguin had not previously encountered. The social circles that had welcomed him back to Paris after five years at sea were cosmopolitan in their taste and education but conventional in the way they lived their lives. The tradition-bound Spanish and the earnest Scandinavians valued marriage and children above all else. But the artists and intellectuals of the avant-garde Impressionist movement tended not to marry and often had personal lives that were either unknown or ambiguous even to those in their social circles. Degas, Cassatt, Caillebotte, and Renoir were unmarried when Gauguin met them. Though highly respectable in their public behavior, as befitted their bourgeois status, their art betrayed sensuality, even open sexuality in their frequent depiction of prostitutes, which invited speculation about their private behavior. Gauguin may have gravitated toward Pissarro, another family man, but he was fascinated with the others, particularly Degas.

Degas in his mid-forties had a seductive manner that beguiled many a new artist entering the Impressionist arena. He had a stable of followers, both men and women, to whom he reached out with a sensual charm that amused and aroused them. His shifting loyalties and fickle embrace caused heated jealousy and anger, and most who became lasting friends went through cycles of distance and intimacy over the years.[13] Gauguin never earned this status with Degas, but the older man held a personal and professional power over Gauguin that ultimately eclipsed that of Pissarro. In their different ways, both Degas and Pissarro pointed out new possibilities to Gauguin, new ways to arrange his life to accommodate the increasingly central role of art within it.

As the April 10, 1879, opening of the group's fourth Impressionist exhibition approached, and the roster of artists crystallized, Gauguin's presence as an exhibitor became desirable. Some of the more important members of the group did not exhibit that year: Renoir, Morisot, Cézanne, and Guillaumin backed out for one reason or another.[14] Gauguin's invitation could not have come because anyone thought he was an adequate substitute for the missing artists or even because his works would occupy some otherwise blank walls, for he contributed only one work, and that was a sculpture. Nor did he have a reputation earned at the Salon, as did some of the artists to whom Degas extended invitations.

Gauguin's invitation must have been purely ceremonial—a tip of the hat to a man who had made himself agreeable in a social setting. Someone, probably Pissarro, must have been to his home to see his work. But since Gauguin entered only the one sculpture, a marble bust of his son Emil (Metropolitan Museum of Art), it can be supposed that the scout, whoever it was, was not impressed with Gauguin's paintings and did not encourage him to submit any. Gauguin's art was sufficiently polished that the group would not have been embarrassed by anything he would send, but they must have been relieved that he was content with a modest contribution.

Gauguin continued to show one or two sculptures with the Impressionists as time went on, but it was painting that was at the heart of his enchantment with his new circle of friends. That summer he began to reformulate his painting style by studying with Pissarro for several weeks and by painting every weekend on his own. He was captivated by everything that Pissarro suggested to him, from how to make his brushstrokes and color livelier to how to stretch his canvases himself. Gradually he dropped the formality of their rapport and addressed Pissarro as a friend.[15]

One reason that Gauguin and Pissarro developed a stronger personal relationship was that Pissarro liked Mette Gauguin and, being a family man himself, liked to see their growing children.[16] Gauguin would have met with the Impressionists at the café Nouvelle Athènes by himself. Neither wives nor women artists were comfortable in that male haven, and besides, Mette was pregnant with their third child, Clovis, who was born on May 10.[17] Pissarro probably came to the apartment to meet Mette and the children and see Paul's paintings. Once the acquaintance was formed, the two Danish citizens became very friendly, and the couples made a congenial foursome when the Gauguins visited the Pissarros in the country. In the correspondence between Gauguin and Pissarro, the wives and families are seldom forgotten.[18]

Gauguin made a sketch of Pissarro, just as he had of the many friends and relatives with whom he and his wife had spent leisurely evenings. On the same page, Pissarro returned the favor by sketching Gauguin (fig. 11). The contrast of the two portraits speaks volumes about the two men and their relationship. Gauguin's portrait of Pissarro, executed in colored pastels, is a graceful and polished image of a serene older man pulling thoughtfully on his pipe. Gauguin must have been taken aback by Pissarro's curt reply: Pissarro sketched Gauguin with rough, black strokes, making

11 Paul Gauguin and Camille Pissarro, *Portrait of Gauguin by Pissarro and Portrait of Pissarro by Gauguin*, ca. 1880. Black chalk and pastel on paper, 14 x 19 1/4 in. (35.8 x 49 5 cm). Musée du Louvre, Département des Arts Graphiques, Paris.

him appear unkempt and overly eager. This was hardly the image Gauguin had of himself in his days of waiting cabs and sartorial splendor at the Bourse. It is no wonder that the honor of keeping the double sketch went to Pissarro. But Gauguin learned the lesson that Pissarro wanted to teach: his crude sketch made Gauguin's seem pretty but bland; Gauguin's facile, polished style lacked expressiveness. Gauguin took Pissarro's deliberate primitivism to heart and spent the next several years unlearning the techniques that he had picked up at the Salons.

After Gauguin had spent several weeks with Pissarro in Pontoise in the summer of 1879, his acceptance into the Impressionist group as a regular exhibitor was assured. Gauguin's progress while painting side by side with Pissarro was sufficient for Pissarro to encourage his new acolyte to prepare paintings for the next Impressionist exhibition. The works that he showed in the fifth Impressionist exhibition held in April of 1880 date from those weeks at Pontoise and from the time after his return to Vaugirard. Gauguin had never before had the opportunity to work toward an exhibition in which he could determine which paintings were shown and how many. Unlike his colleagues, he did not have a long history of showing at the Salon before joining the Impressionists; he may have been submitting every year since 1875, although he was successful only one time. Now he had the luxury of knowing that his works would be shown and that the exhibition would attract extensive critical attention. Suddenly he would be in the spotlight as an artist.

Several of the eight works that Gauguin chose for this important debut are now highly regarded. Of the paintings he did with Pissarro, he exhibited a version of his *Apple Trees (Les Pommiers de l'Hermitage [Seine et Oise]*, Private Collection), and of the paintings he did in Paris afterward, he exhibited *The Market Gardens of Vaugirard* (fig. 12). In addition to the paintings, he submitted a marble bust, similar to the one he showed in 1879, but of his wife: *Portrait Bust of Mette Gauguin* (fig. 13). The paintings were

**12** Paul Gauguin, *The Market Gardens of Vaugirard,* 1879. Oil on canvas, 26 x 39 1/2 in. (66 x 100.3 cm). Smith College Museum of Art, Northhampton, Massachusetts, purchased 1953.

**13** Paul Gauguin, *Portrait Bust of Mette Gauguin,* 1879. White marble, h. 13 1/2 in. (34 cm). Witt Library, Courtauld Institute, London.

more brilliantly colored than his pre-Impressionist work, and he had learned the power of the choppy, visible brushstroke. The sculpture was more realistic than the previous year's angelic head of Emil; it showed Mette's fashionable ruffled collar, her hair slightly mussed, and her overly large nose. Gauguin had made great gains in overcoming his bland style to capture the more expressive irregularities of the world around him.

Unfortunately Gauguin's fledgling offerings met with unfavorable reviews, if they were mentioned at all.[19] Dismissed as being in the second tier of Impressionists, his landscapes were seen as derivative of Pissarro's. The faithful Impressionist critic Armand Silvestre found "qualities in the work exhibited by Gauguin and his *Effet de neige* is exceedingly accurate, but his coarse execution is hideously heavy."[20] No one even mentioned the marble bust of Mette. It was an inauspicious debut for someone who liked to cut a commanding figure, and Gauguin never forgave those critics for humiliating him.

Had Gauguin been welcomed as positively as other newcomers — Mary Cassatt's debut the previous year had caused a stir among the regular Impressionist critics — he might have become a full-time painter immediately.[21] In fact, he may have left the employ of the banker Bourdon sometime in the spring of 1880 with the thought that the Impressionist exhibition would launch his career as a painter.[22] He had other inspiration for this: his old friend Emile Schuffenecker quit his job with Bertin that year and, with a small inheritance (smaller than Gauguin's winnings on the exchange), got married and devoted himself to art full-time.[23] If Gauguin had the same thought, the discouraging reviews must have squelched it, because he was employed again by the beginning of the summer. This time he worked for the Thomereau insurance agency, which traded its funds on the stock market.

Although Gauguin resented adverse criticism, he had the kind of pride necessary to carry on. He was also no doubt consoled by his comrades, who were used to taking such blows and who had, in fact, received worse reviews that year than in the past. Pissarro, Cassatt, and Guillaumin, as well as the exhibition in general, had been skewered by the critics.[24] Bad press always intensified their camaraderie, which now embraced Gauguin. Gauguin traded works with Degas, Cassatt, Pissarro, and Guillaumin and treasured the exchanges as a sign of their respect. He always remembered the kindness of Manet: "Once, seeing a picture of mine (at the beginning), he told me it was very good. I answered, out of respect for the master, 'Oh, I am only an amateur!' At that time I was in business as a stockbroker, and I was studying art only at night and on holidays. 'Oh, no,' said Manet, 'there are no amateurs but those who make bad pictures.' That was sweet to me."[25] Degas was "like a good papa [who] said to me at my début, 'You have your foot in the stirrup.'"[26]

Having weathered his first set of bad reviews through his own grit and the kindness of new friends, Gauguin enlarged his art production without giving up his steady employment. The Gauguins moved that summer to an apartment nearby in Vaugirard that had both a courtyard garden for the children and a studio for Paul. Once again Paul spent as much time as possible painting with Pissarro in the country, preparing for the next annual Impressionist exhibition.

One might say that the pressure of this double life, which now had become regularized, caused the first cracks to appear in the Gauguin household. Paul simply had no time for his family. With his own studio and his own exhibiting group, which met on the other side of Paris, he now took his art outside the family circle and practiced it among strangers. Mette increasingly found herself alone with the children, excluded from the lively intellectual company she had always participated in so fervently. In the past, their young artist-friends had enjoyed coming to her drawing room in the evenings; but now her husband's new colleagues got together in a smoke-filled café or sought the company of the other women artists of the group, Berthe Morisot, Mary Cassatt, and Marie Bracquemond. No doubt Mette was invited with her husband to the dinner parties of the larger Impressionist social group, but this must have been a rare occurrence, for she does not seem to have formed a relationship with any of them other than the Pissarros. Paul may have excluded her deliberately.

The Gauguins did keep up a cordial relationship with Emile Schuffe-necker and his new wife, Louise, especially as they began having children. They also lived on the Left Bank, not far from the Gauguins, and now that Emile was devoting all his time to his art studies and his entries for the Salon, art topics would have been their common bond. The Gauguins also became friendly with their new neighbor and landlord, Félix Jobbé-Duval, a painter and civil servant. Jobbé-Duval was a witness on the birth certificate of the Gauguin's fourth child, Jean-René, in April of 1881.[27]

In the summer of 1880, not long after the move to the rue Carcel, the Gauguins' oldest child, Emil, now six, enrolled in a Danish school under the patronage of Mette's old friend the Countess Moltke, one of the Estrup children for whom she had been governess. Either Mette took Emil to Copenhagen, or a member of her family came to Paris to get him. Her ties to her family had remained strong through frequent correspondence and visits. Her sister Ingeborg Thaulow was living in Norway with her husband and two children, as was her youngest sister, Pauline, who was married to Frits Thaulow's cousin, Hermann Thaulow, who ran the Thaulow family's pharmaceutical business in Oslo. Her two brothers, Theodor and Aage, were establishing themselves in Copenhagen; Aage was studying law and later became a judge. At the age of thirty Mette saw her husband's life in Paris becoming broader and more exciting and her own becoming narrower. As she sat alone in her parlor while Paul was off for an evening at the café Nouvelle Athènes, she must have thought wistfully of the importance she would have had in intellectual Copenhagen circles if she had settled there.

The new works that Paul Gauguin completed for the 1881 Impressionist exhibition attest to the increasing amount of time he was spending with the Impressionists. The previous year he had shown mostly landscapes done under the tutelage of Pissarro. This year he showed only three landscapes; the rest of his ten works were still lifes and figure studies that evoked the fashionable life of Paris rather than the rustic beauty of the French countryside. Like Degas, Cassatt, and others in their camp, Gauguin

attempted to suggest the casual informality of a Paris apartment by painting seemingly unplanned motifs: assorted flowers lying on a chair seat waiting to become a bouquet (*Pour faire une bouquet,* Private Collection, Switzerland) or a musical instrument dropped on a chair in passing and left at a precarious angle (*Sur une chaise,* Private Collection).

Gauguin also showed two carved wood sculptures of Parisian women. One was an almost childishly simple carving called *La Petite Parisienne* (Graphische Kabinett, Munich) and the other was a relief medallion called *The Singer* (fig. 14). *The Singer* wears a dress with low décolletage and holds a bouquet of flowers as if she had just finished her performance and was looking out over the audience, enjoying their applause. Mette Gauguin identified the model as Valérie Roumi when it was exhibited in Copenhagen twelve years later, indicating that the piece was not the result of a clandestine alliance but that Mette probably met the singer when she came to the apartment to pose.[28] A pastel of Roumi given to Paul by his fellow Impressionist Jean-Louis Forain shows that she posed for others as well.[29]

Gauguin also showed for the first time a large painting of a nude woman (fig. 15). He must have painted such a subject before, although none from an earlier date can now be firmly attributed to him. Because this was the first one he exhibited, it was a significant departure and a further sign that his art had moved out of the family parlor. A reference to a model who was posing for him in August[30] probably dates the picture to that time and puts to rest the speculation that he had the housemaid pose for him.[31] With his new studio and his new colleagues, he hired models as any professional would.

Gauguin may have hired this particular model because she was not a standard beauty, but her out-of-proportion body allowed him to explore the intense realism that Degas persuasively preached. Because of the quirks of this woman's body, the painting was heralded, in some of the first critical words of praise for Gauguin, as a modern version of the outworn artistic subject of the female nude.[32] As the Belgian critic Huysmans noted, "It is possible to see in an undraped woman her nationality and the historical era in which she lives, her status, her age, the virginal or deflowered state of her body." For Huysmans, the most intriguing of these characteristics was the "deflowered" state of Gauguin's nude, so visible in her "slightly flabby stomach." The vivid impression that Gauguin achieved of the woman who has known sex and had children allows us, as viewers, to "dream of the sort of life she leads, that we can almost search the marks of childbirth in her limbs and reconstruct her sorrows and joys, identify ourselves with her for a few minutes."[33] That a male critic would claim to identify with such a female experience as childbearing indicates a sophisticated blurring of gender lines in contemporary intellectual circles. Even more, it emphasizes the fascination with the "sexual woman" in Impressionist art, a type who was more frequently shown in paintings with open references to prostitution. Gauguin's more respectable version of the sexual woman—his model even wears a wedding ring—nevertheless had the desired effect of arousing the viewer's curiosity about the woman engaging in the sex act itself.

Another, even more titillating step that the viewer might take would be open only to an inner circle of friends. Although she was clearly not the actual model for the painting, the reference to pregnancy and the sexual act that preceded it was a daring allusion to his own wife's fourth pregnancy and the birth of their son Jean-René only a few days after the opening of the Impressionist exhibition. To bring attention to his own and Mette's private sexuality in this way foretells the even more shocking sexual references that Gauguin employed in his later art.[34]

Aside from Huysmans' observations (which were not published in Paris until 1883), Gauguin was virtually ignored by the critics, and the group in general was castigated for the ugliness created by the realist approach taken by Degas and his followers—underscored by the setting of the show, which was cramped and dark in its odd space on the boulevard des Capucines.[35] But Gauguin was much better prepared for the critical reception this year because his standing among the Impressionists had improved in so many ways. As was typical of the unfolding of his relationships, Gauguin, at first deferential, was now assuming an air of command. He had been instrumental in locating the rooms used for the Impressionist exhibition and acted as a mediator to bring Degas, Caillebotte, and Pissarro into greater harmony. This was not entirely successful, for Caillebotte refused to participate, but Degas and Pissarro managed to revive their old camaraderie.

In addition to his self-important new role in making arrangements, Gauguin had the exquisite pleasure of selling a number of paintings. The Impressionists' dealer, Paul Durand-Ruel, bought three for 1,500 francs, and a Romanian collector in Paris, Georges de Bellio, bought one of the still lifes, which Gauguin borrowed back to put into the 1881 exhibition. The money that Gauguin was paid for these paintings he immediately reinvested in a seascape by Manet, *Vue de Hollande,* which he added to a pastel he had bought from Manet in 1880. Gauguin's reaction to the sale of his works— to turn around and buy other art—shows his speculator's approach even to his own art. Unlike Pissarro, who had to pay bills with the money he earned from his sales, Gauguin used his art to buy more valuable works by artists who were already established. By the end of the year he had bought paintings by Manet, Renoir, John Lewis Brown, Boudin, and Jongkind to add to the Pissarros and Manet already on his walls. In addition, he had traded some of his paintings for works by Degas and Cassatt. His own speculation in works of art fueled the interest of his friends on the stock exchange, such as Emile Bertaux, for whom Gauguin bought paintings by Pissarro and Guillaumin.[36]

Although Gauguin may have been especially driven by his speculator's personality, he was not alone among the Impressionist artists in thinking of the future value of their works and those of their friends. Both Degas and Cassatt, who came from banking families, put their sales money back into works of art, primarily investing in works by other Impressionists.[37] Although Degas may have been motivated by his love for the objects and seldom sold a piece, Cassatt thought a great deal about the future value of her friends' work and did her part to increase the family fortune by investing in paintings. When Gauguin's fortunes plummeted, his collection of Impressionist paintings was the only one of his investments that held its value.

Although the circle of family and friends that had been entertained by Paul's art no longer gathered in the Gauguin parlor, Mette and her household were increasingly put on public view thanks to the Impressionist emphasis on the painting of daily life and Paul's constant search for new and interesting motifs. The family's antiques and decorative ceramics showed up in Paul's still lifes, their furniture became props for portraits, and Emil's recollection that his father used his mother's "best linen tablecloth for canvas or her finest petticoat for paint-rags" was probably not much of an exaggeration.[38]

In 1881, Paul painted two ambitious interiors, one showing Mette at the piano and the other their daughter, Aline, asleep. The human subjects have to compete with the curious decorations in such paintings as *Flowers, Still Life* and *The Little Dreamer:* the odd black dado encircling the lower half of the walls, the wallpaper patterned with birds in flight, and the ceramics and souvenirs isolated in the big space (figs. 16–17). Whereas most Impressionist interiors show cozy fireplaces, food on the table, and fine paintings on the wall to stimulate the senses, Gauguin's idea of an interesting home was one full of strange juxtapositions and confrontations.

In the background of *Flowers, Still Life,* overshadowed by the furniture and decorations, we find Mette playing for an attentive man who leans on the piano and looks down at her. By his round face we can probably identify him as Emile Schuffenecker, Paul's longtime associate and one of Mette's dearest friends. Later correspondence between the two shows how deeply they cared for each other and also how similar struggles in their marriages and with Paul gave them a strong rapport.[39] By placing his wife and his best friend in a classic pose of lovers, Paul may again have given those in his inner circle something intimate and provocative to think about, where the general public saw only an anonymous scene of flirtation. Mette herself must have wondered about the ambiguous personal messages suggested by her husband's paintings, and although she could appreciate Paul's attempt to depict domestic life in a new and haunting way, it must have made her somewhat uneasy.

Gauguin reached his apogee as an Impressionist at this time. Now a regular at the café Nouvelle Athènes, he reversed roles with Pissarro, often giving advice to the older man. He told his friend in the country that "a

painter *must* live in Paris to keep up with the latest ideas."[40] As time went on, he became even bolder in his advice, telling Pissarro whether to paint figures or still lifes, whether to spend more time in the studio or *en plein air*. He even felt confident enough to tease the unusual but highly respected Cézanne, asking if he had as yet "found the formula of painting that would startle the world."[41] When the group talked of the next exhibition to be held in the spring of 1882, he put himself in the middle, busying himself with arrangements and pronouncements about who should or should not be included. He was by no means at the top of the list of preferred exhibitors according to Caillebotte, Renoir, or Monet, but in deference to Pissarro and to avoid having to confront the strong-willed man themselves, they allowed him to have his way. When he threatened to withdraw over the possible inclusion of Degas's favorite, Raffaelli, the threat made hardly a ripple in the discussions of the others, and he quietly let the matter drop and went on as usual.[42]

The seventh Impressionist exhibition opened in early March with only eight exhibitors, most of whom practiced classic Impressionism—using pure colors and broken brushstrokes applied to landscape or rural subjects.

The painters of urban life — Degas, Cassatt, and the others in their group except Caillebotte—either boycotted or were not invited. Thus Caillebotte, Monet, Renoir, Pissarro, Morisot, and Guillaumin represented the original group, while Victor Vignon and Paul Gauguin were the newest members, both having begun exhibiting in earnest in 1880. The show was heralded as a return to the best of Impressionism, and Pissarro was singled out for particular praise. Although once again Gauguin was reviewed unfavorably, at least he was not ignored.[43] Most important to him was that he had positioned himself in the inner circle of a group that had the attention of the press, the support of the dealer Durand-Ruel, and the best chance of success in an increasingly tight art market.

Compared to friends like Marguerite Arosa and Emile Schuffenecker, with whom he had started to paint ten years before, Gauguin felt he was on the fast track. They were both now regulars at the Salon, but neither had the visibility that Gauguin's participation in the notorious Impressionist group had given him. Yet, because of their more careful handling of money, they, as well as most of Gauguin's friends among the Impressionists, were able to paint full-time. As he looked with envy at those around him, he increasingly identified his family as the financial and personal obstacle that stood between him and the pleasures of an artist's life. Only Pissarro had managed to have a large family while working full-time as an artist, and although Gauguin clung to Pissarro as a friend and mentor, his growing resentment of his wife and children was a symptom of his inner determination to follow his desires rather than meet his responsibilities.

The failure of the Union Générale bank in January 1882 had such an impact
on the economy of France that few citizens, including Paul Gauguin, escaped
unharmed. This bank had been formed only five years earlier by speculators playing on the nation's desire for a French Catholic bank to rival the great
Jewish financial institutions of Europe, such as the house of Rothschild.
Using illegal methods to capitalize the bank, the partners stimulated phenomenal growth, which prompted a nationwide frenzy of investing. In late
1881 and early 1882, the bank proved unstable and collapsed in a matter of
days. Small investors were unusually affected, and the collapse brought
some local economies, such as the city of Lyons, to a standstill. In Paris, where
the stakes were highest, traders in stocks and related commodities often
lost everything. Much has been written about the crash of the stock market
in 1882, but the most moving account can be found in Zola's *L'Argent*
(1891): "The catastrophe of the Universale [Union Générale] had been one
of those terrible shocks that make a whole city totter. Nothing had remained
firmly standing. Other establishments had begun to give way; every day
there were fresh collapses. One after another the banks went down, with the
sudden crash of bits of walls left standing after a fire."[1]

Art, inasmuch as it was traded on a free market, was also affected
by the economic depression. It took years, and a great deal of foreign
investment (largely American), for the Paris art market to rebound to the
approximate level of the boom days of the 1860s and 1870s. For the
Impressionists, the loss was compounded by the fact that their primary
dealer, Paul Durand-Ruel, had been financed by a partner in the Union
Générale.[2] Not only did he lose in his own speculations, but his backers
deserted him, calling in their loans. Durand-Ruel abruptly stopped buying
Impressionist pictures, such as Gauguin's, that did not have ready buyers,
and he was no longer able to offer the subsidies he had extended to such
financially strapped artists as Pissarro. Three years later he applied to
the French government for an exemption from French customs for paintings shipped to America, pleading that such an act would save French
art from the "current stagnant state of the art market, which has so cruelly
struck down a great number of our artists."[3] Artists and art dealers were
forced to take extreme measures and go great distances to lure whatever
buyers they could find.

As an employee in Paris's financial district and as an artist, Gauguin
was one of the people at highest risk, and he was profoundly affected by
this unforeseen turn of events. But the crash symbolized for him a more per-

vasive destruction of the old, conventional life in which he had once taken such pride. It set in motion a rough, sometimes violent scramble to assert his own desires over those of the people dependent on him. The transformation took several years and had many false starts; but the calculation and occasional blatant cruelty that emerged in his character in his path toward liberation was so exhilarating that he made little effort to curb these tendencies. The myth of Gauguin — proud individualist — was forged in the period of lawlessness that follows all upheavals.

By June of 1882, Gauguin was complaining that his business commissions were down because of the stalled market and that, despite the accompanying decline in the art market, he thought increasingly about painting full-time.[4] The Gauguins' old friend Marie Heegaard (now the wife of Bjorn Stephensen) had visited Paris with her husband and returned to Copenhagen with one of Paul's large still lifes[5] — a sale that gave Paul the confidence that he could avoid the slump in Paris by developing a market in Scandinavia. He regretted that the painting would be so far away, but bragged to Pissarro that Stephensen was now a convert to Impressionism and would promote Gauguin and his fellow Impressionists back home in Denmark.[6]

Impressionism was attracting some attention in the Danish press; the well-known literary critic, Georg Brandès, had written on Japanese art and Impressionism,[7] and in October of 1882, Brandès's friend Karl Madsen published an explanation of the style and some of its proponents: Manet, Degas, Monet, and Pissarro.[8] Paul's and Mette's ties to the art community in Copenhagen were established through Ingeborg and Frits Thaulow, who lived in Norway but were often in Denmark, as well as through Mette's friendships with such wealthy collectors as Marie Heegaard Stephensen and the Count and Countess Moltke. That the Gauguins also had continuing contact with the Danish and Scandinavian communities in Paris is attested by Paul's pastel portraits of Charlotte Flensborg (Wildenstein 68), a Danish pianist and teacher, and William Lund (Wildenstein 69), a Danish collector.[9] Mette also made the acquaintance of Scandinavian artists during trips north to visit her family. In the fall of 1882, when she was staying with Ingeborg and Frits in Oslo, she met the Norwegian painter Erik Werenskiold and probably the well-known Swedish painter Ernst Josephson, both of whom were frequent guests of the Thaulows.[10]

As Paul faced the real possibility of becoming a full-time artist, he understood better than most that success would come through marketing as much as through artistic effort. He saw an opportunity to gain a foothold with the Scandinavians, who were not so immediately affected by the crash of the French stock market, and he readily seized it. It is interesting that his Spanish circle of friends did not seem to constitute as promising a market for him; that may have been because most of his friends were, like him, employed in the banking field and were also financially strapped. Many of his Peruvian relatives were doubly affected because, in addition to the failure of the Union Générale, they suffered the collapse of the guano market, which had enriched them for so many decades. Decades later, Gauguin told of one such relative, for whom he may have acted as an agent:

In the year 1880, I think, Etchenique came to Paris again as Ambassador, on a mission to arrange with the Comptoir d'Escompte the guaranty of the Peruvian loan (on a basis of guano).

He stayed with his sister, who had a splendid house in the Rue de Chaillot, and, being a discreet ambassador, gave her to understand that everything was going well. My cousin, pleased by this, as all the Peruvians were, hastened to speculate on a rise in the Peruvian loan in the Maison Dreyfus.

But the contrary was true; and a few days later the Peruvian stock was unsaleable. She drank up several millions in that soup!

"*Caro mio*," she said to me, "I am ruined. I have nothing left but the eight horses in the stable. What is to become of me?"[11]

From his vantage point in 1903, Gauguin had little sympathy for his wealthy relatives; but at the time, he shrewdly maintained close ties to everyone who might be in a position to help him. And although few of his paintings seem to have been purchased by his Spanish friends, and none at all by the Arosas, Gauguin was involved in other speculations with these financiers that he hoped would someday pay off.[12]

Among his non-Spanish friends on the Bourse, Gauguin found some who shared his interest in collecting contemporary art. One of these was Emile Bertaux, a clerk to the *coulissier* G. Lafuite.[13] Bertaux extended sums of money to Gauguin so that he might make purchases of paintings based on his insider's knowledge of the Impressionists. Gauguin mainly bought Pissarros and Guillaumins for Bertaux, as well as passing on to him some of his own paintings.[14] Bertaux presumably resold these works to wealthier colleagues and clients. Gauguin may also have used the family's apartment for the display of other artists' work in hopes of making a sale to friends who visited. In a letter to Pissarro in June of 1882, Gauguin reminds his friend to bring him a painting that he had thought about putting in the Gauguin home.[15]

In one curious instance in the fall of 1882, Gauguin paid Pissarro for a large painting of a man sawing wood (*Le Scieur de bois*, 1879, Private Collection) but did not immediately take possession of it. Later he found that he needed the money back and canceled the deal.[16] It is hard to imagine that Gauguin would have been so callous as to ask the financially precarious Pissarro for money back from a sale that was between friends. That Pissarro arranged to have the money repaid to Gauguin without recrimination suggests that the sale was somewhat speculative from the start and that both parties understood that the arrangement might fall through. Gauguin may have paid for the work out of his own pocket, expecting Bertaux or another agent to reimburse him when the painting was passed on; but when the sale collapsed, both Gauguin and Pissarro felt it was only fair that Gauguin get his money back. In January of 1883, after Pissarro had arranged for Durand-Ruel to pay Gauguin the 800 francs in question, Gauguin was again involved in possible Pissarro sales, which, Pissarro had to remind him, must go through Durand-Ruel, with whom he had a contract.[17]

Throughout this period both Paul and Mette Gauguin often visited the Pissarros and were on the most cordial terms. The Pissarros' oldest son, Lucien, was now seeking employment, and Gauguin tried to use his contacts in London to help find him a place in the financial market.[18] Lucien's interest in art, however, eventually prevailed over more practical employment, and his association with a younger generation of artists would affect both his father and Gauguin.

The spring of 1883 brought other radical changes to Gauguin's art world. First and foremost was the absence, for the first time in four years, of the regular Impressionist exhibition. Gauguin had been devoting more and more of his time to painting and was taken by surprise when Durand-Ruel co-opted the group event by holding a series of one-artist shows that spring for Boudin, Monet, Renoir, Pissarro, and Sisley. The artists around Degas—the painters of modern life—were not so affected, because they had boycotted the previous year's exhibition. Gauguin, however, who had so triumphantly taken his place alongside the landscape Impressionists in 1882, now found himself conspicuously excluded from that charmed circle. He could not hide his anger and lashed out even at Pissarro, whom he accused of betraying his socialist principles in abandoning the group exhibitions. Gauguin passionately proclaimed that no matter what happened, *he* would never be so selfish as to put himself above the others with such a "Moi et toujours moi" attitude.[19]

Other changes that affected Gauguin that spring were the deaths of Gustave Arosa and Edouard Manet. Arosa's death was primarily a personal loss, but it also meant the abandonment of any hope of eventual patronage from that influential man. Manet's death may have affected him even more. Not only had Manet offered him encouragement, but he had also shaped the Impressionist movement that Gauguin was so proud to be a part of, and his passing symbolized the ever-increasing fragmentation of the group.

Another development was the threatened divorce of Ingeborg and Frits Thaulow.[20] They were in Paris over the winter of 1882–1883, so the Gauguins were drawn into their marital woes perhaps more than they normally might have been. Mette naturally supported Ingeborg; Paul seems to have drawn closer to Frits. Frits's leadership position among progressive Norwegian artists made him interested in Paul's Impressionism, and Gauguin in return saw Frits as a valuable ally in his attempt to engender a Scandinavian following. He visited Frits's studio often and met Scandinavian artists and critics there. The next year Frits arranged for him to show in a large exhibition in Oslo.[21]

The discussion of divorce between Frits and Ingeborg Thaulow no doubt raised the same possibility in the minds of Paul and Mette Gauguin. Years later, Paul wrote to Emile Schuffenecker that he had gone so far as to write Mette's mother to ask for a divorce, but that he and Mette had reconciled.[22] There is no mention of this in correspondence from the early 1880s, but it would not be surprising if such a temporary break did take place. Perhaps a sign of their estrangement was that in 1883, when summer came and Paul was anxious to spend his vacation weeks painting with Pissarro at Osny, Mette was forced to make independent arrangements for the family to stay nearby with Pissarro's friend Dr. Paul Gachet. Despite Paul's later accusations of Mette's spendthrift ways ("when I managed to earn 35,000 francs in a single year I didn't spend on myself . . . and yet Madame Gauguin contrived to run up debts throughout the *quartier*"), we get quite another view of her in a letter written by a friend at this time.[23] In recommending Mette as a tenant, the collector Eugène Murer wrote, "Madame is charming, very nice, not at all snobbish, and very simple in her tastes."[24]

In August of that year Gauguin made another trip, this time to Cerbère, a seaside town on the Mediterranean side of the border between France and Spain. He went there on a mission for the Republican Military Association, a Spanish group in Paris led by Ruiz-Zorilla, which was dedicated to the overthrow of the Spanish government. Gauguin's part in what was to be an invasion of troops over the border from France is unclear, but was probably arranged by his friend Adolphe Calzado, who was financing the movement. Gauguin later told friends that he had made a surreptitious trip into Spain hidden in a sack of charcoal, but did not explain why.[25] Another trip to the south of France the following April with his friend Bertaux and cryptic dealings with the same group of Spanish rebels in the fall of 1885 indicate that he expected to reap financial rewards from these activities. As he wrote to Pissarro, "I am very interested in some Spanish business dealings in which I have a somewhat active part; I'll explain sometime later in the strictest confidence. At any rate, if this revolution succeeds or lasts for at least a month, I could very easily retire soon with some money."[26] Gauguin may have staked more than he should have on the success of this venture. By September of 1883 his letters make it clear that he no longer had his job with Thomereau and was having a hard time finding another position.

All summer he had been speculating in art, primarily in partnership with Bertaux. He bought two Cézannes from the art supplies dealer Julien Tanguy, which, he complained, he could not get Bertaux to buy from him,[27] although later he was able to sell him some paintings by Guillaumin and Pissarro.[28] In September he tried to establish a relationship with the Galerie Georges Petit (which was handling Impressionist works), primarily for the sale of his own paintings but possibly also to buy and sell the works of his friends.[29] He also called on Durand-Ruel and the smaller dealers Legrand and Portier and tried to interest a patron in Impressionist paintings—a M. Cellot, a financier with whom Gauguin later discussed other business possibilities.[30] Another idea he tried to develop was the designing of Impressionist tapestries; in this he was possibly inspired by his old friend Claude Favre ("le Marsouin"), who worked for Dillies and Company, a Belgian manufacturer of commercial cloth.[31] He no doubt thought that a translation of the Impressionist style into fabric would have commercial appeal. Pissarro shook his head at Gauguin's maneuverings. "Gauguin definitely makes me uneasy; he is such a terrible hustler—at least the way he talks. I don't dare tell him that it's wrongheaded and won't get him very far."[32]

By the fall of 1883, Paul Gauguin was openly expressing his desire to become a full-time painter regardless of the consequences. He spoke of his responsibilities as head of a large household and his dutiful attempts to find another job, but in reality all of his efforts were now focused on making a living through painting. As he wrote to Pissarro in October, "I find myself, my dear Pissarro, at an impasse right now: the love of my art occupies me too much to be a good employee in a business in which one cannot be a dreamer—but, on the other hand, I have a family that's too large and a wife who can't handle poverty. I can't launch myself as a painter without seeing necessity looming. In sum, I must make a living from painting at all costs. I am counting on you; and when you get back, please spend some time with me to help me get started."[33]

Once Gauguin made this declaration, he took action. Too impatient to wait for Pissarro to return from Rouen, where he had been painting all fall, Gauguin went out to see him.[34] He stayed only a day in Rouen, but it was enough to convince him that he would be smart to begin his life as a painter in this small town, where the cost of living was low and the population was wealthy. After several more trips in late 1883, the Gauguins left Paris, their home of ten years, to settle into a small house on the Impasse Malherne in Rouen. Their fifth child, Paul Rollon (called Pola), was born less than a month before they moved, and on his birth certificate Paul Gauguin for the first time recorded his occupation as "painter."[35]

When Gauguin made his preliminary trips to Rouen to visit Pissarro, he made a quick calculation of its sales potential. Pissarro had been staying with Eugène Murer, who had recommended Mette as a tenant; he was the retired owner of a bakery who now devoted his time to collecting art.[36] Although Murer had the reputation of paying low prices for the works he bought, he provided an important source of income for the Impressionist landscape painters. He also organized exhibitions in Rouen that other collectors in the area attended. Gauguin hoped that Murer would be an important ally.

Rouen was also home to a number of wealthy Scandinavians, whom Gauguin could cultivate with Mette's help. As Federico Zandomeneghi, a painter in Degas's circle, wrote jovially to Pissarro, "I heard that Gauguin is with you . . . he has gone to exploit the Scandinavians of Rouen."[37] The principal patrons Gauguin hoped to engage were the Mantheys, the family of the consul for Norway and Sweden. Their daughter sat for a pastel portrait by Gauguin and bought a painting of sailboats (*Les Voiliers*, Wildenstein 120) from him. Gauguin also courted the Rouen jeweler Haslauer and his Danish wife with gifts of paintings.[38]

Gauguin's friendship with Frits Thaulow was useful in his continuing pursuit of a Scandinavian market for his paintings, not only because of the contacts he wanted to make in Rouen, but also because Thaulow had invited him to exhibit in Oslo the following fall. As Gauguin planned which works to send to Norway, he tried to anticipate what would be of interest to that audience. He finally sent eight works, of which two still lifes and one portrait were included in the exhibition. These cannot be identified with certainty, but it is likely that the portrait was of his Danish wife (*Madame Mette Gauguin in Evening Dress* (fig. 18), whose two sisters lived in Oslo. Gauguin acknowledged that he sent works painted in a tighter than usual style, knowing that northerners were swayed more by intellect than by enthusiasm.[39] He also knew that identifiable Scandinavian subject matter would help. Another painting he sent was of Clovis sleeping next to an antique Norwe-

gian tankard (*Sleeping Child*, Private Collection) that Mette owned.[40] While Gauguin lived in Rouen his thoughts were often of the northern countries.

Perhaps it was because Mette Gauguin was a central figure in her husband's pursuit of a Scandinavian audience that Paul backed off from the idea of divorce and, further, insisted on transplanting the whole family to Rouen rather than taking painting excursions by himself, as Pissarro had done. The Gauguins soon found, however, that any money they might have saved in lower living expenses was expended at once in the move itself.[41] They had a reserve large enough to live on for six months: about 5,000 francs, which may have remained from Gauguin's successful investments in the stock market or the payoff from the Spanish intrigue of the summer before.[42] It was a handy sum for a painter to launch himself with, but for a man with five children — one a newborn — the margin was not comfortable. For Gauguin to sell enough paintings to meet the family's expenses after the savings were gone, he would have to sell at least three per month, a quota he had no proof he could meet.

A wiser artist would have waited until his sales were regular before entrusting his family's welfare to painting as a source of income. His friend Schuffenecker had made the move with caution: After receiving his modest inheritance and retiring from the Bourse, he had spent two years (1881–83) studying in the ateliers of Carolus-Duran and others and then became certified to teach drawing in French schools.[43] From 1884 he had a regular income from teaching, which allowed him to play an active role in the Paris art world. In later years, Gauguin looked upon Schuffenecker's security with envy and made barbed references to the privileged life of a drawing teacher.[44]

In spite of Mette's support of her husband's painting and her genuine interest in the arts, she could not disregard the precarious position the family found itself in. To move while she was still recovering from her fifth pregnancy was risky, and although the Gauguins had servants, running a household with four children under eight (Emil was still in boarding school in Copenhagen) was taxing. Mette cooperated with her husband, but she could not help being alarmed at the uncertainty of their future. The couple fought over money from the moment they arrived in Rouen. Paul complained to Pissarro, "My wife is impossible! She finds fault with everything here and sees the future as black."[45] At the age of thirty-three Mette saw everything she had worked for put in jeopardy by a willful husband.

Paul did not want to hear her concerns. Ever since he had chosen his course, everything about his family irritated him. In a letter to Pissarro he complained that he "was writing in the midst of the screams of a crying baby and all sorts of other encumbrances."[46] He envied Pissarro his courageous wife, who was so unlike the complaining Mette.[47] Later he wrote that a man is better off if he marries a servant rather than an educated woman — another reference to Pissarro's wife, a former housemaid.[48] But Mette, who knew Julie Pissarro better than Paul did, was aware of Julie's bitterness at her husband for not providing the family with a steady income. Furthermore, in spite of her efforts to get her Scandinavian friends and family to buy Paul's work, she knew that he was not well received by the Paris critics, nor had he found steady patrons or even a regular dealer. Camille Pissarro had good reviews, a good dealer (Durand-Ruel), and widespread patronage — and still struggled to support his family. When she pointed out these unpleasant facts to her husband, he cried betrayal. In fact, he attacked everyone who opposed this move, including his sister and their old circle of friends in Paris: "My sister and a lot of others have naturally turned my wife's head, [telling her] I don't have a drop of talent, etc."[49]

As the year in Rouen progressed, the situation worsened. Gauguin was able to place seven works with Durand-Ruel, but they were soon returned to him unsold.[50] He maintained his alliance with Bertaux, trading in paintings and taking another speculative trip to Spain. Gauguin also engaged in some questionable practices in selling Impressionist pictures. Durand-Ruel found two works (a Monet and a Renoir) that he had given to Gauguin on commission offered for sale without their frames in a cheap picture shop where the paintings were displayed on the floor. Unbeknownst to Durand-Ruel, a scam was worked whereby the customer paid a certain amount on the spot but was charged extra when it came time for the works to be delivered.[51]

In spite of Gauguin's schemes, the money in the bank trickled away long before the estimated six months. Although he had sold some paintings, the prospects presented by Murer and the Scandinavian community clearly would not provide him a regular income. By the middle of May, to keep the family afloat the Gauguins began selling other assets, such as Paul's life insurance policy and works from their own art collection.[52]

At this point, Mette took action. In July she made the long voyage by sea back to Copenhagen to investigate a move to Denmark. If her contacts among the Scandinavians in France had created a promising market, perhaps relocating to Denmark would be even better. And although Paul complained that she "cried 'Fire!' but did not go get water," she wanted to see what her own job prospects might be in her native country.[53] She came back with good news: she would have no trouble making money teaching French in Copenhagen, and, even better for Paul, the interest in Impressionism in Copenhagen was growing.[54]

At first they decided that she would go with the children and begin working, and he would join her six months later. Gauguin anticipated what others might think of him for letting his wife support the family, but he claimed his conscience was clear. "I have worked for a long time for the family, and if at this moment I can't make a living, it is because of the stupidity of the public."[55] This belligerently defensive tone would characterize most of his future writings about his family. He was keenly aware that he was abdicating his responsibilities, but he dared anyone to blame him for it. Intent on pursuing his own course, he believed that his wife and children should take care of themselves. He said that he would join them in Copenhagen only if Mette made enough to support them all.[56]

Shortly after writing these hot-tempered words, Paul recanted. Agreeing to come immediately to Denmark, he arranged to become a sales representative in Scandinavia for Dillies and Company, the cloth manufacturer for whom his friend Favre worked. He pictured it as an ideal situation because he could earn an income but set his own hours, which would allow him the flexibility to continue painting. And he was optimistic about his reception as a painter, generously writing to Pissarro, "If I succeed in advancing Impressionism in Denmark as I have in Norway [a reference to his recent exhibition in Oslo], I will let you know and arrange for you to benefit as well."[57]

For Mette the future looked bright again. Both she and Paul would be employed, and Paul's success as an artist was still a possibility. She imagined that with their contacts, they could step right in to the highest social and artistic circles of Copenhagen. Before their departure for Denmark, Mette spent a day shopping and saying goodbye to friends in Paris; and in her optimism, she spent over 400 francs on a new dress—money that she had to borrow from the Schuffeneckers.[58] The gesture was extravagant, for respectable dresses could be had for 60 francs,[59] and 500 francs would support the family for a month.[60] But for Mette the dress symbolized their former success in Paris and her belief in their future success in Copenhagen. Photographs taken during their last days in Rouen at the request of Paul's uncle Isidore show Mette and some of the children posing in their finery (fig. 19).[61]

Mette arrived in Copenhagen with the children in early November 1884, and Paul joined her a few weeks later. Their temporary home was with Mette's mother on the elegant, tree-lined street of Frederiksbergallée, in

a residential section west of the center of town. Within a few weeks they found their own apartment a few blocks away, in a building on the shopping street, Gammel Kongevej. This commodious apartment with seven bright rooms and picturesque sloping ceilings served as workplace for both Paul and Mette. Emil (ten) was in boarding school but could often come home now, and Aline (seven) went to school in Oslo, where she lived with her aunt, Phylle. The three youngest, Clovis (five), Jean-René (three), and Pola (one), were at home.[62]

Mette quickly obtained students for her private French lessons. Prime Minister Estrup and his family (her former students, now adults), as well as other friends, recommended her as a French teacher to young men training for diplomatic or naval careers. At thirty-five, her liveliness and no-nonsense language stood her in good stead with this age group. Through her sister Ingeborg she was introduced to members of the literary circle of Copenhagen, including Edvard Brandès, founder of the liberal newspaper *Politiken* and member of the Danish Parliament. Brandès was the brother of the internationally renowned literary critic Georg Brandès, whose writings propelled many new thinkers, like Ibsen and Nietzsche, into the forefront of European intellectual discourse. Ingeborg, her marriage to Frits Thaulow still on shaky ground, was active in these circles and a close friend of Edvard Brandès, whom she would marry in 1887. From this association, Mette found work translating the latest French literature into Danish. Many of her translations of the novels of Zola, among others, were published in *Politiken*.[63]

Paul's assimilation into the new intellectual environment in which he found himself was less wholehearted. He certainly knew Edvard Brandès—

57

Brandès bought one of his paintings (*Les Vases et l'éventail,* Wildenstein 178)—and very likely met his brother Georg. But in all Gauguin's letters to his friends in Paris, the famous literary figures are remarkably absent. In fact, Gauguin, who normally painted portrait sketches of everyone around him, painted only one in Copenhagen—of himself (fig. 20).

The snobbish French radical dismissed even the collectors like Count Frederick Moltke and his wife, Magda (Mette's former student), who were known all over Europe, and the prominent Danish painters who welcomed him into their homes.[64] Gauguin sneered at young progressives like S. Peder Kroyer, who was a central figure in contemporary Danish art. Kroyer had led the group that splintered off from the Academy, and formed an alternative school and exhibiting group, Society of the Friends of Art, much like the Impressionists. Gauguin felt, however, that their understanding of the goals of Impressionism was shallow because they admired French masters whom Gauguin considered second-rate. As he wrote to

Pissarro in outrage, "Kroyer told me that it seemed to him that de Nittis and [Bastien-]Lepage had brought what the Impressionists started to the height of perfection."[65]

Gauguin's first and most damning impression of the thoughtful, cosmopolitan people in his social context in Copenhagen was of their deplorable taste in interior decoration. In one of his first letters back to France he launched into this favorite theme: "You would not believe the Danish parlor—The freshly varnished walnut furniture, the busts of poets in the corner hung with flowers and ribbons, photographs everywhere—on the tables and on the walls—and on the floor a pot of ivy sends up delicate shoots to curl among them. The chairs are covered with tiny needlework patterns—very difficult, very complicated, and horrendously ugly. It's obligatory, for example, to have landscapes in oils painted to look like chromolithographs."[66] Yet, for all his snobbishness about the Danes, Gauguin's writings over the next twenty years often reflected ideas that came directly from the Scandinavian intelligentsia. In "Avant et après," his last major treatise and memoir, for example, Gauguin revisited social issues hotly debated in the North: democracy, feminism, and the workings of such social structures as marriage and the family.

Even Gauguin's interest in Eastern mysticism, which he shared with Schuffenecker and many artists of his circle in France, can be related to interests of Edvard Brandès, whose thesis was on Indian literature, "Ushas and the Hymns of Ushas in the Rigveda."[67] Although Gauguin had explored abstract methods of interpreting human character, such as handwriting analysis, before his acquaintance with Brandès, it was during his stay in Copenhagen that he began developing elaborate theories of mystical understanding, which he outlined to Schuffenecker in his letters.[68] He was fascinated, for instance, with what he felt was Cézanne's "Eastern nature": "In his methods, he affects a mystery and the heavy tranquillity of a dreamer; his colors are grave, like the character of Orientals."[69] At some point in the next year he even wrote what he called the manuscript of Vehbi-Zumbul Zadi (Bibliothèque Nationale)—advice on painting from an Eastern mystic who has never been identified and is presumed to have been invented by Gauguin.[70]

Gauguin's musings on character led him to declare that "the great artist is synonymous with the greatest intelligence; he is the vehicle of the most delicate, the most invisible emotions of the brain."[71] The secret of this genius was, for Gauguin, "sensation"—an inborn knowledge that predates mental function or education. Gauguin's belief that genius emerges naturally out of the undistinguished masses was remarkably similar to Georg Brandès's revelation in 1884 that he was not in favor of democracy but supported what he would later term Aristocratic Radicalism. Taking his cue from Nietzsche, he believed in the "great personality full of ideas." Further, "True art is no longer that which is satisfied with ideas and ideals for the average and the mediocre; great art tears itself away from the multitude, seeks defiant independence, 'aristocratic absolutism.'"[72]

Gauguin in turn and without attribution argued that greatness could not be taught; otherwise, why doesn't every studious artist paint masterpieces? His answer: "Because it is impossible to create a nature, an intelligence, a heart."[73] Art reflects what the artist is inside, and only a natural-born genius could paint like one. Gauguin took his argument one step further in declaring that the patron of art must also be an aristocrat. He disagreed with the populist Pissarro about the outcome of greater education and advantages for the masses: "I think that the more the masses are equal the less need they have of art. For such needs, it is necessary to have contemplation, a love of luxury born of nobility, a feeling for irregularity in the social scale, and less petty money-grubbing."[74] The ideas that flowed around Gauguin, no doubt politely expressed in French for his sake since he spoke no Danish, were challenging and exhilarating. Whether or not he acknowledged his debt to these intellectuals, they helped his art and his thought rise to a new level.

Gauguin spent his days in Copenhagen painting and writing letters. The enormous task of developing a market for the Dillies waterproof cloth in a country that already had established sources for such a product was beyond Gauguin's patience or interest. He had been a bookkeeper and a speculator—never a traveling salesman. He found making sales calls, even on the sympathetic friends and relatives of his wife, demeaning. To make matters worse, the Dillies company was cautious. It was unwilling to stake Gauguin with money or goods until he could prove that the venture would be lucrative. Gauguin must have known that this would be the case, but he may have overestimated his persuasive powers either in selling or in changing the company's mind.[75] At any rate, despite the efforts of both Paul and Mette (who solicited favors from her relatives and wrote Paul's letters in Danish and Norwegian), the income from this work remained pitifully slight. After only four months the Gauguins were forced to move to a less expensive apartment closer to the center of town.[76]

Life was increasingly confining. The decision he had made to quit the Thomereau agency and not to seek another position was based on a persistent intolerance for any work other than painting. Poverty had less and less power to change his mind. Before the Gauguins came to Copenhagen, Paul had already voiced the idea of leaving his family to fend for themselves, and gradually this thought came back in full force. With his own interests now uppermost in his mind, everything about living in Copenhagen rubbed him wrong.

It is hard not to sympathize with his dilemma. Gauguin was a talker who found himself unable to speak the language. He was a flamboyant man of affairs used to frequenting the Bourse who now spent every day at home. As an artist he was a radical—smug and belligerent—who now found himself surrounded by insufferably genial liberals. The bourgeois taste in clothes and furnishings made him wince. He expected the provincial Danish artists to look to him for the latest styles, but instead they politely rejected the second-hand offerings he submitted to local exhibitions (fig. 21) and passed over the one show he had at Kroyer's Society of the Friends of Art (May 1–6, 1885) without comment.[77] After six months in Copenhagen, Gauguin was seething.

If Gauguin had been genuinely determined to make the best of a bad situation and keep his family together, he might have handled things dif-

ferently. Although he would have realized at a glance that the Danish art world would not understand or appreciate the radical character of his art, he could have made more of his opportunities in Paris even while living in Denmark. He refused, for instance, to exhibit in Paris with the new group called the Indépendants, which Schuffenecker helped to found in 1884. Even though the Impressionists were not holding their own exhibition that year, Gauguin could have found other ways to have his pictures seen at the smaller galleries or in the proliferating exhibition societies. Frits Thaulow was doing something very similar in Paris while he remained in residence in Norway.[78] Since money was not immediately forthcoming from his art, Gauguin might have taken a position in the Danish financial district that was more suited to him than selling commercial cloth. With more funds he could have returned to Paris regularly and perhaps moved his family back there once the economic climate had improved.

But from Gauguin's actions in Copenhagen, it is clear that remaining with his family was not one of his priorities. Aside from their financial plight, Gauguin put the family in jeopardy in other ways. He expressed his ideas so aggressively that people took offense. Apparently his extreme antagonism toward the organized church caused his wife's friend and Emil's patron, the Countess Moltke, to cut off Emil's tuition at his boarding school, forcing him to return home abruptly.[79] Another incident at the seashore during the early days of the summer also caused great pain to Mette Gauguin. Her husband told the story with glee in his memoirs and probably to rowdy groups of men many times over the years, although the incident was petty. It was the custom for Danish men and women to bath nude, so the beaches were segregated, and a polite averting of the eyes was practiced. Gauguin thought it extremely funny to stare at a pretty woman, an acquaintance of Mette's and wife of a Danish government minister, walking into the water with her young child. Gauguin's offensive gaze caused the woman to retreat, making him laugh all the harder: "[She showed] me all the front after having shown me the back. I confess that the front again, at a distance, made a very good effect. It was a great scandal. What! To have looked!!!"[80]

Gauguin's delight in manipulating and humiliating women in public was unacceptable to the Danes whom he had offended in so many other ways. But it was his behavior in private that finally caused the breakup of the family. The enforced intimacy of the Gauguins' apartment brought matters to a head. Never before had he spent all day with his wife and children. His wife was pressured to earn more since he was earning less, and tried to get him to help with the French lessons. As he wrote to Schuffenecker, "You will laugh, me, lessons in French!"[81] Mette was harried, but determined to be successful among her own people, regardless of the stigma of having to live from hand to mouth. It was a bitter pill for the woman who had only months before bought a fancy Parisian dress for the brilliant life she thought she would lead once again. As time went on, she had less and less energy to assist her helpless husband or to sympathize with him. The tension in the home was surely aggravated by the presence of three little boys under the age of five. For Gauguin, who could not bear the cries of Pola when he was a baby, home life was intolerable. He lashed out at them all, but particularly at Mette, whose own patience was at an end. The carping tone that had surfaced while they lived in Rouen escalated into bullying. Emil saw his father attack his mother, and he never forgot it: "When I was ten years old in Copenhagen . . . I saw my father bloody my mother's face with his fist."[82]

In June, at the urging of her family, Mette forced Paul to leave. He had wanted to go for some time, but it rankled that she had stood up to him. Out of spite he took one of the children—the beautiful blond Clovis, whom they still kept in dresses and long hair—and returned to Paris. Paul's cruelty to his wife and children, as well as to any woman who happened to make herself vulnerable to him (such as the woman on the beach), was probably not new, but once he left his family, it seemed to loom larger in his life. In the years to come, not only does he desire a kind of revenge, but increasingly he seems to derive pleasure from inflicting pain. If, at the age of thirty-seven, he had freed himself from the conventions of family and employment, he had also eliminated the last vestiges of self-control that had kept the more violent aspects of his personality in check.

When Paul Gauguin returned to France without his family, old friends noticed
that his behavior had become flamboyant and unpredictable. Outbursts
alternated with spells of self-justification and a honeyed, calculating charm.
In the past he had been a wage earner, a husband, and a father—a "man"
as defined by his culture. But when he left his regular employment and failed
to earn a living by his art, he lost a large part of his social identity. Then,
when he drove away his wife, who had not only helped him earn a living but
conferred upon him his respectability as a husband and father, he found that
he had jeopardized his fundamental masculinity in the eyes of the world.[1]

As intensely as he had desired what he got—freedom from his responsibilities and a life of art—he could not have anticipated the price that society would force him to pay. Paris was particularly hard on him. It was his
home and the home of his illustrious ancestors, as well as the adopted home
of his wife and the birthplace of his children. It was the site of his success
in the financial world. It was the capital of the international art community
in which he had carved out a niche among the Impressionists. It was full of
people who knew him and felt qualified to judge all aspects of his life and
work, and for a year after he returned from Copenhagen he encountered
disapproval on all fronts; indeed, Paris never again embraced him as unre-
servedly as it had when he had established himself there in the 1870s.

Now that Gauguin could participate in art as fully as he wanted, without the burden of a job or a family, he no doubt expected that he would
quickly receive the personal and professional rewards that had made art so
attractive to him in the first place. Instead, he encountered a cutthroat,
competitive community that had already forgotten him in its rush to adopt
the newest fad and lionize the latest prodigy. Now that he no longer collected art, nor had active contacts among art collectors in the financial district,
neither artists nor dealers were as warm toward him as they had once been.
Nor did a group of sophisticated, avant-garde personalities, like the Impressionists, welcome him. Within a year he began retreating from Paris to
increasingly remote and exotic locales where he found once again the personal pleasure that he felt art should bring him.

Mette Gauguin's role in the shaping of Paul's self-image has always
been misunderstood. Because he berated her, it has been easy to believe, as
he did, that she was a villain. Men who are batterers often convince others
that the victim is to blame.[2] But lashing out is consistent with the behavior
of an abusive husband, who typically blames his wife not only for all his
troubles but even for the violence that he perpetrates against her.[3] Although

63

Gauguin's physical abuse of his wife can be documented only one time—in Copenhagen in 1885—his verbal and emotional abuse was already evident in Rouen and probably began shortly after their marriage. However, as is typical of abused wives, Mette seems to have been persuaded by Paul to overlook his behavior, probably by a renewal, after each violent outburst, of the extremely romantic pursuit that had won her heart.[4]

Before Denmark the couple was always able to neutralize the effects of the violence and stay together. Paul cared too much about his standing in society to have such an intelligent and charming wife leave him, and Mette, with her own pride and a growing number of children, was eager to forgive. It wasn't until Mette was back among her family and old friends, developing a career of her own, that she could conceive of life without her husband. She could end the threat of physical abuse by forcing him to leave. Unfortunately for both, the separation did not end the marriage.

This halfway method of resolving abuse in a marriage harms the wife because she never steps out of the shadow of her husband.[5] But the effect on the husband is also unsettling. His guilt is acknowledged, but his wife does not forgive him, nor is he punished by losing her. He pays dearly for managing to elude responsibility for his unseemly acts: "Being acquitted from responsibility for the violent act means being freed from responsibility for a large part of one's individual life. . . . This way of neutralizing the act transforms the man into an irresponsible child."[6]

The Gauguins' inability to either reunite or make a clean break kept them both in a constant state of emotional turmoil. Mette clung to the hope that Paul would make his fortune and save the family. Always in the position of responding to her distant but dominant husband, she would sometimes beg his forgiveness and at other times get so angry that for months she would refuse to write to him. Paul alternated between his belief in himself as a good family man and his rage toward his family for rejecting him. He wanted to be perceived as a man but found himself acting more often like a child.

At this point in his life, his behavior might have been more stable if he had had the example of his own father to look to. But there was no one in his life whose performance as husband and father affected him personally. Although he had had the protection of his uncle Isidore during his childhood, Isidore himself was a single man and may have reinforced his nephew's attraction to the bachelor life. Furthermore, Gauguin's pride in his own achievements, despite the lack of a father, no doubt led him to his belligerent belief that his wife and children should be able to survive just as well as he and his mother had.

Ironically, the next ten years (1886–96), when he was racked with defensiveness and guilt, were the most innovative and creative of Gauguin's career. He found a way of using his bitterness and desire for revenge to give a sharp new edge to his art. The previously bland beauty of his ideas, pointed out to him by Pissarro in their 1880 drawings of each other, erupted after 1885 into an almost caricatural distortion of form (particularly in his drawings of women), combined with a forceful, almost reckless use of color. Gauguin's innate sense of the decorative was brought to a higher level of expressiveness by his ability to channel into it the violence of his emotions.

Having failed according to society's construction of manhood, he struggled to assert social power in other ways. One of the most blatant was through phallic imagery, including snakes and the long necks of geese, as well as the signature "PGo" (French slang for "prick").[7] But he also reveled in his freedom *from* accepted norms of manhood. He wore capes and ostentatious jewelry and grew his hair long. He preferred the company of other men, particularly those who were also at odds with their wives, such as Emile Schuffenecker and Daniel de Monfreid. He even courted the affection of many men who were homosexual or impressionably young, and basked in their adulation. Male or female, adult or juvenile—Gauguin's behavior defied classification. He impressed and mystified his audiences by speaking in parables and riddles. Paradox had become central to his life.[8]

The darkest side of Gauguin was immediately revealed in the hissing, vituperative letters to his wife written in the first year after their separation. These letters show him consumed by his need to punish and humiliate her for having rejected him. He placed in her hands all his unfinished business for the Dillies Company in Denmark and Norway. He gave her orders on how to handle the problems he left behind; he clearly had no intention of fulfilling his obligations any further. When Mette's brother-in-law in Oslo, Hermann Thaulow, went bankrupt and had to cancel the small order he had placed, Gauguin considered this a problem for Mette to solve. As if it were her fault, he complained that he might lose his reputation as a businessman, but he did not even try to straighten it out himself; "To salvage the messes of others and start all over again is beyond me."[9] Because her sister Ingeborg and her younger brothers had united in forcing Gauguin to leave Copenhagen, he spoke of the whole family with the utmost scorn.

People who had known Gauguin in his former life recoiled from him in his new guise. Many a letter went from Paris to Copenhagen from the Schuffeneckers, Paul's sister Marie, and other friends trying to get a sense from Mette of how they should treat her errant husband. Knowing that people trusted her opinion, Paul tried to enlist her to help him get employment as a sculptor's assistant from their old friend Jules Bouillot by keeping up her correspondence with his wife.[10] But Bouillot stayed clear of Paul, as did Paul's friends at the Bourse when he dropped by to renew old acquaintances and see if he might arrange some picture business or find a regular position there. His approach was nonconciliatory, however. In December of 1885 his reckless criticism of his old associate Cellot even caused Cellot to challenge him to a duel. Cooler heads prevailed, but Gauguin bragged to his wife, "At the last minute Cellot bowed out, not wanting to fight with an outlaw like me."[11] Regardless of how this incident was really resolved, Gauguin got a reputation among *boursiers* for being a violent man. Schuffenecker remembered many years later that Gauguin had "beaten within an inch of his life an unfortunate clerk who had dared to make him the butt of an innocent joke."[12]

Even the Impressionists, who tolerated unusual, often hurtful behavior, shrank from Gauguin in this raw state of mind. When he joined the crowd of artists in the fashionable seaside resort of Dieppe that August, he was snubbed by Degas and closed out of the circle around him. The young painter Jacques-Emile Blanche, in Dieppe with his family, recalled that "his strange features (of which he did such fine self-portraits), the extravagance of his dress, and a certain haggard appearance, which my father had all too often pointed out as the symptoms of megalomania, made me keep my distance from him. If that man was not a lunatic, he must at least be a frequenter of those medieval brasseries in the Pigalle quarter, to which we went with our poet friends."[13]

Perhaps the saddest victim of Gauguin's vindictiveness was his six-year-old son, Clovis. Mette would not have been able to stop her husband from taking the child, but no doubt she believed that Clovis would be safe in a good boarding school in or near Paris, for Emil and Aline had been sent away to school at the same age. She also believed that Clovis's aunt Marie would be able to watch out for him. This plan might have worked if Paul had been able to make the income he promised he would, and if Marie had not herself been so strapped for money (the Uribes were also casualties of the crash) and so angered by Paul's irresponsibility that she washed her hands of him.[14]

When Paul and Clovis returned to Paris, Marie took the child out to the country for a summer with her family.[15] At summer's end, however, Paul had not raised enough money to put Clovis in a private school. Marie was appalled to see that the child was to live in a squalid apartment with his Bohemian father and attend the public school next door.[16] Gauguin did not curtail his daily activities to care for the boy but put him in the hands of friends, neighbors, or the concierge.[17] It is not known whether Gauguin beat his children, but the picture of Clovis that he drew for Mette must have wrung her heart: "He is a really good boy and plays all alone in his little corner without bothering me. Sometimes he asks where his mother is and when she's going to come. He has good memories of you; let's hope that the others will not be raised ignorant of their language and homeland and their poor father—I won't stand for that."[18] Perhaps Paul was needling Mette with his pathetic descriptions of their poverty; still, Clovis's life with his father seems to have been one of neglect, little food, and insufficient clothing. "Don't worry about Clovis, at his age he isn't bothered by things as long as he has a little affection and a little food. . . . With an egg and a little rice, he eats very well—especially when there's an apple for dessert."[19]

In the spring of 1886 Marie finally despaired of Paul's ever taking proper care of Clovis and, in spite of her own financial difficulties, paid for the boy to be put into a good boarding school, where he spent the next year. When she did so, she spoke to her brother with a vehemence and directness that Mette could never achieve; but Paul believed that the two women were in league against him, and he struck back at Mette: "I saw my sister, to whom you write such long letters. Her way of comforting me was to shout from the rooftops what a beast I am—that I left Bertin just to paint, that my poor wife who is without a home, furniture, everything, was abandoned for this ridiculous art."[20] He also took his revenge on Clovis. For the next year, his father rarely visited him or brought him home for school breaks. Even during the summer vacation Clovis stayed at the school while his father enjoyed himself in the resorts of Brittany. Paul kept Clovis from his mother,

refusing to allow Mette to come when she begged to see him "even for a couple of hours" because *he* (Paul) couldn't bear to see her.[21] This was how Gauguin treated his favorite child. The portrait of Clovis that he painted that year shows an uncertain, spartan boy (fig. 22). Both his beauty and his long golden curls were a thing of the past.

During the first year of Gauguin's life as social misfit, he produced very little art. He was included in the eighth and final Impressionist exhibition in May–June 1886, but many of his nineteen paintings were from Rouen or Copenhagen, and those that had been done since his return to France showed no striking novelty.[22] This is surprising given the ferment in the Parisian art world caused by the debut of Seurat and his circle of Neo-Impressionists, which now included not only the young Lucien Pissarro but also his father, Camille. Because of the distinctive new pointillist style that the Neo-Impressionists, or "Néos," proposed, scientific color theory was hotly debated in Gauguin's old haunts. He distributed two theoretical writings himself at this time, his "copy" of the so-called teachings of a Turkish poet Vehbi Mohamed Zunbul-Zadé and his "Notes synthétiques," a treatise on the superiority of painting over literature.[23] Gauguin argued that painting was superior because all the elements are "synthesized" into the image on the canvas and thus can be grasped at once rather than gradually unfolding over time. But because Gauguin's own theories did not visibly alter the "unscientific" Impressionist style that he had been working in for the past six years, and because he aggressively rejected Neo-Impressionism, he was ignored by the radical artists and once again overlooked by the critics.

Georges Seurat, who had established the leadership position within the avant-garde that Gauguin wanted for himself, became his bête noire. At first, he courted the handsome young man whose habit of dressing neatly in black attracted attention at the café Nouvelle Athènes, pressing upon him his "*papier*" (essay) of theoretical writings.[24] But Seurat had no patience for Gauguin's aggressive manner and deliberately provoked him by locking him out of Signac's studio, which Gauguin had arranged to borrow when Signac went out of town for the summer.[25] The quarrel resulted in Gauguin's lifelong enmity toward Seurat and his group, the Néos, and the final break between Gauguin and Pissarro.

The only artists in Paris who seem to have accepted Gauguin after the breakup of his marriage, when he was at his most erratic and violent, were Emile Schuffenecker and Félix Bracquemond. Probably at the prompting of Mette, the Schuffeneckers were the first to provide shelter for her husband and her son, Clovis, when they returned to Paris in the summer of 1885. Their long association with Gauguin both professionally and as family friends accounts for their initial hospitality. But Emile Schuffenecker's desire to maintain a friendship for years to come with a man whom he knew to be "hard to get along with" at best and violent at worst requires more of an explanation.[26]

It is clear from the letters Gauguin wrote to Schuffenecker that Gauguin made an effort with "Schuff" to make him feel like a special confidant and an artistic equal (fig. 23). This certainly accounts for Schuffenecker's loyalty when others fell by the wayside. Gauguin relied too much on Schuff's regular purchases of his paintings and other periodic infusions of cash to neglect their friendship. Schuffenecker stretched his income as a teacher at the Lycée Michelet to make many purchases of works of art from avant-garde artists like Gauguin, including Guillaumin, Pissarro, Redon, and Van Gogh. His purchases and his role in the founding of the Société des Indépendants in 1884, whose regular exhibitions gave many young or rejected artists a public forum, conferred on Schuffenecker an importance in the avant-garde world that Gauguin could not overlook.

As for Schuffenecker, he gravitated toward artists with leadership potential. His early support for the Neo-Impressionists, Redon, and Van Gogh shows an ability to evaluate artists that has been underestimated in recent discussions of Schuffenecker's role in Gauguin's career. Schuffenecker, furthermore, was not just interested in collecting and supporting the avant-garde; he was eager to make his own mark as an artist. In addition to his role in the unjuried exhibitions of the Indépendants, he wanted to be accepted in the more prestigious group of the Impressionists. When the group committed to one more exhibition in 1886, he used Gauguin as a conduit to the other members in his vigorous campaign to be included.[27] Gauguin was relatively silent on the matter, but their friendship gave Schuffenecker cred-

ibility, and he achieved the desired goal. In 1889, Schuff again used
Gauguin's greater visibility to organize and include himself in the famous
exhibition of Impressionists and synthetists at the Volpini Café on the
grounds of the International Exposition. Schuffenecker's well-known mod-
esty hid, to some extent, his ambition. His continuing friendship with
the aggressive Gauguin opened many doors for him.

Beyond issues of self-interest, the friendship of Gauguin and
Schuffenecker was based, finally, on a personal affection unusual in Gauguin's
life. They both enjoyed the endless discussions about art that took place
in the studios and cafés around town. Both natural teachers, they held forth
for each other and the younger men they gathered around them. Schuffenecker, unlike Seurat, was an interesting companion but not a threat. He never
challenged Gauguin's superiority, and he allowed Gauguin to pirate his
more erudite ideas. Schuffenecker's interest in Buddhism and other forms
of mysticism was particularly useful to Gauguin as the avant-garde leaned
in this direction in the later 1880s; Gauguin was not patient enough to acquire
the knowledge himself.[28] Because their art discussions were unusually
meaningful to both, they took extra steps to nurture their relationship.

The long-standing friendship between Gauguin and Schuffenecker
was the model for many of Gauguin's intimate relationships with other
men. As the letters between them demonstrate, Gauguin's affectionate tone
suggested a level of trust and dependency that persuaded Schuffenecker
to respond in kind, often in spite of his better judgment. Gauguin expressed
his vulnerability—both artistically and financially—in such a touching
way that few (certainly not the kindhearted Schuffenecker) could remain
unmoved. As a result, Gauguin both bullied and clung to men like Schuffenecker in his paradoxical way; he intertwined with them as if they were lovers.

The almost erotic intimacy that Gauguin engendered with Schuffenecker[29] was complicated by Gauguin's several portraits of Schuffenecker's

wife and daughter and the later accusation (seemingly unfounded, given Madame Schuffenecker's distaste for Gauguin) that Gauguin had had an affair with his wife.[30] The very real affection between Mette Gauguin and Emile Schuffenecker, which is documented by their letters to each other and suggested obliquely by Gauguin's painting of them at the piano (see fig. 16), makes the relationship between the two men even more charged with complicated romantic attraction. Whether Gauguin's homoeroticism in relationships like this was accompanied by actual sexual intimacy is unknown, but Gauguin's liaisons with men were far tenderer than those he had with women.

On the opposite end of the scale, the other artist who helped Gauguin, when most others were staying out of his way, was the ceramic designer and printmaker Félix Bracquemond. Bracquemond, unlike Schuffenecker, who had already had a long and complex relationship with Gauguin, knew Gauguin very slightly and only for a brief time; but his support in the days during and after the Impressionist exhibition of 1886 set Gauguin onto a new course. After going to the exhibition and seeing Gauguin's paintings and the carved relief he had executed and given to Pissarro in 1882, Bracquemond suggested that Gauguin attempt painting on porcelain and designing other art ceramics in the studio of the renowned designer Ernst Chaplet.[31] Bracquemond's introduction resulted in Chaplet's engaging Gauguin to work in his studio during the following winter months. Suddenly and almost accidentally, Gauguin's desire to work in a three-dimensional medium was to be realized.

Gauguin also renewed his acquaintance with Félix's wife, the artist Marie Bracquemond, who had exhibited alongside Gauguin in the Impressionist exhibitions of 1879 and 1880, as well as the current one in 1886. Together the Bracquemonds acquired two of Gauguin's paintings, one of which was apparently painted during a visit to their house in Sèvres that summer; it is inscribed to her.[32] Through Marie Bracquemond Gauguin met the painter and printmaker Henri Delavallée, who was in the habit of spending his summers in the artists' colony of Pont-Aven, near the southern coast of Brittany.[33] Delavallée had already met several of Marie Bracquemond's fellow Impressionist exhibitors, including Pissarro and Seurat, with whom he painted in the summer of 1887, and may have provided the immediate stimulus for Gauguin's decision to visit Pont-Aven. Delavallée's memories of Gauguin at Pont-Aven in 1886 provide one of the earliest descriptions of Gauguin in the artist's colony that he later made famous. Félix and Marie Bracquemond, who stayed out of avant-garde politics in Paris and probably knew little of the commotion that Gauguin was causing among the Impressionists and Indépendants, exerted a beneficial influence over his career at a crucial time.

As summer commenced, Gauguin realized that he was not welcome in the places the Impressionists typically gathered. He had been snubbed by Degas in Dieppe, and he could no longer spend the long summer days painting with Pissarro. Seeing so many other artists head for the picturesque villages of Brittany, he decided to do the same. Consequently, on June 27, 1886, a year after his breakup with his wife — during which time he did little except vent his rage in the financial and artistic communities—he boarded the overnight train from Paris to Quimperlé, then caught the horse-drawn stage to Pont-Aven.[34]

When he descended from the coach at eight o'clock that summer evening, he had finally found an environment that was ideal for him. A tourist town with relaxed social rules, Pont-Aven treated artists royally. To add to his satisfaction, Gauguin soon found that he had no competition in the avant-garde arena. The local artists were mainly conservative French painters and eager but unsophisticated foreigners, including English, Americans, and Scandinavians. Here Gauguin could forget the jockeying for position with Seurat in Paris and the homage demanded by Degas and Pissarro. In Pont-Aven he could be master of all those who had heard of the new styles but were too far out on the fringes to learn more than a few superficial details. Gauguin loved this hungry audience, and they loved him. One by one the eager acolytes put aside their Salon ambitions and succumbed to the utter freedom of being so removed from professional and social pressures: they became Impressionists. Gauguin, who was pleased to influence others but unwilling to lose his avant-garde superiority, cultivated an air of mystery and danger. In Paris, where the stakes were high, his rough behavior irritated and alienated people; in Pont-Aven, where a holiday atmosphere prevailed, it was considered intriguing.

Archibald Hartrick, a Scottish painter in his early twenties, came away from Pont-Aven that summer with a typical view of Gauguin. Hartrick, who had been studying in Paris, was knowledgeable about avant-garde styles but stayed somewhat removed from the controversies. He later met Vincent van Gogh in Cormon's studio. That summer he had joined the group of other young painters in their twenties, which included Charles Laval and Ferdinand du Puigaudeau, both of whom had struck up a friendship with the older Gauguin. Through Laval and du Puigaudeau (nicknamed Piccolo), Hartrick had access to Gauguin, but he kept a respectful distance. He was struck with how Gauguin made his presence felt in the small tourist town. Gauguin had adopted the local costume—beret and blue, embroidered sweater: "His general appearance, walk and all, was rather that of a well-to-do Biscayan skipper of a coasting schooner."[35]

Gauguin made himself at home in this harbor town. When he wasn't imitating a local sea captain, he played the tourist, oblivious to humdrum standards of genteel behavior. Hartrick's most vivid memory was of Gauguin being towed by a boat rowed by two Breton oarsmen and containing du Puigaudeau and a female friend with her five children. Gauguin was holding on to a rope and gliding nearly naked through the water "like a dead porpoise, but evidently enjoying himself hugely."[36] Behavior that raised issues of propriety was now an established part of Gauguin's public life. Only the summer before he had stared inappropriately on the beach in Denmark. But in Pont-Aven, unlike in Copenhagen, he had no job or family to lose and no one to challenge him. The local population had seen much worse from the crowds of footloose young artists who came every summer, and Gauguin's willingness to fight made everyone back off. "Most people were rather afraid of him, and the most reckless took no liberties with his person. 'C'est un malin [He's a devil]' was the sort of general verdict. He was distinctly athletic in his tastes and had the reputation for being a formidable swordsman. I believe it was truly earned; anyway it added to the caution with which he was usually approached, for he was treated as a person to be placated rather than aroused."[37]

Gauguin was indeed active as a swordsman and boxer in Pont-Aven. According to his own account, he helped open a fencing school and then gave lessons to the fencing master.[38] He loved to discuss the technical aspects of both fighting with various types of swords and boxing. In addition, he had advice for winning against all types of opponents and for losing when clearly outmatched by a strong one: "At the least forward movement on his part, present your arm to his point. Honour is satisfied and you get off with a trifling wound."[39] His interest was not academic. He was ready to fight with swords, fists, or words.[40]

Nor were his special friends safe from his temper. Achille Granchi-Taylor, who had also left the stock exchange to become an artist, found this out. To help Gauguin financially, Granchi-Taylor had commissioned a portrait from him in 1885, upon which Gauguin had inscribed, "A il signor Achille, amicalement" (To Monsieur Achille, with friendship). They had come to Pont-Aven together in the summer of 1886 but soon had a violent argument. Granchi-Taylor told Gauguin that in spite of their split, he would treasure the painting—to which Gauguin responded, "fine, but the dedication is null and void." Granchi-Taylor subsequently painted it out.[41]

Another acquaintance in Pont-Aven that summer, Marie Bracquemond's friend Henri Delavallée, also came away a little frightened of Gauguin. When he was asked years later for his recollections of the painter, he described him as "proud, a little naive, a great trickster, and incredibly sly. You often had to ask whether or not he was kidding."[42]

Surprisingly Gauguin's physical and verbal menace did not result in his rejection by either his fellow artists or the local people, as it had in Copenhagen. Although very few became close friends, many observed him at a distance and were fascinated by his painting and his unusual pronouncements on art. He spoke about synthesis—a concept that he seems to have defined vaguely in conversations with other artists—and about technique.[43] He rejected the Neo-Impressionist "dot," preaching the merits of pure color applied with a sable brush stroke by stroke to a carefully prepared canvas.[44] Delavallée referred to his canvases as "striped"; Hartrick recalled a panel that Gauguin had painted for the dining room of a guesthouse (most hotels in French artist colonies were decorated with paintings by their artist-guests) that seemed extreme at the time "in its crude exaggeration of purple and gold."[45] Gauguin's style and manner were so liberated that few artists could resist his influence.

> I well recall, too, the attack made on him by V. [Hubert Vos], a Dutch painter, who, on the strength of a medal in the Salon, was more or less cock-of-the-walk among the painters then in Pont-Aven. He swaggered about the village, with long carroty locks, on the top of which was set a green velvet cap of Rembrandt pattern, and laid down the law on everything to everybody. Gauguin, shortly after his arrival, a stranger to most, came back for déjeuner one

day and passed through the crowd at the door of the auberge. He was carrying a canvas on which he had been painting some boys bathing on a weir [now lost], painted brilliantly with spots of pure color in the usual impressionist manner.

V. started by asking, in the rudest way, what game was this he was playing . . . while the majority crowded round to enjoy the fun of the newcomer being baited. Gauguin, however, only smiled grimly, and elbowing his way through, went about his business without explanation or retort.

The sequel to this was really funny. Within a fortnight V.'s special pupil, P. [du Puigaudeau], went off to Gauguin for instruction, leaving V. altogether. . . . Within a month V. was secretly consulting his former pupil on Gauguin's methods and theories; finally, he went over a large picture he had just completed, taking out the blacks in the shadows and substituting spots of pure color in their place.[46]

Gauguin was thrilled at his unexpected success in Pont-Aven. In his letters to his wife, he positively crows about the leadership position he has found himself in: "My painting stirs up a lot of discussion and, I must say, is well received by the Americans. There's hope for the future."[47] "Everyone considers me the best painter in Pont-Aven and they all (Americans, English, Swedish, French) fight for my attention and advice."[48] "All the artists fear me and love me: none can hold out against my theories and it is very funny to see Hagborg [Swedish painter] and company ask my advice, fear my critiques, and never challenge anything I do."[49]

The glow of success even softened Paul's tone toward Mette, which had been unrelentingly harsh in the past year. "What a shame we didn't come here earlier," he sighs. "I'm sure with 300 francs a month, a family would be very happy."[50] His reawakened family feelings were of short duration, however, because when Mette responded warmly to his new mood, he backpedaled. "My heart is as wooden as this table, and now that I am hardened against adversity, I have feelings only for my work, for my art."[51] Many such negative statements by each notwithstanding, in the following months both began to think about the possibilities of reconciliation. The seesaw of emotions was far from over.

That Gauguin's first thoughts were for his family whenever he arrived at a place he liked (this happened again when he arrived in Martinique and later in Tahiti) indicates that he harbored an ideal image of himself as a respectable citizen surrounded by a family that he was able to support adequately. This ideal was not compelling enough for him to sacrifice his art and related free lifestyle for his family, but it was reawakened whenever he saw an opportunity to start over. Furthermore, it explains why he clung to the shell of his marriage. In the first year of their separation, he briefly worked for an advertising poster firm in Paris with the promise of eventually heading a branch office in Madrid. As ever, the possibility of financial success stimulated thoughts of family.[52] In those first raw months after leaving Copenhagen, he threatened to leave Mette for good and find a "real" wife in Spain. When the job didn't materialize, neither did the wife. As time went on and financial success still eluded Gauguin, at least he had the remnants of a marriage to give him what he saw as importance in the eyes of society.

For actual companionship, Gauguin preferred the company of young men. Although there were several women artists working in Pont-Aven, the free and easy artists' culture was largely dictated by the men. They drank freely, claiming that drinking helped them to paint. One man "never attempted to paint . . . until he had drunk three glasses of absinthe and bathed his face in ether."[53] Their amorous adventures were also typical of a group of young men unencumbered by social restrictions. But Archibald Hartrick noticed that Gauguin refrained from engaging in this aspect of Pont-Aven revels. Not only did he preach "Pas de femmes," but Hartrick remembered him as "sardonic and sarcastic" about the others' relationships with women, describing "the fatter mistress of a fat painter as his 'slop bucket.'"[54] Hartrick doubted "if women, certainly no educated women, ever got on well with him."[55]

Gauguin's credo, Pas de femmes, is evident even in his paintings from that summer. In the seventeen paintings that were probably executed during the four months that Gauguin spent in Pont-Aven, the few figures of women are small and subordinate to landscape. The painting that Hartrick remembered best was of boys playing on the rocks of the Aven River, a theme that Gauguin returned to every succeeding summer in Brittany. Even though he did not make women an important part of the paintings he worked on in Pont-Aven, however, he did do a number of drawings of women in Breton costume that he later used as the basis for *Four Breton Women* (fig. 24). He painted this large canvas back home in Paris, and, unlike the paintings of the previous summer, it goes beyond Gauguin's competent but uninspired Impressionist style and shows the compelling direction he took for the next fifteen years.

New sources of stylistic inspiration, along with his bitter feelings toward women, make this painting both appealing and jarring—a combination that Gauguin probably arrived at by accident, but he was astute enough to recognize it and develop it into a mature style. Curiously, while Gauguin was shedding restraint in the various arenas of his life, his art had continued to be fundamentally "correct" and conventional. Though based on the radical tenets of Impressionism, it was cool in color and regular in its hallmark broken brushstrokes. Now, allowing himself to vent his strong feelings, he arrived at an art that used unconventional drawing to convey an intriguing message. The four Breton women, heavy and distorted by their costumes and poses, seem to be writhing from the exchanged gossip, which, one suspects, is intimate, scandalous. Like his earlier "pregnant" nude, these women seem distorted by their unladylike knowledge of base sexuality.

While he was at Pont-Aven, Gauguin was introduced to one of the most popular tourist books on Brittany, Henry Blackburn's *Breton Folk: An Artistic Tour of Brittany* (1880), illustrated by Randolph Caldecott.[56] Caldecott's entertaining cartoonlike style, mainly used to illustrate children's books, had captured the imagination of French avant-garde artists and writers who were eager to promote lively, nonacademic drawing styles to show their contempt for the ponderous methods taught in the official French system. According to Hartrick, Gauguin began imitating Caldecott's style in drawings he made that summer.[57]

While Gauguin was in Pont-Aven, new trends in Paris reinforced his interest in "naive" and antiacademic art. At the second exhibition of the Indépendants in August 1886, the self-taught painter Henri ("Douanier") Rousseau captured the attention of the avant-garde, including Pissarro, who likened Rousseau's art to that of his four-year-old son, whose drawing he was carrying in his pocket.[58] Experimental artists, both trained and untrained, began to use a crude, simplified style to imbue their work with ancient, non-Western, folk, or simply childlike purity. Such experiments ranged from Seurat's large, serious canvases, which drew on Egyptian art, to the satirical exhibitions of a group called the Incoherents, who, starting in 1882, showed only works of art done by people who had never created art before.[59]

Gauguin's *Four Breton Women* has the charming, naive quality of Caldecott's illustrations for children's books, with the extra ingredient of satirical exaggeration. When Gauguin transferred his carefully finished drawings to the large format of the painting, he exaggerated certain features of the four women to the point of caricature. The large, white shapes of their headdresses and wide collars distort their heads and shoulders so that the sturdy young women appear hunchbacked and misshapen. Their faces, which in the drawings are rather pretty, are now dull and vacuous. Because of the bright colors and fairy-tale quality of the costumes, the painting provides an attractive glimpse of Breton life; but the awkwardness of the poses and the ugly, staring faces have a mocking quality consistent with Gauguin's openly sardonic attitude toward women. Gauguin saw that the combination of purity and malice was fascinating—and an extremely original way of recasting overused subjects, such as Breton peasants. Bracquemond told Pissarro that he found Gauguin's new direction to be good "but . . . strange. . . . A little confused, but after all interesting."[60] Some people he showed the paintings to "became literally angry, conceiving that they were being taken in."[61]

After Gauguin returned to Paris from Pont-Aven in mid-October, he was further encouraged to branch out into nontraditional styles and subjects when he began working for the ceramic designer Ernst Chaplet.[62] Chaplet had studied the pottery of the Far East, as well as European folk styles, and reintroduced stoneware into contemporary ceramic production. He put Gauguin to work adapting the Brittany drawings to glazed paintings on stoneware vases. He also allowed Gauguin to experiment freely in making his own clay vessels, which, from the first, were both charming and grotesque. Freed from the conventions of sculpture that lay behind his earlier carvings in wood and stone, Gauguin squeezed, stroked, and cut the clay into organic shapes decorated with protruding figures, faces, knobs, straps, and handles. Although some are extremely beautiful in color and incised drawing, most are merely puzzling. One, which pleased him immediately, is now lost but can be seen in a painting of his young friend Charles Laval (fig. 25). The large, brown vessel has a human shape, the "chest" of which is open like a mouth, from which a limp tongue hangs down. Laval's gaze is fixed on this biomorphic form that permits so many organic interpretations. This pot was no doubt signed, like the others that Gauguin produced over the winter of 1886–87, with his proud new logo, PGo.

Ceramists commonly used initials or other symbols, rather than full names, to sign their work. Ernst Chaplet used a circle of beads from which hung a tiny cross—a *chapelet,* or rosary.[63] Inside the circle were the stamped initials of his employer, Haviland and Company, or the initials of his various collaborators, such as Gauguin, which were scratched into the clay. Gauguin's PGo inside the circle was a crude retort to Chaplet's saintly rosary and a warning to the Paris art world that he was still the malin (devil) of Pont-Aven.

Paris was still not impressed with Gauguin. None of the dealers he knew from the old days—Durand-Ruel, Portier, Legrand—would take on his work. Nor could the old Impressionist exhibitions be revived. The important exhibitions now were at the Petit Gallery and those held by the emerging avant-garde group in Brussels, Les XX (The Twenty). The more salable Impressionists were invited to exhibit, like Monet and Pissarro and, in the second tier, Seurat, but not Gauguin. Although he again frequented the café Nouvelle Athènes, his anger at the Néos grew so uncontrollable that he finally refused to speak to any of them. One night at the end of November,

Gauguin snubbed even Pissarro, an affront that reverberated through the whole group.[64] By the end of January 1887, Pissarro was writing to his son, "Gauguin is gone . . . completely disappeared."[65]

By default, Gauguin fell back on Emile Schuffenecker, who had found him an apartment near Chaplet's ceramic studio, on the rue Blomet in Vaugirard, and was extremely interested in his new painting style and pottery. The Schuffeneckers also visited Clovis at school (Gauguin did not) and corresponded with Mette.[66] They may have represented to Gauguin some remnant of his former life. Yet Gauguin also kept up with his two friends from Pont-Aven, Charles Laval and Ferdinand du Puigaudeau, who were back in art classes at the Julian and Cormon studios. The contact with the art student crowd was novel to Gauguin, who had skipped this phase of art training. Gauguin's young friends continued to be flattered by his attention, and they probably helped him financially out of their parents' liberal allowances. Laval's portrait, for instance, may have been a commission.

After the New Year, Gauguin was spending all his time with Laval and du Puigaudeau and seemed to be working exclusively on his pottery, for no paintings survive from the first three months of 1887. In fact, he may have been spending all his time on Chaplet's pieces to earn as much money as possible. Once again he had failed in Paris and needed to find a new, more appreciative environment. This time, instead of going to Rouen, Copenhagen, or Pont-Aven, he went to find his fortune on the Panama Canal. It had been almost fifteen years since he had embarked on a great sea voyage, but the memories of sexual experimentation in distant ports and Paris's warm embraces upon his return were too beguiling to resist.

Gauguin talked about exotic travel for a long time before he left for parts unknown. He consumed the popular travel magazines and investigated every scheme that might take him to Spain, the South Seas, or Madagascar.[1] Not only did he seek to escape his professional and personal difficulties, but also, after suffering through a long winter in Paris, he craved the heat of the sun and the sensual pleasure of the sea. To live in a tropical climate was one of his deepest desires and became a recurring theme in his letters to his wife. But how to earn the kind of money he would need to live in southern climes had, to this point, eluded him. Finally he saw his opportunity arise the same way all previous employment had—through his family. His sister Marie's husband, Juan Uribe, had returned to his native country to set up a retail business in Panama City, which was then still part of Colombia. The Uribes had apparently lost badly in the market crash of 1882 and perhaps also in the Peruvian stocks based on guano. But Juan was not a stockbroker like his friends; he was a merchant, and he devised a plan to capitalize on the money flowing into the Panama Canal project that France had launched in 1880. Marie mentioned to her brother, when he returned to Paris from Pont-Aven, that Juan needed someone to handle the finances of the company, and suggested that he might take the job.[2] Despite their quarrels, Marie was anxious to help her brother resume a normal life with his family.

Although Paul doesn't seem to have had any further conversations with Marie or Juan about this, he grew to believe that his future lay in Panama— or, more precisely, Taboga, a small island off the Pacific coast, near Panama City. He imagined working for Juan only long enough to make enough money to retire to the island to paint.[3] This scheme sounded plausible enough to his young confidants, Laval and du Puigaudeau, and the three of them soon decided to set out on this adventure. Once the decision was made, the arrangements came together rather quickly. In March 1887, Paul announced to Mette that he was leaving in a month and that she should come and get Clovis.[4]

Although she was delighted to have Clovis back, this surprising development put an additional strain on Mette's limited budget. Not only did she have to find the money to pay for the trip, but she also had to pay Clovis's school bills.[5] She no doubt pointed out to her husband that if he had enough money to sail to the Caribbean (the steamer ticket alone cost 750 francs), he had enough to support his family for two months; but he, in reply, made it clear that he was unwilling to share any of his funds with his wife or children.[6] Finally, under pressure, Paul offered her some of his less important art works—both paintings and pottery—to see if she could sell them in Copenhagen.[7] This was the beginning of a peculiar monetary arrangement between them: he gave his family very little money (regardless of how much he made), and Mette became skilled at promoting, selling, and bartering his works in Scandinavia.

Paul did arrange for Mette to have his power of attorney so that she could claim the inheritance that was earmarked for the children if his aging Uncle Isidore should die while he was out of the country. Ever since the family had moved to Copenhagen in 1884, Mette kept Uncle Isidore informed of the children's activities and updated their photographs periodically. It is clear from the frequent mentions of him in their correspondence that both Paul and Mette hoped that someday their inheritance from Uncle Isidore would put them on their feet again. Paul's thoughtfulness in granting Mette power of attorney was consistent with the increased affection he had felt for her recently, but he did not grant it without goading her: "If he [Uncle Isidore] should die, the money you would receive is for the children: I think you are now too smart to keep it for yourself."[8] This admonition was unnecessary, for Mette was already the sole support of the children, as well as ironically prophetic of the fact that it was Paul who kept it all for himself when Uncle Isidore died at long last in 1893.

Paul and Mette spent a little time together before he left Paris for the dock at Saint-Nazaire; Mette's feelings for him continued to be warm, and now that he imagined himself employed once again, he considered the possibilities of a reunion upon his return. He closed his letters sweetly: "Je t'embrasse mille fois bien tendrement, comme je t'aime."[9]

When the time came, only Laval and Gauguin set sail; their third companion, du Puigaudeau, stayed behind, expecting to join them later. Mette was still on Paul's mind when he and Laval landed in Panama. Gauguin immediately saw that the country before him presented more problems than he had anticipated; but on the voyage over he had glimpsed paradise— the island of Martinique in the French Antilles, where the ship had made a stop. Gauguin's response to Martinique during this brief layover was identical to that he had had in Pont-Aven: with a little money the family could have a wonderful life there. The vision of a "family" paradise—Martinique— quickly overshadowed the possibilities of Panama and reduced his experience there to one long effort to get out.

The French presence in Panama during the 1880s has been largely forgotten. For a period of about ten years, the two countries most likely to build an interocean canal on that site—Colombia, which owned the territory, and the United States, which had the resources and the most to gain—became bystanders as French engineering imperialism took its final bow on the world stage. Thanks almost entirely to the success of the French-led Suez Canal project (1856–66) and the entrepreneurial spirit of the French financial market around 1880, a private company was formed and financed to undertake this glorious feat of engineering.[10] Work began in 1881. After the failure of the Union Générale, investors saw this project as a bright spot on an otherwise dim financial horizon.

Gauguin had shown no personal interest in Panama before his brother-in-law, Juan Uribe, set up a business there in 1885. But he was frequently drawn to opportunistic schemes in other countries, as he was to the Spanish uprising in the early 1880s and to an ongoing project in Madagascar that is mentioned in letters from 1887 to 1891 but never fully explained.[11] Madagascar, like Panama, was the site of recent French territorialism. The French had fought a war from 1883 to 1885 to establish their claims over the island and to oust the British, the conclusion of which opened many new opportunities to French traders and investors. Gauguin does not name his connections to the Madagascar scheme, but they may have been either his old friends from the Bourse or his Norwegian connections through Frits Thaulow. Norwegians played a little-known but very prominent role in the political and economic development of Madagascar.[12]

The Madagascar project was put off temporarily, so Gauguin proceeded to Panama, although he harbored great hopes that he could combine the two schemes by bringing Juan Uribe into the Madagascar project as well.[13] Gauguin's decision to go first to Panama may have come from his greater knowledge of the country and the Panama Canal construction. His Colombian relatives, the Uribes, were a useful source of information about the negotiations and about the impact of the canal on the country. Furthermore, he knew the geography because he had sailed along the Pacific coast of the isthmus during his voyage aboard the *Chili* in 1866–67.

His firsthand knowledge did not keep his expectations from far outstripping the reality of the situation, in terms of both the possible financial rewards and the art he had hoped to produce. He blamed his error on the false descriptions of others, most likely the fond viewpoint of his brother-in-law ("Que le diable emporte tous les gens qui vous renseignent de travers!" [The devil take those who give you the wrong information!]).[14] Some details may also have come from Charles Laval, who had family connections to Henri Cottu, an administrator of the private company building the canal, the Compagnie Universelle du Canal Interocéanique de Panama.[15] Cottu had promised the young artist letters of reference to help Laval and Gauguin find employment within the company.

However ignorant Gauguin and Laval may have been about Panama, the society they encountered when they stepped off the boat in Colón had seen many men like them before. The majority of the people drawn to Panama in the 1880s were laborers, men and women—mainly blacks from the islands of the West Indies. But white American and European professionals also came. Many young French engineers hoped to establish their reputations on the canal, and subcontractors from all over the world were hired by the company to carry out various facets of the construction. After those who actually worked on the canal came adventurous businessmen like Juan Uribe, as well as doctors, lawyers, and the inevitable journalists, writers, and artists of all kinds.

But clerks—Gauguin had recently been one himself—composed the largest category of skilled labor. There were so many that they glutted the market. One anonymous correspondent to the *New York Tribune* reported: "The class of adventurers who are always more numerous—the men who rely upon their supposititious intellect rather than upon their muscle—are today to be found in Panama and Colón literally starving. Most of them are swindlers or clerks. The former class, unless they are expert gamblers, find little scope for the exercise of their talents; and the latter oscillate between feeble efforts to emulate the unremunerative practices of the former and a fruitless beggary, until they die in the street or stow away on some homeward-bound vessel."[16] Gauguin, who had come to Panama primarily to resume his career in finance, fell right into this category of surplus clerks and swindlers.

Upon arriving, Gauguin and Laval took the short train ride to Panama City, on the other side of the isthmus, to see Gauguin's brother-in-law. Unlike Colón, headquarters of the Canal Company, Panama City was the capital of the province and a well-established center of colonial Spanish culture in the New World. The Uribe family may already have had roots there. Not surprisingly, by the time Gauguin arrived, Uribe had filled the position that Gauguin had heard about months earlier. Uribe decided against placing his wife's brother in his business in any capacity. Furthermore, he soon made it clear that he would not bankroll Gauguin's schemes in either Panama (allowing him to live "like a savage" on Taboga) or Madagascar. Although at first Uribe was generous, the two men quickly reached the end of their goodwill toward each other, and Gauguin left abruptly, taking with him some of Uribe's merchandise. Paul wrote indignantly to Mette, "My imbecile brother-in-law . . . couldn't have spent more than a few pennies on a welcome for us and was as nasty as possible. I was so mad I cheated him out of some clothes he was asking 35 francs for but which were worth only 15."[17]

Gauguin's money was slipping away. He and Laval had checked into the Grande Central Hotel, owned by the Canal Company, which was at the heart of social life in the old city of Panama.[18] All the rooms looked out over a central courtyard, which was outfitted with billiard tables, a gambling casino, and a huge, American-style bar. A young French engineer, visiting in 1881, was in awe: "There is every diversion at hand in this hotel lobby. Besides, it would be useless to go out to look for other pleasures; they were nowhere to be found. In this city there is neither theater nor concert nor café, nothing but the lobby of the Grand Hotel, to which one must always return."[19] Gauguin's fantasy of being a champion billiard player may have had its origins in this lobby: "They say I am the champion billiard player, and I am French. The Americans are furious and propose that I should play a match in America. I accept. . . . In a great luxurious room (American luxury), the famous match takes place. My opponent plays first. He scores a hundred and fifty. America rejoices. I play . . . two hundred, three hundred. America is beaten. And still I yawn. They say I am happy. Perhaps."[20] Gauguin had a great desire to triumph over Americans (including his brother-in-law) and to avenge the cool welcome he received in this part of the world.

The colonial society that Gauguin and Laval found themselves in was cutthroat. His vision of buying land and living off tropical fruits was not even a remote possibility in this speculators' market; in fact, getting any kind of job was difficult. According to the *Tribune* correspondent, "It is no unusual matter, this sad spectacle of educated men starving in the streets of Panama. Nowhere else does there seem to be less of the milk of human kindness than on the isthmus."[21]

Given the rough conditions, it must be seen as a triumph of sorts that Gauguin and Laval managed to find positions working on the canal within two weeks of their arrival. Surely their success was due to their connections—Gauguin's to Juan Uribe and Laval's to Henri Cottu (even though the actual letters of reference came later)—and to their education, and, in Gauguin's case at least, management skills. They were hired as temporary clerks by the Société de Travaux Publics et Constructions, one of the six subdivisions of the Canal Company.[22] Their division was in charge of building a dam across the Chagres River so that the dangerous and unpredictable flooding of these waters would be diverted away from the canal.

The inhumane conditions under which the manual laborers worked became legendary. But however bad the conditions at the work site, neither Laval nor Gauguin would have had to put up with them, for they both worked in the headquarters located in Colón. Even though they were hired as temporary employees, they made good money (almost 600 francs a month) because of the inflated wages of the canal zone, and they were able to save at least half of it toward their return trip to France. Laval was also apparently able to obtain some portrait commissions for 500 francs each. Gauguin was not, because, as he wrote his wife, "they have to be done in a special and extremely awful manner, something I am incapable of doing."[23] Actually, Gauguin, like Laval, had done portraits of a marketable type before—Gauguin's Rouen portraits of his wife and other Scandinavians are evidence of this—but Laval may have had more success through his connections than Gauguin had.

Although Gauguin's life was not easy in Panama, it is significant that he exaggerated his hardships to the point of falsehood in letters to his wife. Instead of describing his real job, he told her he had become a manual laborer: "Tomorrow I start to swing a pickax on the canal. . . . Don't complain about your work; every day I dig from 5:30 in the morning until 6:00 at night under the tropical sun and in the rain."[24] He was obviously feeling guilty that he was off spending much-needed money while she shouldered a heavy workload to support the children. Gauguin had spent over 1,000 francs on this fruitless trip to Panama. Now he was making 600 francs a month and still had no intention of sending any home. To divert her attention from the money, he fabricated the tale of "swinging a pickax" and then casually doubled the mortality rate on the canal: "The blacks, who have the worst jobs, die 9 out of 12, but the others die at only half that rate."[25] Mette was the only one of Paul's correspondents to be treated to this vivid and gory tale of his misfortunes, a sign both of his guilty feelings about her and his delight in worrying her.

Gauguin's and Laval's lucrative jobs with the canal ended suddenly, as was typical of the temporary positions they held. The Canal Company had come to the end of what seemed like limitless funding for the project; the next month, in July 1887, a bond issue to raise an additional 220 million francs failed.[26] This was the beginning of the end of the French effort to pierce the isthmus. Gauguin and Laval had worked for only about two weeks, but their income and their reserves amounted to enough to purchase tickets part of the way back to France—to the island of Martinique.

Martinique was a thriving port of call for the many ships sailing between Panama and France in the early 1880s, and enjoyed much of the prosperity created by the canal enterprise without enduring the mess of construction itself. When Gauguin had disembarked in the harbor of Saint-Pierre on the trip over, he had glimpsed the lively colonial society on Martinique, and had kept it fixed in his mind until he could return.

Martinique, like Pont-Aven, was basically a tourist society. The scenery was interesting, the climate was mild, and the hard work was done by somebody else. The French colonists lived well off their sugar plantations and fruit orchards and were delighted to welcome visiting artists, writers, and educated tourists of all kinds.[27] The boom of the canal had made these visits more frequent, and many tourists found houses in and around the cosmopolitan coastal city of Saint-Pierre, cultural capital of an island whose population was close to 200,000 in 1890, intending to stay for months or years and enjoy the perpetual holiday atmosphere. An artist or writer could make something of a living selling painted or written travel sketches of this tropical paradise to the public back home in France or in the nearby United States.

The most prominent writer was Lafcadio Hearn, an American of British parentage who had been educated in France. Hearn lived in Saint-Pierre from July to September 1887 to gather material for a long essay, "A Midsummer Trip to the Tropics," which was bought by *Harper's Magazine*. Hearn returned to Martinique later that fall for a stay of about a year and a half, during which time he wrote two novels and the travel book *Two Years in the French West Indies* (1890). Hearn's delight in the nonwhite residents and their customs, as well as in the dramatic landscape, also led him to take extensive photographs of Martinique. No documentation affirms that Gauguin and Hearn met, although it is quite likely that they did. Both were interested in island folklore, which may have been the result of actual acquaintance or, if not, may show that artistic tourists were attracted to the kinds of tales and ideas commonly discussed on hotel verandas and in cafés and other visitors' meeting places.

After the grim, hardworking society of Panama, Martinique was a relief. Gauguin envisioned a successful life here, complete with money and family, and wrote of it to his wife. "I very much hope to see you here with the children one day. Don't panic: there are good schools on Martinique, and the whites are as pampered as white blackbirds."[28]

Although Martinique was not an artists' colony, as Pont-Aven had been, Gauguin and Laval surveyed the situation and got to know local and visiting artists, illustrators, photographers, and art teachers. Because both artists had Salon credentials, they would have been treated with respect by a society that was in close touch with Paris through frequent visits and subscriptions to French newspapers. Their association with Impressionism may also have opened doors in the more avant-garde circles of colonialists and tourists. Gauguin imagined that if he were to establish his family here, they would be able to take the trip to France often: it was a voyage of only about twelve days.[29] Gauguin even wrote enviously to Schuffenecker of the art professor at the Lycée de Saint-Pierre, who, he had already discovered, made 400 francs a month for working only half days. "Some people have all the luck!" he groused to the similarly employed Schuff.[30]

Having no connections, Gauguin and Laval no doubt assumed their most important airs to make contacts and set up the life they wanted to live in Martinique. The clothes from Gauguin's brother-in-law's shop certainly helped. In a port like Saint-Pierre, Gauguin's sailing credentials would have been as useful as his Salon acceptance. Gauguin no doubt swaggered around the harbor front in the pose of a sea captain, as he had in Pont-Aven. Laval's success at the Salons of 1880 and 1883, as well as the fame of his father, Ernst Laval, a prominent architect in Paris, would have stood him in good stead.

The two artists soon rented from one of the wealthy landowners what they called a "Negro hut," along the coast toward Le Carbet, the premier suburb of Saint-Pierre. It is doubtful that these two self-important Frenchmen would have been offered or would have accepted a dwelling of the kind occupied by the poor black population. Their rented cottage was no doubt simple, but was most likely of the type typically rented by white tourists or city dwellers wanting a seaside vacation. The area along the coast road to the small town of Le Carbet, a distance of less than a mile, was thick with such small cottages owned by the wealthier inhabitants of Saint-Pierre and local plantation owners.[31] As in Pont-Aven, the two men took advantage of the holiday atmosphere: they swam in the sea and set their own hours to walk into Saint-Pierre to shop, visit the cafés, and pick up their mail.

At first everything went well, and both wrote glowing letters back home about the delightful scenery and the easy living. But soon reality set in, and they once again found that even the fruit from the local coconut farms had to be paid for. Their money dwindled, and, unlike in Panama with its Canal Company, they were not able to replenish their purses with lucrative temporary jobs. As Laval soon wrote to du Puigaudeau, "All we need is our dear Piccolo and a little more money."[32]

It took less than three months after their arrival in Martinique for Gauguin to become completely disillusioned. He wrote plaintively to his wife, "Right now I'm in a Negro hut, lying on a seaweed mattress, my strength gone, and completely without funds to return to France."[33] At the same time he was writing to Schuffenecker to send him enough for the ticket home. "I must leave here or I'll die like a dog!"[34]

Gauguin's agitated state can be partly accounted for by a bout with yellow fever, which left him weak, but partly, too, by the impact of receiving his first mail from home. Powerful emotions aroused by various correspondents (Gauguin's wife, his old friend Claude Favre, and Laval's brother Nino) made Gauguin long for familiar faces and surroundings.

Mette's letters were loving and open about the painfulness of her life. To her, Paul wrote, "Oh, my poor Mette, I wish I were dead and it would all be over. Your letters bring me pleasure but, at the same time, unbearable sadness. If at least we hated each other (hatred is bracing), but you are wishing for a husband just when it is impossible. And poor Mette, buried by work, you ask me to help. But I can't."[35] Paul's guilt about letting Mette and his children down at this point was clearly genuine. But his impulse was, as always, to make excuses, to exaggerate his own difficulties so that she couldn't hold him accountable. Ignoble though it may be, his guilt prompted him to provide a vivid picture of his illness and suffering—so vivid that one cannot help but be moved, even knowing that the account is largely false:

> During my stay at Colón, I was poisoned by the malarious swamps of the canal, and I had just enough strength to hold out on the journey, but as soon as I reached Martinique I collapsed. In short, for the last month I have been down with dysentery and marsh fever. At this moment my body is a skeleton and I can hardly whisper; after being so low that I expected to die every night, I have at length taken a turn for the better, but I have suffered agonies in the stomach. The little that I eat gives me atrocious pains and it is an effort to write, as I am light-headed. My last shillings have gone to the chemist and for doctor's visits. He says it is absolutely necessary for me to return to France if I am not to be always ill with liver disease and fever.[36]

To Schuffenecker he wrote a (somewhat) toned down and more believable account:

> "I have been mortally ill from dysentery, liver trouble, and marsh fever—for eight days I rose only to eat, and I am just a skeleton. I shall not in fact be any better until I am on the sea and in sight of my native land, and if I had the money for the voyage, I would leave at the same time as this letter."[37]

The eight days during which the fever ran its course were in July, for Laval mentions Gauguin's illness to du Puigaudeau in a letter early on.[38] Over a month later Gauguin re-created the experience for those he wanted to feel most sorry for him, particularly his wife.

Other letters that Gauguin received at this time agitated him, although not all touched his heart. Some correspondents criticized him severely for this extravagant and futile trip to the Caribbean, principally Favre, le Marsouin. As recounted in Gauguin's indignant summary for Schuffenecker, Favre apparently told Gauguin that if he disgraced himself, it was his own fault, and that he didn't know whether to laugh or cry at the situation Gauguin had created. Favre believed in scaling his efforts to what he knew he could handle without imposing on anyone else.[39] His criticisms were right on target; and many people over the years leveled similar ones at Gauguin. Each time Gauguin shrugged them off and redoubled his efforts to win the sympathy of those less critical of him, primarily his wife and Emile Schuffenecker. He closed his letter to Favre telling him that if the Dillies Company asked his whereabouts, he was in China and would be out of touch for ten years.[40]

To Schuffenecker, from whom he had not yet heard, Gauguin wrote a letter devoted half to his sufferings and half to requests for money. Because Schuffenecker held his better art works (those not given to Mette) and had promised to put them on the market, Gauguin could ask for money in advance of future sales without the request seeming like a personal loan. In fact, Schuffenecker often loaned Gauguin money and ended up with his artworks in return. Schuffenecker had gotten himself too entangled in Gauguin's finances to be able to tell Gauguin off as neatly as Favre had done, much though he might have wanted to.

Gauguin, after reading his first mail from home, was overwhelmed with homesickness, longing, and anger—all giving him a sudden, acute dissatisfaction with Martinique and a desire to be back in Paris. Besides, Laval's brother Nino had written that a collector was interested in Gauguin's pottery and would be willing to set him up in business.[41] Gauguin lunged at the opportunity—as he did at any business proposition, no matter how slight. Once again he saw his future grow rosy: this time the long-awaited triumph would be over old enemies in Paris.

Gone were his ideas about settling in Martinique; the scenery and exotic people were no longer to be his future. He was now desperate for someone to give him enough money for the boat trip. Because it took a month for a reply from France, he had to give up catching the next month's boat home, which would sail sometime around September 25. But by October 25 he had gone, leaving Charles Laval behind to paint and nurse his frail health for another year.

Only after the change of heart about the Martinique paradise did Gauguin produce, in the remaining two months he was there, a number of paintings to take back to France. Although he had packed a complete outfit of painting supplies, he doesn't seem to have even attempted to paint in Panama. Upon arrival in Martinique, before he was laid low by yellow fever, he made pencil sketches, but he doesn't refer to paintings in his letters until well into the fall.

The dozen or so canvases he began in Martinique built on his breakthroughs at Pont-Aven the summer before. The unusual new figure studies he had done of black women on the island, a more decorative palette reminiscent of tropical fruits and flowers, and an evocative calmness in the compositions made these paintings arresting to the Parisian eye. Like his letters, the paintings were based on a reality that was filtered through Gauguin's obfuscating lens. He wanted to make the simple tropical scenes enticing in their remoteness. As he wrote to Schuffenecker, "I have never been able to do such clear, lucid painting (and yet very much from my imagination!)."[42]

It is not hard to see which aspects of island life inspired Gauguin to take his painting into a more imaginative realm. He was hardly there a week before he had absorbed some of the popular island tales with sexual themes. Always uncomfortable about sexual advances made by women, Gauguin was struck by how the black women made themselves available to visiting white men. He couldn't help going into detail about this to Mette, all the while claiming that he nobly preserved his virtue. The thought of making her blush may have heightened his dramatic delivery.[43]

> I can tell you that a white man here has all his work cut out to keep his clothes intact, for Potiphar's wives are not wanting. Nearly all are coloured from ebony to dusky white, and they go as far as to work their charms on the fruit they give you to compel your embraces. The day before yesterday a young negress of 16 years old, damnably pretty, offered me a split guava

[mango] squeezed at the end.[44] I was about to eat it as the young girl left when a light-skinned lawyer standing by took the fruit out of my hand and threw it away. "You are European, Monsieur, and don't know the customs of the country," he said to me. "You must not eat fruit without knowing where it comes from. This fruit has a spell; the negress crushed it on her breast, and you would surely be at her disposal afterward." I thought it was a joke. Not at all; this mulatto (who had nevertheless passed his examinations) believed in what he said. Now that I am warned, I will not fall, and you can sleep soundly, assured of my virtue.[45]

The actual facts of the event cannot be ascertained from Gauguin's colorful tale; but it was common enough for Europeans to develop liaisons with willing local women of African descent. A letter from Hearn to a friend in New Orleans describes the ease with which it was accomplished: "As, under a perpendicular sun, I wandered down the narrow, curious, yellow painted streets of Martinique, I looked about me; . . . In a little while I ceased to be in the street; under the guidance of a half-naked mulatto I had found my way into the upper chamber of a queer building, overlooking a court full of cabbage-palms and breadfruit trees;—there was a girl there,—the tallest and most generally appetizing possible to conceive,—a Martinique octoroon."[46]

Gauguin's story of the seductive spell placed on a mango by a young woman suggests the swapping of tales of sexual conquest in a smoky café where bohemian tourists might gather. Few visitors to Martinique would have understood the Creole patois well enough to get such stories from the natives themselves. But someone like Lafcadio Hearn, who had studied Creole and published a book of Creole proverbs, *Gombo Zhèbes,* in 1885, might have shared such fascinating tidbits with his fellow whites.[47]

Gauguin attributed the story to a man of mixed heritage who acted as an interpreter between the two cultures, but who, Gauguin emphasizes, believed in magic spells himself. Like most whites, Gauguin felt that the black culture on Martinique operated on irrational principles—which made that world separate but highly intriguing. Although Gauguin never painted the woman either holding a mango to her breast or offering it to her intended victim in Martinique (he returned to the idea in Tahiti), he did paint only black women, suppressing most signs of white culture on the island, so that his compositions would evoke that alternative, mysterious other world.

Creole folklore and proverbs, like those compiled by Hearn, also suggested to Gauguin the importance of the snake in the metaphorical and actual lives of the Martiniquans. Although no snakes appear in the drawings or paintings he created on Martinique, they assumed an important role in the images of Eve and the Temptation that Gauguin explored in the years after his visit to the island. His fascination with fruit and sexuality at this time (seen in such stories as that of the enchanted mango and such works as *Among the Mangoes at Martinique* in which women pick and lustily eat fruit off the trees) call to mind the biblical Fall of Adam and Eve and the implied presence of the snake (fig. 26). Snakes were in fact very common on the island and were the only indigenous creature that posed a mortal threat to the human population.[48] Hearn gave the snake a large role in his novels and short stories of Martinique, often placing it in a sexual or romantic

context. The language of black Martinique, the Creole patois, based as it was on French but governed by rules of grammar and pronunciation that stymied the European French speaker, was another colorful device that Hearn and others took as a symbol of the island's mysterious nature.[49]

The women he painted on Martinique suggest another world in ways besides evoking its sexual magic. Whites believed that in the black community of Martinique traditional European gender roles were reversed. The men were often considered too lazy for heavy labor—stay-at-homes supported by their wives.[50] The women, on the other hand, were strong and enterprising. They worked as laborers and farmhands and operated the transport system. The terrain did not allow horse-drawn carts. Instead, the tall, powerful women carried whatever needed to go from one part of the island to the other, usually balanced on their heads. Many women made a good living by their own labor and by organizing other women into transport companies under their supervision. European men were fascinated by this female industry (and role reversal), and the *porteuses* were one of the most remarked-upon aspects of island life. In his paintings, Gauguin depicted them as if they were descendants of ancient Amazons.

Hearn's famous essay on these women, published in *Two Years in the French West Indies* (1890), paints a similar picture: "You find less the impression of a scene of to-day than the sensation of something that was and is not. Slowly this feeling strengthens with your pleasure in the colorific radiance of costume,—the semi-nudity of passing figures,—the puissant shapeliness of torsos ruddily swart like statue metal,—the rounded outline of limbs yellow as tropic fruit,—the grace of attitudes,—the unconscious harmony of groupings,—the gathering and folding and falling of light robes that oscillate with swaying of free hips,—the sculptural symmetry of unshod feet."[51] These lithe, vigorous women were to Hearn like Atalanta, queen of the Amazons.[52] Gauguin's friezelike arrangements of the figures in his paintings, the draped forms silhouetted against the blue of the ocean, suggest that he, like Hearn, used Greek, Egyptian, or Assyrian reliefs as a way to cast the Martiniquan culture in the mold of an ancient world.

Gauguin's idea that Martinique scenes could be so used may have come from Hearn, who wrote stirringly to the American audience back home of the "ancient" sights on the island: "When you find yourself for the first time, upon some unshadowed day, in the delightful West Indian city of St. Pierre,—supposing that you own the sense of poetry, the recollections of a student,—there is apt to steal upon your fancy an impression of having seen it all before, ever so long ago."[53] Mount Pelée, the volcano that rose majestically behind Saint-Pierre, recalled for Hearn and many other visitors that other volcano, Mount Vesuvius, that cut short the life of the thriving resort town of Pompeii. "And all at once the secret of your dream is revealed, with the rising of many a luminous memory,—dreams of the Idyllists, flowers of old Sicilian song, fancies limned upon Pompeiian walls. For a moment the illusion is delicious: you comprehend as never before the charm of a vanished world,—the antique life, the story of terra-cottas and graven stones and gracious things exhumed: even the sun is not of to-day, but of twenty centuries gone;—thus, and under such a light, walked the women of the elder world."[54]

There even appeared to be scientific proof that Martinique and its sister islands in the French Antilles were vestiges of the sunken continent of Atlantis. Nineteenth-century botanical research had been unable to explain the strange seaweed found only in that area, and, as a consequence, the romantic theory had grown up that it was a "floating waif" now separated from the gardens that once grew on the lost continent. "It was the Atlantis which is mentioned by Plato; the land in which the Elysian Fields were placed, and the Garden of Hesperides, from which the early civilizations of Greece, Egypt, and Asia Minor were derived, and whose kings and heroes were the Olympian deities of a later time. The poetical idea prevails that this plant, which once grew in those gardens, having lost its original home, has become a floating waif on the sapphire sea of the tropics."[55]

The frequency with which the antique theme was used in literature about Martinique struck a chord that resonated with ideas and issues growing steadily more important in the avant-garde circles of Paris, from which Gauguin was a refugee. Gauguin, Pissarro, and their friends had often talked of finding inspiration in the nontraditional art of the past, both

Western and non-Western, and folk art of all kinds. Seurat had based his stylized, geometric forms on ancient reliefs, and Rousseau had created a similar exotic and naive art. In symbolist circles, Redon's fragmentary compositions inspired dream images evoking the ancient world.

The previous summer in Pont-Aven, Gauguin had discovered the power of caricature to bring the odd Breton costumes and shapes to life. He had taken this novelty one step further in his experimental pottery after his return to Paris. In Martinique he used his caricaturist's eye to study the women before him, but gave them a haunting dignity consistent with their kinship to an ancient race. Their large, masculine bodies and aggressive eroticism satisfied Gauguin's own nontraditional interests. He took a chance that his reference would be understood by the avant-garde Parisian audience, which was made up of many men, like Degas, who avoided marriage and the clichés of heterosexual sensuality in their art. Gauguin knew that the dealers, patrons, and critics, as well as the other artists of this circle, would also be looking for the kind of experimental subjects and styles that the Neo-Impressionists had recently introduced. He wanted to show that he was aware of the emerging trends, but at the same time, he wanted to create something entirely new, something uniquely his own — that would earn him the fame he knew he deserved. Ironically, he managed to accomplish this feat on the island of Martinique only after he had abandoned the idea of living there permanently and had begun looking at the local motifs through the eyes of an artist who was already mentally back in Paris.

Gauguin could not have guessed the significance Martinique would have for the rest of his career. As he shivered in the gray November cold of Paris, he managed to turn the tropical sun—its heat even more than its light—into a metaphor for his artistic as well as his physical needs. In the many variations of the sun theme that he developed in the months to follow, he portrayed the sun's heat not as nurturing but as all-consuming and all-powerful— a force to be feared as much as it was desired.

In an intellectual community growing increasingly symbolist, Gauguin's skillful use of the sun metaphor impressed artists and writers alike and satisfied his own love of language and paradox. He incorporated it into his new pottery, emphasizing the immense burning heat of the kiln necessary in the creative process. He also enlarged upon his earlier adoption of the naughty signature PGo by starting to portray himself as a man of the sun—a savage Inca from Peru—who preached a return to the tropics to chart the true course of modern art. He found a ready audience in the younger Parisian avant-garde, who had never known him when he was a prosaic clerk on the stock exchange or a married man with five children. To them he came straight from Martinique, a haughty, bronzed sun god who appeared in Paris in the fall of 1887 to show them a new path.

It is doubtful that Gauguin's construction of his new identity as a man of the tropics occurred to him before he returned to Paris. But two things happened almost immediately. First, he found a huge exhibition of art pottery being held at the Union Centrale, where the new styles practiced by his former employer Chaplet were causing a sensation.[1] Gauguin's own pottery from the previous winter began selling in the wake of interest in this exhibition.[2] Although the scheme of setting up a business with Chaplet (proposed to him by Charles Laval's brother Nino while he was in Martinique) fell through, he sold more of his pottery than ever before. Naturally, he fired up the kilns and sat down to make more. And, feeling close to his wife and family, he took the unexpected proceeds and sent off 100 francs to Copenhagen as a token of his good intentions and his optimism.[3] It was the first money he had ever sent to his family.[4]

The second auspicious occurrence was that a respectable dealer, Theo van Gogh of the internationally prominent Goupil Gallery (which had recently changed its name to Boussod and Valadon), was interested in representing him (fig. 27).[5] It had been more than four years since a gallery (Durand-Ruel) had taken on some of his works, and although he still had some things placed with the independent agent Portier, he wasn't optimistic about selling them. But now, instead of having to scratch for sales by making the rounds of the independents and the dabblers, such as Bertaux and other friends from the Bourse, a well-established dealer who managed his own inventory and exhibition space for Boussod and Valadon was coming to *him*. Along with Theo came his artist-brother Vincent van Gogh, and Gauguin's association with both of them profoundly altered the course of his career. Looking back, Gauguin would claim that his favorite paintings of Vincent's were his sunflowers; Gauguin may have believed that the bright yellow flowers that turned to follow the sun were painted in tribute to him.

Indeed, Vincent may have been waiting for Gauguin to come back from Martinique.[6] How and where the two men first met is unknown, although Gauguin wrote that it was in 1886, the year the Dutchman came to Paris.[7] After trying out various professions—art dealer, teacher, and evangelist minister—Vincent had become a full-time artist in 1880, at the age of twenty-seven. He, like Gauguin, was largely self-taught, although he had sought the advice of various artists over the years and spent short periods of time at the Brussels Academy and the studio of Cormon in Paris. In fact, his intention in coming to Paris was to receive instruction in certain technical aspects of painting that he didn't feel he could learn on his own. Once enrolled in Cormon's studio, however, he learned far more from his fellow students about avant-garde techniques and ideas than he did of traditional academic methods, and was soon an active presence in the circles of radical artists. He did not return to Cormon's studio after his first session in the spring of 1886.

Vincent was in Paris for the last Impressionist exhibition, held in May and June of 1886, where the Neo-Impressionists had made such a splash. He sought out the Néos—Signac, Lucien and probably Camille Pissarro, and Emile Schuffenecker; he did not meet Seurat until 1888. He was introduced to Guillaumin by the agent Portier upon his arrival in Paris. He met Toulouse-Lautrec in the class at Cormon's and also got to know the larger circle of former Cormon pupils, such as Emile Bernard and Charles Laval. He was a temperamental person whose outbursts and odd quirks were soon familiar to the artists around him, but he was at the same time so articulate and, at heart, so kind that he was quickly accepted into a surprising number of the avant-garde cliques. The many portraits of Vincent van Gogh painted by artist friends over the years attest to the affection he inspired.[8]

It did not hurt, of course, that his brother was a prominent art dealer and that at times he acted like one himself by organizing informal exhibitions of his friends' work in restaurants, facilitating exchanges among artists, and encouraging collectors and smaller dealers to buy from the struggling radicals. While he took his own work very seriously and believed in his ultimate success, he did not display competitive behavior toward his colleagues. Because his brother supported him financially and because he felt that he could have an exhibition in Paris whenever he felt ready to make his debut there,[9] he was content to put others ahead of him, unlike his fellows in the cutthroat profession he had chosen. Even artists like Edgar Degas, Claude Monet, and Mary Cassatt, who had by this time become finan-

cially secure and often helped those who were struggling, jealously promoted their own sales first and foremost. But Vincent van Gogh did not; and this refreshing absence of competitiveness won him something he valued even more than success—the affection of his colleagues.

If Vincent had not actually met Gauguin before he returned from Martinique, he certainly knew of him. Gauguin's contentious behavior in Paris among the Impressionists and Neo-Impressionists made him a frequent topic of conversation among mutual friends, like the Pissarro father and son, Guillaumin, Signac, and, of course Schuffenecker. Furthermore, during the summer of 1886, Gauguin had made disciples of the Cormon students Laval and du Puigaudeau and had met Bernard and Hartrick, both of whom knew Vincent well. Vincent could have seen Gauguin's paintings at the Impressionist exhibition and at the homes of Guillaumin and the Pissarros, as well as the Schuffeneckers. He may not have been so taken with Gauguin's art, which was as yet relatively unadventurous compared to that of the Néos, but when Gauguin and Laval left for Panama and the tropics, the boldness of their adventure would have made all the Parisian devotees of modern art sit up and take notice.

The paintings Gauguin brought home from Martinique, which were presented to the art crowd in Schuffenecker's home, where Gauguin had temporarily taken up residence, did not disappoint. The joint efforts of Gauguin, who no doubt spoke enticingly of the woman with the bewitched mango and the lost continent of Atlantis, and of Schuffenecker, whose affectionate enthusiasm was unbounded (and who also hoped to recoup some of the money lent to Gauguin), turned all who came into admirers.[10] Vincent, whose own work was on display with his friends Toulouse-Lautrec, Bernard, Anquetin, and others in an exhibition at the Grand Bouillon restaurant, immediately suggested an exchange with Gauguin.[11] That Gauguin agreed to this is more likely due to his desire to court Vincent's brother, the art dealer, than to his belief that Vincent's work was worthy of exchange with his own. Whereas Vincent certainly knew Gauguin's work from the time he came to Paris, it is doubtful that Gauguin knew, much less had come to admire, Vincent's. Whatever Gauguin's motive in exchanging with someone little known to him, the gesture paid off handsomely.

Within a month after Gauguin's reentry into the Paris art world, he had no fewer than nine works on view at Theo's Boulevard Monmartre branch of Boussod and Valadon, and, soon after that, a Pont-Aven painting was sold through the same gallery.[12] Furthermore, he received his first positive review from Félix Fénéon, champion of the Néos and a trendsetter among the young critics. In early January, Theo bought three paintings for a total of 900 francs and put more on view.[13] Gauguin was stunned! He knew the Martinique paintings were good, but the response was more than he had any reason to expect. He began his mental calculations—how soon could he go back?

Would Gauguin's evolution as an artist have proceeded as it did without the impact of Vincent and Theo van Gogh? Their enthusiasm for his Martinique pictures and Vincent's subsequent belief that tropical light facilitated the development of modern art through the liberation of color and the suppression of shadow encouraged Gauguin to develop his artistic vision in the tropics. He never forgot the sweetness of success that the brothers provided for him in Paris, after years of lukewarm acceptance, when he returned with the island pictures under his arm. His later trips to Tahiti and then the Marquesas were in some ways attempts to re-create the heady moment when he began to believe that he could conquer Paris after all.

Theo van Gogh helped many avant-garde artists at this time. Pissarro, Guillaumin, Bernard, and other lesser-known but struggling artists were able to sell an occasional painting through Theo when none of the other dealers in Paris would or could handle their work. Theo also learned to benefit from the success of Impressionists like Degas and Monet, whose prices were rising and whose work was in demand by several dealers at once. But of all the radical artists Theo handled (and they accounted for a very small proportion of his overall stock, because Boussod and Valadon mainly dealt in Salon artists), it was Gauguin whose life and career were most significantly altered by Theo's support.

Although Gauguin was strong-willed and driven by his own inner desires, he was not an artist who sought inspiration solely from within. From the first, he practiced art in a social context, changing and altering his style to speak to an intended recipient or audience. With his own background on the Bourse, he was extremely aware of market forces and, as a result, was unusually sensitive to the interaction of artist and dealer. Theo's willing-

**28** Paul Gauguin, *Sketches After Degas's Nude Bather, Album Briant*, 1888–89. Musée du Louvre, Département des Arts Graphiques, Paris.

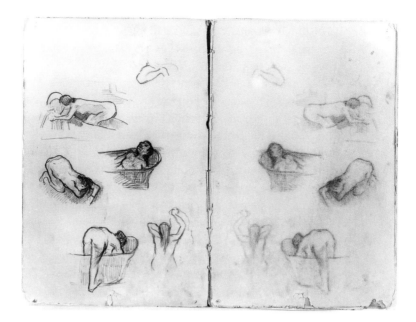

ness to take on Gauguin's Martinique paintings and unusual art pottery encouraged Gauguin to follow these directions perhaps more than he might have if there had been no market for them, and even to branch out into other directions that he knew Theo approved of and thought promising.

Among the radical artists Gauguin knew to be handled by Theo were his three old colleagues Pissarro, Guillaumin, and Degas—all of whose works Theo exhibited alongside Gauguin's in his gallery in December 1887 and January 1888. Gauguin knew Pissarro's and Guillaumin's art all too well, and the reunion of the three former painters of the countryside was an ironic juxtaposition of the three different directions they had recently taken—Pissarro into Neo-Impressionism, Guillaumin into his own impasto color studies, and Gauguin into studies of the exotic women and island landscape of Martinique.

In January, Gauguin was flattered to be paired with Degas, who had continued his series of nude women bathing and dressing in the setting of ordinary Parisian apartments.[14] Gauguin was once again fascinated with Degas's skillful grasp of the telling pose or gesture, which suggested much but revealed very little. His sketches of Degas's pastels show that he could not resist pushing them into caricature by exaggerating the jutting rear ends of the women and making Degas's "ordinary" poses seem lascivious and somehow unflattering (fig. 28). The critic Huysman's opinion of Degas's nudes as misogynist has been hotly disputed over the years, but Gauguin's version is less defensible on this score.[15]

Knowing that Theo admired Degas's work and respected Degas's opinion about the work of others, Gauguin fell back into his old mentor's orbit

95

to a certain extent. Although he wasn't in Paris long enough to socialize with him extensively, Gauguin carried his impressions of Degas's latest art along with him during his travels in the next year and increasingly introduced nudes into his work. An important early portrait by Degas, *Woman with Chrysanthemums* (Metropolitan Museum of Art) was in Theo's gallery at this time,[16] and the pose of the woman appears in Gauguin's *At the Café* (Wildenstein 305) in 1888.

Aside from his personal fascination with Degas as a sexually ambiguous unmarried man, Gauguin had previously courted him because he held such a powerful position in organizing the Impressionist exhibitions. But now that those exhibitions had ceased, Gauguin hoped to benefit from Degas's new role as an adviser on modern art to dealers and collectors. There is no question that he admired Degas's art greatly and would have incorporated some elements without any ulterior motive. But at this time Gauguin had gone beyond Degas's realism into a more symbolist art and thus looked to Degas primarily for his connections in the Parisian art market, particularly Theo van Gogh.[17]

Gauguin's relationship with Theo was relatively straightforward. They were very different types—Theo was the self-effacing, efficient art dealer whose gentle manners offended no one, whereas Paul Gauguin was the flamboyant, self-centered artist. They fit together in a traditional artist-dealer relationship. But Gauguin's association with Vincent van Gogh was more complex and potentially volatile, primarily because the two men had so much in common.[18]

Each had started his adult career in business—Gauguin in the stock market and Vincent in the art market; Vincent was an employee of an uncle who at that time was a partner in the Goupil Galleries, the same organization that Theo now represented. Even though both had left business (Vincent in 1876 after seven years of service, Gauguin in 1883 after eleven years), they still thought of themselves as knowledgeable in highly speculative fields.[19] In fact, Gauguin's experience in buying and selling art on his own made him feel as much an expert in the art market as he had been in the stock market. Because so much of the work both men did while they were in business was clerical, they both had unusual patience in list making, letter writing, copying, and generally writing things out by hand.

Their business experience could not help but affect them as artists. No matter how personal their artistic inspiration was, they understood that their paintings were products that would ultimately be sold to appropriate buyers. Since self-expression would create a more attractive commodity, it was a means to an end, not an end in itself. Vincent wrote often about the monetary value of the growing number of works he handed over to Theo and how someday it would be realized, as with any other kind of investment.[20] For his part, Gauguin explained his travels to increasingly distant lands as not so much an aesthetic necessity as a response to the market's unrelenting demand for novelty.[21]

Although neither Van Gogh nor Gauguin started out as artists, they both came from families that had been involved in the trade. Two of Van Gogh's uncles had had galleries in Holland; Gauguin's grandfather André

Chazal had owned a lithographic shop in which his grandmother Flora Tristan had worked. Gauguin's great-uncle Antoine Chazal was a moderately successful painter in Paris; Van Gogh's cousin was married to one of the most famous Dutch painters of the time, Anton Mauve. In spite of—or perhaps because of—the family connections, however, neither Van Gogh nor Gauguin followed the traditional course of artistic training, and, as was typical of self-taught artists, both had contempt for the academic system. They both found a natural home in the avant-garde when they discovered it.

Once within avant-garde circles, their strong personalities attracted attention. Although Gauguin's inclination toward hierarchical relationships, with himself at the head, made him a more visible leader and teacher in Paris, Van Gogh also had a magnetic personality, drawing around him a circle of artists and amateurs. In Holland he had had several informal pupils, all of whom respected him as a teacher, and in Arles he gave drawing lessons to at least one friend.[22] His love of art and the passion with which he articulated his artistic theories drew many to him, much the way Gauguin attracted disciples. Also, Vincent's and Gauguin's unusual dress made them readily identifiable as artists, especially in that they had a tendency to paint designs on their clothes and shoes. Both liked to create artistic environments and paid a great deal of attention to the decorative arts.

Finally, their decisions to give up regular employment to become full-time artists cost them both a family life. Like Gauguin, Van Gogh had established a home at one time; he had lived with a woman and her two children in The Hague. Although they never married, he had desired a long-term life together. She, on the other hand, felt that she could support herself and her children better on her own and had refused to follow him when he moved to a remote section of northern Holland to paint.[23] Because of his own painful experience of losing a family over art, he was very sympathetic over Gauguin's estrangement from his own.

The conversations between Van Gogh and Gauguin in the early days of their relationship, in the winter of 1887–88, must have been warm indeed. Van Gogh's admiration for Gauguin was based on many shared traits and experiences that few, if any, of their friends could match. Van Gogh also saw qualities in Gauguin's paintings from Martinique that fit his own beliefs and values without recognizing the possibility that he might be imposing his own interpretations. For instance, Van Gogh interpreted Gauguin's choice of models of African descent as evidence of social liberalism and love of the lower classes, feelings that were genuine in his own heart but not necessarily in Gauguin's. Van Gogh traded one of his works for one of Gauguin's Martinique pictures; he got Theo to buy another and encouraged others to do the same, even though he fervently wished he could have them all. He thought he saw in Gauguin's art a high-minded spirit. As he wrote to Emile Bernard, "There's great poetry in his pictures of negresses: everything he does has something gentle, heartrending, astonishing."[24]

Gauguin took care not to disabuse him of this notion. With his followers, Gauguin could be the noble character Van Gogh thought he was. He saved the venomous PGo persona for those who crossed him: his wife, sister, and most other women, his former friends Granchi-Taylor, Favre, and

Pissarro, his competitors Seurat and the Néos, and the rest of the Parisian art world that insisted on ignoring him. To his disciples he showed nothing but kindness and the bittersweet smile of a martyr.

Charles Laval, for instance, whose money, connections, and adoration sustained Gauguin for more than six months in the Caribbean, saw nothing but good in his master. He and Gauguin had become so close that Laval addressed him as "tu" while old friends like Schuffenecker still said "vous." In a letter written from Martinique after Gauguin's departure, Laval poured out his love and gratitude for favors that Gauguin did for him once back in Paris and for the generous guidance he gave while they painted together. "In this day and age your generosity is heroic; you are an example, and I will follow you with all my might."[25]

With his primary admirer, Laval, still on Martinique, Gauguin found a replacement in Vincent van Gogh. Vincent's unalloyed approval, not to mention his useful connections, brought out the best in Gauguin. He in turn did not peer deeply into Vincent's character. He accepted the adoration without noticing that Vincent was a much more mature artist and person than the twenty-two-year-old Laval. Vincent was gracious enough to accord Gauguin a superior place in art temporarily, but he believed strongly enough in his own abilities that whether he wanted to or not, he would eventually challenge Gauguin for dominance.

For the moment, Vincent was content to drink in everything he could of this sun god from Martinique. He might also have been attracted to Gauguin's public eroticism, which had begun modestly enough with the PGo signature on his pottery of 1886–7 but was becoming more overt in the images he used in the pottery of 1887–8. The most striking of the new works were vases in the shape of heads, most of which were actual portraits. The idea seems to have come from Gauguin's study of Peruvian anthropomorphic vases on view at the Musée d'Ethnologie (now Musée de l'Homme), a study that was probably sparked by the display of Chinese and Japanese ceramics at the current Union Centrale exhibition and by Gauguin's memories of the collections of Peruvian antiquities made by his mother and many others with ties to South and Central America.[26] Two vases portraying Emile Schuffenecker's wife, Louise, and another of his daughter, Jeanne, show that Gauguin had a very personal symbolism in mind. As Gauguin's hosts, the Schuffeneckers, and their friends, were his intended audience; one wonders what must they have thought when Gauguin portrayed Louise once with a snake around her waist (Bodelsen 31)[27] and another time with a goose in the suggestive pose of Leda and the swan (Bodelsen 34; see fig. 40). Although Louise, whose patience with her husband and his friends was rather short,[28] was probably not amused, Emile and the other artists delighted in the shock value of a respectable woman portrayed as an antique temptress.

Regardless of the imagery, pottery had an erotic character for Gauguin owing to the sensual molding of the clay with his hands and to the immense heat of the kiln, to which he and many other ceramists of the day had a visceral reaction. The making of family portraits in this context, therefore, has a peculiarly perverse significance that was not beyond Gauguin's range of shocking erotic impulses. In his *Intimate Journals* he relates a favorite story, undoubtedly told many times before, about a Japanese family making a cloisonné vase in the small kiln of their peasant hut. Rejecting other, more refined stories of Japanese craftsmen, such as can be found in Pierre Loti's *Madame Chrysanthème* (serialized 1888, published 1893), Gauguin describes how this family—father, mother, and children—feed the fire with charcoal and devotional offerings until it is unbearably hot:

> The pledges are trinkets and combs, quickly offered and quickly lost. They grow warm, the fan becomes more and more active; the infernal work is nearing completion in the retort. Songs and laughter accompany this sham revel. Soon there is nothing left to forfeit and the combatants end by being as beautifully naked as when they were born. Not so much as a vine-leaf! Having nothing left to give, they give themselves, and I assure you that neither the notary nor his honour the mayor regularizes these loves of the moment that could not be eternal. . . .
>
> P.S. I once related this to someone whom I thought intelligent. When I had finished he said to me, "But your Japanese are vulgar pigs!"
>
> Yes, but in the pig all is good.[29]

To Gauguin, heat swept away all taboos, but perhaps for him an even greater pleasure was watching the reaction of an innocent listener to his unrepentant telling of the tale.

The use of erotic subject matter had been a standard feature of avant-garde art for years, but Gauguin had a knack for testing its limits without losing his ability to be appreciated by the average viewer. His erotic, often perverse meaning would be understood only by those in his inner circle, so he could suggest sex with children, adultery, exhibitionism (PGo), and androgyny without openly admitting to such themes. Other artists in his circle, such as Emile Bernard and Toulouse-Lautrec, were also exploring the theme of illicit sexuality in their scenes of bohemian life and brothels, but in comparison to Gauguin's hints of more perverse and forbidden practices, their images of adult female prostitution seem tame indeed.[30]

Van Gogh was not close enough to Gauguin during the two months the latter spent in Paris that winter to understand fully the nature of Gauguin's eroticism, but it certainly played a part in his fascination. When Gauguin left Paris at the end of January for Pont-Aven, Van Gogh could not forget him. A few weeks later, Van Gogh's own health and his desire to get out of the city took him to the south of France, where he settled in the small Roman town of Arles, near Marseilles. As soon as he rented a home of his own, he began thinking of inviting Gauguin to stay. "I could quite well share the new studio with someone, and I should like to. Perhaps Gauguin will come south?"[31]

Meanwhile Gauguin, who had seldom traveled alone and never in the middle of winter, had resolutely packed up and left the Schuffeneckers for the deserted resort town of Pont-Aven, where he would be without the heat of the kiln and the adoration of his disciples. He stayed there in relative isolation for five and a half months before his coterie trickled out to the country from Paris and other points. The few letters he wrote give very little information about his life during this time.

What enticed him into such an exile was the promise of money. In a letter to his wife in early January 1888, Gauguin summed up his financial situation by listing the extraordinary string of recent sales and some pressing debts. The timing seemed urgent to him: "Now that I am being launched, I must put supreme effort into my art, and I am going to go to Brittany, to Pont-Aven, for six months to do some paintings."[32] Theo's success in selling Gauguin's latest works was enough to convince Gauguin to paint more. With the approximately 1,400 francs that Theo paid him in December and January, Gauguin could easily live through the summer at an inexpensive place like Pont-Aven.[33] And with the money he would make from the sales that were certain to come, he would have the reserve he had always longed for.

Once again he found it difficult to part with any of the money he had in hand. As with his trip to Panama and Martinique, he justified neglecting his family with the argument that sacrifice today would bring a brighter future. But this year Mette was tired of the old story and suggested that he come to a resort town in Denmark if he needed to get away.[34] There at least the family could be together, and the expense of the children could be shared. Gauguin scoffed at the idea and listed all his objections in a rambling, scornful letter: (1) Travel to Denmark was too expensive (he had made her bear the burden of the same trip the previous year). (2) The children would disturb his work, and besides, he doesn't have the proper clothes. (3) They would bore each other and quarrel. Her family would object. She might get pregnant again. (4) He has suppressed all emotions as a stoic Indian does who is focused only on the path ahead, and he doesn't want the sight of the children to reawaken them.[35] Not only did he refuse to share any of his time or money with them, he categorically refused to ask or allow Mette to ask Uncle Isidore to send Emil to engineering school or spend any of the money (that would one day be Paul's) on the children.[36] After a year of relatively cordial exchanges, Mette must have been taken aback by such a thoughtless dismissal of her and the children while Paul claimed to be working for the good of the family.

Paul charged in the same venomous letter that her suggesting he should help support the family showed that she was obsessed with money and unable to appreciate art or artists.[37] These accusations were so unfair and so typical of an abusive husband that she could hardly bring herself to write to him again. Dutifully she sent him the sweaters that he had requested at the end of the offensive letter, but in her note she couldn't resist reminding him of how difficult it was to carry the weight of the family alone. In reply he complained of his own loneliness while living in a resort town in the off-season. "What about me, alone in a hotel bedroom from morning to night in absolute solitude. Not a soul with whom to exchange a thought."[38] Seeing that Paul was incapable of feeling pity for his struggling family, Mette's next letter was a straightforward plea: they were desperate for any help he could give them. To this Paul did not respond at all.[39]

Incredibly, the money that should have lasted Gauguin through the summer at Pont-Aven seems to have been spent by the end of February, which is when he began the familiar begging letters to Schuffenecker and his new sympathetic pal (*copain*), Vincent van Gogh.[40] Gauguin was not begging from Vincent—who he knew lived off an allowance from his brother—but asking for Vincent's intercession with Theo.[41] Vincent was more than happy to help and immediately wrote to his brother of Gauguin's plight. He also arranged for a fellow artist and collector from Cormon's, the Australian John Russell, to see Gauguin's paintings. Although Russell never did buy a Gauguin, Theo put one of Gauguin's Martinique paintings on display in the window of his gallery during the month of April.[42]

As the spring progressed and Gauguin received attention but no major funding through either Schuffenecker or Van Gogh, he began to use his poor wife as extra leverage in his campaign to get his friends to support him. To Schuffenecker, he wrote, "Oh yes, we need a guaranteed income—you're telling me! My wife writes me desperate letters asking me to help out a little. Me—I don't even know how to support myself."[43] When Schuffenecker received this letter, he offered (anonymously) to buy Gauguin's Cézanne still life for 300 francs, probably because he worried about Mette and the children. But apparently Gauguin was not so desperate for money that he didn't flatly refuse this offer, believing that the painting would eventually sell for much more.[44]

By the first of May, Vincent had found another way of helping Gauguin. Unlike his friend in Pont-Aven, Vincent was unhappy staying indefinitely in a hotel, and impulsively rented a four-room apartment in a yellow house not far from the train station. Such a large space demanded more than one occupant. It only made sense that the other should also be an artist and that, together, they could start the community of artists that had been discussed in the cafés of Paris for a decade. Although Vincent proposed many other artists for the honor, such as an American painting nearby, Dodge MacKnight, and the young Emile Bernard, Gauguin was, from the beginning, his first choice. But he didn't act on the idea until coincidentally Gauguin wrote to Theo again asking for money a few weeks later.

Gauguin's humble tone—addressing Theo who was almost ten years younger as "Cher Monsieur"—and his kind words about Vincent's painting were calculated to charm: "Your brother, is he still in the South sunning himself? He must have done some interesting things. He has a curious eye, and I hope he is not going to change it."[45] But he could not have known what effect this letter would have. By the end of May, Vincent, with the backing of Theo, proposed an end to Gauguin's money troubles for at least a year. If Gauguin would come to Arles and live communally with Vincent, Theo would support both of them. In return, Gauguin would send Theo one painting a month.[46] It was roughly the same agreement Vincent had with Theo, only Vincent sent Theo all his paintings that he didn't give away or exchange with other artists. In short, the Van Goghs were offering the guaranteed monthly income that Gauguin had always yearned for.

Much to the surprise of Vincent and Theo, Gauguin put them off. On the one hand, he wrote pathetic letters about illness and debts, yet, on the other, he always seemed to have the wherewithal to turn down offers of money that didn't suit him. Whether he had sources of income that he did not reveal or whether he thought he could force a higher offer, his reluctance to take either Schuffenecker's offer to buy the Cézanne or the Van Goghs' offer of support makes one question his candidness in financial matters. The excuse that he made to the Van Goghs was that a new opportunity to go into business had just arisen. He claimed that he had just been offered the capital (600,000 francs) to become a dealer in Impressionist paintings.[47] This plan, which was concocted by Gauguin and Nino Laval (Charles's brother was staying in Pont-Aven during May and June waiting for Charles's return from Martinique), was immediately recognized as a "fata morgana" (mirage) by the Van Goghs, whose family business was art galleries, but Gauguin continued to make them wait while he considered it.[48] By the end of the summer, after Gauguin had changed his mind many times about coming to Arles, Vincent also discerned that Gauguin was pitting the two families (the Lavals and the Van Goghs) against each other to see which would offer him the best deal.[49] Gauguin's leverage was the intense personal stake Charles Laval and Vincent van Gogh both had in being close to him.

It is no wonder that by the time Gauguin and his wife next exchanged letters, in June 1888 on the occasion of Paul's fortieth birthday, he flung her pale, Danish, female affection back in her face. She had written after not hearing from him for six weeks.[50] She no longer asked for any money; she wanted only to find out if she still had a husband at all. Irritated by the guilt feelings her questions provoked but buoyed by having two financial deals on the table at once, Paul sent her letter back to her—after first subjecting it to the laughter of his friends, who naturally agreed with him that it was the work of an unworthy woman.[51] He charged her with being boring and unappreciative of his talent compared to those around him. He ended with a diatribe against marrying educated women: "When your son is old enough, do you dare advise him to marry anyone but a kitchen maid? If she is genteel, she won't talk to him about anything but domestic concerns. . . . If this good boy is more intelligent than his wife, he will be hated. Only a kitchen maid will be proud of her husband, respect him, and find it natural that he should be the boss."[52] In spite of all Gauguin's protestations that he had gone out on his own for the ultimate good of the family, the evidence indicates the opposite. The plight of his family had become a useful device in his periodic campaigns to win sympathy and cash from his friends, but when he saw improved financial prospects, his first response was to protect his assets from any claim that his wife and children might make on them.

As abusive as he was to Mette during the summer of 1888, for instance, he nevertheless continued to find it useful to present himself as a struggling husband and father. About the same time he wrote this letter, he was also writing to Vincent about how he was tempted to take the Lavals' offer for the sake of his family. Kindhearted Vincent struggled with his disappointment at this news: "I am very curious to know what Gauguin will do, but to risk *persuading* him to come—no—for I do not know now if it would suit him. And perhaps when you consider his large family, it is more his duty to try to bring off something that would bring in enough to let him be the head of the family again."[53]

During this period of constantly shifting personal alliances, Gauguin was right to call himself an "Indian"—an unemotional man focused solely on the path before him.[54] He had certainly lost his increasingly erratic affection for his wife, as well as the most basic paternal feelings concerning the care and comfort of his children. In addition, despite his openly flirtatious, if not seductive, behavior with the men who craved his company, he apparently did not return the regard of either one. As charged as his relationships were with the Van Goghs and the Lavals (as well as with his own wife), what mattered most to him was producing art and establishing himself in the Parisian art world. The emotion that might naturally have been expressed in his personal relationships was channeled instead into the sensual act of painting and the exhilarating pursuit of success. Everything revolved around this goal, and the more than eight months he spent in Pont-Aven in 1888 constituted the longest stretch of uninterrupted work he had ever accomplished. At the end of it, when he finally did go to Arles in October, he had arrived at a style and an identity that remained essentially unchanged for the rest of his life.

His letters from Pont-Aven stress his loneliness and protracted bouts with an illness that lingered from Martinique. But Pont-Aven in the winter was not as deserted as he liked to portray it, nor was he as sick as he often claimed to be. In fact, with a small community of sympathetic townspeople and the few artists, mostly foreigners, who stayed on in provincial places like Pont-Aven because they had no winter home in Paris, Gauguin led a reasonably happy and productive life. In those eight months he painted almost sixty known finished canvases, which, because he worked relatively slowly, indicates that he took few holidays or extended sick days. The absence of throngs of painters meant that he could concentrate more on the character of the local people who were his models and develop a set of telling gestures and poses that would, to the sophisticated eye of an avant-garde Parisian viewer, bring this rural society to life.

Gauguin could take advantage of the country setting even in the middle of winter because he worked mainly indoors. He sketched landscape motifs and may even have used photographs to provide a basic composition and filled sketchbooks with drawings of people to place into the landscapes. He painted the landscape elements in his old Impressionist style but had learned with the Martinique paintings to use his figures to add a touch of mystery.

In the summer, however, he reversed the process by using stock landscape backgrounds to insert behind freshly observed figural compositions. The most important of these were of children: a scene of three girls dancing in a circle (Wildenstein 251), two boys about to swim nude in the Aven River (fig. 29), and a similar bathing scene with two of the boys wrestling (Wildenstein 273). The painting of the three girls is probably Gauguin's most charming and popular painting; but the scenes of the bathing boys are the most intriguing.

Gauguin had seldom painted nudes since his monumental *Woman Sewing* of 1880, and never before a male nude. Rather unexpectedly, Gauguin has included the adolescent stub of the young boy's penis profiled in dark against one of the lightest areas of the background. Gauguin presents this part of the model's anatomy so naturally that the viewer is hard pressed to find any erotic content or any hint of undue exploitation. But because Gauguin cited Japanese prints as his inspiration, in addition to deriv-

Paul Gauguin, *Young Bretons Bathing*, 1888. Oil on canvas, 36 1/4 x 28 1/4 in. (92 x 73 cm). Hamburger Kunsthalle.

ing poses from Hokusai and Hiroshige, he may have had in mind the graphic representations of both male and female anatomy in the more pornographic images of that traditional art form. For many nineteenth-century observers, the portrayals of courtesans and various sexual positions in these colorful woodblock prints made the whole genre seem morally questionable, and Gauguin's reference to this source of inspiration would have carried more than stylistic significance.[55] The related painting of two boys wrestling shows them modestly covered with loincloth-like underwear, but the young combatants are locked in a quiet wrestling stance that strongly resembles an embrace. As the competition between the Van Goghs and the Lavals swirled around him, Gauguin, rather than accepting either proposal, filled his canvases with the ambivalent, tender eroticism of young boys.

When he wrote about his excursion into this new territory to Schuffenecker, he boasted about the novelty of the images: "I have also done

some nudes, you will be glad to hear, and not at all in Degas's style." Referring to the simplified color planes of the background and the unexpected
male sexuality, he went on to say, "The last is a fight between two boys near
the river, completely Japanese." When the irony of this struck him, he
continued, "Completely Japanese by a Frenchman," and then amended the
sentence once more, scratching out "Frenchman" and ending the sentence
with "completely Japanese by a savage from Peru" (fig. 30).[56]

The evolution of Gauguin's identity, so clear in the changes made to
this sentence, was unfolding in his own mind. In the past he had called
himself an Indian and a savage, but never before had he brought his Peruvian heritage so prominently to the fore. He was not actually Inca or of
any Indian descent, but he was from Peru and he was a savage—an uncivi-
lized person—by anyone's standards. He had proved this to the art world
in general in his preference for Pont-Aven over Paris, in his interest in
native models in traditional poses and dress, and in the simplified, almost
crude style of his painting. His inner circle knew about the further proof
offered by his abusive, combative temper, his delight in the shock value of sly
obscenities, and the ignoble treatment of his family. He was certainly
entitled to call himself a savage, but because he now saw his Peruvian heritage as linked to the power of the burning sun, he took a perverse pride
in proclaiming it.

When Charles Laval returned from Martinique in July 1888, he immediately went out to Pont-Aven to join his brother Nino—who had been there since May—and his dear friend Paul Gauguin.[1] It was the beginning of Pont-Aven's high season. Artists from Paris were trickling out to the countryside in June after the culminating events of the Salon and the smaller group exhibitions officially closed the artistic year; by August the resort towns throughout Brittany would be packed. Even though Gauguin had written encouragingly about Arles to Theo at the end of June,[2] he became so caught up in the festive atmosphere of Pont-Aven at its peak that the Van Gogh brothers didn't hear from him again until the end of July; and then he wrote only in the vaguest terms about coming to live with Vincent.[3]

By mid-August, Gauguin was surrounded by a diverse group of young painters ranging in skill from Henry Moret, who had studied at the Ecole des Beaux-Arts and exhibited at the Salon, to Ernest de Chamaillard, a twenty-six-year-old lawyer who had taken up painting that summer under Gauguin's tutelage.[4] Paul Sérusier, a promising art student at the Académie Julian, looked from afar upon this renegade band until late September, just before he was to return to Paris, when he asked Gauguin for a critique and received a lesson in painting that revolutionized his style. He took the precious trial painting (which he referred to as "the talisman") and Gauguin's memorable words back to his friends at Julian's, where they formed a Gauguin satellite group called the Nabis, or prophets.

The most charismatic member of Gauguin's group in Pont-Aven that summer was the twenty-year-old Emile Bernard, a former Cormon student and a well-known figure in avant-garde circles. Bernard's friends already included Laval, Toulouse-Lautrec, Emile Schuffenecker, and Vincent van Gogh. He had begun his artistic training in 1884 at the age of sixteen; by the age of eighteen he was established as a radical artist and, because he also wrote poetry, as a literary symbolist; and by the age of twenty he was considered a major theorist on modernist painting and literature.

In spite of his slight build and ingratiating manner, Bernard had an authoritative voice when speaking of aesthetic issues and a firm belief that he was destined to transform the pictorial arts as symbolism had already transformed literature.[5] Loudly rejecting Neo-Impressionism as a dead end, he argued instead for an art drawn exclusively from the imagination so that forms and colors could convey a rich symbolic significance beyond simple description or narrative.[6] He and his friend Louis Anquetin had taken their inspiration from Japanese prints, medieval stained glass, and various other decorative arts. They were able to exhibit the fruits of their experimentation in November 1887 in the exhibition organized by Vincent van Gogh at the Grande Brouillon restaurant, which also featured the work of Toulouse-Lautrec and other friends. As Bernard recalled, "It really looked quite new, by far the most advanced thing in Paris."[7]

Bernard had known Gauguin since the summer of 1886 and had verbally sparred with him during the few months they were both in Paris after Gauguin's return from Martinique.[8] When Bernard appeared in Pont-Aven in August, the two were mentally poised to make the most of each other. Since the spring Bernard had been painting in Saint-Briac-sur-Mer on the north coast of Brittany, but he went to Pont-Aven in mid-August because of Gauguin and the group of radical artists assembled around him.

Bernard had been urged to do so by Vincent van Gogh, who thought that Bernard and Gauguin would benefit from painting together.[9] Van Gogh also no doubt thought that Bernard, a more faithful correspondent, would provide him with another link to the elusive Gauguin. Indeed, Van Gogh's letters to Bernard, which Bernard dutifully shared with Gauguin, gave Van Gogh a presence in Pont-Aven that he would not have otherwise had. With Bernard's help, he nudged them all into painting self-portraits to exchange with his own, sent drawings of his most recent canvases, and selected canvases to give as gifts to each of the artists in Gauguin's circle.[10] Van Gogh hoped they would invite him to join them in Pont-Aven, and when they didn't, he participated in their discussions as much as he could. As he wrote to Theo, "I have just had a letter from Bernard, who went some days ago to join Gauguin, Laval, and somebody else at Pont-Aven. It was a very decent letter, but not one syllable in it about Gauguin intending to join me, and not a syllable either about wanting me to come there. All the same it was a very friendly letter."[11]

As for Gauguin, he took the connection between Bernard and Van Gogh very seriously. If he won Bernard to his side, the young pundit would help him keep the good opinion of Vincent and Theo. He found that Bernard was susceptible to his charm, which he had by now practiced on many young men, and soon he had another disciple. But Bernard was much more than that. In spite of, or perhaps because of, his extreme youth, he spoke and painted much more freely than anyone Gauguin had known before. As Gauguin wrote to Schuffenecker soon after Bernard's arrival, "Here is someone who has no fear."[12]

Gauguin was energized by Bernard's forceful rejection of the old tenets of naturalism and his desire to found an art based on completely new principles, which Bernard wanted to call pictorial symbolism. Gauguin had preached much the same message himself, and his "Japanese" bathing boys, painted just days before Bernard arrived, were in this spirit. But even though Bernard was mostly confirming ideas that Gauguin already held, it is surprising how swiftly Gauguin assimilated Bernard's new verbal and pictorial language. The letter to Schuffenecker quoted above, written shortly after Bernard appeared, shows that Bernard had persuaded Gauguin to renew his opposition to the Neo-Impressionist dot, a battle he had fought two years earlier. It also shows

Gauguin adopting the term "abstraction" and repeats Bernard's clearly stated opposition to naturalism in his advice to Schuffenecker "not to copy too much after nature—art is an abstraction." Gauguin also suddenly began using Bernard's religious phraseology, telling Schuffenecker to appreciate art as a creation and thus become more like the divine Creator. Gauguin closed his letter with the uncharacteristically pious "May God take you in his holy keeping and reward your efforts."[13] A new force had definitely taken hold of the old PGo.

It is not surprising, therefore, that by September, Gauguin was working on a religious painting (fig. 31). The new spiritual exhilaration he felt for having freed himself from naturalism following Bernard's example led him to try his hand at painting the religious ceremonies of French peasant villages, a favorite subject of Pont-Aven artists.[14] But Gauguin was going to do his from imagination and let the lines, shapes, and colors convey a symbolic message. The painting would be a rebuke to the dull, detailed naturalism of all the other painters in Pont-Aven, from the Salon academics to the unimaginative Impressionists. At the same time it would point the way to true spirituality in art by borrowing the simple, primitive beliefs of

Breton folk culture.[15] Gauguin and Bernard even imagined it hanging in a Breton church.

The painting was called *The Vision After the Sermon,* implying that the red field out of which the green tree grew was an imaginary stage upon which a vision of Jacob wrestling with the angel was enacted in the minds of a Breton congregation. Although by rights the congregation itself was not imaginary, Gauguin distorted the shapes of the faces and headdresses to signify that the pious women were in a state of trance.

While the religious references and the frankly visionary "reality" indicated by the startling red field were new to Gauguin, much of the personal symbolism was familiar. Gauguin's caricatural treatment of the women and the priest are consistent with his recent portrayals of women in general and costumed Breton women in particular. Despite the flowery religious language Gauguin used in his letters during August and September 1888, the excesses in drawing betray Gauguin's satiric tendencies and undermine the viewer's ability to take his spiritual concepts seriously.[16] It is hard to believe that the Gauguin whose irreligious statements in Copenhagen nearly lost his son Emil the support of his patron in 1885 had three years later become a convert to the conventional beliefs of a country parish. The wrestling Jacob and the angel were also personal symbols, referring to Gauguin's interest in martial arts of all kinds and his special interest that summer in the more subtle meanings of physical contact between men, boys, and other masculine creatures, including angels.

Bernard told the story of Gauguin's offering the painting to the priest of the nearby church at Nizon. Gauguin, Bernard, Laval, and possibly the whole group had hiked the few miles across the fields to the old stone church.

> Laval and I had carried the painting; when we arrived in Nizon the church was open, and Gauguin himself picked out the place to hang his work. We lifted it there and he judged the effect. I went to find the priest in the presbytery, to let him know about the gift of great worth that he was receiving. He rejoiced at what I told him and walked faster and faster. We entered the ancient sanctuary.
>
> Gauguin came respectfully before the old priest, pointing with his extended hand to the work, which was resting on a bench. . . . [The priest] must have been suspicious of some artist's caricature, since Pont-Aven had that reputation. . . . The first words he spoke were those of polite refusal. Gauguin insisted, speaking of the relationship between his art and the old church's wooden saints, which seemed to call the parish priest to witness. Then the priest inquired as to the subject and declared the interpretation nonreligious and uninteresting for the faithful.[17]

Bernard, writing this account in 1911, after he had become a convert to orthodox Catholicism, still fervently believed in the sincerity of Gauguin's and his own efforts in 1888. But if we picture the parade of Gauguin and his ragtag followers into the church and their vocal indignation upon being refused by a parish priest (who was, in their minds, only one step above the superstitious women he preached to), it seems more like one of Gauguin's pranks than a serious attempt to contribute to the spiritual life of this community.

Certainly many artists did offer paintings to local churches, just as they decorated inns and hotels throughout the French countryside. Such an event occurs in the most popular book published about the artist colonies of Brittany, *Guenn, a Wave on the Breton Coast,* by Blanche Willis Howard, which was in its fifteenth edition by 1883. Although the book was written by an American about American artists painting in Concarneau and nearby towns like Pont-Aven, Gauguin would surely have been familiar with its contents through the endless discussions and pilgrimages it inspired. In *Guenn,* the protagonist, an egocentric and brilliant painter named Hamor, offers to paint a picture for a small local chapel. The priest agrees but dictates the subject: "'It is good for us to realize that he suffered. I want a Crucifixion. And make the agony as terrible as you can,' he said fiercely."[18] Hamor, a good artist, but without religious sensibility, never completes the painting. Howard's moral in *Guenn* is that artists can wreak havoc in the rural communities they love to paint because their worldly values contrast so greatly with the values of the local population. Gauguin, in spite of his professed love of the primitive and his adoption of local dress, confirmed Howard's point.

Gauguin's *Vision After the Sermon* gained more notoriety by being rejected than it ever would have from being politely accepted by the priest and just as politely put into a closet. It became the subject of outraged letters to Van Gogh, Schuffenecker, and other sympathetic friends, and the event was so memorable that the painting became the focus of much later controversy. Bernard, who went on with Gauguin to explore further religious imagery the next year, recognized the importance that this painting had gained by Gauguin's rash gesture, and struggled in later years to be recognized for the role he had played in the evolution of the unusual work.[19] Largely because of the attention Bernard brought to it in his many writings and memoirs until his death in 1941, it became one of Gauguin's best-known and often-reproduced paintings.

Bernard also pointed out that originally Gauguin had signed the work and added in blue on the white border "A Gift of Don Tristan de Moscoso," as if Gauguin were the heir to the ancient Peruvian title of his great-grandfather. This impressive inscription, according to Bernard, made the priest hesitate for a moment. "He read the title of the noble who donated it—it seemed somewhat Romanesque to him; then he looked at the painting, which terrified him."[20] The exquisite delight with which Gauguin, the malin, watched the priest assimilate the various facets of this work can easily be imagined. Knowing that his aristocratic claims would bring him respect but that the avant-garde novelty of his painting would shock and confuse, he no doubt hoped for a noble rejection. His new Peruvian identity was proving useful once again, although this time he invoked the upper class rather than the savage aspect of his proud pose.

While Gauguin's efforts to shock the unsophisticated viewer gave him a certain amount of private amusement, they must be seen primarily as public acts staged for the benefit of an avant-garde audience and calculated to advance his own standing in that arena. In Pont-Aven that audience was the group of followers who accompanied him to the Nizon church that day carrying his large painting by hand. Through these young men he could be sure that the story would make the rounds of the cafés, small galleries, and academies when they all returned to Paris in the fall. Gauguin himself spread the word to Vincent van Gogh and Schuffenecker by mail, knowing that they would repeat it in the avant-garde circles they inhabited. Gauguin was determined to stand out both as a personality (a savage from Peru) and as an artist.

Vincent van Gogh, who had similar aspirations but less drive to achieve them, partly because he had more money and better connections, commented on Gauguin's struggle: "I think that Gauguin will never give up the fight in Paris, he has it too much at heart, and believes in a lasting success more than I do. That will do me no harm; on the contrary, perhaps I am too pessimistic. Let's leave him this illusion then, but let's realize that what he will always need is his daily bread and shelter and paints. That is the crack in his armor, and it is because he is getting into debt now that he will be knocked out in advance. If we two come to his aid, we are in fact making his victory in Paris possible."[21]

Ultimately, this is what Gauguin needed to hear from the Van Goghs. Shelter and monthly support, though appealing, were not enough to entice him to Arles, where he feared he would be cut off from the traffic of the Paris art world that came regularly through Brittany. Offering a painting to a church in Arles, a town without a large, Parisian artists' colony, would not be worthwhile. Vincent had written to Gauguin early in the summer about leasing a storefront in Marseilles where their pictures could be exhibited and offered for sale, but it wasn't until Gauguin heard from Theo at some point in the fall that Theo would take a large number of Pont-Aven pictures from Gauguin and exhibit them in Paris, that the deal was finally sealed.[22]

Even so, nothing they could do would pry him loose from Pont-Aven until all the other artists had left. Schools and businesses in Paris didn't start up again until mid-October, and it was only then that Gauguin boarded the train to leave the now-deserted resort town. Why was he not tempted to put Arles off yet again so that he might make a triumphal entrance into Paris, as he had done the year before? He obviously had decided that he could let others spread his fame—Theo would exhibit his paintings, Sérusier and Bernard would carry his aesthetic message, Schuffenecker would handle the storage and access to his growing stock of art works. Besides, he truly hated cold weather and did not like (and could not afford) to live in Paris. For these reasons he let absence enhance his mystique in Paris that fall.

By the end of September, Vincent was sure that Gauguin was coming. Although Gauguin had said so before, this time he clearly meant it, because Bernard, Laval, Moret, and Chamaillard all suddenly wanted to come too.[23] Vincent was good-natured about his new popularity, offering to exchange works with them but emphasizing that it was Gauguin who would be at the head of the often-dreamed-of community of artists. He saw, too, that the others had less freedom—Bernard was facing his mandatory military service, Laval would only be able to come in February—so he needn't take their promises seriously. As for Gauguin, Van Gogh could think of very little else but the fact that he was really coming.

Vincent's letters to Theo trace and retrace the type of business arrangement they should have with Gauguin, settling matters of Gauguin's debts in Pont-Aven, the cost of his travel to Arles, and expenditures on furniture for the house and making demands on Gauguin in return. Vincent emphasized how important Gauguin would be to Theo's increasing business in Impressionism and how he could help Theo leave Boussod and Valadon and set up business on his own. "In the end what you are doing privately will be a far bigger thing with his collaboration than with my work alone. . . . Later on, if someday perhaps you are on your own with impressionist pictures, you will only have to continue and encourage an already existing concern."[24] Vincent's knowledge of the art business and his tremendous need to justify the financial support that Theo gave him (and would soon give Gauguin) made these monetary issues extremely important.

Vincent's personal and artistic needs could not, however, be entirely hidden under the cool veneer of his endless discussions of business matters. Vincent's isolation in the south had taken its toll on a man who had finally found his spiritual home in the Paris avant-garde. To make up for the lack of intellectual stimulation among his local friends in Arles, he devoured art journals, from the conservative *Revue des deux mondes* to such radical *petits journaux* as *L'Intransigeant*. He read popular fiction by Pierre Loti, Zola, Hugo, and Daudet, as well as the poetry of Walt Whitman and philosophical tracts like Thomas Carlyle's *Sartor Resartus*.[25] When not reading, he carried on a voluminous correspondence with artist friends and family members. It had been many years since he had lived alone, and recently he had spent two happy years sharing an apartment with Theo. In Arles he made the most of the few artists working in the area, one of whom, the Belgian Eugène Boch, was connected through his artist-sister to the avant-garde group Les XX in Brussels.[26] And he was friendly with a local army officer, Milliet, and the family of the postmaster, Roulin. But they did not replace his Paris friends, and he was desperate for his intellectual solitude to end.

Vincent was not eager to admit that, although he would appreciate like-minded companionship of any kind, in his heart he craved only Gauguin. Once the plan had been formulated, he tried to accept every setback philosophically—Gauguin had to think first of his family, he should take support from the Laval camp if he could get it, he wasn't worth all the worry, and Bernard would do just as well—but Gauguin's reluctance irritated the normally soft-spoken man, and he was not always able to hide his pique.

When Gauguin persisted in his rash plan to establish a new Impressionist gallery, not only did Vincent dismiss it as amateurish, but he was uncharacteristically impolite about Gauguin's backers, referring to them scornfully as "Jewish bankers"[27] and to the cooperative arrangement with their artists as a "Jew Society."[28] Later, after Gauguin's second false promise to come, Vincent wrote, "As for Gauguin, perhaps he is letting himself drift with the current, not thinking of the future. And perhaps he thinks that I shall always be here and that he has our word. But it is not too late to withdraw, and really I am strongly tempted to do so, because failing him, I should naturally think of another partnership."[29] By mid-September, when Gauguin began hinting again, Vincent's inclination was to protect himself. "Why then such a noise about this Gauguin business? He will do well to come to us, and we would like him to come. But neither he nor we are to let ourselves be crushed. On the whole there was a fine calm about that letter of his, although he left his intentions where we are concerned in the air. . . . Gauguin is married, and we must thoroughly realize in advance that in the long run it is not certain that our various interests will be compatible."[30] And finally, Vincent revealed that he understood the real Gauguin: "I feel instinctively that Gauguin is a schemer who, seeing himself at the bottom of the social ladder, wants to regain a position by means which will certainly be honest, but at the same time, politic."[31] Vincent the former art dealer understood Gauguin the speculator probably better than most of their fellow artists did. But whether he could always accept Gauguin would soon be tested.

Through the several episodes of Gauguin's false promises and his own anger and despair, Vincent never wavered in his desire for Gauguin. He waited and forgave, periodically renewed his offer, and finally got what he wanted. Now, as he waited for Gauguin's imminent arrival, he stepped up the pace of his painting and his letter writing. It is hard to tell whether Vincent was aware how warm an attachment to Gauguin is revealed in those paintings and letters. Lovers are a frequent theme; bedrooms are another. Although he notes that regular visits to brothels will be part of their routine, he also confesses that he has little use for them—he has become impotent.[32] In fact, since coming to Paris, his old desire for women and his dream of a wife and family had been replaced by his newfound passion for art.[33]

Whether Vincent was truly impotent or whether, like Gauguin, he simply discovered erotic satisfaction in his friendships with the unconventional men of the Parisian avant-garde, he clearly expressed more love for his male friends than he did for the women he knew. The tender language he used in speaking of his two best friends in Arles, Milliet and Boch, portrays them as lovers, and he hung the portraits he painted of them above his bed. Of Milliet he said, "He is a very good-looking boy, very unconcerned and easy-going in his behavior, and he would suit me damned well for the picture of a lover."[34] Vincent's reference was perhaps to Milliet's performance at a brothel the night before he had to take an officer's examination. As for Boch, he described the portrait he wanted to paint showing the artist as a dreamer: "I want to put my appreciation, the love I have for him, into the picture."[35] In none of the descriptions of his female models, toward whom he was generally affectionate and respectful, does one find the same sweet references.

Vincent had every reason to believe that Gauguin had the same feelings toward other men that he did. Without assuming that Gauguin was homosexual—in fact he assumed the opposite by including trips to the brothel in his proposed agenda for their communal life—Vincent was nevertheless aware of Gauguin's famous motto Pas de femmes as well as his close friendships with male disciples and his fascination with gender reversal and androgyny.

Gauguin's mocking courtship of Emile Bernard's sixteen-year-old sister, Madeleine, enacted in front of Bernard and the entire artists' community that summer, reveals the unexpected path that Gauguin's erotic interests typically followed. Though not an artist herself, Madeleine was as preco-

cious as her brother in embracing modern art, and gamely modeled for sexually suggestive paintings by Bernard and Gauguin (fig. 32).[36] She demonstrated the freewheeling spirit of Pont-Aven by wearing the Breton dress and coif. Gauguin was clearly delighted with her boldness but does not seem to have been attracted to her in the traditionally heterosexual fashion. A patronizing letter that he wrote to her later that fall advised her that to *"be someone,* to find happiness solely in your independence and your conscience," she must think of herself as androgynous, a slave neither of the body nor of money.[37] The message not only underscores the nature of Gauguin's ideal woman— as much like a man as possible—but implies that, to Gauguin, androgyny was an intriguing guise for both men and women.

In the same letter, Gauguin advises her to be proud and yet, at the same time, not be afraid to ask for help—advice based on his own contradictory behavior. It suggests that he did not so much love her as identify with her. He was willing to prove his own androgyny by signing her name, "Madeleine B.," to a still life he painted as a birthday present for the local hotelkeeper.[38] Ironically, Charles Laval, who wanted but could not have Gauguin, wooed Madeleine a few years later, and they were engaged for a short time.[39] Without going so far as to practice (or at least announce) homosexuality, the men in the group around Gauguin openly embraced the concept of androgyny and formed attachments with each other that defied social conventions.

Van Gogh pictured Gauguin and himself wandering in the gardens near his yellow house like Petrarch and Boccaccio, as close as two men could be. Vincent would be Boccaccio, the earthy observer of the high and low of human society, while Gauguin would be Petrarch, the noble creator of refined verse.[40] Compared to Gauguin, Van Gogh claimed, he had always had "the coarse lusts of a beast." Van Gogh became obsessed with

decorating the house, which was ample enough to allow each man to have his own bedroom and studio. In his own room he created the effect of utmost simplicity with humble furniture and portraits of men. Gauguin's room, on the other hand, he first decorated with paintings of sunflowers so it would look "like the boudoir of a really artistic woman" and later with four paintings of gardens—the poets' gardens, or the gardens of love (fig. 33).[41]

Van Gogh yearned for a portrait of Gauguin to hang with the paintings of the other beloved men in his yellow house. He proposed to Bernard and Gauguin that they paint each other and exchange these works for a portrait Van Gogh would do of himself. But Bernard begged off the assignment, telling Vincent candidly that he was too afraid of Gauguin to paint him.[42] Besides revealing much about the nature of Gauguin's relationships, Bernard's honesty explains why there are so few portraits of Gauguin by other artists (unlike the many that exist of Van Gogh).[43] Gauguin took the matter into his own hands and painted for Vincent a dramatic self-portrait that he hoped would convey the sophistication of his new artistic identity (fig. 34).

He wrote to Vincent before he sent it, explaining the symbolism and abstract allusions.[44] Knowing that Vincent was suspicious of art that required too much explanation, he claimed that it was necessary only because he was afraid his ideas had not been completely realized in the painting.[45] When he wrote the same explanation of the portrait to Schuffenecker, who was much more open to symbolism and abstraction, he made no such polite disclaimer.[46] The portrait, he asserted, was not just of him but of the generic Impressionist painter, downtrodden and forced into so-called crimes by the conservative Ecole des Beaux-Arts; it was a portrait of the Jean Valjean of painting. By referring to Victor Hugo's saintly hero of *Les Misérables* (1862), Gauguin not only tapped one of the noblest characters ever created in the history of literature but evoked one that Vincent himself

had often spoken of as a favorite.[47] Gauguin knew his audience well. Vincent immediately sent Gauguin's letter to Theo: "Enclosed is a very, very remarkable letter from Gauguin. Do put it on one side as a thing of extraordinary importance. I mean his description of himself, which moves me to the depths of my soul. . . . Do you realize that if we get Gauguin, we are at the beginning of a very great thing, which will open a new era for us."[48]

A few days later, when Vincent opened the carton containing Gauguin's self-portrait, he was shocked. "Gauguin looks ill and tormented in his portrait!!" he cried to Theo. "He must not go on like this."[49] As Vincent came to terms with the frightening image before him, he felt sure that because he knew the real Gauguin, this portrait must represent him in an unnaturally tormented state. A few restful weeks in Arles, Vincent believed, would bring him back to health, to how he had been when he returned, godlike, from Martinique: "He must become again the richer Gauguin of the 'Negresses.'"[50]

What Vincent wasn't ready to admit was that the portrait accurately captured Gauguin's fierceness, the mien that frightened even close friends like Bernard. Certainly Gauguin had the elegant, feminine side that Vin-

cent was so in love with. He evoked it in the delicately flowered wallpaper that Gauguin said referred to his virginal artistic state, meaning that he was untrained, "unsullied" by academic teaching. But Gauguin's face, also an abstract floral pattern, was aggressive. His eyes, nose, and mouth were twisted into a glare and colored with purplish tones like glazes still molten from the fire of a pottery kiln, symbolizing the dangerous fires that burned within him. Gauguin must have felt that Vincent would be moved by this demonstration of his passion, as the thrill-seeking young men in his Pont-Aven entourage had been. And Vincent was moved—he responded powerfully to Gauguin's visual language—but he immediately fought to regain his long-cherished vision of a gentle, humanitarian Gauguin. Vincent's own self-portrait, painted in response to Gauguin's, showed a calm monk, eyes slightly altered to look Japanese, bathed in the most neutral of colors (fig. 35).[51]

If Van Gogh's self-portrait was intended to be a response to the violence of Gauguin's, it echoes a similar response that he had to a caricature that Gauguin drew on a letter from Pont-Aven.[52] It was a cartoon of a man seated on the tip of a rock, busy painting the sun. It referred to Vincent's love

117

of the brilliant light in the South of France, but it may also have referred to Vincent's extreme admiration for Gauguin, the man of the tropics. But Vincent was again taken aback. "The artistic gentleman in the letter who looks like me—do you think it's me or someone else? The face certainly suggests that it is me, but in the first place I always smoke a pipe and secondly I have the utmost horror of sitting like that on precipitous rocks overhanging the sea, it makes me giddy."[53]

It was becoming clear that the two men had fundamentally misunderstood each other. Vincent had long had a false image of Gauguin, and Gauguin, who was interested in Vincent only insofar as he would promote his career, had a mistaken idea of what would please. Because Vincent spoke of himself as having the coarse lusts of a beast, Gauguin naturally assumed that he was as physical and fierce as Gauguin himself.[54] Not only did he emphasize this aspect in his self-portrait, but he came to Arles prepared to expose his earthy side. After a few days together, Vincent wrote to Bernard, "Without a doubt, we are in the presence of a virgin creature with the instincts of a wild animal. In Gauguin, blood and sex prevail over higher aspirations."[55] Vincent could no longer harbor the illusion of Gauguin's refined Petrarch to his genial Boccaccio.

Gauguin was also quickly disabused about Vincent. Vincent was gentler and shyer than Gauguin had expected him to be. In some ways Gauguin was chastened by Vincent's refinement, as shown, for example, in a sudden improved treatment of his wife.[56] But Gauguin also discovered that Vincent's earnest approach to all aspects of art and life meant that he was far more judgmental than Gauguin liked his friends to be. Although Vincent was steadfast in his support of Gauguin and the paintings he produced, a certain wariness crept into his letters to Theo after Gauguin arrived. Gauguin is "interesting as a man,"[57] his experience as a sailor gave Vincent "an awful respect for him,"[58] and "it does me a tremendous amount of good to have such intelligent company as Gauguin's, and to see him work."[59] This is lukewarm compared to the fervor with which Vincent had anticipated Gauguin's arrival.

At times Vincent even went so far as to disagree with Gauguin's opinions of art and artists. Vincent loved the masters of color and brushstroke, such as Rembrandt, Delacroix, and the Marseilles painter Monticelli; Gauguin preferred the elegant draftsmen, like Raphael, Ingres, and Degas. Above all, Vincent looked for art that conveyed the nobility of the land and the common people, whereas Gauguin, who also used rural themes, was looking more for novelty in style and subjects that were exotic and intriguing. Too often Gauguin felt that his Parisian sophistication was looked down upon by his wholesome companion. And it irritated him to have another artist criticize his work, as he wrote to Bernard. "He likes my paintings very much, but while I'm doing them he always finds that I am doing this or that wrong."[60]

After his summer at Pont-Aven, Gauguin was too accustomed to adoration to accept Vincent's polite dissent. His instinct was to reassert the hierarchy of a relationship and to become defiantly flamboyant in the face of disapproval. He immediately took control of their lives together, just as a controlling husband might do, doling out the money to Vincent, improving the quality of their food, and insisting on a higher standard of cleanliness in the house.[61] He attempted to undermine Vincent's confidence in his own art and opinions by criticizing important aspects of his style. Knowing that Vincent had waited almost a year for feedback from an artist he admired, Gauguin, who was normally very kind to those seeking his advice, could be very cold. As the days went by and Gauguin did not comment on the decorations that had consumed Vincent during the month before Gauguin's arrival, Vincent wrote meekly to Theo, "I do not yet know what Gauguin thinks of my decorations in general, I only know that there are already some studies which he really likes, like the sower, the sunflowers, and the bedroom."[62]

Gauguin was aware of the romantic nature of Vincent's attachment to him. Because this was evident from the passion of Vincent's pursuit over the previous five months, Gauguin must have come to Arles confident he could handle yet another young man's adoration. As he wrote to Schuffenecker, he understood that the plan was basically a business arrangement, and he referred to Theo's (and Vincent's) passion as mercenary. "Rest assured that as much as [Theo] van Gogh desires me, he has not agreed to support me in the south because of my pretty eyes. He has taken the lay of the land like a cool Dutchman and expects to promote me exclusively."[63] But when he settled in Arles, Vincent's expectations were more personal and more difficult to manage than, for instance, Laval's had been. Vincent, in his analogy to Boccaccio and Petrarch, had imagined a bond between equals.

Seeing that Vincent wanted more from him than he wanted to give, Gauguin asserted his independence. To Gauguin, it felt as if Vincent were pursuing him day and night. He claimed that several times he woke up in the middle of the night to find Vincent by his bed.[64] Although male affection was not distasteful to him, and he even courted it frequently, in this case he wanted to discourage it. He did so by turning to women, as he had not done in several years. He discovered that Vincent, even though he often talked of taking necessary trips to the brothel, was shocked when Gauguin formed liaisons with women he met there. Typically, Gauguin got much pleasure out of the shock value of his amoral behavior. The effect on Vincent was immediate; it was so gratifying that he decided to try it out on Schuffenecker. "Make love often and avoid irregularity—these and the freedom to work are what pulls a man through. Virtuous Schuff, I can see your big eyes growing wider at my scandalous words. Calm down, eat right, have good sex and good work, and you will die happy."[65]

But Vincent, unlike Schuff, who was used to Gauguin's jesting, took Gauguin's behavior much more seriously and personally. In relating Gauguin's "success with the Arlésiennes" to Theo, he said somewhat priggishly, "*We* are not such fiends [*malins*] in that regard."[66] He went on to wonder about the sincerity of Gauguin's frequent references to his wife and family when discussing money matters. He felt that Gauguin's interest in the local women had significant consequences. "He is married, but he doesn't keep up the appearance of it."[67] Vincent's concern about Mette and the children surpassed that of Gauguin's usual friends, who were too young and thoughtless to

**36** Paul Gauguin, *The Wine Harvest at Arles*, 1888. Oil on canvas, 28 3/4 x 36 1/4 in. (73 x 92 cm). The Ordrupgaard Collection, Copenhagen.

see more than one side to a relationship. But Vincent, with Gauguin throwing his indiscretions in his face, could relate to her suffering at the hands of a belligerently independent husband.

Gauguin's painting in Arles was closely intertwined with Vincent's because they sketched the same sites and often responded to each other's works by copying or revisiting the same ideas. But one work Gauguin painted in mid-November stands out from the group. Called *The Wine Harvest at Arles* or *Human Misery*, it shows a raw-boned peasant woman, her red hair loose around her face, sitting amid huge piles of grapes (fig. 36). The absence of the traditional folk coif indicates sexual abandon, and the harvesting of the fruit symbolizes pregnancy.[68] It echoes a lithograph Vincent had done several years before of his pregnant mistress, Sien, which Vincent had titled in English, *Sorrow* (fig. 37). The plight of the women in both Gauguin's and Vincent's renditions is explicit, but the clear emotional content of Vincent's *Sorrow* makes the viewer empathize with the forlorn woman, whereas the eerie calm of Gauguin's *Wine Harvest* suggests symbolism beyond pure emotion. The women in black and the odd pose of the central figure in imitation of a famous Peruvian mummy on view in the Ethnographic Museum in Paris cast the specter of death over the scene.[69] But typical of Gauguin's delight in personal symbolism, the red hair of the woman abandoned by her lover seems emblematic of Vincent, whose own passion for Gauguin would lead only to ruin. Gauguin wrote of this and another painting, *Les Cochons,* when he sent a batch of his latest works to Theo. "These two I think are very male. But if they are a bit gross, it's the hot sun of the South that puts us in heat, like animals."[70]

**37** Vincent van Gogh, *Sorrow*, 1882. Lithograph on tinted paper, 15 1/8 x 11 1/2 in. (38.5 x 29 cm). Van Gogh Museum (Vincent van Gogh Foundation), Amsterdam.

After the two men had lived together for about six weeks, an unspecified episode frightened Gauguin into calling an end to their experiment. He wrote suddenly to Theo that he could no longer stay with Vincent. But within a day or so, they made up; and Gauguin joked to Theo, "Consider my trip to Paris pure fantasy and the letter I wrote you just a bad dream."[71] Vincent also wrote to Theo: "Our arguments are terribly *electric*."[72]

Gauguin was the only one to write about what happened in the last days of their living together. He told how Vincent threw a glass of wine in his face and later threatened him with a knife, but given the tendency for abusive men to blame their victims and Gauguin's past history of such behavior, it could easily have been the other way around.[73] Neither Van Gogh nor Gauguin recorded any physical abuse that Vincent might have suffered at Gauguin's hand, but the emotional abuse inflicted upon Vincent was evident. Gauguin's tendency to fight when provoked or when made to feel guilty is also well documented. He had even brought his fencing gear—masks and swords—to Arles, expecting to be able to keep up his skills. Vincent referred to these weapons derisively as his "toys." If Gauguin bloodied Vincent's face the way he had Mette's, the damage, both physical and emotional, could easily have pushed Vincent into the psychotic episode during which he cut off his ear.

This is how Gauguin told the story:

> Vincent, at the time when I arrived in Arles, was in the full current of the
> Neo-impressionist school, and was floundering about a good deal and suffering
> as a result of it. . . . I undertook the task of enlightening him . . . [and] from

that day my van Gogh made astonishing progress; he seemed to divine all that he had in him, and the result was that whole series of sun-effects over sun-effects in full sunlight. . . .

During the latter days of my stay, Vincent would become excessively rough and noisy, and then silent. On several nights I surprised him in the act of getting up and coming over to my bed. . . . [One night] we went to the café. He took a light absinthe. Suddenly he flung the glass and its contents at my head. I avoided the blow and, taking him bodily in my arms, went out of the café, across the Place Victor Hugo [and put him to bed.]

[The next day while taking a walk] I had almost crossed the Place Victor Hugo when I heard behind me a well-known step, short, quick, irregular. I turned about on the instant as Vincent rushed toward me, an open razor in his hand. My look at that moment must have had great power in it, for he stopped and, lowering his head, set off running towards home. . . .

With one bound I was in a good Arlesian hotel, where, after I had enquired the time, I engaged a room and went to bed. . . .

Van Gogh had gone back to the house and had immediately cut off his ear close to the head. . . . When he was in a condition to go out, with his head enveloped in a Basque *beret* which he had pulled far down, he went straight to a certain house where for want of a fellow-countrywoman one can pick up an acquaintance, and gave the manager his ear, carefully washed and placed in an envelope. "Here is a souvenir of me," he said. Then he ran off home, where he went to bed and to sleep. . . .

I had no faintest suspicion of all this when I presented myself at the door of our house and the gentleman in the melon-shaped hat [policeman] said to me abruptly and in a tone that was more than severe, "What have you done to your comrade, Monsieur?" . . . .

Anger, indignation, grief, as well as shame at all these glances that were tearing my person to pieces, suffocated me, and I answered, stammeringly: "All right, Monsieur, let us go upstairs. We can explain ourselves there." . . . Gently, very gently, I touched the body, the heat of which showed that it was still alive. For me it was as if I had suddenly got back all my energy, all my spirit. . . .

Once awake, Vincent asked for his comrade, his pipe, and his tobacco; he even thought of asking for the box that was downstairs and contained our money. . . . Vincent was taken to a hospital where, as soon as he had arrived, his brain began to rave again.[74]

That day, December 24, 1888, Gauguin telegraphed Theo, who took the next train to Arles. There is some question whether Gauguin waited for Theo to arrive and returned to Paris with him or whether Gauguin left alone the next day.[75] At any rate, Gauguin had no intention of continuing his stay in Arles and broke the agreement he had made with Theo.

When Vincent recovered over a week later, his first concern was for Gauguin. "Have I scared him? In short why doesn't he give me any sign of life? . . . Tell Gauguin to write me and that I am always thinking about him."[76] But his old anxiety about money and the well-being of his brother made him testy when he wrote Gauguin himself. "Tell me—was my brother Theo's journey really necessary, my friend? Now at least do reassure him completely, and please be confident yourself that after all no evil exists in this best of worlds in which everything is always for the best."[77] From Vincent's point of view, the cutting off of a piece of his earlobe

(Gauguin exaggerated when he said it was the whole ear) was a relatively minor occurrence. Indeed, looking back at Gauguin's account, it was the accusation of the police that he had killed Vincent that shook him up, not the cutting off of the ear. As for Vincent having threatened him with a knife, this was not part of the original account he had given Bernard when he first returned to Paris; then, he described Vincent as "running after him." This scared him because Vincent had been acting strangely for some time.[78] Gauguin's tendency to exaggerate the sins of those he abused and then abandoned make it very likely that the story of Vincent's threats with a razor evolved as time went on.

Finally, on January 9, 1889, Gauguin wrote to Vincent, and the two exchanged several letters in the next few weeks. The renewed dialogue rekindled Vincent's anger toward Gauguin, which had built up during the time they spent together. On January 17 he wrote scathingly of Gauguin's greed, which resulted not only in some unwise expenditures in Arles but also in his taking two sunflower paintings and requesting a third.

Even more unsettling to Van Gogh were Gauguin's own mental lapses. "If Gauguin stayed in Paris for a while to examine himself thoroughly, or have himself examined by a specialist, I don't honestly know what the result might be."[79] These lapses were mostly on moral issues, as he pointed out to Theo: "On various occasions I have seen him do things which you and I would not let ourselves do, because we have consciences that feel differently about things. I have heard one or two things said of him, but having seen him at very, very close quarters, I think that he is carried away by this imagination, perhaps by pride, but . . . practically irresponsible."[80]

Vincent commended Gauguin for his businesslike and orderly approach to things like daily expenses, "but his weakness is that by a sudden freak or animal impulse he upsets everything he has arranged."[81] Greatest among Gauguin's weaknesses, Vincent felt, was that he left Vincent in his hour of need. "Do you stay at your post, or do you desert it?" he asked, and questioned Gauguin's reputation for generosity. "If Gauguin has so much real virtue, and such capacity for charity, how is he going to employ himself? As for me, I have ceased to be able to follow his actions, and I give it up in silence, but with a questioning note all the same."[82]

When Gauguin asked for his fencing equipment back, Vincent sneered. "I shall hasten to send him his toys by parcel post. Hoping that he will never use more serious weapons." And then, musing on Gauguin's physicality, he came to the subject of Gauguin's oft-told desire to reunite his family and his conflicting plan to return to Martinique. "It is frightful, all the welter of incompatible desires and needs which this must cause him. I took the liberty of assuring him that if he had kept quiet here with us, working here at Arles without wasting money, and earning, since you were looking after his pictures, his wife would certainly have written to him, and would have approved of his stability."[83] Vincent could now fully sympathize with Mette.

But also like Mette, Vincent could not make a complete break with Paul. Two days later, on January 19, Paul was writing for more money, and Vincent was already planning how they might live together again. "I dare

say that basically Gauguin and I are by nature fond enough of each other to be able to begin again together if necessary."[84] They never did live together again, but they continued to correspond until Vincent's death in 1890. Months before his death, when Vincent looked back on the park scenes he had painted in anticipation of Gauguin's arrival, describing them as the gardens of love, he forgot that they had been painted in a spirit of optimism. He wrote wistfully about his own identification with Boccaccio to Albert Aurier, who had published an article on Van Gogh in the *Mercure de France*: "a melancholic, somewhat resigned, unhappy man who saw the wedding party of the world pass by, painting and analyzing the lovers of his time — he, the one who had been left out of things."[85]

Gauguin, on the other hand, interpreted their time together as positive, regardless of its violent end (fig. 38). He felt that they had both done good work, and even he had gained from the exchange. "I owe something to Vincent, and that is, in the consciousness of having been useful to him, the confirmation of my own original ideas about painting."[86] But his most eloquent and provocative summary of the situation came in a haunting letter to Schuffenecker on December 20, 1888, just as the crisis was coming to a head. He explained that he couldn't leave Vincent, who was obviously in pain, and besides, he needed Theo too much. In addressing Schuffenecker's fear of receiving criticism for his new work, he spoke to Vincent as well as Schuff: "Be patient, and stay calm. If you have wings of wax, you have to be careful how close you fly to the sun. The Incas, according to legend, came straight from the sun and will return there. But not everyone comes from the sun."[87]

## 9  The Martyr
### 1889

Returning to Paris in late December 1888, after almost a year in the provinces, Gauguin was able to make yet another dramatic appearance. This time he was pleased to find himself viewed as a brave martyr, just as he had portrayed himself in his self-portrait for Vincent, *Les Misérables,* the previous fall. The portrait was still in Arles, but enough artists in Pont-Aven had been present during its genesis that it served as a convenient reference. Two dramatic testaments to his sufferings were now circulating in Paris — the rejection of *The Vision After the Sermon* by the priest at Nizon and, more recently, his noble actions toward and flight from poor, mad Vincent van Gogh.

Gauguin's friends rallied around him. Schuffenecker again took him in until he found his own studio nearby, on the rue du Saint-Gothard. Bernard, Laval, and now Sérusier introduced him to the younger set. He seldom ventured back to his old Impressionist haunts around the place Pigalle on the Right Bank; students and poets were making the Latin Quarter and the Montparnasse section the new centers of intellectual bohemianism. Charles Morice, Gauguin's later collaborator and biographer, met him around this time.

It was in 1889, at a small restaurant down the street from the Odéon where poets, impartially described as symbolists (still) or decadents (already), would meet.

That evening, arriving late for dinner at the Côte d'Or, I spied a new face amid my group of friends, a large, bony, bulky face, with a narrow forehead and a nose not beaked, not curved, but broken-looking. The mouth was straight and thin-lipped; the eyes were lazy, heavy-lidded and slightly bulging, with bluish pupils that glanced and swiveled from right to left in their sockets, their owner making only a token effort to move his head and body in concert.

This unknown individual seemed thoroughly lacking in charm; but nonetheless he exercised a definite attraction on account of his singular expression. This was a blend of natural nobility, pride, and a simplicity that verged on the commonplace. One quickly perceived that the mixture translated as strength, the moral strength of an aristocrat among the common people.[1]

The reaction to Gauguin, the result of the previous year's cultivation of his image as a Peruvian noble / savage, tended to be sympathetic. The doubts that might have been expressed by his wife or Vincent van Gogh were not heard above the admiring voices of the young crowd he had successfully wooed. In the absence of the self-portrait *Les Misérables,* Gauguin made another one in ceramic (fig. 39). The pathos of his tortured features, shaped to suggest an ancient Peruvian portrait vase, was accentuated by closed

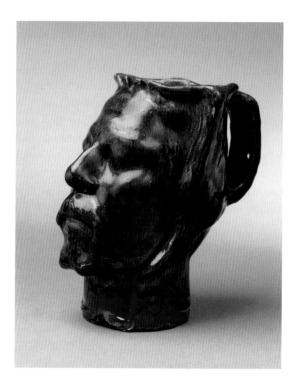

eyes, ears cut off, and a red glaze dripping down his face like blood from a crown of thorns.[2]

Despite this pose of noble suffering, Gauguin had as little actual reason to complain as he had ever had in his artistic career. Thanks to Theo van Gogh, not only had he had no living expenses for the past two months, but during the same period he had sold approximately 3,000 francs' worth of paintings and pottery. This was more than he had ever made from his art in a year, much less in two months. It brought his total sales for 1888 to almost 4,000 francs.[3]

The contretemps in Arles did not seem to have damaged his relationship with Theo, as he had feared it might. Theo reimbursed Gauguin for his expenses in Arles according to their agreement and continued to promote Gauguin's work. For the next two years he represented Gauguin and provided a key link to other patrons, such as Vincent's friend Eugène Boch, who promoted Gauguin's sales in Brussels, and Jacob Meyer de Haan, the wealthy Dutch businessman-turned-painter who later supported Gauguin for over a year. The two difficult months with Vincent had certainly paid off.

Although it has never been unusual for artists to be supported by dealers or wealthy patrons, the relationship can be more or less dignified, depending on the personalities involved. In Gauguin's case, the pattern that evolved was a complicated one. Because of his strong, authoritarian manner, much of Gauguin's patronage came in the form of tribute to him as master of a new movement or, as with Vincent, payment in exchange for instruction or guidance. But his authoritarian manner masked Gauguin's other recurrent tendency, which was to be wheedling, self-pitying, and flirtatious. He took full advantage of the attraction that other men felt toward him and encouraged in them a protective attitude, which paid off in offers of money, shelter, and favors of all kinds.

The noble face of Gauguin's Janus-like persona—which incorporated both strength and weakness—was the martyr, the guise that Gauguin shaped brilliantly in the late 1880s. The ignoble face, which Gauguin did not acknowledge in himself but repeatedly commented on as characteristic in modern society, was the prostitute. Gauguin's willingness to court the affection of men who could do favors for him frequently had an undercurrent of sexuality, as it had with Vincent. Whether such relationships were ever consummated is not known, but the erotic connection between sex and money, a long-standing one in Gauguin's life, was never so evident as it was in this period of growing success.

Gauguin, who had not intended to be in Paris at all that winter, stayed only about six weeks before returning to Pont-Aven. But while he was in Paris he did everything he could to maintain his momentum. With Theo's encouragement, he created a set of ten zincographic drawings based on his paintings from Martinique, Brittany, and Arles (fig. 40). About fifty sets were printed from zinc plates by a professional printer.[4] Although little is known about how they were intended to be sold, it is likely that Theo kept a few sets in his gallery. Degas, Pissarro, and others had had a certain success with this type of inexpensive but fine print related to their paintings.

In a spirit of generosity, Gauguin began a large portrait of the Schuffenecker family, no doubt inspired by Vincent's series of portraits of the Roulin family, which he had been working on in December. The Schuffenecker portrait was intended to repay them for their hospitality, just as the ceramic portraits of Louise Schuffenecker and daughter had been last year, and it offered a similarly puzzling interpretation of husband and wife, son and daughter.[5]

During this time Gauguin was thinking once again of his own family. Mette had kept up her usual communication with old friends, including Paul's sister, Marie, and the Schuffeneckers.[6] Despite Paul's attempts to ridicule her appreciation of art, she was an active member of the Copenhagen art world.[7] She sent a young Danish painter, J. F. Willumsen, to Emile Schuffenecker, who had in turn introduced him to Theo van Gogh. Willumsen stayed in Paris until the summer of 1889; although he had paintings in the Salon des Beaux-Arts and the Exposition Universelle, he did not meet Gauguin until 1890.[8] The collection of Gauguin's own early Impressionist paintings and the remaining works by Pissarro, Degas, Cassatt, and others hanging in Mette's apartment were a resource for a number of Danish painters trying to learn the newer styles, and she lent them to exhibitions of modern French art in 1888 and 1889.[9] Her French lessons and her willingness to put Danish artists in touch with her old friends in Paris also won her their respect.

Mette had refused to write to Paul ever since he had scornfully sent her letter back in June of 1888. In August he had written again, puzzled by her silence and blithely asking for news of the children. When he hadn't received a reply by mid-December, he sent money, very likely at the suggestion of Vincent van Gogh. Making the letter as insulting as possible, he neglected any sort of greeting, starting the letter with "Here's 200 francs."[10] The fact that he had intended to send 300 but crossed the number out and kept 100 francs for himself could hardly have added to the charm of the letter. But Mette dutifully acknowledged the receipt of the money and once again relented and brought Paul back into the family with an affectionate, newsy letter, a note in French from Emil (now fourteen), and a recent photograph of them all (fig. 41). In reply, Paul criticized the way everyone looked in the photograph, ridiculed Emil's French,[11] and accused her of responding only when he sent money.[12]

In spite of his carping, the receipt of Mette's letter and photograph after receiving no news since June had its usual impact on Paul. As in Martinique, he had a sudden desire to see his family and proposed combining a trip to Brussels, where he would be showing some work, with a quick visit to Copenhagen. However, as before, the familial impulse was of short duration. In his next letter he dismissed Mette's suggestions about dates and

times, saying that he had neither the right clothes nor enough money to make the trip after all.[13] He decided to go to Pont-Aven with Laval instead.

Gauguin's contradictory impulses concerning his family surely had to do with the large amount of money he had just made. Most of it came in December, while he was living with Vincent, who expected and encouraged him to send money home after everything he had said about needing money for his family. He had managed—ungraciously—to send 200 francs, but he perhaps had it in mind that this was the time to spend the money on a trip home and share the fruits of his labor with them. Not only Vincent but Theo, Schuffenecker, even Laval, not doubt expected him to do this. Surely *he* wanted to do this, if only to prove to his wife's family that he was now a success. But other forces prevailed. In his speculator's heart he believed that if he kept the money himself, he could spend another year at Pont-Aven and would have twice as much to give them the year after that.

All of Paul's indecision and waspishness about the trip and his family must have been puzzling to Mette, who had no direct way of knowing he had earned all that money. She was just glad to be back in touch with him. But she could easily have surmised through Schuffenecker and through Scandinavian friends such as Willumsen that Paul's reputation was improving and that there might be some hope of his eventually being able to support the family after all. Her own pride, as well as the practical matter of supporting five teenagers, caused her to wish for his success. In Copenhagen she did all she could to bolster his importance as a leader in the new French artistic movements that were of increasing interest to Scandinavians. Therefore, from this point until the final break in 1895, she kept corresponding with him no matter what he said to her, always hoping that, if he would not love her, he could at least make her proud of him.

The exhibition in Brussels that he proposed combining with a trip to Copenhagen was the annual exhibition of the avant-garde Les XX.[14] Organized by the critic and publisher Octave Maus in 1884, the group included such Belgian artists as Ensor, Knopff, Toorop, van Rysselberghe, Rops, and Anna Boch (Anna was the sister of Vincent's friend from Arles, Eugéne Boch). From the beginning, the exhibitions also included certain invited foreigners, which gave them an interesting international flavor. In 1884, for instance, the exhibitors included Rodin from France, Chase and Sargent from the United States, Whistler "from England," and Vincent's cousin Anton Mauve from Holland.[15] As time went on, the invited French artists tended to come from Impressionist circles. Bracquemond, Monet, Renoir, Redon, Morisot, Pissarro, Seurat, Caillebotte, Toulouse-Lautrec, Signac, and Guillaumin had all been invited by 1888. Gauguin's brother-in-law Frits Thaulow was invited in 1887.[16]

This was an exhibition that Gauguin was pleased to participate in because he had seen many of his friends and rivals included before he was. Even Mette Gauguin was probably aware of the significance of the invitation and somewhat relieved to see her husband for once as successful as her sister's.[17] Gauguin was particularly pleased when Anna Boch (probably at the suggestion of Vincent van Gogh) bought one of his large Brittany paintings from the exhibition, adding another 400 francs to his coffers.[18]

The experience in Brussels whetted Gauguin's appetite for major exposure of some kind in Paris. All over town, plans were being drawn up for art exhibitions to coincide with the Exposition Universelle, which would open in May. The official art pavilion would display modern painting, sculpture, and decorative arts from all over the world. The dealers were hosting their own exhibitions: the Galerie Georges Petit organized a joint show of Monet's painting and Rodin's sculpture; Durand-Ruel hosted the Society of Painter-Printmakers, which constituted a reunion of sorts of the Impressionist group.

Vincent and Theo had long talked of an exhibition organized by and for Vincent's group of radical artists at which Vincent would finally unveil his Arles paintings. "I want," Vincent wrote Theo in September 1888, "to make enough pictures to hold my own when the others are making a great show for the year '89. Seurat with two or three of his enormous canvases has enough for an exhibition of his own, Signac is a good worker and has enough as well, and Gauguin and Guillaumin too."[19] While all these artists were friends of Vincent's, they weren't necessarily friendly with each other; and so it is not surprising that this exhibition did not materialize. Perhaps if Vincent had not suffered his bout of illness, he might have been able to bring all these factions together, as he had in organizing the Grande Brouillon exhibition in 1887.

Or perhaps the idea for an exhibition of "new" art had been Schuffenecker's all along. Even more than Vincent, it was Schuffenecker who tended to be the organizing force for this circle of artists. He had been a founder of the successful Salon des Indépendants in 1884 and continued to bridge a

number of avant-garde factions. While he was a Neo-Impressionist he had kept up with Gauguin; and lately, now that he was more in Gauguin's camp, he still maintained ties to the Néos. In planning the 1889 exhibition, Gauguin had to remind him lest he follow his natural inclination to be inclusive: "Only remember it is not an exhibition for the others," and, "For my part, I decline to exhibit with *the others*, Pissarro, Seurat, etc."[20]

In mid-March, while Schuffenecker was searching for an appropriate space, as Degas had once done for the Impressionists, he approached the manager of the well-known Café Riche, who was named Volpini, who had the contract for the Grand Café des Arts on the fairgrounds opposite the Fine Arts Pavilion.[21] The decor of the temporary building was to have included mirrors; but a mix-up left the manager facing the grim prospect of bare walls on opening day. A deal was struck whereby the respectable Schuffenecker—art professor and former Salon painter—would provide amusing decorations of the Brittany countryside painted by a select group of modern artists as quickly as possible. The group would arrange for their own catalogue, posters, and publicity in several newspapers. It was a coup.

**43** Paul Gauguin, *In the Waves*, 1889. Oil on canvas, 36¼ x 28¾ in. (92 x 72 cm). Cleveland Museum of Art, Gift of Mr. and Mrs. William Powell Jones.

Schuffenecker wrote immediately to Gauguin in Pont-Aven. Of all the arrangements that had to be made (who to invite, how to arrange for the catalogue and the publicity) the most important issue to Gauguin was what to show. The paintings would potentially get more exposure here than if they were hung anywhere else in Paris. Gauguin had been in Pont-Aven about a month when he heard the news. He then stayed another month, until he felt it was absolutely necessary to go back to Paris. Judging from the works that appeared in the catalogue and on the walls, he had not produced a series of blockbusters to equal those of the previous fall. But the four works—three small works on paper and one large canvas—established the theme of Eve that would be his signature theme for the rest of his life.[22]

Two of the new works attracted most of the attention—a small pastel of Eve and the snake, inscribed "Pas écouter li li menteur" (Don't listen to the liar; fig. 42), and the large oil called *In the Waves* (fig. 43). Though separate works, they were related in theme, and on the cover of the catalogue Gauguin had drawn a new design combining the two. Both featured nude women of classical proportions that resembled the bathers by Degas that Gauguin had sketched so irreverently the year before. Even the use of pastel, which was rare for Gauguin, suggested Degas's influence. But the women were as imaginary and symbolic as Degas's were ordinary. Gauguin's bather was not stepping gingerly from her tub; her bath was a life-and-death struggle with the sea.

Gauguin's discovery of this new motif—the female nude as Eve—allowed him to express ideas of primitivism and inner emotion in a form that was familiar to all audiences. His new Eve was a virtual replica of the seated peasant woman among the harvested grapes that he had painted in the fall (see fig. 36). But *The Wine Harvest at Arles* used such personal symbolism that it was virtually incomprehensible to anyone not privy to the artist's explanation. Eve, on the other hand, was the biblical version of that very theme—sexual downfall—and needed no explanation. The peasant woman, now nude, became "the first woman" and the presence of the snake transformed the scene into the Fall.

Once the basic message had been established, Gauguin tailored it to make it more provocative. The pose was slightly altered from the version he had used in *The Wine Harvest* so that it conveyed more anguish than misery but still had the overtones of death. In Gauguin's new rendition, the woman's hands cover her ears rather than prop up her chin, and her body is contracted and tense rather than resting listlessly on the ample base of her lower limbs. In *The Wine Harvest,* Gauguin depicts the harvest of shame after the fall, but in his Eve he shows the moment of terror just before. She is powerless to stop the hovering snake's advance. Seduction has become rape.[23]

Gauguin's reinterpretation of the temptation of Eve was one of many "modernizations" of the traditional Christian themes that had fascinated artists in the nineteenth century as the church lost its power to dictate religious art. Double-entendre paintings of women picking fruit could be found throughout the exhibitions in Paris that summer, from the most conservative art to the most liberal.[24] But Gauguin, in his version, eliminated the role of the symbolic apple and Eve's subsequent seduction of Adam. He also ignored the fact that Eve's terror would have been impossible according to the biblical account, because she had not yet acquired the knowledge of what was in store for her. Brushing the details of the story aside to create a stunningly original reinterpretation, he concentrated on the raw truth of the pushy snake and the terrified virgin. The victim—as Gauguin suggests in his inscription, "Don't listen to the liar"—has a choice but cannot exercise it; she fears yet allows the rape that is presented in the guise of love. The simultaneous horror of and yet desire for rape were both titillatingly perverse and worthy of PGo at his best. Yet the theme of the temptation of Eve was familiar enough that those who did not share PGo's interest in such taboos could see instead the typical moral lesson of the Fall.

What was more visible, and in many ways more disturbing to Gauguin's viewers that summer, was the inscription. Gauguin wrote it in Creole French, or "Nègre." His point of reference was Martinique, where he had become familiar with the lilting patois, which a native French speaker had trouble understanding. But Creole was spoken throughout the French colonial world wherever a large African population assembled, from New Orleans to Algeria.[25] It was easily recognized by knowledgeable Parisians as the language spoken by the black colonials who had come to live in Paris. Gauguin's use of Creole in this case made the suggestion, shocking to many in racist Paris, that God and therefore Eve (in his image) were black. As one critic indignantly asked, "What document supports M. Gauguin's assumption that Eve talked pidgin?"[26]

Gauguin hoped the reference to Martinique would be well received by those in his inner circle. He had not forgotten how important his Martinique paintings, with their intriguing black women, had been in establishing him with the Van Gogh brothers and such hitherto hostile critics as Félix Fénéon. To remind the public of these important canvases, he borrowed one from Theo for the exhibition, *Among the Mangoes at Martinique* (see fig. 26). In that canvas, as in many modern versions of the Garden of Eden, the women pick and carry fruit, and the seated central figure eats one of the mangoes. Gauguin very likely hoped that his new Eve would be viewed by his friends, including the all-important Theo van Gogh, as a continuation of the Martinique series. The emphasis on Martinique paid off when Theo sold *Négresses causant* (Wildenstein 227) to the painter and friend of Degas's, Henri Lerolle, in June, not long after the exhibition went up.[27]

On a personal level, the use of Martiniquan patois for the title was a reference to his companion that spring in Pont-Aven, Charles Laval. They had explored the island together in 1887 before Gauguin's departure, and Laval's lengthy stay had made him more a master of Martiniquan language and culture than Gauguin. Their discussions of the experience prompted Laval's friend Albert Dauprat to visit Martinique himself in 1889.[28] The use of Creole in the title of the painting may have been prompted by Laval. Even the aggressive snake in the painting may have been suggested by the legendary poisonous snakes of Martinique that threatened the native women traversing the island.

If *The Wine Harvest* was a conscious or unconscious reference to the misery that resulted from Van Gogh's love for Gauguin, the Eve should be seen as a reference to Laval's passive horror of and desire for the snakelike PGo. It is reminiscent of Gauguin's portrait of Laval from 1886, in which he depicts his young friend hypnotized by the grotesque, organic pottery with its giant tongue (see fig. 25). According to friends, Laval was unable to work the whole time he was with Gauguin that spring and passed his days in a "somnambulant" state.[29] By the time he left Brittany in the fall of 1889 he had spent most of the past three and a half years at Gauguin's side, yet so little is recorded of the presence of this man that one is easily persuaded that Eve's masochism was based on Laval's own.

Once the exhibition had been hung on the pomegranate-red walls of M. Volpini's café (ever since it has been referred to as the Volpini exhibition), Gauguin headed back out to Pont-Aven. He had every reason to be pleased with his standing in Paris. He and seven others (Laval, Schuffenecker, Bernard, Anquetin, Louis Roy, Léon Fauché, and a friend of Schuff's, Daniel de Monfreid) had filled the café walls with more than a hundred colorful paintings under the nose of the official exhibition. Because of Bernard's contacts with the radical press, the show received some attention in print, and both Gauguin and Bernard were able to publish their own editorializing articles on art in Paris that summer.[30] The show did not get the publicity in other quarters that they had hoped it might, but the younger artists in Paris made it their Mecca. Never before had Gauguin exhibited so many works (seventeen) for such a long period of time (the exhibition was up until October). And even though others, like Bernard, showed more canvases, Gauguin was clearly the central figure of the group.

Because of the definitive statement that the show made about his style and his leadership, Gauguin gained two new disciples that summer in Pont-Aven. The first was Paul Sérusier, who had painted briefly with Gauguin in the fall and carried back his teachings to the radical clique at the Académie Julian. Sérusier was struck anew with Gauguin's power when he saw so many canvases together. Not only did he lead the others on frequent pilgrimages to Volpini's café, but he followed the master himself out to Pont-Aven. Through his influence as a writer and theorist, Sérusier became one of Gauguin's most important apostles.

The second of Gauguin's conquests was a Dutchman, a friend of Theo van Gogh's: Jacob Meyer de Haan.[31] De Haan had had a relatively successful career as a painter in Amsterdam before moving to Paris in October 1888 at the age of thirty-six. Supported by a wealthy family, he was able to take the time to learn the new Parisian styles without the constant pressure of exhibiting and sales. His connections in the Dutch art world, including the painter and critic J. J. Isaacson, with whom he traveled to Paris, led him to such important figures as Theo van Gogh, who took de Haan and Isaacson into his apartment as roommates. In April, de Haan moved out to Pont-Aven, and when Gauguin returned to Brittany after hanging the Volpini exhibition, de Haan solicited his advice and friendship.

Gauguin, always willing to accommodate a friend of Theo van Gogh's, took him on as an informal pupil and found him to be an enjoyable companion. They worked together in Pont-Aven and then began spending more and more time in Le Pouldu, a nearby resort on the seacoast. After his experience with Vincent, Gauguin must have hesitated at first. But de Haan was not as competitive as Vincent and seems to have shared more of Gauguin's ribald tastes. Gauguin's many portraits of de Haan with his features fiendishly distorted show at the very least his ability to share Gauguin's harsh brand of humor (see fig. 47). One sculpted portrait of de Haan (National Gallery of Canada, Ottawa), which maintains the phallic shape of the log from which it was carved, shows a rooster perched on the Dutchman's head, referring to the meaning of "de Haan" — "rooster" in Dutch and, thus in slang, "cock." PGo and de Haan, the two cocks, made a charming pair.

We glimpse the raucous style of their friendship in André Gide's account of his evening with Gauguin and friends in Brittany:

> There were three of them and they soon made their appearance with their easels and paintboxes. Needless to say I had asked to dine when they did—that is, if they had no objection. They soon made it very obvious they were not in the least put out by my presence, by showing not the least concern for it. They were all three bare-footed, in brazen dishabille and with clarion voices. During the whole of dinner, I sat gasping with excitement, drinking in their words, longing to speak to them, to tell them who I was, to find out who they were and to tell the tall one with light eyes that the tune he was singing at the top of his voice and in which the others joined in chorus, was not Massenet, as he thought, but Bizet.
> I met one of them later on at Mallarmé's — it was Gauguin.[32]

To strangers Gauguin wore a rather forbidding mask. Another acquaintance from that time explained that "his slow gait, his sober gestures, his severe facial expression gave him much natural dignity and held unknown and foreign people at bay."[33] Yet in the company of close friends, as Gide describes, his behavior was extraordinarily uninhibited. He was known for his ardent temperament and was always in search of new sensations. He continually invoked his early life as a sailor to explain his rough manner and his crude motto, "Wine, tobacco, and love."[34]

Yet observers also admitted that this bohemian reputation was largely talk. Of the three sailors' vices, Gauguin was remembered as being most addicted to tobacco.[35] Aside from speculation about his nocturnal visits to a hotel maid, Gauguin was considered quite repressed about "love" and was not known to drink beyond moderation.[36] From the evidence available, it seems most likely that Gauguin's "ardent temperament" burned brightest in the company of his male companions and, at that, had a quality of public rather than private indulgences.

This obviously suited de Haan far better than it had suited Vincent van Gogh. Little is known about de Haan's private life except that he was unmarried and, like Vincent and Gauguin, also traveled with male companions. He painted a striking portrait of Marie Henry, the owner of the hotel where he and Gauguin stayed in Le Pouldu, and was said to have lived conjugally with her for a year, leaving her pregnant with his child. Because she identified him as the father of the child, it is difficult to dispute this fact; but since the child was born at least seven months after he left Le Pouldu, it is also possible that he (or even she) did not know of the pregnancy at the time of his departure. It would not be impossible that the paternity of the child was a safe guess on Henry's part because de Haan had already left and could not contradict her. The stories of both Gauguin's and de Haan's amorous adventures with women in Brittany are, upon examination, rather thin, and deflect attention from their mutuality: they gained creative and emotional sustenance primarily from each other. The first summer they painted together, Gauguin produced a sequel to his paintings of nude boys from the summer before (fig. 44). This time the child is lying on the ground in full frontal nudity, his face flushed and his eyes narrowed into the same fiendish gaze that Gauguin would use for his portraits of de Haan (see fig. 47).

During the summer of 1889, while his exhibition was on view in Paris and he was becoming acquainted with his new companion de Haan, Gauguin encountered indecision in his work for the first time. Now that he was receiving feedback from a variety of sources and not just his own circle, he was unsure what direction his work should take in the future. As he wrote to Bernard, who was at Saint-Briac, on the north coast of Brittany, "I have been more than a month at Pouldu with de Haan because I am floundering in a slough of despond and struggling with work that requires a certain time for completion. I find pleasure, not in going farther along the lines I established formerly, but in trying something fresh. I feel it even if I cannot explain it. I am certain to get there eventually, but slowly in spite of my impatience. In these conditions, my tentative studies yield only a

maladroit and amateur result. Anyhow, I hope that this winter you will find in me an almost new Gauguin."[37]

    This is an unusual confession of uncertainty in light of Gauguin's normal didactic tone in letters to Bernard, Schuffenecker, and others. It perhaps indicates that his new companion de Haan did not insist on answers from him, but encouraged him to reexamine and test his often-repeated tenets. It is also a new expression of his old belief in an intuitive rather than a theoretical approach to art. During this time he could briefly claim victory in the struggle for dominance in Paris and allow new ideas to form in his mind and on his canvas. He felt that they would surface without the intervention of intellectual constructs.

    He began to produce paintings this way at Le Pouldu: "[His] method consisted of spending a long time contemplating the points of view [he] wanted to paint—studying its lines, harmonies, colors, and light until [he was] satiated—and taking abundant notes, pencil in hand. Gauguin liked to say that a work of art has to be entirely completed in the painter's mind before he begins his canvas. . . . The artist would then jump to his brushes, and face to face with nature, in one sitting he would draw the poem out of his dream."[38]

    This account of Gauguin's working method is consistent with the duality of other aspects of Gauguin's character at this time. At first glance, he was an aloof analyst of the people and places around him; but eventually, in a burst of almost orgasmic physical or intellectual activity, he would take control of the scene before him, redefining it in his own terms.

Unfortunately many of the works he painted in this manner in the summer of 1889 were, as he said, tentative and amateurish. For the most part they were landscapes and views of peasants working, with very little allegorical or symbolic content. He got a rude awakening when he sent Theo van Gogh a batch of paintings at the end of August. The paintings of the past year had not found a market, and the attention he had gained during the summer did not translate into sales.[39] Quickly changing gears, Gauguin returned to the themes that he thought had been successful in the past year —martyrdom and human misery. At once hoping to regain approval in Paris and to garner sympathy for himself, he returned to the vehicle of the self-portrait, this time painting himself in the guise of the ultimate martyr, Christ.

Gauguin and de Haan came back to Pont-Aven from the seacoast at the end of August, at the very height of the resort season. This year there were more artists and vacationers than usual in Brittany because the Exposition Universelle had attracted visitors from all over the world.[40] In the midst of the milling crowds, Gauguin painted three religious paintings— two referring to religious sculptures in local churches (called *The Yellow Christ* and *The Green Christ*) and the portrait of himself as Christ, called *Agony in the Garden* (fig. 45).

As with *The Vision After the Sermon* from the previous year, these were produced as a kind of theater for the benefit of the French and foreign artists who now came to Pont-Aven hoping to catch a glimpse of the avant-garde leader. Showing himself as Christ, Gauguin acknowledges his new leadership position but stressed the suffering he has experienced at

the hands of officialdom, which he fears will ultimately lead to his crucifixion.[41] The Garden of Olives theme, however, brings in the added element of anticipated betrayal at the hands of a Judas among his own disciples. Unlike a similar painting by Bernard that was not a self-portrait but does depict Gauguin as Judas, Gauguin includes only two small indistinct figures in the background, whose identities cannot be established.[42] That fall Gauguin complained of many "supporters" who had recently betrayed him—Theo, Degas, and Guillaumin—because they had found fault with the Volpini exhibition or with recent paintings.[43] But Gauguin's suspicion may also have included others closer to him who had shown signs of dissent, and the painting may have been a ploy to get them to reaffirm their loyalty. At any rate, the public setting in which this work was created was ideal for sparking controversy beneficial to Gauguin and his group.

Another remarkable work that Gauguin carried out in the public arena of Pont-Aven was a painted wood sculpture carved in relief on a specially milled wood panel (fig. 46). It also revisited the theme of the fallen woman that he had been developing for the past year with *The Wine Harvest* and the Volpini Eve. Continuing his fascination with the interrelationship of sex and pain, in this new piece he shows the nude woman physically captured in the strong grasp of a monstrous man—another self-portrait. Although not an Eve, it is the Volpini temptation taken one step further, into the rape itself. Gauguin now reveals that he is the snake and the "liar" (*li li menteur*) who utters the words carved at the top: "Soyez amoureuses, vous serez heureuses" (Make love [or: be a lover], and you will be happy).[44]

To both Van Gogh brothers he explained the work in terms sympathetic to the woman: the tempting words are shown to be false by the sadness of the other figures, particularly a "desolate old woman" who is in the anguished pose now familiar from *The Wine Harvest* and the Volpini Eve.[45] Gauguin meant to remind them of the woman who is the innocent victim of a bad upbringing and a corrupt society and whom Vincent first portrayed as pregnant and abandoned in *Sorrow*. But Gauguin's meaning was, as usual, not so simple. To Theo he stressed that the meaning was not important, and went on to describe, tongue in cheek, the woman "who struggles despite the good advice of the tempting inscription."[46]

As with the Volpini Eve, the woman fears the pain of inevitable sex but cannot avoid it. The many traditional representations of rape in the history of art, from the theme of the Rape of the Sabines to the sculpture of a gorilla carrying off a nude woman (*Troglodytes Gorilla* by E. Fremiet) in the Exposition Universelle of 1889, suspend the viewer between sympathy for the victim and the perverse thrill of sexual violence. Gauguin's deliberate ambiguity about the woman's rejection or acceptance of the rape made his version, like his Eve, puzzling but arresting. His history of physical abuse of his wife and his later comments on sexual practices give strong evidence that he himself found pleasure in violence—whether real or fantasized. In a section of his memoirs he imagines himself in the circus:

> The great royal tiger is alone with me in his cage; nonchalantly he demands a caress, showing by movements of his beard and claws that he likes caresses. He loves me. I dare not strike him; I am afraid and he abuses my fear. In spite of myself, I have to endure his disdain.
>
> At night my wife seeks my caresses. She knows I am afraid of her and she abuses my fear. Both of us, wild creatures ourselves, lead a life full of fear and bravado, joy and grief, strength and weakness.
>
> At night, by the light of the oil lamps, half suffocated by the animal stenches, we watch the stupid, cowardly crowd, ever hungry for death and carnage, curious at the shameful spectacle of chains and slavery, of the whip and the prod, never satiated of the howls of the creatures that endure them.[47]

In this passage Gauguin shows his identification with both victim and wild beast; he abuses the stupid, cowardly crowd for its taste for violence but is obviously one of them. He had too many conflicting identities (monster, Christ) to take or represent a clear, valid moral stance. But he could weave all the ingredients—sex, violence, morality—into something breathtakingly new. As he wrote to Bernard, this was his aim, after all—to create a work that fulfilled a higher imperative in Gauguin's set of values than morality or narrative. "I am glad you have seen the carving and that you understand it; nobody else appears to. But what does it matter? It is either a work of art or not."[48]

Gauguin spent the month of September producing this controversial group of works, which he immediately shipped off to Theo. In early October he and de Haan returned to Le Pouldu, where de Haan had rented the vacation villa of a family that had returned home to Quimperlé for the winter.[49] This commodious building offered a large room overlooking the ocean. The two men set up their easels there, but since the servants of the house were gone, they found it more comfortable to lodge once again at the small hotel run by the entrepreneurial Marie Henry. Gauguin was happy with the arrangements, especially now that de Haan was his sole source of support. De Haan received a modest but reliable monthly income (300 francs) from his family in Amsterdam as his share of the prosperous business. In Brittany this sum went much further than did the 200 francs that Theo had arranged for Vincent and Gauguin to live on in Arles. De Haan was apparently not only generous but supplied Gauguin with whatever he needed without calling attention to Gauguin's state of dependence. In the case of tobacco, for instance, "De Haan would buy huge one-pound packages of it that he would put in a ceramic vase especially used for this purpose. Gauguin would help himself to it according to his needs. When the receptacle was empty, out of discretion he would refrain from asking that it be refilled. But he became sad, quiet, somber."[50]

**48** Paul Gauguin, *Self-Portrait*, 1889. Oil on wood, 31 1/4 x 20 1/4 in. (79.2 x 51.3 cm). National Gallery of Art, Washington, D.C., Chester Dale Collection.

For four months, from October 1889 until January 1890, the two men lived together quite happily. Although the isolation of Le Pouldu in winter did not stimulate Gauguin to create the major works he had just produced in bustling Pont-Aven at high season, he did occupy himself with some colorful paintings of Breton children and other local scenes. The monument most evocative of this brief period of calm, however, was the painted dining room of Mary Henry's inn, to which he and de Haan applied themselves with zeal. The hotels in the more populated artists' haunts like Pont-Aven or Concarneau were already full of paintings donated over the years by guests. Gauguin's offerings to Madame Gloanac, his hostess at Pont-Aven, were always at odds with the more conservative works already hanging there. But in Le Pouldu, Marie Henry's inn was new, her tastes were bold, and Gauguin and de Haan had the unique opportunity to dictate the entire decor. Sculptures, ceramics, and paintings added to the decorations that soon covered both walls and woodwork. The primary motifs were Breton scenes, but the three people responsible for the decorations were given pride of place: the large portrait by de Haan of Marie Henry and her daughter hung in the middle of one wall, and portraits by Gauguin of himself and de Haan were painted on wood cupboards on either side of another wall (figs. 47–48).

De Haan, his features distorted because of the odd, high point of view, fixes glowering eyes on a plate of fruit on the table in front of him. This composition echoes Gauguin's earlier depiction of Laval similarly hypnotized by pottery surrounded by apples (see fig. 25): both men seem to be contemplating forbidden fruit. Gauguin's matching self-portrait shows him looking back over his shoulder toward de Haan with a delicate, tame snake held gently between his fingers.[51] The depiction of himself as tempter refers to the panel he had just completed, *Soyez amoreuses vous serez heureuses,* but this time he is benign, even angelic, as the halo above his head suggests. Sexual violence has been replaced by a jesting caricature of devil and angel, temptation and fulfillment, which was the key to the relationship between the two men. The casual nature of these portraits, painted in off-season with no expectation of being shown in Paris, shows a side of Gauguin that he seldom revealed in the combative, challenging art he created for public consumption. Charming, witty, and affectionate, it is the Gauguin that captivated de Haan and the other men who stayed at his side for as long as they could.

Ironically, the pose of impoverished artist that Gauguin had so disingenuously created for himself in 1889 became a reality in 1890. One after another, he lost the stable of regular bill payers he had cultivated over the years — de Haan, Laval, Vincent van Gogh (with money from Theo), and Schuffenecker. Nor were his sales good: Theo van Gogh was unable to earn more than 1,000 francs for him, less than a third of what he needed to live on. In spite of his extensive exposure during the 1889 Exposition Universelle, both at the Volpini exhibition and in the press, his exhibition opportunities in 1890 were minimal, and almost nothing about him appeared in print. When he tried to halt the dwindling of his funds, none of his schemes — from obtaining a government post in the French colony of Tonkin to selling his work in bulk — worked out.

By the end of the year, he was like a "cornered dog"—harrying friends, proposing new schemes—until finally he developed the right strategy to capture the attention of the Paris art market.[1] He would, he proclaimed in the newspapers, sell off his remaining art at auction so that he might sail to the romantic isle of Tahiti, made famous by one of the most popular novels of the day, *The Marriage of Loti* (1880), and let the Paris public see in pictures what Pierre Loti had described in mere words. It was a desperate measure, taken by an artist who was scrambling to reverse a series of misfortunes, but it worked: on April 7, 1891, Paul Gauguin found himself on the dock in Marseilles, boarding a ship, alone, headed for the end of the earth. How had this come about?

Eighteen eighty-nine had been such an extraordinary year in so many ways for Gauguin that only as it came to a close did it strike him that he had made only a fraction of the money he had made the year before. Whereas he had started 1889 with a comfortable nest egg of 4,000 francs, he was approaching 1890 with less than 1,000 francs.[2] The major difference was that this year Theo van Gogh had not held an exhibition of his works, as he had when Gauguin went to live with Vincent. Nor was Theo able to sell the more esoteric works that Gauguin had recently painted, including the scenes of himself as Christ and the violent *Soyez amoureuses vous serez heureuses*. Nevertheless, Theo valiantly kept these works on view at the gallery because even if they didn't sell, they did bring in many visitors who were interested in Gauguin's latest creations. As Paul wrote to Mette, "I am exhibiting my works at Goupil's in Paris, and they are creating a great sensation; but it is difficult to sell them. When this will happen I cannot say, but what I can tell you is that today I am one of the artists who attracts the most attention."[3]

In the fall of 1889, although Gauguin was becoming concerned about his lack of sales, he was not yet desperate, because he was still enjoying the hospitality of Meyer de Haan at Le Pouldu. When he learned that his nine-year-old son, Jean-René, had been injured in an accidental fall from a third-floor apartment window, he asked with uncharacteristic generosity that Theo send the 300 francs he hoped to receive for a wood carving directly to Mette. It is unclear whether this sale and thus this monetary gesture were realized, but the desire to help was that of a financially confident man.

Only weeks later, however, Gauguin's comfortable world at Le Pouldu collapsed. De Haan's family threatened to stop de Haan's monthly stipend if he couldn't demonstrate that he was using the funds in a re-sponsible way. Gauguin's anxiety was expressed in a barrage of letters after the New Year to all his friends proclaiming his profound despair and im-mediate need for funds. All thoughts of sending money directly to his wife were forgotten, but not the horror of his child's accident, which became more vivid in each recounting of the story. In his initial letter to his wife he had hardly mentioned it except to scold her for writing only when she had bad news.[4] To Vincent van Gogh, however, who had already heard of the accident from Theo, Gauguin wrote, "Life is awfully long and awfully sad. . . . For the last three months I've been in Le Pouldu I've only had 30 francs in my pocket and can hardly face going on with my painting. . . . I almost lost one of my children who fell from the third floor onto the street. . . . Ah, why paint?"[5] Vincent, as in the past, was moved by Gauguin's family woes and wrote sympathetically of him to his sister. "I am so fond of my friend Gauguin because he has found the means of producing chil-dren and pictures at the same time; at the moment he is horribly distressed and uneasy in his mind because one of his children met with an accident and he was not there, and unable to assist."[6]

Before the end of January, Gauguin was in real need of assistance. De Haan was forced to stop supporting Gauguin entirely and faced a com-mand to return at once to Holland. Gauguin had no choice but to fend for himself. Unable to bring himself to write directly to Schuffenecker beg-ging for asylum yet again, he instead wrote to Bernard and asked the young man to forward his request to Schuff. He needed to return to Paris; he must once again be taken in by the Schuffeneckers.[7] As Bernard put it wryly in urging Schuff to be his old generous self, "You know what a hothead he [Gauguin] is. Do what you want, but I know you to be generous and good. Won't you take in one more time this egotistical spoiled brat?"[8]

For the next four months, Gauguin availed himself of the Schuffe-neckers' hospitality in Paris, the longest period of time he had ever stayed with them. The family had recently moved to a larger house with a garden, on the rue Alfred Durand-Claye, that was closer to the growing Montparnasse section of the city. The house had two floors, the second of which was mainly taken up with Emile's large studio. On either side of the studio were two rooms—on one side was the maid and on the other was Gauguin.[9] Visitors to the house reported that Gauguin made himself completely at home: "That spring one could, by the large open window, see at the family table a person with an unusual manner who sipped with visible satisfaction the classic mixture of mocha, martinique [rum], and bourbon as the last course of a bountiful lunch. A bottle of fine champagne was within reach, and from a cigarette held between his yellow fingers curled delicate spirals of smoke. It was Gauguin . . . temporarily at peace thanks to the ministrations of people attentive to his slightest wish. With the impassivity of someone who has seen it all, he conducted himself—this will not surprise anyone who knew him—not as a guest whose wishes were being indulged but as the true master of the house."[10]

Gauguin's comfortable life with the Schuffeneckers partly explains the length of his stay, but a genuine lack of funds precluded other options. For the past few winters in Paris he had stayed with the Schuffeneckers only until he found his own apartment (as in 1889) or until he could get back out to Pont-Aven (as in 1888). But this year he couldn't afford independence, and all his attempts to improve his situation that spring failed.

Since his return from Martinique, he had talked of taking another exotic trip from which he would bring back a fresh batch of unusual paintings. He was aware that the Martinique trip had made him as an artist, thanks to the interest of the Van Gogh brothers and the intrigued response of the younger avant-garde crowd in Paris. The work he had done in Brittany was successful in attracting attention but did not sell as well as the Martinique paintings. But during the summer of 1889, when he had had a chance to study foreign cultures in the various pavilions at the Exposition Universelle, he switched his planned destination to Tonkin, the northernmost of the three French protectorates in what is now Vietnam.

Judging from the fact that he collected photographs of Cambodian and other Asian art available at the fair, it seems that he was impressed with the decorative style of Asian art and imagined himself adapting the motifs to good effect in his painting. He also believed that the people, whom he also saw in the Asian pavilions, would make good models. On a practical note, Gauguin restricted his prospective destinations to French colonies because he believed he would be able to get government support to subsidize the trip. The more distant French colonies needed people to fill the government posts, and Gauguin felt himself qualified to obtain one of them.

Gauguin's travel aspirations were encouraged by a Countess de Nimal, an apparently wealthy and well-connected woman whom Gauguin met vacationing at Le Pouldu in the fall of 1889. With her assistance Gauguin applied for government support for his trip and a colonial post.[11] In January he discovered that the government was not easily convinced that there was a post for a man who had been a full-time artist for the past five years, and Gauguin began to feel that his chances would be better if he could apply pressure in person.[12] Once back in Paris he pulled all the strings he could, unsuccessfully, and the matter was soon dropped.

Gauguin was not without alternative plans. His wife had written to him of the success of the recent exhibition of modern French painting held at the Society of the Friends of Art in Copenhagen from October 31 to November 11. She had lent many of the works in their collection, by Degas, Manet, Cassatt, and Pissarro, and several of Paul's canvases dating from before 1887—the last time he had shared any of his work with her.[13] This event whetted his appetite once again for a northern audience, and he considered the possibility of returning to Copenhagen to cultivate the interest in modern art that had been increasing steadily in that city.[14] He also proposed to Van Gogh and de Haan the idea of having their group relocate to Antwerp, another city with activity in modern art, where they might also establish their own gallery as a branch of Theo's Goupil Gallery.[15]

Gauguin's travel schemes all required that he raise substantial capital, and as a corollary, he talked of selling off the batches of work that had been accumulating at the Schuffeneckers' and Goupil's. He used the term "bazarder," which illustrates his desire to sell his works at prices more appropriate to a bazaar than to a respectable art gallery.[16] During his months in Paris he searched for a speculator, probably among his old friends from the Bourse, who would be willing to take forty or fifty canvases for a lump sum. Gauguin could thus raise 5,000 or more francs quickly, and the speculator could sell off the works individually over time and recoup at least twice as much. In May he found such a speculator, Charles Charlopin, a former naval surgeon and an inventor who expected to sell one of his patents and make a fortune.[17] This deal, like his application for Tonkin, dragged on for several months and ended with equally disappointing results.

Throughout the spring Gauguin thought primarily of taking drastic steps to improve his situation—foreign travel and major financial deals. Working hard and cultivating his known audience seemed to be too slow. In the face of the huge inventory of unsold works, making more art seemed less important than relieving himself of what he had. The Wildenstein catalogue raisonné indicates that there are fewer than twenty known paintings from 1890, the least he had produced since he had turned to art in earnest ten years before.

The person most shocked by Gauguin's rejection of art making was Vincent van Gogh. After almost a year of trying to regain his mental balance at the asylum of Saint-Rémy, he was as furiously productive as ever, pausing only for the unpredictable episodes of mental shutdown that incapacitated him for a week or more. Ironically, while Gauguin was experiencing a downward slide in his career, Van Gogh's was surging upward. In January, Van Gogh was invited to show with Les XX in Brussels (Gauguin was not), and in March he sent several works to the Indépendants' exhibition, which Gauguin still snubbed. Thanks to low-key efforts by Theo and the more overt machinations of the well-connected Bernard, Van Gogh's work was becoming known and beginning to sell. In January a major article on Van Gogh by Bernard's friend Albert Aurier appeared in *Mercure de France*.[18] For all Gauguin's publicity the year before, he had not yet received such recognition himself.

Gauguin's feelings upon seeing his former disciple so honored are not recorded, but they can be imagined. Vincent himself was so conscious of Gauguin's reaction—whether it was voiced to him or not—that he bent over backward to assure everyone in their circle that it was Gauguin who deserved the attention and praise, not him: "I think they ought to say things like that of Gauguin, and of me only very secondarily."[19] Vincent's humility went only so far, however; he sent the article to everyone, including Gauguin, if only to point out how little he deserved the praise.

Gauguin's campaign to rally support in his new hour of need brought Vincent back into his orbit after a year of relative coolness. Vincent not only responded to Gauguin's family troubles but saw that he could once again be useful financially to the magnetic martyr. He wrote to mutual friends, such as the Australian John Russell, who might be able to buy from Gauguin, and encouraged Theo to do as much for Gauguin as possible, probably prompting him to show Gauguin's pottery and sculpture (including the carved relief *Soyez amoureuses*) in an exhibition of Pissarro's paintings in February. He himself once again offered to set up housekeeping in the little house in Arles with him. Gauguin declined with what must have been a painful but still respectful honesty: "It doesn't seem prudent to begin living in an isolated town where you would lack immediate care if you had another episode."[20] Vincent accepted the rebuff without pressing Gauguin, especially since he was not as confident as his doctor was of his ability to manage on his own. But Gauguin was on his mind frequently that spring, encouraged by Gauguin's attentions, which were, as usual, partly calculated to raise his own profile with Theo.

Because Van Gogh was interested in copying works by his favorite artists at that time, he became intrigued by a charcoal drawing of a woman done by Gauguin while they lived together.[21] He went about making a painting based on this drawing that he called "a work belonging to you and me . . . a summary of our months of work together."[22] He tried to copy the drawing as scrupulously as possible but at the same time interpreted it by means of color. The very act of communing with Gauguin through his drawing and reliving their time together was enough to trigger a new mental episode. As he put it to Gauguin, "I paid for doing it with another month of illness."[23]

By the time Vincent recovered from the devastation caused by his reminiscence of Gauguin, spring was almost over. His doctor at Saint-Rémy felt that he was strong enough to go north again—to Paris and then perhaps back to Holland. Vincent himself was hesitant to go so far away from his doctor but compromised by arranging to spend the summer in Auvers, the small town outside Paris near Pissarro's old home. This lovely setting would be restful and yet provide ample opportunity to paint. It had an additional advantage in the presence of Dr. Paul-Ferdinand Gachet, the homeopathic doctor who had nursed Pissarro's mother in her last days and who was a valued friend of Pissarro and other artists in his circle.[24] When Van Gogh arrived in Paris on May 17, after over two years in the south of France, he was overwhelmed by the urban environment and moved out to Auvers after less than four days.

One of the disappointments of his time in Paris was that Gauguin did not come to see him, even though they were in neighboring parts of the city.[25] Gauguin claimed he did not know that Vincent was in Paris; but his uncharacteristic neglect of Vincent (given his normally unceasing efforts to hold Theo's attention) was probably due to having finally put together a deal with Charlopin to sell a group of his works for 5,000 francs.[26] This was to be the long-awaited answer to all his problems. Not only would he be relieved of the now cumbersome inventory of work, but he would have the kind of money necessary to take a second trip to an exotic land. Since February, when his efforts to gain government support to go to Tonkin failed, he had shifted his attention to another French colony, Madagascar.

Eagerly he wrote to all his friends about his new plans and the advantages of this new proposed destination. Apparently, it was the "primitive" qualities of Madagascar that appealed to him. Unlike Tonkin, which offered an exotic but highly refined culture, he imagined life in Madagascar to be extremely basic: he could build a native hut on a plot of ground, grow his own food, and paint and sculpt in peace.[27] Contemporary accounts, as well as the display seen at the 1889 Exposition Universelle, described typical dwellings. "The best of the houses are built of wood, but the majority of bamboo split and plaited, or of rushes dried and kept in their places by means of two or three long pieces of split bamboo driven through each. Nearly all are thatched with the leaves of the travelers' tree. In fact, this tree in some places supplies all that is necessary for the house-building."[28] In addition to such a house, Gauguin said to Bernard, "a woman out there is, so to speak, obligatory, which will provide me with an everyday model."[29] The woman would also, no doubt, care for the house and the garden so that life would indeed be simple.

Aside from the personal advantages of choosing Madagascar over Tonkin, Gauguin may also have been persuaded to switch destinations by the recent news that France would soon supplant England entirely in its official protection of Madagascar. In August 1890, the long-awaited agreement was signed whereby Britain recognized the French resident general as the ruling authority in Madagascar. This agreement was greeted with jubilation by French traders, who foresaw a new era of prosperity.[30] In Paris it must have seemed like an equally good omen to Gauguin, whose interest in business and a wealthy local clientele was unabated.

Expectant as he was of a rosy future, thanks to Dr. Charlopin, Gauguin neglected or did not notice Vincent's return to Paris. In fact, soon after making the arrangements with Charlopin, which would not go into effect until Charlopin's patent was sold, in a month or six weeks, Gauguin left Paris himself for a short vacation in Le Pouldu.[31] By now Meyer de Haan had pacified his family sufficiently to host Gauguin again, and the two were reestablished at Marie Henry's inn by early June. As the art schools and end-of-year exhibitions closed for the summer, Gauguin and de Haan were joined by other artists from Paris, including the now-regular Sérusier and two new disciples, Paul-Emile Colin and Charles Filiger.

Gauguin was in a jubilant mood as the summer festivities began. He was so little concerned with work of any kind that he had not even brought his painting gear. As he wrote to Bernard, "I . . . walk about like a savage, with long hair, and do nothing. I have not even brought colors or palette. I have cut some arrows and amuse myself on the sands by shooting them just like Buffalo Bill."[32] When swimming weather arrived, he joined the vacationing families on the beach enjoying the sun and the surf. Colin reminisced about those days to Charles Chassé, one of the first Gauguin scholars, thirty years later. "I can still see Gauguin swimming at Le Pouldu beach with his eagle's-beak nose, his clear sailor's eyes, his black, slightly long hair, his beret, his swimming trunks, his forty-year-old man's belly; he made you think of a buffoon, a troubadour, and a pirate, all at once. . . . Tremendous energy sprung forth from his whole being; he seemed to be hatching a huge work."[33]

After a month of relaxing by the ocean, Gauguin and his friends drove six miles inland to Pont-Aven to spend Bastille Day with the holiday crowds there. Several artists at Pont-Aven remembered meeting him as he passed through the streets with his retinue, attracting attention wherever he went. Maxime Maufra, who later became a member of the larger Gauguin circle in Brittany, gives a sketch of the theatrical antics of the group:

> I had been [at Mother Gloanec's inn] for a few days when, on July 13, an old cart that seemed to carry a band of gypsies drove into the square and stopped at the doorstep of the inn. . . . One by one from this old peasant conveyance descended an evil-looking redskin, a young blond man with a Christ-like face, and a little hunchback wearing a scarlet fez. Another big man with a frozen smile came last. It was Gauguin and his disciples: Filiger, de Haan, and Sérusier.
>
> After dinner at the inn, the group stayed on alone, talking in the dining room. Maufra decided to go in and introduce himself, but when he got to the door, the young blond (Filiger) stopped him:
>
> "If you desire to hear the words of the master, come in."
> "Certainly," I said, and I entered. . . .
>
> Opposite the master sat the little hunchback de Haan. Dutch by origin, he spoke French with some difficulty, but he understood it perfectly, and he offered me this metaphor:
>
> "We here are merely cut glass, while Paul Gauguin is the diamond that sparkles and casts its reflection on us all." . . .
>
> The evening ended late, after everyone drank enormously.
> The next day was the holiday with its festivities and its ball.
> Paul Gauguin, a child at heart, had a great time and inspired everyone else to do the same.[34]

The artist with his exotic appearance—now deeply tanned from his month in the sun—and his retinue of slavish admirers was ridiculous; but he was also inspiring to the young artists who had just escaped for the summer the rigid regimens of their Paris art academies. The social and artistic freedom he preached, tinged with a masculine sexuality that few dared to acknowledge was attractive, made Le Pouldu an increasingly popular destination for the summer inhabitants of Pont-Aven.

Paul-Emile Colin remembered that Gauguin likened himself to Balzac's sinister character Vautrin, whose presence in several novels of the *Comédie humaine* was as a seductive but punishing Satan.[35] Vautrin preyed on beautiful young men, such as Lucien Chardon in *Lost Illusions* (1837–43) and *A Harlot High and Low* (1839–47). A tall, dark Spaniard resembling Gauguin in appearance, Vautrin seemed to have a supernatural power to affect the lives of Lucien and other innocents. Whether Balzac intended Vautrin to be interpreted as a homosexual is debatable, but by the

1890s this interpretation was not uncommon, and Marcel Proust referred to him as a pederast.[36]

The self-drawn parallel between Gauguin and Vautrin must have seemed especially apt in the summer of 1890 when Gauguin and Filiger appeared for the first time together in the artists' haunts of Brittany. As blond and innocent in appearance as Gauguin was dark and sinister, Filiger was twenty-seven that summer. After gravitating from the study of decorative arts to fine arts, Filiger had just begun attracting attention with his pointillist watercolors.[37] He may have been introduced to Gauguin by Louis Roy, a mutual friend who had been a coexhibitor in the Volpini exhibition. Gauguin had traded a set of his 1888 zincograph prints for a watercolor that Filiger had shown at the Indépendants show in March 1890. Sometime in June, Filiger joined Gauguin and de Haan in Le Pouldu and became as slavish as de Haan in his devotion to the master. A measure of Gauguin's returned devotion was his petition to have Filiger included in the invitation to exhibit with Les XX the next winter, a unique instance of Gauguin's championing another artist.[38]

The close relationship of Gauguin and Filiger during 1890 is significant because Filiger was the only openly homosexual artist of the many with whom Gauguin shared his life during these years.[39] The extent of their physical affection is impossible to document, but that affection existed is equally impossible to overlook. The openness of this relationship was yet another mesmerizing quality that drew artists to Gauguin during the height of his visibility in those circles.[40] Gauguin liked to refer to his group at Marie Henry's inn as PGo and Company.[41]

With this situation in mind, it is intriguing to take a look at the ceiling decoration the group painted that summer to finish the scheme they had started the winter before. The ceiling design is organized around a central motif of four large geese placed in a symmetrical pattern that emphasizes their long, phallic necks. An inscription corrupts the heraldic legend of the Knights Templar, "Honni soit qui mal y pense" (Shame on him who thinks evil of it). Gauguin's version, "Oni soie ki mâle y panse," is a nonsensical phrase substituting "mâle" ("male" or, in slang, "cock") for "mal" (evil) to produce a different sort of admonition: "Shame on him who thinks of the cock."

The idea that the goose should be interpreted as female, and thus as a reference to Marie Henry, is unlikely, given Gauguin's penchant to use the long-necked creature as akin to the Jovian swan (as in Leda and the swan).[42] He used the goose in such a phallically suggestive manner in a zincograph from 1889 that also bears the inscription "Homis [*sic*] soit qui mal y pense" (see fig. 40). At Marie Henry's inn during the summer of 1890, it was the phallic goose, not the female "goose" (silly person), who was thinking of the cock (mâle) as the four artists played out their erotic theatricals for each other and their awestruck artistic audience.

Gauguin's extraordinary flaunting of sexual innuendo may have been prompted by his belief that he would soon be off to Madagascar and need not be overly concerned about the consequences of scandalous behavior. Before this time, as much as he enjoyed and courted the attention of attractive young men and liked to make veiled allusions to illicit erotic themes in his art, he had been reluctant to be known publicly as anything other than a husband and father. His reckless public behavior (albeit in the more forgiving resort towns of Brittany) was as daring as he would ever make it in displaying the pleasure he derived from male company.

The prospect of Madagascar had other consequences. It brought back into his fold those who had wandered off, disillusioned. Emile Bernard, for instance, when he heard of Gauguin's plans for Madagascar, forgot that he had called Gauguin a hot-tempered spoiled brat and invited himself on the trip. Gauguin was not optimistic about the success of this plan, especially since Bernard would have difficulty raising the money, but he encouraged him because he could be useful in many ways. Gauguin soon had Bernard doing errands for him in Paris, visiting various government offices, finding a Malagasy dictionary, and checking with Charlopin to monitor the progress of the important deal. He also asked Bernard to use his influence with the writer Aurier to get a major article published on Gauguin along the lines of the one Aurier had recently written on Vincent.[43]

Vincent van Gogh was another who invited himself to Madagascar to join the "Studio of the Tropics" he had long dreamed of.[44] Going along was a vague notion, but he mentioned it both to Gauguin and to his brother in letters from Auvers. He still felt the disappointment of having missed Gauguin in Paris, and being back north reminded him keenly of his elusive friend. "Since my return I have thought of you every day," he wrote to Gauguin in early June.[45] Once again he took up Gauguin's drawing *L'Arlesienne,* in which he had invested so much mental energy the previous spring and which had precipitated a severe breakdown. This time he used it to inspire an etching, which he executed and printed with the help of Dr. Gachet, an amateur printmaker. He sent an impression of this new "collaboration" to Gauguin in Brittany, along with the request that he be allowed to visit Gauguin and meet de Haan, about whom he had heard so much.[46] But once again Gauguin rebuffed him, pointing out that Le Pouldu was much too remote for someone needing a doctor's care.[47] Van Gogh did not write again, although, after a visit to his brother's gallery, he wrote wistfully to Theo, around July 23, "I noticed with pleasure that the Gauguin from Brittany which I saw was very beautiful, and I think that the others he has done there must be so too."[48] On July 27, Vincent van Gogh shot himself—he died of his wounds two days later.

Gauguin heard the news several days after the funeral, probably from Bernard, who, with Laval, had attended the ceremony and burial in Auvers. Gauguin wrote his condolences to Theo, although he was not overly saddened by the loss. He wrote to several friends that he thought it a blessing that Vincent would now be freed from his suffering.[49] But in a painted wood carving that he was just starting at the time (fig. 49), he revived the theme of the tragic red-haired woman diving into an engulfing wave, which he had first formulated in 1889, a few months after his stay with Vincent. The woman turns her back on a dark-haired figure with his/her hand up in a gesture of blessing and looks up to see her own red-haired reflec-

tion in the round shape of the sun. Gauguin titled the piece *Soyez mystérieuses* (Be Mysterious) and put on it a price more than three times what he had ever received for any work.[50]

The death of Vincent coincided with the evaporation of the Charlopin deal. For some time Gauguin had preferred not to notice that the deadlines they had set had long passed and that the news from his friends in Paris was not encouraging. He continued to plan a monumental voyage but, in something of an admission of defeat, asked Schuffenecker to send him his art equipment from Paris.[51] The stay in Le Pouldu would not be a short vacation after all; he now saw that it would be necessary for him to get back to work. The fall art season in Paris was approaching, and he would need to send Theo a respectable group of new paintings. With Charlopin out of the picture, he needed Theo more than ever.

In September, to make matters worse, de Haan again began getting threatening letters from his family. Suddenly Gauguin not only had to face the immense burden of providing for his future, but he had to pay his present bills as well. Marie Henry would not let him leave the inn without settling his summer's account of 300 francs, which he had assumed either Charlopin or de Haan would take care of. Letters were quickly shot off to Schuff and Theo in Paris, apprising them of his pressing debts and asking for whatever help they could give him.

To Theo he outlined again his scheme of finding a collector who would buy a large number of works at a bargain price to bankroll Gauguin's travel to exotic lands.[52] Although Theo does not seem to have replied to this letter, he kept Gauguin's dilemma in mind as he resumed his duties at the gallery after Vincent's tragic death. He honored Vincent's attachment to Gauguin, despite the many disappointments Vincent suffered at his hands, and he truly believed in the greatness of Gauguin's art. But the stress of losing his brother triggered in Theo a similar mental breakdown, which manifested itself by the beginning of October. He began to have violent outbursts in the gallery, arguing savagely with his employers over minor incidents. When the same uncontrolled behavior began at home—he threatened to kill his new wife and infant son—he was put under a physician's care.[53] During this descent into madness he did not forget Gauguin, but imagined that he had found a way to subsidize Gauguin's trip. About October 9 or 10 he sent the following telegram: "Your departure for the tropics is assured; money to follow."[54]

If Gauguin was taken in by Theo's fantasy, his euphoria would have been quashed by the news of Theo's breakdown and his confinement on October 12. Only days later, de Haan was finally forced to leave Le Pouldu to face his angry family.[55] Because the summer season was over, the rest of Gauguin's adoring followers had also left (with the possible exception of Filiger, although he was equally poor). Gauguin had hit bottom. Without de Haan or Theo van Gogh, whom he had counted on after the Charlopin deal collapsed, without reason to expect money from any of his other friends, he was stuck in a deserted resort town with a persistent landlady who would not overlook his debt. Now would have been the time to paint the self-portrait *Les Misérables*.

Yet this extraordinary string of misfortunes, rather than defeating Gauguin, actually energized him. As he wrote to Schuffenecker, "I have to say, my life as an artist has been singular in its hopes and illusions, loves and hates of all sorts. I am extremely tired of it and yet full of energy to carry on the struggle in art as long as I can."[56] From Le Pouldu he drew up his battle plan. Without Vincent and Theo to fall back on, he became his own dealer and publicist. He enlisted everyone he knew, from Sérusier and Laval to Schuffenecker and Redon, to look out for potential buyers. He impressed upon anyone who would listen the importance of sending him to the tropics, where he would revive his muse and come back with art that would increase his reputation and thus the value of all his previous work. Finally, on November 8, he left Marie Henry after handing over an assortment of works of art as collateral against future payment of his debt, and returned to Paris.[57]

Even before he left, things had already begun to look up. At first, it seemed certain that Theo's bosses, Boussod and Valadon, would clear out all the works by progressive artists that Theo had accumulated over the years. Theo's successor at the gallery, Maurice Joyant, had written to the organizer of Les XX, Octave Maus, that any help would be welcome in finding homes for Gauguin's works.[58] Maus quickly found purchasers for five works at the reduced price of 100 francs each. But even before this purchase was completed, Gauguin got the news that Boussod and Valadon had decided to continue their representation of Gauguin. He was amazed—and wondered if he owed this change of heart to one of his old friends, such as Pissarro or Degas, whose opinions meant a great deal to the gallery.[59]

With 500 francs in his pocket, Gauguin was not dependent on Schuffenecker for hospitality this time, although, as usual, the Schuffeneckers' home was his first stop in Paris. Instead, he took a small room in the Hôtel Delambre, a favorite of artists because of its proximity to the Académie Colarossi and other artists' studios in the burgeoning Montparnasse quarter. Being away from Schuffenecker forced him to develop other friendships and enlarge his sphere of influence. One of the most important of these new friendships was with Georges Daniel de Monfreid, a friend of Schuff's from his days at Colarossi (1882–83), who had some independent means and was attempting a career as an artist.[60] Monfreid invited Gauguin to share his painting studio some blocks away on the rue du Château.[61] Not only would Monfreid inspire Gauguin to paint the few important paintings he accomplished that year, but he would be the single most loyal friend Gauguin would have for the rest of his life.

Gauguin also renewed the summer's friendship with Sérusier and through him was introduced to the Nabis group that had formed at the Académie Julian. They had haunted Theo van Gogh's gallery on the boulevard Monmartre and listened to Sérusier's stories of the master long before they met him. In person they found him equally intriguing. He was "the uncontested Master, whose paradoxes we recorded and retold, about whom we admired everything—his talent, his articulateness, his gestures and physical prowess, his nastiness, his inexhaustible imagination, his tolerance of alcohol, the romanticism of his life style. . . . He wanted above all to express character, the inner being, even in its ugliness."[62] Gauguin's connections with the Nabis paid off in later years in the pages of their sympathetic organ, *La Revue blanche,* and in the attention of the publisher of their prints, Ambroise Vollard.

But the most important professional connection Gauguin had in Paris when he returned to the city in November 1890 was with the poet Charles Morice. Morice had established himself as one of the most important of the younger symbolist writers, and his ambition was to join the constellation of the greats, including Mallarmé, Mirbeau, and Verlaine. Listening to the talk of the young artists of avant-garde circles, Morice understood Gauguin, the Master, to be in that upper echelon himself. In lending a sympathetic ear to and sponsoring Gauguin in symbolist literary circles, Morice could only improve his own standing.

One night at the Café Voltaire, where on Saturdays a large group of poets and artists gathered around Verlaine, he [Gauguin] confided to me his desire for a new exile.

"The experience that I had in Martinique," he said to me, "is decisive. Only there did I really feel like myself, and it is in what I brought back from there that one has to search if one wishes to find out who I am. . . . In Brittany I am now too well known . . . I have to talk, to discuss things, and not get anything done. . . . These are the inconveniences of glory," he added with his bitter smile. "And really, I want to go to Tahiti [his new destination], but I need money. About 10,000 francs. . . . I think that a properly prepared sale of about thirty works . . . would raise that much. But the preparation is tricky. I cannot imagine anything better than a resounding article in a large newspaper . . . but by whom?"

The next day I went to see Mallarmé.[63]

Gauguin's subsequent introductions to Stéphane Mallarmé and, in turn, to Octave Mirbeau, were decisive events in his career. In spite of the regard his followers held for him, he had not yet captured the attention of any extremely influential figures in the Paris intelligentsia. His relationships with the Impressionists, particularly Pissarro and Degas, had been checkered over the years. As a result, no powerful artist had been willing to advance Gauguin's career to the extent that these literary figures were offering to do. Mallarmé and Mirbeau, who had sponsored many artists in the past, including Degas, Pissarro, Monet, and Morisot, were always happy to find that their symbolist ideas had resonated in other arts.

In addition to Gauguin's obvious adoption of symbolism in his painting, the literary world was also taken by his proposal to make Tahiti his next artistic destination. Up to the middle of the summer, Gauguin had set his sights on Madagascar. But, apparently at Bernard's suggestion, another French colony, Tahiti, had subsequently come under consideration.[64] The information they discussed about the island came primarily from Pierre Loti's extremely popular novel *The Marriage of Loti*.[65] This 1880 novel by the naval captain Julian Viaud, writing under a pen name, might not have been uppermost in the minds of the avant-garde if not for the astounding announcement that summer that Pierre Loti had been nominated to a newly vacant *fauteuil* (seat) in the Académie Française. The candidacy of Loti, the consummate popularizer, aroused mixed reactions in the Parisian literary world.[66] He was supported by such established figures as Anatole France, Alphonse Daudet, and Edmond Goncourt. But the younger, more progressive symbolist writers found much to criticize in Loti's romantic narratives.

Gauguin's mission, to paint in a symbolist manner the island life that Loti had made his own, was a gallant challenge to the Académie, which he saw as the literary equivalent to the Salon. The literary avant-garde could appreciate this compelling opportunity to counter a controversial but popular writer. Charles Morice would go so far as to collaborate on a book, *Noa Noa,* based on Gauguin's trip.[67] Written in his symbolist poetic style but revisiting many of the romantic features of Loti's novel, Morice hoped that the book would make both of them famous.

Morice's enthusiasm persuaded his friend Mallarmé to speak to the critic Mirbeau. But Gauguin was not content with only one agent acting on his behalf. He also got de Haan to persuade Pissarro to write to Mirbeau.[68] Gauguin understood that articles by influential critics came about by pulling strings behind the scenes, and he was going to pull every string he could. As was his style, he emphasized his desperate financial situation and the crippling emotional despair that would be alleviated only by a drastic change of scene. This was the right tack to take with Mirbeau, who was completely charmed by Gauguin when he finally came face to face with him. As Mirbeau explained to Monet, "He [Gauguin] has a sensitive nature and is truly tormented by his artistic sufferings. Besides, he has a magnificent head. He pleased me very much."[69]

During Gauguin's visit to Mirbeau's home in the country and Mirbeau's subsequent examination of Gauguin's art inventory in Paris, the artist was able to impart to the writer what he thought were the most salient points about his art and life, and Mirbeau took from this information what he felt would be most interesting to the Parisian public. Unlike the other writings on Gauguin at this time, the two articles that Mirbeau published were not colored by the complicated personal and professional rivalries that ruled the avant-garde press. Intended for a wider circulation—daily newspapers rather than the little journals—they give a straightforward version of the story as Gauguin wanted it to be told and as a sympathetic but disengaged outsider wanted to tell it.[70]

Curiously, the image Gauguin presented and Mirbeau shaped for the public was not that of last summer's swaggering gypsy or of the charismatic Master but that of a man of good family and former employee of the stock exchange, whose love of art was drawing him inexorably toward the Pacific, which represented home to him. Most of Mirbeau's first article was biographical. It stressed the political importance of Gauguin's newspaperman father and reminded the public of his grandmother, Flora Tristan, and her writings and work on behalf of social causes. It stated erroneously that Gauguin's mother was born in Peru; but in doing so it established Gauguin's spiritual home in the Pacific. His desire to flee modern urban life was thus associated with the universal urge to retire to the site of one's origin. As Gauguin matured, Mirbeau wrote, "he would become nostalgically obsessed with those suns, those races, that flora, and with the Pacific Ocean, where he was surprised to find the cradle of his own race and which seems to have rocked him in bygone times with familiar lullabies."[71]

Gauguin's trip to Martinique, which had turned out to be pivotal for him, was given special emphasis and lengthened from four months into two years. But, Mirbeau points out, Martinique was where Gauguin went beyond naturalism to represent forms with incipient symbolism. "The forms . . . revealed the state of the spirit of the one who understood them and expressed them thus."[72] The magical success of the Martinique paintings, which Gauguin hoped would be duplicated with the paintings from another exotic trip, could not be overemphasized. Mirbeau ended his paean to Gauguin by tying the themes of Martinique and family values together. "The same need of meditation, of absolute solitude, that drove him to Martinique this time takes him even farther, to Tahiti, where nature is better adapted to his dream, where he hopes that the Pacific Ocean will have for him caresses more tender, that he will have the old and true love of a regained ancestor."[73]

In conjunction with this interpretation of Tahiti as Gauguin's ancestral home, one might place the two rather mysterious paintings of Gauguin's mother, *Portrait of the Artist's Mother* (see fig. 3) and *Exotic Eve* (Wildenstein 389), based on a photograph of Aline Gauguin in his possession.[74] Both exaggerate the features of his mother into a Polynesian lushness—large, soft lips, dark skin, and thick, black hair; and in the "Exotic Eve" his mother's head has been inexplicably placed on a nude body in an Eden-like setting. This is consistent with the rather far-fetched tale of Gauguin's tropical origins, which was taken to such lengths by Mirbeau. It isn't hard to imagine Gauguin painting his mother as a tropical Eve in an entertaining spoof of the whole contrived notion and shocking his friends with such an eroticized image of his own mother.[75]

**50**  Paul Gauguin, *Portrait of Stéphane Mallarmé*, 1891. Etching with pen and wash on paper, 5 7/8 x 4 1/2 in. (15 x 11.7 cm). Dr. and Mrs. Martin L. Gecht Collection.

Gauguin was producing a large number of art objects of all kinds now that he was back in Paris. His energetic pursuit of critics and collectors seemed to inspire him to do more artwork than he had done during the five relaxed months he had spent in Le Pouldu. Most of it was in reaction to the lively intellectual circle he now found himself frequenting. He etched a portrait of Mallarmé intended to illustrate an article that Morice planned to publish (fig. 50), and he drew an illustration for the playwright Rachilde's book *Le Théâtre*. He spent several days in February in the Musée Luxembourg making a large copy of Manet's *Olympia,* which had recently been purchased by donations from many artists and intellectuals and given to the French state. He painted a portrait of a dark-haired woman, who has never been adequately identified, sitting in front of a large Cézanne still life (Wildenstein 387). Like the copy of *Olympia,* this canvas is a tribute to one of the artists heralded at that time as a father of modernism and shows Gauguin's desire to be seen as part of the latest artistic currents in Paris.[76]

Another painting of a dark-haired woman—the same one could in fact have been the model for both works—shows a slim young nude lying in the foreground of a Brittany landscape, a golden fox cuddling on her shoulder (fig. 51). Gauguin titled it *La Perte du pucelage* (The Loss of Virginity). The model was remembered by Gauguin's friends as "a dark, skinny girl who cannot have had many suitors. He had a lot of trouble persuading her to pose—and when she did, how great was the disappointment!"[77] Subsequent memoirs have suggested that this model was Juliette Huet, a young seamstress and the friend of Monfreid's mistress.[78]

Since Gauguin's separation from his wife, Huet is the first woman Gauguin is known to have expressed affection for. But information about her is scarce. From the letters written to Monfreid after Gauguin's departure for Tahiti we know that she had a child that Gauguin acknowledged to be his,

and from other sources we know that when he returned to France in 1893, he renewed his acquaintance with her in a limited way. Years later their daughter, Germaine Bizet, who was interviewed by Charles Chassé, stated that Gauguin had given Huet some money before he left for Tahiti to help with the child but that her mother had not wished to make the connection public and had burned all his letters and other memorabilia.[79] The only eye-witness account of their intimacy comes from the Danish painter J. F. Willumsen, who visited Gauguin in Paris in the winter of 1889–90: "The studio was completely empty except for an iron bed which stood in the middle of the room and on which Gauguin was playing a guitar while at the same time a woman was sitting on his lap."[80]

In the absence of information that would make Huet come to life as an individual, she has been viewed as the generic model cum lover; one imagines an artist like Gauguin, separated from his wife and family, would have had many such. But because Gauguin was known by his contemporaries more for his relationships with young men than for his relationships with women, models or otherwise, her presence in his life at this moment, however shadowy, is unusual. Given that it coincided with his campaign to win the support of important literary figures and given, too, Mirbeau's article presenting Gauguin as thoroughly bourgeois in his personal life, one cannot help but note the convenient appearance of a presentable woman at Gauguin's side at this time. Huet's recognizable face and nude body in *The Loss of Virginity* and her quick pregnancy would have reestablished Gauguin's "manhood" and counteracted whatever stories might have been circulating in Paris about his incautious summer with Filiger. Gauguin hints at the somewhat infrequent and unromantic nature of their trysts when he writes to Monfreid from Tahiti, "Poor Juliette with a child, and now I can't help her. . . . It happened in spite of everything. God knows the conditions under which I did it." [81] Gauguin's relationship with Huet, if viewed in this context, seems contrived and unconvincing as a major event in his personal life.

But Huet did become pregnant, giving more evidence of Gauguin's actual sexual practices outside marriage than can be had from elsewhere. Huet's pregnancy was the first in a series; several similar young women became pregnant by Gauguin in the next ten years, proving that he was attracted to women in spite of his frequently expressed misogyny and his erotic attachments to men. Their appeal was undeniably in their androgynous appearance, but, at the same time, Gauguin was also interested in their strictly female characteristics. As suggested by his previous series of submissive Eves, which now included *The Loss of Virginity*, he was inflamed to have budding creatures yield their youthful innocence to a man now past forty. As Gauguin got older he followed the path of many men in desiring sexual liaisons with increasingly younger partners. And unquestionably Gauguin found pleasure in the possibility of pregnancy—the most public sign of his sexual power. Finally, Gauguin's relationships with women were eroticized by a real or imagined triangle, as in his romantically charged portrayals of his wife, Schuffenecker, and Schuffenecker's wife. His affair with Huet was tied to his friendship with another man, Monfreid, whom he reminds in his first letter after his departure for Tahiti to "kiss Juliette for me with all your heart." [82]

Another tantalizing triangle emerges when one notices that Gauguin's relationship with Juliette Huet coincided with the annual renewal of correspondence with and affection toward his wife in the winter of 1890–91. As had happened in previous years, Paul had ceased writing to Mette in the spring after it became clear that he would again not be going to Copenhagen. As usual, the summer season in Brittany was so engrossing that Paul simply could not be bothered to keep in touch with her. Mette eventually stopped writing when she saw that she would not receive a reply. But every year something triggered a note from Mette—last year it had been Jean's accident—and they would once again exchange news. In November of 1890, Mette sent a promising young Danish avant-garde painter, Mogens Ballin, to Paris with letters of introduction to all her old friends, including Pissarro, Schuffenecker, and her husband. [83]

Mette may have heard of Paul's troubles that fall, because her letter introducing Ballin commiserated with him and mourned their broken lives. Things hadn't become easier for her. That year they had moved into a second-floor apartment in the lively downtown area, above a photographer's studio and a café frequented by artists (see fig. 41). [84] Money was tight —the younger boys, who did not have patrons, were not able to go to private schools as Emil had done. Aline, now thirteen, attended a school run by her great-aunt. In the summers they felt fortunate if friends invited the children to spend vacations at their summer homes in the country. Mette herself was seldom able to get away. But their lives were nevertheless privileged in that, thanks to Mette's intelligence and sociability and their ties to the Brandès circle, they were still part of the Copenhagen intelligentsia. Artists increasingly came to study the French Impressionist paintings hanging in the apartment and to talk to Mette of her husband and the other avant-garde artists with whom she was still in touch.

Once the Gauguins began writing to each other in the winter of 1890, the letters became warm, and once again Gauguin began thinking of visiting Copenhagen. He would be showing with Les XX in February of 1891; perhaps he could continue on to Copenhagen from Brussels. This time Mette knew better than to suggest alternative dates, and no other offer arose that Paul found more attractive. As the newspaper articles by Mirbeau and others appeared, Paul sent them north, sharing his genuine excitement with his wife. He also, of course, hoped she would translate them and have them republished in Scandinavian papers. All that remained was to see if the sale itself would be successful. He not only needed the money for the trip, but he wanted to present himself to her and her family as an important man. He did not want to be accused of being less than serious. "The day will come when *your* children will be able to present themselves to anyone anywhere with the name of their father for protection." [85] In his imagination he was already internationally famous—"I shall pass my days in Copenhagen incognito," he assured her.[86]

The sale upon which so much depended had been scheduled to take place at the Hôtel Drouot, the major auction house in Paris, on February 23. This is where the Arosas had sold off their collection of Barbizon paintings so profitably in 1878; this is where the great Manet sale had been held in 1883. An auction was the riskiest method of selling a body of works and was usually chosen as a last resort. If the auction failed, Gauguin's prices, already low, would surely plummet. He would have to accept the fact that his work was no longer salable. But publicity was the best protection against a total failure, and Gauguin's ceaseless efforts paid off. As he wrote to Mette, "The articles have created a big stir in Paris, and there is a buzz throughout the art world; even in England a newspaper has called this an event." [87]

The preview the night before the auction was exciting, bringing together the many factions of the Paris art world that Gauguin had courted in the past few months, including the Impressionist old guard like Degas and his circle, the Nabis, the poets around Morice, Schuffenecker and his crowd, Filiger's effete friends, like the Comte de la Rochefoucauld, and the Scandinavians. The next evening, by the time the gavel went down on the last of thirty paintings, Gauguin was not ecstatic, but he was happy. Those thirty paintings that he would have sold to Charlopin for 5,000 francs had brought almost 10,000. Granted, he sold most of them for the relatively low prices that Theo van Gogh had already placed on them—in other words, he had not made a fortune—but he had sold them quickly and had established his art as a good investment on the open market.

Gauguin had every reason to believe that the desperate measures he had taken in the last year had finally borne fruit. As he wrote later to Monfreid, he was a man who took chances. "I stand at the edge of the abyss, yet I do not fall in. When [Theo] van Gogh went insane I was just about done for.[88] Well, I got over it. It forced me to exert myself."[89] Indeed, just as Theo's initial enthusiasm for the Martinique paintings was a turning point, his incapacitation and eventual death four years later was another one. Gauguin's career had become mired in the inbred artistic circles of Brittany and Paris. He needed to move on. After the auction, all that was left was to say good-bye and go.

It took Gauguin little more than a month to make his preparations for Tahiti. This was a remarkably short time to prepare for a trip that he thought would last several years, but because he had not had a stable home since he returned from Martinique in 1887, personal arrangements were minimal. The care and storage of his art had been simplified by the sale of so many paintings in February, and the remaining objects were safe where they were—with Monfreid, Schuffenecker, and the Boussod and Valadon gallery. He trusted these caretakers of his art to handle any future sales in his absence. He added to this core group his new friend Charles Morice, with whom he entered into a financial arrangement from which he expected a regular income during the time he would be in Tahiti. It is difficult to tell the nature of the agreement from existing letters, but it would seem that Gauguin had left part of his proceeds from the auction with Morice to be invested and then repaid to Gauguin over time.[90]

Other matters requiring Gauguin's attention during the short period before he sailed were those having to do with obtaining government support for his project. Because one of his motives for choosing Tahiti over other South Pacific islands was the availability of subsidies for French citizens willing to go to the colonies, he systematically petitioned appropriate government offices to obtain privileges as an official French visitor to Tahiti. As a result, he was granted a 30 percent discount on his fare to Nouméa (where he would transfer to a ship bound for Tahiti), which amounted to a savings of over 500 francs. This grant was only good with the French Compagnie des Messageries Maritimes, which limited his travel options and thus dictated the early departure date and the roundabout route he had to take. He was also given an official mission "to study and then paint the customs and landscapes" of the island, which carried with it no funding, but which implied that a painting would be bought from him by the French government upon his return.[91]

At last, he needed to say his good-byes to all those in Paris who had contributed to the success of this grand venture. This was the most important step because it would prepare the way for his eventual triumphant return. To this end he planned a banquet in his honor to be held at the Café Voltaire, where he had established himself in the midst of the symbolist literary crowd. He personally wrote the invitations that yielded some forty guests and, with Morice's help, engaged Mallarmé to preside. These frequently held artistic dinners were important tokens of the importance of their honorees, and the write-ups in the small journals provided an additional form of publicity.

All of these arrangements for departure were consistent with Gauguin's habits and goals of the past few years. The biggest surprise and the most unusual step he took in preparation for the grand journey was taking a trip to Copenhagen to see his family. To have been consistent with his past behavior, he would have called off the planned trip at the last minute, begging yet again for a little more time to parlay his success into the nest egg that would allow him to retire from the artistic fray and be reunited with his family.

But somehow circumstances were different this time. Perhaps something in Mette's letters sparked his desire to see her and the children; perhaps his relationship with Juliette Huet reminded him of the pleasure he had once had in female company; or perhaps the 10,000 francs made him disregard the cost of the trip and convinced him that now was the time to parade his success in front of his doubting in-laws. Or the impetus might have been professional. His recent contact with Danish artists like Willumsen and Ballin might have made him decide that the Scandinavian market was ripe for his art; or maybe he really did combine the trip to Copenhagen with a stop in Brussels, where five of his works were on view in the exhibition of Les XX. Any and all of these may have contributed to his decision to go to Copenhagen. Whatever the reasons, the result was an extraordinary and completely unexpected renewal of affection between husband and wife.

Copenhagen had changed little since Gauguin had been there in 1885, but like all European cities in the late nineteenth century, there was a bustle that marked the emergence of modern urban technology— electricity, telephones, and tramways. The apartment that Mette had moved to was in the heart of the city, where the heightened activity was most marked. When Paul arrived on March 7, he was met at the train station by Mette and the two oldest children—Emil, sixteen, and Aline, thirteen. As they had arranged, Paul checked into a nearby hotel. But for the next week, he spent all his waking hours in the small apartment of his family at 47 Vimmelskaftet, where he conversed with his oldest children in their school-learned French and stared mutely at the three younger boys, who spoke only Danish.

Paul had not corresponded with the children over the years, nor had he made any attempt to notice their birthdays or Christmases. But Mette had kept them in touch with their father by reading them what letters she received (passing over any abusive passages) and by speaking of him with respect. Because Paul had ridiculed their attempts to write in French and could not read Danish, Mette did not encourage them to write their father but made her own letters speak for them all. By carefully monitoring the children's relationship with their father, Mette had brought them up to have remarkably tolerant feelings toward him, which is noticeable in their later writings.[92] Seeing that he did not have to overcome the hostility that he had expected from his years of neglect, Paul flirted freely with them, particularly the two teenagers. Emil hung back, no doubt remembering his father's violence toward his mother, but Aline was captivated by the attention, and Paul teased her about being his wife someday.[93]

Mette arranged as best she could for her family and friends to renew their acquaintance with Paul now that they could perceive him as success-

ful. The publicity surrounding his auction in February had been noticed in Copenhagen, and his arrival was duly recorded in the newspaper, *Berlingske Tidende.* With his embroidered Breton sweater and longish bohemian hair curling over his ears, he struck an artistic pose when receiving callers in the afternoon. It was this attire that he immortalized when he took Emil and Aline downstairs to the photographer's studio for a photograph showing the similarity of their "Gauguin" profiles (fig. 52).

His newfound wealth allowed him to refresh his formal wardrobe: this time he did not complain about lacking the proper clothes for Copenhagen. In a more respectable guise, he apparently attended the theater with the rest of the extended Gad family to see Mette's translation of Zola's novel *Pot Bouille,* which had been turned into a play.[94] He also made contact with the few Danish artists he was still on good terms with who had not moved to Paris, including Theodor Philipsen.[95] He was so impressed with the interest that the Danish artists, critics, and collectors showed in him—largely based on the pre-1887 works that Mette displayed in the apartment and had lent to recent exhibitions—that he arranged with Mette that she should go to Paris as soon as she was free in June and bring back some of the paintings in storage there. After Mette's patient cultivation of the Danish market over the years, it seemed to both of them that the more recent work should be made available in Copenhagen.

Paul Gauguin must have been surprised to find that the demon wife he had castigated over the years was still the levelheaded, kind, and interesting woman he had fallen in love with almost twenty years before. The family lived just as she said they did—in a very simple manner made possible by her hard work and the occasional generosity of friends. The children were shy but obviously brought up to honor their father rather than to despise him, his frequent accusations notwithstanding. Furthermore, Mette was up-to-date in her reading and tastes and genuinely appreciated his art, as

165

much as she knew of it. Her original ideas and engaging conversation charmed him, as they did the intellectual circle she moved in. He came away smitten with her: "My adored Mette, . . . I know how difficult the present is for you, but now the future is assured and I shall be happy—very happy—if you want to share it with me. . . . Good-bye, dear Mette, dear children, love me well. And when I return, we will be remarried. It is therefore a betrothal kiss that I send you today. . . . Your Paul."[96]

The sudden and profuse affection that Paul displayed for Mette after so many years of scorn is not an uncommon occurrence in violent marriages such as theirs. Paul, defensive about his questionable behavior toward her (which couldn't be entirely hidden from their circle of friends and family), was relieved to be received warmly by his family and, in a sense, forgiven. Mette, anxious and careworn from her struggle to support the family, was grateful for any sign that her husband would again take up his half of the responsibility. She wanted desperately to be proud of him.

Furthermore, their now sexless relationship suited them both. Mette, with her hair cut short, had the androgynous appearance that titillated Paul but did not require any action on his part, and Mette was relieved that she was no longer expected to engage in what may have been sex tinged with violence, which was a recurring theme in her husband's art. Paul could also see that his wife was popular with important people and, somewhat jealous, teased her about the attentions of a Danish captain. This turn to their relationship surprised yet pleased Mette, who was still wondering about it when she wrote to Schuffenecker a year later. "I have also had a letter from him [Paul]—sweet and tender, as they have been since his visit to my home here. Perhaps he has come to see that I am worth something and that the 'cook' [that he wishes he had married] would not have managed as well as I have."[97]

In addition to everything else, what made Paul leave Copenhagen with such long-lasting affection for Mette was what pleased him most: she did not ask him to part with any of his newly won 10,000 francs. Once again, swayed by honeyed promises about their future financial security and family reconciliation, Mette let Paul leave without contributing a sou to the support of their children. Instead, they agreed between them that she would bring some works back from Paris to sell in Copenhagen, and that would fulfill his obligation. What Mette could not know was that Paul, despite his promises, would eventually ask for and receive most of the profits from those sales. But for the time being, they had formed a pact that both believed would provide for the future of the family. As Paul wrote to Mette, "In three years' time I shall have won a battle that will enable us—you and me—to live at our ease. You will rest and I will work."[98]

Paul Gauguin's resolution of his feelings of guilt and defensiveness that had resulted from his abusive behavior toward his family over the years was the crowning achievement of his spring of successful ventures. With money in his pocket and acclaim in the press and from avant-garde intellectuals, he could go off to Tahiti with a sense of well-being. This optimism can be seen not only in the affectionate letters written to his wife over the next two years but also in his enthusiastic embrace of all the new experiences of his travels. Although he inevitably slipped back into his old pattern of self-pity to persuade his friends back home to send more money, overall he enjoyed Tahiti — much more than his abortive trip to Panama and Martinique — and the contentment of a man newly at peace with himself shows in much of the art he produced there.

## 11   Tahitian Tourist
1891–93

If Gauguin approached the island of Tahiti at night, as almost all travelers on large ships did (to take advantage of the morning tide to enter safely into Papeete harbor), he would have missed the most spectacular beauty of the island—its majestic mountainous profile seen from a distance.[1] Once the tourist is within the harbor and onto dry land, Tahiti offers some of the least impressive scenery of any oceanic island. As Gauguin wrote in his autobiographical travelogue, *Noa Noa,* "To a man who has traveled a good deal this small island is not . . . a magic sight."[2] Tahiti is strongly reminiscent of Martinique in the thick undistinguished green foliage that grows down to the edge of the beach, obscuring the outlines of the land and views of the ocean. Most tourists to Tahiti quickly exhaust the few natural wonders the island has to offer and sail off to the more dramatic terrain of neighboring islands, like Mooréa, Huahine, and Bora Bora.[3]

Instead of being spectacularly beautiful, Tahiti's charm, then as now, lay in its more prosaic qualities, such as its pleasant climate and the legendary friendliness of the local population. It was a comfortable, rather than exotic, place to be. Those who made lengthy stays on Tahiti, like Gauguin, were not true adventurers, but people who enjoyed being in an attractive, out-of-the-way spot (like Pont-Aven or Le Pouldu) that had the relaxed mores of a large tourist population. Contrary to popular perception, Tahiti, the "Paris of the Pacific," was remote in its geographical location but not in its culture. By the time it became a French protectorate in 1844, it had already been westernized by the efforts of British missionaries and through its convenience as a mid-Pacific stopping point for shippers from Australia, New Zealand, South America, the United States, and Asia (fig. 53). At the turn of the century, Tahiti also hosted small but recognizable communities from French colonies all over the world, including Martinique and Tonkin. A symbol of the international flavor of Tahiti was that the accepted currency in the 1890s was the Chilean dollar.

Also defying popular perception was the prominent role played by the native Tahitians in the government and culture of the island.[4] Rather than being a tragic race, removed from their land and traditions by the encroaching Westerners, the Tahitians were comfortably ensconced in all levels of the social hierarchy. Upper-class Tahitians tenaciously preserved their Polynesian heritage, but at the same time they often displayed more cosmopolitanism than their Western counterparts. This remarkable state of affairs had arisen because they still owned most of the land on the island and thus did not suffer the typical marginalization of native populations during the period of European colonization.[5]

Schools, courts, and government agencies of all kinds, including the
official (and only) newspaper, were largely bilingual—Tahitian and French.
The population of the island was relatively steady at about ten thousand
(which was probably down from the population in the eighteenth century,
when European "discoverers" began recording it), but since it had been
taken under the protection of the French government, there had been no
major decimations through war or disease. In fact, ever since Tahiti's ele-
vation to capital of the French possessions in the South Pacific, it had attracted
members of native aristocratic families from other islands of French Polynesia who wanted to lobby for their districts in the territorial legislature
and partake of the sophisticated pleasures of Papeete. Many of the residents
of Tahiti, therefore, brought with them the flavor of other islands—Tonga,
Bora Bora, the Marquesas.

When Gauguin was campaigning for funds for his trip, he frequently
cited the primitive living conditions on Tahiti as his reason for choosing it
as a destination, quoting a travel brochure that portrayed the natives as
living only "to sing and to make love."[6] If he actually believed such propa-
ganda, rather than using it mainly to impress his more gullible correspondents (his wife,[7] Schuffenecker,[8] Willumsen[9]), he would surely have been
surprised to find the educated mix of Westerners and Polynesians living in
conditions of modern ease and moderate prosperity. But rather than complaining of being misled by false information, as he had when he went to Panama, he saw all the advantages of the island upon which he had rather
arbitrarily chosen to spend the next two years.

On a professional level, these advantages included local interest in and
assistance with his painting, as well as the convenience of regular ship-
ments bringing mail, newspapers, and art supplies to the island and finished
paintings away from it. On a personal level, Gauguin soon re-created his
circle of admiring young men and was able to indulge in swimming, sun-
bathing, and a daring degree of public nudity. Finally and most importantly,
he found irresistible the open encouragement of sexual practices that had
always intrigued him but were frowned upon in Europe. Among them were

169

those involving adolescent girls and the open tolerance of violent behavior toward them. Gauguin left Europe in an optimistic mood, but his success there was only a prelude to the paradise he found in Tahiti—not one of biblical purity but one that allowed him to indulge his deepest erotic fantasies of pleasure and pain. There can be little wonder that the South Seas captured his imagination.

What is fascinating about Gauguin's life on Tahiti is that the realities of the situation differed from his representation of them in his art and

writings and, further, that the island is virtually unrecognizable in them. From the rich, flowerlike colors to the nude bathing figures, Gauguin's paintings show that his imagination was so stimulated by the extraordinary sexual opportunities he encountered there that he transformed the mild, ordinary island into a land of rare beauty.

Two paintings that seem to epitomize all that is exotic about Tahiti, *Vahine no te Vi (Woman of the Mango)* and *Fatata te Miti (By the Sea)*, are actually based on ideas and motifs that Gauguin had been working with for years before he came to the South Seas (figs. 54–55). *Vahine no te Vi*, for instance, gives visual form to the story of the young woman with the enchanted mango that he had first used in a letter to his wife from Martinique in 1887. *Fatata te Miti* reuses the pose of the woman in the waves, which he first formulated in 1889 (see fig. 43). In this painting he has replaced the drab brown volcanic beach of Tahiti with a fantastic decorative foreground of pinks and purples. Neither painting is based on what Gauguin *saw*. Still, Tahiti triggered his use of the vivid colors and sensual poses that explode on his canvases during this time. In Martinique, when the young woman offered the mango, Gauguin presumably declined. But in Tahiti he, like Adam, was happy to succumb to the temptation of the forbidden fruit. It was not by accident that the pose of the woman in this painting was based on the Joseph in a drawing of the biblical story of seduction, Prud'hon's *Joseph and Potiphar's Wife,* that Gauguin knew well.[10] Gauguin changed the gender of the figure from male to female and changed the seduced to the seducer: he reveled in all the possibilities of erotic encounters that he found in Tahiti.

On the surface, Gauguin's experiences, as far as they can be reconstructed, were those of a typical Western tourist to the island. He stayed in the usual hotels and guesthouses described in travel guides, visited the recommended sights, and socialized with the hospitable upper-class community. But his intimate and erotic experiences were such that when he painted his glowing canvases and wrote about his Tahitian experiences in *Noa Noa,* taking the familiar tourist route was transformed into an odyssey of primitive travel and forbidden passions.

The outline of Gauguin's life on Tahiti from 1891 to 1893 is relatively simple. After spending a few months in Papeete, he arranged to rent a house in Mataiea, on the south side of the island, where he stayed until his return to Paris. He received a warm welcome, and throughout his stay the Tahitian residents did their best to help him accomplish his artistic mission. The Paris news was particularly well disseminated, albeit six weeks late, and Gauguin found that Mirbeau's article on him in *Le Figaro* had preceded him.[11] As on Martinique, many residents of Tahiti kept abreast of art and literary news and were eager to welcome such a famous Impressionist to their shores.

The French and British residents on Tahiti were mostly business and professional people whose families had been established on the island for years, if not generations.[12] Their children were sent to school in France, England, or the United States and returned to marry and enter the family occupation. It was also relatively common for these Europeans to marry into the important Tahitian families, which still owned most of the land and ruled the local provinces.[13] The higher government posts were filled with political appointees from France, who changed with some frequency, as did the military officers in their normal rotations between France, Tahiti, and the rest of the French colonial world.[14]

Gauguin found that this temporary French population of high status was sophisticated in its tastes and familiar with developments of the Parisian avant-garde. He immediately befriended the naval captain, Swaton, with whom he had sailed on the last leg of his trip from Nouméa to Tahiti.[15] He also availed himself of the friendship and willing service of Swaton's young lieutenant Jénot, with whom he recapitulated the aesthetic debates that had previously engaged so many similar young men in Paris and Brittany. Jénot's apartment, conveniently located along the gracious, tree-lined curve of the Papeete harbor, served as a meeting place for Gauguin, Swaton, and others who entertained themselves in the time-honored custom of talking and drinking.

But Gauguin had not come to Tahiti to while away his days among the young French officers in imitation of Parisian café life. Always mindful of the steps necessary to achieve fame and fortune, he was eager to establish himself among collectors, patrons, and others who might be useful to him in the new setting. To this end, he managed, with Jénot's help, to make the acquaintance of the local moneyed class, including such prominent citizens as the mayor of Papeete, François Cardella; the lawyer and businessman Auguste Goupil (he had no connection to the Goupil Gallery); and the premier physician of the island, Charles Chassaniol, who was also the intimate friend of Marau, queen of Tahiti, whom Gauguin met in turn.[16] Because of his official French mission, Gauguin also had access to the French territorial governor, Etienne Lacascade, upon whom he called the day of his arrival.[17]

Gauguin's rank as an official painter and his fame, established by Parisian newspapers, helped to make him acceptable in the upper circles of Tahitian society. But it is also true that most tourists to Tahiti, who, like Gauguin, exhibited the hallmarks of gentility and prosperity, recorded meeting the same people and being welcomed into Tahitian society.[18] The educated local population was eager for contact with interesting people from the outside world and showed surprisingly little suspicion of foreigners. A survey of the writings of travelers to this part of the world around the time of Gauguin's residence on Tahiti, by Pierre Loti, Robert Louis Stevenson, Henry Adams, and the many other less famous authors of Tahitian travel literature, reveals that Gauguin's experiences with local society were typical.

There was much interest in Gauguin's art, particularly since he must have let it be known that he was something of a portraitist. He boasted to Mette, "I think I shall soon have some well-paid commissions for portraits: I am bombarded with requests to do them. I am making the utmost difficulties about it at present (the surest way of getting good prices). In any event, I think I can earn money here, a thing on which I did not count."[19] The potential patrons could not have known Gauguin's style, because he does not seem to have brought any work with him except perhaps the recent etching of Mallarmé, but from Mirbeau's article in *Le Figaro,* they would have been aware that his work was avant-garde, and thus they should be given credit for even considering such commissions.[20] As time went on, and Gauguin's experimental style was fully revealed, the enthusiasm for portraits by this visiting artist waned, but Gauguin did eventually complete several portraits of people from Tahitian society (Captain Swaton, Suzanne Bambridge, Atiti Suhas, and Vaïte Goupil); and although their family traditions had it that the portraits were "quickly relegated to the attic," the patrons must have chosen such a portraitist with their eyes open.[21] Gauguin provided a link to the Parisian intelligentsia, which otherwise they would only have been able to read about in their slow-to-arrive newspapers and journals.

The hospitality of local society in and around Papeete soon persuaded Gauguin to drop his bohemian pose and conform. His uniform of embroidered Breton vest and felt cowboy hat, which he defiantly wore as he disembarked from the ship expecting to encounter the hostility of narrow-minded colonialists, was soon replaced by the white tropical-weight suit that had been adopted in such locations for its combination of respectability and comfort.[22] Gauguin found that formal dress was not a burden, and when not in public, he, like most Westerners, adopted some version of the loose, cool cotton apparel (shirts and the wrapped skirts, or *pareus,* for men, missionary gowns for women) usually associated with native Tahitians.[23]

As soon as he established himself socially and rented a small house in the residential neighborhood behind the cathedral, Gauguin applied himself to his work. Lieutenant Jénot was fascinated by Gauguin's artistic process and participated to the extent of his abilities. He offered his own apartment as a studio and watched as Gauguin set up his stock of paints and canvases—measuring, stretching, and priming—and as he finally painted.[24] Gauguin was thrilled to find someone to do his errands, as Schuffenecker and Monfreid had in Paris, and Jénot became involved in finding local substitutes for materials that Gauguin ran out of or ordering them through the local shippers who ran the regular shuttle to San Francisco.

Jénot also went in search of models for Gauguin, who was primarily interested in people and scenes indigenous to Tahiti, as dictated not only by his aesthetic preferences but also by his official mission, which he no doubt made known to as many people as possible. He took lessons in the language and accumulated information about the culture. He soon realized that the melting-pot society, pleasant as it was, made it difficult to isolate what exactly was native to the island; only by delving into Tahiti's history could he clarify what the Tahitian characteristics were before the advent of the Europeans. Because many people he met were also interested in this topic, he had no trouble obtaining both oral and written histories. Few households were without copies of such classics on Tahitian culture as *Voyages aux îles du Grand Océan* (1837) by J. A. Moerenhout or, at the very least, Loti's famous novel *The Marriage of Loti.*

Coincidentally for Gauguin, the French government had recently introduced a formal registry of land ownership on the island that required everyone to establish their right to the property they claimed.[25] For those who had acquired land before the French protectorate began in 1844, primarily the Tahitian ruling families, it was necessary to put into writing the genealogies that traced their hegemony into the distant past. Thus the past was very much on the minds of prominent members of Tahitian society, and the exercise of recording it swept many visitors to the island into the romantic narrative. Henry Adams, the American historian and writer, who visited Tahiti with the painter John La Farge in 1890–91, was tapped by Queen Marau (fig. 56) to write down the elaborate history of her family, the Tevas, as it tumbled musically from the lips of her grandmother Hinaarii.[26] Meanwhile, Marau, who was herself a conscientious preserver of island history, was writing out the songs and legends that she had heard over the years.[27]

Gauguin met Queen Marau only months after Adams and La Farge left Tahiti and was himself impressed with the cultural heritage that was still very much on her mind. The death of her husband, Pomare V, on June 12, 1891, only a few days after Gauguin's arrival on Tahiti, put the past in an especially elegiac light, because Pomare was the last to occupy the largely honorary throne. Marau, even though she and Pomare had divorced in 1887, was in charge of the ceremonial decorations for the king's lying-in-state. Knowing that the recent arrival Gauguin was an official artist, a government

functionary politely asked his advice on the decorative scheme that Marau was carrying out; Gauguin, just as politely, deferred to her superior qualifications in this matter.[28] As Gauguin came to know her better, he saw in her "the remembrance of her ancestor [that] the great chieftain Tati conferred on her, on her brother, on the whole of that family in general, a real impressiveness. In her eyes, a sort of vague presentiment of those passions which shoot up in an instant — an island rising from the Ocean and the plants beginning to burgeon in the first sunshine."[29]

But even Queen Marau, whose maiden name was Joanna Marau Salmon, was more typical of the hybrid Tahitian of her generation than of the fictional purebred that Gauguin and other romantic Westerners came in search of. Daughter of a Jewish British banker, Alexander Salmon (who came to Tahiti in 1841), and a princess of the ruling family of the district of Papara, Marau was one of several Salmon siblings who dominated Tahitian business and society in the 1880s and 1890s. Her brother Tati Salmon maintained the grand family home in Papara, where she joined him as hostess after her estrangement from King Pomare. Although they preferred English-speaking society to French (Adams and La Farge, as well as numerous other American and British tourists, visited them in Papara), it would be surprising if Gauguin had not also been invited to join them for days of sightseeing in their district and for the long discussions of Polynesian culture and history that had charmed so many others.[30]

Invitations such as these to visit the country houses of prominent Tahitian families were freely given to important visitors to the island. And visitors could easily avail themselves of such invitations. Transportation

175

to all but the most remote areas of the far end of "Little Tahiti," the bulbous peninsula attached to the southeast coast of the main island, was simple and efficient. A road substantial enough to support all manner of horse-drawn carriages and trucks had long encircled the main island, and a public conveyance for mail and passengers left from Papeete to traverse the road on a regular schedule several times a day. Since the farthest town on the main island, Taravao, was only about forty miles from Papeete, a traveler never had to plan on taking more than a few hours to reach any destination. If public transportation was not desirable, a tourist could find horses and carriages for hire at several stables in town.[31]

It is likely that Gauguin—after learning that information about the history of this culture could be procured on visits to the country homes of the important district families, and after scouting the island himself from a buggy or the mail coach—became convinced that the customs and landscapes of the island could best be studied during a lengthy stay in the country. This was to his taste anyway, because he had been staying in the French countryside for most of the past four years. By the end of the summer he was happily ensconced in the district of Mataiea, one district beyond Papara, as the guest of the local ruling family there.[32]

Gauguin's hosts, Tetuanui and Haamoura Tavana, were both from distinguished families in Mataiea.[33] Tetuanui became chief of the district in 1890, following in the footsteps of his father, and the land upon which the couple built their two-story Western-style house with sweeping verandas overlooking the sea had been given to them by Haamoura's family. The couple had no children of their own but, in the Tahitian fashion, adopted twenty-five from other families, whom they raised and launched into the upper spheres of Tahitian society.[34] They had gone as representatives of Tahiti to the Exposition Universelle of 1889 and may have dined at the Café Volpini surrounded by Gauguin's paintings. Although they spoke French, the preferred language *en famille* was Tahitian, and their guests were expected to use their time in Mataiea to perfect their skills in speaking this language.[35]

The French system of government of the island preserved the traditional Tahitian districts, which had each been ruled by chiefs in a hereditary system. Traditionally in Polynesian culture the chief was primarily responsible for the judicious use of the resources of his district—both land and sea—and oversaw local agriculture, fishing, and manufacturing.[36] In return, the chief was entitled to signify his rank with an elaborate dwelling and large guesthouses.[37] In the 1890s, the guesthouses were an important part of a district chief's compound, because most chiefs charged their guests for their hospitality and thus ran a kind of resort. The 1906 travelogue by Clement Wragge, *The Romance of the South Seas*, gives a clear picture of the situation for travelers like Gauguin: "So to Papara, and here we are at the south-western extremity of Tahiti. No hotels are round the island, only what may be termed 'guest-houses.' Accommodation here can be got at a beautiful bungalow down by the beach, belonging to Tati [Salmon], our friend at Papeete. He is Chief of the district, and deservedly beloved by all his people. Then there is Lehertal's restaurant, even more handy; and if one desires to prolong the stay, a villa can be rented at a reasonable price."[38]

Some guests of the chief of Mataiea, like Frederick O'Brien, an American journalist who wrote many books on his travels in the South Seas, stayed in the main house with its elegant Parisian furnishings during his lengthy visit in the early 1910s.[39] But O'Brien found that the family itself stayed in the many smaller dwellings scattered about the ten acres of the homestead with its freshwater stream meandering toward the ocean. O'Brien reports that he ate at a table set with the silver, glass, and linen that the family eschewed for its own daily use.[40]

When Gauguin went to Mataiea to stay with the Tavanas, he chose instead to take one of the outlying buildings, which had two rooms and a simple porch and faced a flowing stream. He lived as did Tetuanui and Haamoura, their twenty-five adopted children, and other members of their extended family.[41] Somerset Maugham, who visited Tahiti in 1917 in preparation for his fictional account of Gauguin's life, *The Moon and Sixpence,* went to Gauguin's dwelling in Mataiea. He bought from the current owner the glass panes of a door that Gauguin had painted on and photographed the building.[42] Although the photograph doesn't bear it out, Gauguin described his hut as walled in with reeds in the traditional fashion: "The reeds of my hut in their spaced rows were visible from my bed with the moonlight filtering through them like an instrument of music. . . . My hut was Space, Freedom."[43]

O'Brien found this same sense of well-being at Mataiea: "In the house of the chief, Tetuanui, I knew a peace of mind and body as novel to me as my surroundings. For the first time since unconcerned childhood I felt my heart leap in my bosom when the dawn awoke me, and was glad merely that I could see the sun rise or the rain fall."[44]

Like Gauguin, O'Brien was intensely interested in what Tahiti had been like before contact with Europeans. He turned to his hosts for answers. "Over the breakfast we talked, Tetuanui and Haamoura answering my questions and taking me along the path of my inquiry into far fields of former customs and ancient lore. They were, as their forefathers, gifted in oral tradition, with retentive memories for their own past and for the facts and legends of the racial history. . . . On rainy days, when Chief Tetuanui did not oversee the making or repair of roads in his district, and always when we were both at leisure, I sat with him, and the elders of the neighborhood, and queried them, or repeated for correction and comment my notes upon their antiquities—notes founded on reading and my observation."[45]

Although Gauguin knew Tetuanui and Haamoura almost twenty years earlier than O'Brien, the custom of aristocratic Tahitians reciting their family histories and ancient lore was already well established. With this wealth of information at his fingertips, Gauguin was to find in Mataiea everything he needed to fulfill his mission and allow him to paint the masterpieces that have established for him a lasting fame. He spent most of the remaining year and a half on Tahiti living and painting peacefully in Tetuanui's guesthouse.

Most of the other artists and writers who visited Tahiti within a decade or two of Gauguin's stay there tried to capture the relaxed atmosphere of tropical life, the bewitching individuals who spoke so eloquently of their island's past glories, or the curious flora and fauna of the island. But

Gauguin was unmoved by such conventional tourist imagery and shrugged off the normal responsibilities of the foreign correspondent. Once, when Schuffenecker asked for details of Tahiti, he explained with some irritation, "If I were Madame de Sévigné, I would write you four long pages describing my house, the local landscape, and the shape of the noses of the people around here. But sorry, I am not Mme. de Sévigné and you will have to be satisfied with this type of letter. One day a painting will come and you will read my 'description' in a couple of seconds."[46] Even Gauguin's paintings were not truly descriptive, however, for he combined and invented motifs in a symbolist manner rather than accurately transcribing them. By nature and by aesthetic philosophy Gauguin resisted straightforward communication of his experiences either in his writing or in his painting, and his admonition "Be mysterious" (*Soyez mystérieuses*) came from the heart.

Gauguin's transformation of his life in Tahiti was the result of more than his well-established stylistic preferences. His desire to place his erotic adventures at the center of his representation of the South Seas not only served his own predilections but directly fed what he knew would be the unacknowledged hunger of the European audience for a fantasy world of unfamiliar sexual sensations. Thus he did not merely suggest, as most artists and writers did, that these "primitive" people practiced an unselfconscious nudity and open sexuality; he showed practices that were often perverse and painful, yet strangely beautiful. If Gauguin had produced only visual images of Tahiti, this sensation would have been too subtle to define with any certainty; but he also wrote about his trip, and the paintings together with *Noa Noa* give the full effect of Gauguin's erotic Tahiti (see fig. 60).

Because of the disjointed structure of his book and the different times that incidents were added to the manuscript, it is difficult to rely on *Noa Noa* for factual information and chronology. However, certain passages are descriptive enough of what he actually encountered that the writing seems rooted in his actual experience. Gauguin's depictions of Queen Marau and the funeral of Pomare, for example, are evocative of his life upon settling in Papeete and the people he associated with.[47] Similarly, the stories of his adventures around the island—hikes he took in the mountains, his trip halfway around the island to Hitiaa, his visit to the Maraa fern grottoes, a fishing expedition, and his attendance at a Tahitian wedding—were common experiences for tourists.[48] He was obviously trying to take in all the sights recommended to him. But the eerie light in which he casts these activities —his encounters with eels, *tupapaus* (ghosts), tale-telling fish—helps to raise his account above the standard tourist literature to something resembling symbolist fiction.

Indeed, it is soon clear that he is not just the average Westerner exploring for the sake of broadening his understanding of the world—he is, more than anything, a sexual tourist. Even the title *Noa Noa*, which means "fragrance," is used by Gauguin to indicate the aroma of a human body, particularly in sexual situations. Although sexual liaisons similar to those described by Gauguin were regularly reported in other contemporary travel accounts, Gauguin makes them central to the story and, in doing so, transforms the normally pedestrian Tahitian sojourn into an erotic holiday.

Gauguin makes his relationship with Tehamana (also called Tehura), his thirteen-year-old "wife," the shocking and sensual core of the book. He tells of traveling around the island to Faaone, not far from the tourist destination of Hitiaa, where a young girl is offered to him by her mother: "The old woman returned, followed by a tall young girl carrying a small parcel. Through her excessively transparent dress of pink muslin the golden skin of her shoulders and arms could be seen. Two nipples thrust out firmly from her chest."[49] When *Noa Noa* was published in 1901, even his collaborator, Charles Morice, was sensitive about the age of Tehamana and introduced a note into the text explaining that thirteen in Tahiti was like being eighteen or twenty in Europe.[50] Most subsequent commentators on *Noa Noa* have similarly tried to soften what Gauguin intended as pure titillation. Given his previous forays into sexual taboos (such as *Nude Breton Boy;* see fig. 44) and the story of a Japanese family having sex in front of their kiln (in *Intimate Journals*), it is certain that Gauguin emphasized the youth of the girl for dramatic effect.

It is also quite probable that Gauguin did indeed have a vahine who was in her early teens. The shocking evidence is that Western tourists were commonly offered young girls, usually by the girls' parents, to serve as companions for the duration of their stay on the island.[51] Loti's "marriage" to Rarahu, as well as his brother's "marriage" to a young island woman, was not fiction but a practice that was almost de rigueur for the French military, particularly officers, and other temporary European and American visitors who found themselves in similar situations. One young American reported that while staying with a family on the farthest coast of the island, the parents of an eleven-year-old encouraged her to get in bed with him: "'Go,' said Tema. 'We live here alone and very far from the white people. Perhaps never again will you have this opportunity. Go, sleep beside the white man, small daughter.'"[52] In fact, he found that a Western visitor to Tahiti living alone was viewed with suspicion and that eventually someone would introduce a young woman into every white man's lodging.[53]

Westerners in their travelogues accounted for this phenomenon in a variety of ways. Some believed that it was motivated by greed, and Gauguin himself wondered whether Tehamana's "mother had ordered it, with her mind on money."[54] Because the man was expected to support the girl while she lived with him, there certainly was an economic basis to the arrangement. And although Gauguin took offense at a local Frenchwoman's description of Tehamana as a whore, there was some truth to the appellation as it was understood by Westerners. Gauguin's later addition of a story about Tehamana wheedling a pair of copper earrings from him hints that Gauguin thought her behavior manipulative and mercenary. "Vahine," which means "woman," is usually translated into English as "wife," and Gauguin's use of the term implies that he felt a conjugal bond to Tehamana; but it should be pointed out that Gauguin also referred to Titi, a woman he knew in Papeete and whom he clearly thought of as a whore, as his vahine.[55]

Other explanations of the youth of these young Tahitian lovers and their inevitable pregnancy pointed to the common Polynesian practice of adopting each other's children, which guaranteed that all children conceived would be adequately cared for. In Western societies young girls were discouraged from getting pregnant in part because they would be unable to care for their offspring. In Tahitian society no child would be denied proper care, no matter what the capabilities of his or her mother were. One Englishman even concluded that "they esteem it an honour to have children, especially if the father is a European."[56] Many observers also commented on the fact that Polynesian husbands would offer their wives to European men, whereas they were murderously jealous of other Polynesian men.[57]

When Gauguin's real-life Tehamana was pregnant, he wrote to Monfreid, "Good Heavens, I seem to sow everywhere! [referring to Juliette Huet's pregnancy in early 1891]. But here it does no harm, for children are welcome and are spoken for in advance by all the relatives. It's a struggle as to who should be the mother and father nurses. For you know that in Tahiti a child is the most beautiful present one can give. So I do not worry about its fate."[58] Indeed, there is no further mention of the baby in Gauguin's letters; it was probably adopted from its teenage mother and raised in another home.[59]

This letter to Monfreid, written at the end of the summer of 1892, establishes that Gauguin's relationship with the young woman was in effect by January of that year or, at the latest, six months after his arrival in Tahiti. Although the story in *Noa Noa* of his journey by horseback around the island to Faaone to look for a wife is colorful, the real story of the arrangement may have been more prosaic and in line with other tourists' experiences. After living on and off with Titi at Mataiea for a few months, Gauguin would finally have been persuaded to take in a young relative of one of the people on Tetuanui's compound. In his *Noa Noa* story of Tehamana's infidelity while he is off fishing, Gauguin refers to a neighboring "mother-in-law" who brings them coconuts. "She questioned Tehamana with a look. She knew."[60] This mother-in-law may have been his hostess, Haamoura, who had adopted so many children. When O'Brien stayed at their house, he was waited on by a fourteen-year-old girl who may have been intended to become his companion: "I ate alone mostly, at a table on the veranda in front of my chamber, waited on by Tatini, a very lovely and shy maiden of fourteen years. To her I talked Tahitian, as with all the family, in an effort to perfect myself in that tongue."[61]

Gauguin's decision to take in a vahine may have had a more practical side as well. If related to the host family, she may have been his housekeeper and provider of food. She may also have had to care for him when he suffered a sudden hemorrhaging in his lungs that sent him to the hospital in Papeete for a brief stay.[62] He left the hospital early to save money and no doubt required some nursing during his convalescence. Finally, he would have found it convenient to have a model in his household, even though he often talks of painting from his imagination. Artists in Tahiti found that Tahitian women were very reluctant to pose in the nude unless it was considered part of lovemaking. O'Brien encountered the American artist George Biddle on Tahiti and reported that he "had to make love to his girl models to induce them to pose in the altogether, for money would not make them adopt the garb of Venus."[63] When Gauguin's neighbor asked if Manet's

*Olympia* (a reproduction of which was hanging on Gauguin's wall) was a painting of his vahine, he did not comprehend that, in her eyes, only a woman who was sexually involved with the artist would let herself be painted in the nude.[64]

Gauguin's genuine delight at having an adolescent lover pervades *Noa Noa* and most likely colored his perception of life in Tahiti. The submissiveness of the girl was highly erotic to him. In *Noa Noa* he admits to rape fantasies about all the local girls: "I saw plenty of calm-eyed young women, I wanted them to be willing to be taken without a word: taken brutally. In a way a longing to rape." He found that such fantasies were acceptable in this society: "The old men said to me, speaking of one of them: 'Mau tera (take this one).'" [65] When he meets Tehamana, she follows him without question, and though at first "impenetrable," she gradually yields more and more. With, no doubt, some twisting of her arm, she follows the monster's admonition to all women, "Soyez amoureuses."

When Tehamana confesses to an episode of infidelity, she begs him to beat her, and the sight of the abject submission of this beautiful creature delights him. "'You must beat me, strike me hard,'" she implores. "A beautiful golden flower, whose Tahitian *noa noa* filled all with fragrance, and which I worshipped as an artist, as a man . . . I kissed her."[66]

Visitors to Tahiti knew that women were often beaten by their *tane* (men or husbands), and most Western men reported this with some amazement. A 1901 account of Tahiti describes how the "half-caste" son of the prominent lawyer (and friend of Gauguin) Auguste Goupil attacked his girlfriend in a jealous rage: "He pulled out half her hair, blacked her eyes, and gave her a most fearful hiding. I must tell you that a Tahitian girl does not seem to care for a man unless he proves his affection by hammering her at least once a week."[67] Given Gauguin's previous interest in the interrelationship of sex and violence in his art, as in the 1889 panel *Soyez amoureuses,* he would have felt an affinity for this society. Some years later, he titled a brilliantly colored painting of a man beating a woman *Tahitian Love.*[68]

The painting that monumentalizes Tehamana's delicious abject submission and fear is the famous *Manao Tupapau (Spirit of the Dead Watching),* dated 1892 (fig. 57). It is a direct descendent of Gauguin's previous series of frightened Eves from 1889. This time, the monster or snake is the artist (or the viewer) — at whom Tehamana/Tehura turns her head cautiously to peek. Tehamana's fright is the central motif of the painting, as Gauguin explained in a letter to his wife. "I painted a nude of a young girl. In this position she is on the verge of being indecent. But I want it that way; the lines and movement are interesting to me. And so, I give her, in depicting the head, a bit of a fright."[69]

Having established the important things — the marginal indecency, the fright, the interesting lines and movement — he then must invent a pretext for the girl's emotions. He finds this in a narrative about a Maori girl's fear of spirits of the dead, which he represents by the head of an old woman in the upper left.[70] The story took on a different form when he wrote the first draft of *Noa Noa* (a year later), because he inserted it into his "erotic life" with Tehamana. In that account, he had just returned late one night from Papeete and struck a match in the dark room, only to find Tehamana con-

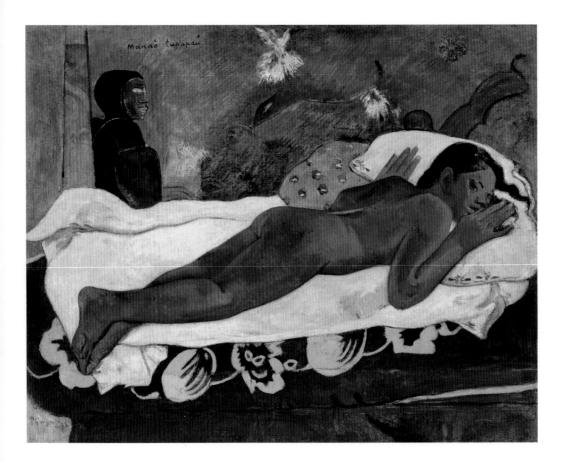

vulsed with fear from having been alone in the darkness.[71] Gauguin left that part of *Noa Noa* unfinished in that draft, so the next version includes a much more complex explanation of her fear and his reaction to it: "Tehura, immobile, naked, lying face downward, flat on the bed, with her eyes inordinately large with fear. She looked at me, and seemed not to recognize me. As for myself, I stood for some moments strangely uncertain. . . . Never had I seen her so beautiful, so tremulously beautiful. . . . How could I know what at that moment I might seem to her? Might she not with my frightened face take me for one of the demons and specters, one of the Tupapaus, with which the legends of her race people sleepless nights?"[72]

It is too simple to attribute the girl's terror to her belief in spirits and irrational fear of the dark.[73] Gauguin clearly gave himself a role in that fear in his old guise of devil (malin), monster—and now tupapau. Gauguin's previous battering of Mette suggests that despite his innocent rejection of Tehamana's pleas to punish her in *Noa Noa,* he very likely did abuse his Tahitian vahine, the submissive fear in her eyes being his erotic reward. His ability to convey in visual terms his erotic attraction to her fear confirms the underlying mixture of sex and violence that has made his series of Eves so intriguing over the years.

In *Manao Tupapau,* Gauguin also brings to fruition an almost gothic fascination with horror, which is evident in some of his favorite fiction over the years. An avid reader of Edgar Allen Poe,[74] he also enjoyed French stories of the macabre, such as Balzac's *Séraphita* (1836), de Maupassant's *Le Horla* (1887), and Maeterlinck's *L'Intruse* (1890).[75] Ghosts, sleep terrors, and androgyny figure strongly in the nineteenth-century gothic novel and continued through twentieth-century film in a form that has been called artificial horror. Whether real or artificial, the sensation is primarily a physical one, with all its orgasmic connotations.[76]

Gauguin suggests in *Noa Noa* another element to his celebration of the sensuality in Tahitian society that helps to explain the intention of the painting *Manao Tupapau*. This comes in the story of a hike into the mountains in which he expresses his homosexual desires, mainly in his wish to experience the "female" role, which he interprets as submissive: "To be for a minute the weak being who loves and obeys."[77] His erotic fascination with submission suggests that he identifies with the young girl in the painting, who, he imagines, receives pleasure from her fear and obedience. In the painting, her androgynous body is made more so by showing her from the back. Her buttocks are slightly raised and turned toward us; and a visible curved stroke of orange paint calls attention to the point of entry between them.

One final taboo in Europe, homosexuality, Gauguin presents so sensually in *Noa Noa* that his ultimate condemnation of it tends to be forgotten. Like sex with young girls, homosexuality was an accepted part of Tahitian eroticism. Traditional Polynesian cultures included openly homosexual men called *mahus,* who had been noted by the earliest European explorers. Travelers in Gauguin's era were still talking about the cross-dressing mahus, who could be seen throughout Papeete and the districts.[78] According to Lieutenant Jénot, Gauguin himself was labeled *taata vahine* (man-woman) when he first arrived in Tahiti with hair down to his shoulders.[79] He cut his hair short when he realized that he was attracting attention, obviously as reluctant to be branded a homosexual in Papeete as he had been in Paris. But the exhilaration of such a declaration stayed with him and found its way into *Noa Noa,* where he must have known it would raise eyebrows.

Two stories from the book tell of Gauguin's attraction to Polynesian men, and both come before his "marriage" to Tehamana. The men are extremely handsome and generous to Gauguin, helping him in some fundamental way. The first story is about a man with an ax: "The nearly naked man was wielding with both hands a heavy ax that left, at the top of the stroke, its blue imprint on the silvery sky and, as it came down, its incision on the dead tree, which would instantly live once more a moment of flames—age-old heat, treasured up each day." This man locks eyes with Gauguin and sees that he is hungry. After arranging for a child to bring him food, he "went by and with a kindly expression, without stopping, said to me a single word: 'Paia.' I understood vaguely. 'Are you satisfied?'"[80] Gauguin's

translation of "paia" as "satisfied" is curious because as an adjective it actually means "slippery," and as a noun it means "sodomy."[81]

Gauguin's use of this word with its homosexual connotation was likely to have been intentional. He uses it in such titles as *Landscape at Paia* and *Woodcutter of Pia* (*sic*) that have been associated with paintings of the man with the ax (fig. 58). Tahitians were known for their salty language, and Gauguin probably learned this and other sexual terms in the Tahitian language early in his stay.[82] With his typical sly humor, he uses the term in *Noa Noa* to refer to eating, which a general audience will take without suspicion, but those in his smaller circle would recognize it as sexual.

The second story is about Gauguin's infatuation with a young Tahitian man who was very interested in his art: "The young man was faultlessly handsome, and we were great friends. Sometimes in the evening, when I was resting from my day's work, he would ask me the questions of a young savage who wants to know a lot of things about love in Europe, questions that often embarrassed me."[83] One day the young man offers to guide Gauguin into the mountains, where he can find wood suitable for carving. As Gauguin follows him along a narrow path, he is intoxicated by the scent (*noa noa*) of the youth: "His lithe animal body had graceful contours, he walked in front of me sexless. . . . And we were only . . . the two of us—I had a sort of presentiment of crime, the desire for the unknown, the awakening of evil. . . . I drew close, without fear of laws, my temples throbbing."[84] Although the man turns around at that moment and Gauguin comes to his senses and is chastened ("it was a young man, after all"), he realizes that his companion "had not understood. I alone carried the burden of an evil thought; a whole civilization had been before me in evil and had educated me."[85]

Gauguin's protestation that his evil desires were shamed and dissipated by the innocence of his companion is belied by the orgasmic conclusion of the journey when they reached the heights of the mountains. "Savages both of us, we attacked with the ax a magnificent tree that had to be destroyed to get a branch suitable to my desires. I struck furiously and, my hands covered with blood, hacked away with the pleasure of sating one's brutality and of destroying something."[86] As they returned, Gauguin again admired the beautiful back of his friend and compared it to the graceful rosewood that they were carrying for Gauguin's sculpture: "The tree smelt of roses, *Noa Noa*. We got back in the afternoon, tired. He said to me: 'Are you pleased?' 'Yes'—and inside myself I repeated: 'Yes.'"[87]

As with Tehamana, it is impossible to identify Gauguin's friend, whom he named Totefa in later drafts of the manuscript. Possibly he had such a warm relationship with one of Tetuanui's adopted children who lived in the chief's complex. In Lieutenant Jénot's reminiscences, on the other hand, Jénot describes how fascinated he himself was with Gauguin's art making and how they would talk for hours about aesthetic principles. Furthermore, it was Jénot who led Gauguin up into the mountains to the home of an old man who could supply wood for Gauguin's sculptures.[88] Jénot's youth and eager inexperience, though not the result of upbringing in another culture, may nevertheless have been intoxicating to Gauguin. If, in *Noa Noa,* Gauguin transformed his French lieutenant into a Tahitian, it may have been to protect the man who later returned to France and married, and it may also have been to add the spice of interracial coupling to an already provocative story.

The heightened sensuality of *Noa Noa* with its carefully framed stories of forbidden sexual practices was surely calculated to intrigue a French audience. But those who observed Gauguin after his return from Tahiti testify to his genuine excitement about his experiences there. Thadée Natanson, editor of the journal *La Revue blanche,* in which *Noa Noa* was published in installments in 1897, remembered hearing Gauguin recite the stories in his apartment while he was working on the manuscript. Natanson described how Gauguin's eyes shone when he spoke of Tahiti, a place where "both male and female [seemed] to have none other than sensual love."[89]

Gauguin repeated the story of the excursion into the mountains many times, and his listeners wondered at the sexual implications: "Without the story-teller stressing it at all, we were disturbed, indeed more than he, by the ambiguous sensuality that radiated from the brilliant back of the youth to the teeth of his smile, of which the painter only said that they were hardly different from the body and smile of his companions [in France] of the same age."[90] As Gauguin inserted into a later version of *Noa Noa,* "Even after this long time I still take pleasure in remembering the *true* and *real* emotions in [Totefa's] *true* and *real* nature."[91]

Gauguin's encounter with exotic sensuality in Tahiti was by far the most important aspect of his journey there, and it is no wonder that he was reluctant to leave and, once back in Paris, thought only of returning. As Natanson noted, "Nothing was more touching than the attachment he maintained to the enchantment of those happy isles."[92]

The paintings that Gauguin sent back to Europe from Tahiti convey in visual form the enchantment he felt. There is not a martyr-image to be found in the more than seventy finished paintings and sculptures. To borrow Gauguin's term from *Noa Noa,* the "calm-eyed" young men and women in his paintings are striking in their physiognomy, monumental stature, and rich coloring. Gauguin's tendency to caricature folk costume and peasant features, seen throughout his Brittany paintings, is seldom in evidence when he paints Tahitians.

One of the first paintings he finished in Tahiti, *Vahine no te Tiare (Tahitian Woman with a Flower),* represents a kind of welcome (fig. 59). The *tiare* is a sweet-smelling flower, akin to a gardenia, which is used for making the crowns, necklaces, and other decorations that are traditionally conferred on new arrivals to the islands. On Gauguin's first day in Papeete, Jénot took him to the club for French military and government officials, Le Cercle militaire, where he and Swaton were crowned with flowers by the vahines.[93] The fragrance of these welcoming flowers is part of every visitor's first impression of Tahiti and makes Gauguin's title, *Noa Noa,* imply that the book is a greeting or an introduction to Tahiti in the manner of a tiare.

The flowers were worn for other festive occasions, particularly when a romantic tryst was planned. Pierre Loti explained in *The Marriage of Loti* that the tiare, normally worn behind the ear, had a sexual connotation. "Whenever it is offered by a Tahitian girl to a young man, it has about the same significance as the handkerchief tossed by the sultan to his favorite concubine."[94] Thus, in Gauguin's painting, the woman seemingly has plucked the tiare from behind her ear and is not only welcoming the viewer with her noa noa, but offering to confer sexual favors as well.

The story from Gauguin's text that is meant to go along with *Vahine no te Tiare* is about a neighbor woman of pure Tahitian extraction whom Gauguin desires to paint. He is amused that she resists at first, but she finally returns after she has dressed in her finest gown and placed a tiare behind her ear. Gauguin interprets this as coquetry, or "the attraction of the forbidden fruit," harking back to his paintings of Eves helpless to resist seduction. Although he does not claim to have slept with this woman, he boasts of his conquest through the symbolic act of painting: "Without delay I began work, without hesitation and all of a fever. I was aware that on my skill as painter would depend the physical and moral possession of the model, that it would be like an implied, urgent, irresistible invitation."[95]

Gauguin suggests that this episode takes place in Mataiea and that the woman is unsophisticated in the conventions of Western portraiture. But by his own statement, this was one of the first paintings he executed in Tahiti, which would mean that it was one of those portrait studies mentioned by Jénot as having been executed in Papeete. The study for *Vahine no te Tiare,* which stayed in Jénot's hands long after his return to France, was identi-

187

fied by Jénot as a portrait of a woman named Teuraheimata of Potoru.[96] This portrait study was probably painted in Jénot's apartment, in accordance with Gauguin's custom in Papeete, and the model may have been one that Jénot procured. She is interesting not only because of the similarity of her name to Gauguin's vahine, Tehamana or Tehura in *Noa Noa*, but also because she was very unlikely to have been the naive country woman portrayed in the story. He may even have executed the finished painting in Papeete many months after he had begun living in Mataiea, because the painting was sent with a naval officer returning to France in March 1892, when Gauguin was having an extended stay in the capital.[97]

Gauguin had started out the new year of 1892 with alarming physical symptoms. For the second time since he arrived in Tahiti, he began hemorrhaging and spitting up large quantities of blood, which the doctor in the hospital in Papeete diagnosed as heart trouble and managed to get under control with digitalis. It is also possible that this was a symptom of the syphilis that would wreak havoc with his body and that he would finally admit to having contracted.[98] If he already feared that this and other bouts of illness he had suffered in the past few years were due to syphilis, the tragic disease of his generation, it may explain his attention to whether his sexual partners were sick. Knowing, for instance, that Titi was sick did not stop him from sleeping with her.[99] On the other hand, he was happy to find that Tehamana was not sick;[100] he may have had in mind the age-old superstition — still repeated in Asian countries — that sex with a virginal girl will pass a venereal disease on to her and cure the man who had it.[101] In Gauguin's case at least, following this prescription was not as callow an act as one might think. Until fairly recently, historians of medicine believed that syphilis had originated in the New World, and the indigenous peoples of the Americas and Oceania were resistant to the fatal symptoms that afflicted Europeans.[102]

Along with health problems came inexplicable financial problems. Perhaps staying at Tetuanui's guesthouse was more expensive than he thought, or perhaps he squandered his money in Papeete, or perhaps he made unwise investments in Paris through Morice.[103] By the time he was in the hospital, after only half a year on Tahiti, he was already complaining about his lack of funds. Letters home began harping on this theme by March of 1892, and when the recipients of the letters opened them that summer, they were stunned. "I don't see how he spent so much so fast," Mette wrote to Emile Schuffenecker, who had received the same disturbing news.[104] As usual, letters flew between Paris and Copenhagen as everyone involved in Gauguin's life tried to raise money for him. In Tahiti, Gauguin began petitioning the governor and writing letters back to the Ministry of Public Education and Fine Arts in Paris to garner free passage back to France.

The local community also did its best for Gauguin; one ship captain paid him 400 francs as a down payment on a portrait of his wife.[105] During the summer of 1892 he sold two wood carvings for 300 francs.[106] With this amount he claimed he could live for three months, which makes the dissipation of his original fortune especially difficult to believe. It is hard not to suspect, as Vincent van Gogh had, that Gauguin was less than candid about the true state of his finances. In the fall he received 300 francs from Monfreid.[107] These small contributions seemed to keep him going until his request for a free voyage home was approved in late 1892, and he began to plan for a summer departure. All of the anxiety about money that runs through his letters, however, did not dim his enthusiasm for the South Seas. If he could afford to stay, he would, he said; and if he could amass a large enough amount (1,000 francs), he would go to what were considered the most exotic islands in the Pacific, the Marquesas.[108]

In the meantime, he lived peacefully in Mataiea, taking frequent trips into Papeete and painting. While in Tahiti he sent home nine canvases, and he calculated that he had completed another seventy paintings and a number of carvings, which he would bring back with him. He would leave for France in early June of 1893. At forty-five, he considered himself to be in reasonably good health, albeit much thinner than when he arrived and, he lamented, with nearly gray hair. After two years in the South Seas, he had much to feel pleased about. These years were the pinnacle of a life spent pursuing erotic sensations for personal and professional reasons, and he had every reason to believe that with these provocative paintings, he would now be able to dictate his own terms in the tough art world of Paris.

Although Paul Gauguin regretted leaving Tahiti, he looked forward to a cordial homecoming. Remarkably, he had managed to maintain a good relationship with his wife and important friends, such as Daniel de Monfreid, during the two years he was away. And because of the several paintings he had already sent, he had had strong indications that the work done in Tahiti would be well received. Europe seemed poised to welcome both the man and his art back into the fold. But what should have been a triumphant return, allowing him to take his rightful place as a recognized artist and a peaceful family man, turned into a morass of misunderstanding and disappointment on all fronts.

The crisis was not precipitated by a lack of artistic or monetary success, because, on the whole, his successes outweighed his failures. Rather, it was a matter of his old faults, exaggerated by the effort necessary to engineer his return to Parisian society, that forced him into a marginal position in the world of modern art that he had hoped to dominate. His arrogance cost him many potentially influential friends, and his penchant for questionable social and sexual behavior raised too many eyebrows for him to be embraced in the circles of successful modern artists to which he felt he belonged. As much as he wanted to be accepted in Paris, the motivation for him to subdue his more offensive impulses, which had never been overly strong, was now permanently eroded by his pleasant experience in Tahiti. He had had a taste of the more tolerant and accepting society of the islands and, thus armed with the alluring option of escaping for good, he made even less of an effort than ever to meet the standards of accepted European conduct.

It was during this period of conflict, as his ambitions for a successful European life faded, that he began *Noa Noa,* the first of several semiautobiographical manuscripts written to convey the life he wanted his public to think he had lived (fig. 60).[1] Always conscious of his image, he had previously assumed many guises (Breton ship captain, Peruvian noble/savage, martyr, gypsy) and at times written letters in an exaggerated and misleading fashion. But *Noa Noa* was the first book-length essay, written for publication, to spell out his life on Tahiti—and, in the process, to set a standard for originality and sensuality against which all future artists' lives would be measured. Paradoxically, Gauguin's creation of an erotic life came when his own was becoming less so.

What fell apart almost immediately was Paul and Mette Gauguin's dream of a reunion. Looking back, we can see that this dream had been tenuous at best—formulated during a heady week of reacquaintance and

kept alive through monthly letters that often chased each other across two oceans. Mette had conscientiously gone about building Paul's reputation in Copenhagen in preparation for what she believed would be Paul's eventual return to his family there. She went to Paris twice while Paul was in Tahiti to arrange for his works to be sent to Copenhagen.[2] At home, she courted collectors and began preparing for a large one-person exhibition. Paul was so pleased with her efforts that he graciously allowed her to keep the proceeds of her sales, showing an extraordinary understanding of her precarious financial situation. When he reported these sales to Monfreid after describing his own lack of funds, he wrote, "There is my money, you will say. But the poor woman is hard up. It doesn't matter, and things are coming my way in Denmark."[3] Nevertheless Mette did manage to send him 700 francs when he complained of poverty.[4]

Mette had been skeptical of the dream of reestablishing their marriage, but over time she came to believe in it wholeheartedly. She never lost sight of Paul's faults; but she hoped his success as an artist, which she had seen building in Paris before his trip, would mitigate, if not cure, the worst of them. She imagined that with more money he would be able to support the family once again, and with more public recognition, he would be less domineering in private. Mette wrote reassuringly to Emile Schuffenecker, with whom Paul had quarreled before he left for Tahiti, "If he really is to succeed some day, I think that you will reconcile with him; his immense pride, so difficult to bear, will be subdued, perhaps, with success."[5]

Husband and wife had their usual problems communicating by mail—they each accused the other of being vague and of not answering important questions—but they managed to work together quite well in matters of business while Paul was in Tahiti. Charles Morice and Paul's other new friends in Paris let him down as agents during his absence, but Mette proved to have the connections and management skills to promote him at a crucial time. In addition to the sales she made in Denmark, she also watched for exhibition opportunities. Apparently Paul and Mette had discussed organizing a solo exhibition in Copenhagen during his stay there in 1891, and it is often mentioned in their correspondence. As Mette wrote to Emile Schuffenecker after receiving a shipment of Paul's paintings from Paris, "My paintings are here, but I don't think I'll hold the exhibition until spring. Paul promised me some works from Tahiti by then."[6] By the end of 1892, frustrated by Paul's vagueness, Mette had abandoned the idea of an exhibition: "I talked to him many times, but since he generally does not respond [when] I ask him something, I gave up the idea until his return, [and it is] something he no longer talks about."[7]

Paul, on the other hand, may not have responded directly to Mette, but to his other correspondents he presented the exhibition as a fait accompli and worked diligently during the fall of 1892 to put together a good group of canvases to send.[8] Eight paintings were duly shipped off in the care of an artillery officer returning to France who, upon arrival, put them on the train to Monfreid in Paris, C.O.D.[9] Monfreid was to show them informally to all interested parties before shipping them to Mette in Copenhagen. Because of the miscommunication with his wife, these paintings arrived in Paris after Mette had given up the plan for an exhibition.

Yet only a few weeks later another opportunity for an exhibition arose. It would be organized by the Danish painters Theodor Philipsen ("the only friend Paul made here")[10] and Johan Rohde, whom Mette had sent to the Schuffeneckers' home in Paris with a letter of introduction the summer before.[11] Philipsen and Rohde had identified Vincent van Gogh and Paul Gauguin as the two most interesting painters of the new style and were making arrangements to borrow as many works as they could from the artists' families and other private collectors for a show that would open in March of 1893. Theo van Gogh's widow, Jo van Gogh–Bonger, was now back in Holland with two hundred of the paintings that Vincent and Theo had so carefully accumulated in anticipation of Vincent's eventual debut in Paris. She agreed to lend twenty paintings and a number of drawings.[12]

At the same time Philipsen approached Mette for an equal number of loans.[13] Aware that there wasn't enough time to discuss this new possibility with Paul by mail, Mette made the decision to lend works she already had on hand in Copenhagen and wrote Schuffenecker and Monfreid to send on the new batch from Tahiti: "I can hardly refuse [to lend to the exhibition], because [Philipsen] assures me that it will be a great opportunity to sell, and that's why I ask you to tell M. Daniel to send me the works you talked about a few weeks ago. . . . I would like to be able to send something to Paul again, from whom I receive letters that are sad and discouraged."[14]

Mette's optimism soared when the Tahiti pictures arrived and were acclaimed by Philipsen, Rohde, and the increasingly important modern artists of Copenhagen (who had organized their own exhibiting group, the Frie Udstilling, under whose auspices the Gauguin–Van Gogh exhibition was held). Actually Mette was hopeful that the new canvases would sell at the rather high prices that Paul had placed on them. She herself seemed to be genuinely impressed, and she reported to Schuffenecker that "everyone finds [them] superb!"[15] She was not fazed by the sexuality of nudes like *Manao Tupapau,* for many of his male and female nudes passed through her hands over the years, and in fact, she may have been one of his more liberal viewers.[16]

As it turned out, the exhibition helped Mette to sell several of Paul's earlier canvases, but surprisingly only two from Tahiti—and one of those to her faithful brother-in-law, Edvard Brandès. She concluded rather sadly, "I don't think that Paul's art is understood by the public—most of [the paintings] are still hanging."[17] But the enthusiasm of the modern art community in Copenhagen never wavered, and she was still hopeful that she would sell more after the exhibition closed and that the tide had turned for her and her husband. She had come to believe in him as an artist and as a man, and her desire was now to see "something good result for this great man of a husband I have."[18]

By April of 1893, Gauguin's wife and friends in Europe had begun to get letters promising that he would return shortly. But inexplicably, when his plans were set, he did not write to anyone of his travel schedule. Consequently, they spent the summer trying to guess when he would set foot again in France.[19] As might be expected, when he did disembark in Marseilles on August 23 with no money in his pocket, no arrangements had been made to welcome him, and everyone was still out of town for the summer.[20] Mette was expecting to see him in the countryside—"Naturally I would like to see him, and I understand he wants to see us all"—but was worried about being in Denmark when he arrived.[21] She was right to be concerned; the difficulties he encountered upon his return brought out the worst in him.

The last letters Gauguin had received from Europe before he left Tahiti had been written in February and March, just after the batch of Tahiti paintings had arrived. Everyone he knew in Paris and Copenhagen had written glowingly of them, raising his hopes for the Copenhagen exhibition and the prospect of having a substantial sum of money waiting for him. With this in mind and with optimistic notions of other sales that might have been made in Paris, he allowed himself to arrive in France with very little cash on hand.[22]

A few telegrams from Marseilles to friends yielded enough in loans for him to get to Paris, and once there he expected to find money from sales waiting for him at his gallery, Boussod and Valadon. When he discovered that they had made no sales, he severed the relationship on the spot and took all his paintings and ceramics out of the gallery.[23] His last and greatest hope was that his wife had sold a large number of paintings in Copenhagen and that she would send him a sizable bank draft as soon as she heard from him.

But to his supreme annoyance he waited about three weeks to hear from her, all the while sending her nastier and nastier notes complaining about her silence.[24] About September 12, he began to receive her letters, which she had addressed to his first stopping point in Paris—the Schuffeneckers' house.[25] These letters had efficiently been forwarded to the Schuffeneckers at their summer home in Dieppe and from there to Monfreid in the Pyrenees and then back to Paris to Gauguin's new address. Once he saw that Mette wasn't to blame, his tone became conciliatory, but the damage had already been done.[26] Husband and wife were now once again on guard against each other. When Paul learned that few paintings had been sold from the exhibition in Copenhagen, money again arose as an issue between them.

Because of the roundabout route that Mette's letters were taking, Paul received a telegram from her before he received any letters. The telegram (sent to the correct address once she learned it) was to inform him of the event he had expected for several years—the death of his uncle Isidore in Orléans. Paul was not directly informed of his uncle's death, because his uncle did not have an address for him; rather, ever since Paul had gone to Martinique, his uncle had had instructions to correspond with Mette in Copenhagen. Thus it was Mette who had gotten the official notification of Uncle Isidore's death, and she passed on the news to Paul. To Mette, the inheritance that they had waited for so long was the answer to her prayers. It was she who had corresponded with the uncle, sent him pictures of the children, kept Paul's family in the will when Isidore might easily have decided to leave his entire estate to Paul's sister, Marie, and her family.

But when Mette wrote to fill Paul in on all that the money might mean for the education and improvement of their children, her husband's selfish reply destroyed in one stroke all the goodwill that had arisen between them in the last two years. "I swear—at this moment I am more than furious!" she confessed in an angry letter to Emile Schuffenecker.[27] "He never thinks of anything but himself and his welfare; he prostrates himself in complete admiration before his own magnificence. . . . I have been very worried about Emil's future, I mentioned it to Paul, who tells me that we should not worry ourselves about anything, the boy being big enough to make his own way. . . . He does not even mention giving me a part of the 15,000 [sic] francs."[28] All Mette's hopes of being relieved of her duties as sole breadwinner and all her dreams for her children were dashed at this moment. As a result, Paul did not go to Copenhagen, nor did Mette come to Paris. They continued to correspond, and Paul eventually sent her 1,500 francs from the 13,000 francs he inherited.[29] Mette was now irrevocably disillusioned after all the years of clinging to her hopes; she was especially devastated after the crescendo of optimism of the past two.

When Paul realized that he could no longer talk her out of her anger with promises for the future, and now that he had the financial security he had always wanted, he grew equally angry at her. Censure from his more responsible friends also increased his guilt and annoyance. He managed to keep almost all his uncle's money for himself, but over the years he paid a high price for his cavalier treatment of his family. Not only have his critics kept this issue alive, but the anger and bitterness of his tarnished self-respect ate away at him until the day he died. "I hate the Danes!" he repeated in his memoirs in 1903, a few months before his death. He wrote this while looking out onto tropical foliage on the island of Hiva Oa in the South Seas: time and distance only increased his obsession with his wronged wife.

In the first few months after Gauguin's return to Paris, the drama developing between husband and wife was temporarily obscured by the flurry of activity surrounding his bid for lasting recognition. After he made a break with his old gallery, he went to Paul Durand-Ruel, with whom he had not done business in almost ten years. To his surprise and delight, Durand-Ruel agreed to exhibit his new Tahiti works that fall.[30] It is generally believed that Durand-Ruel's decision was influenced by Degas's enthusiasm for Gauguin's new work.[31] Degas had bought a painting from Gauguin's auction in 1891 and bought more in the next several years.[32] The older man never became personally close to Gauguin, especially since he avoided the more bohemian fringes of the art world whenever possible, but he did not hesitate to admire Gauguin's bold, sensual paintings and spoke highly of them to others.

For Gauguin to find support so quickly among the upper echelons of modern artists and dealers in Paris was extraordinarily encouraging to him. He began to feel that the effort to build his reputation, which had been prematurely terminated when Theo van Gogh died, would at last be carried to its logical conclusion in the hands of the masterful Paul Durand-Ruel. The decision to go to Tahiti had been the right one, he thought, and all those who had doubted his talent in the past, like Durand-Ruel in the early 1880s, would now rally behind him. He would repeat the triumph of his return from Martinique.

But Durand-Ruel had promised him just an exhibition; he had not yet committed to represent Gauguin, so everything hinged on the success of the show. As Paul wrote to his wife, explaining why he would not visit her that fall, he was about to "strike a huge blow, upon which his whole future would rest."[33] He was aware of the pressure placed on him but was optimistic: "I think that with a few notices in the newspapers, this exhibition will be a success. And if this goes well, I believe that Durand-Ruel will promote me."[34]

In the two months Gauguin had to prepare for his exhibition, he attended to the usual tasks of stretching and framing the canvases and see-ing to the publication of the catalogue. In addition, he launched a cam-paign similar to the one in 1891 to assure plentiful coverage of the exhibition in the press. To this end he renewed his friendship with Charles Morice, who had proved so inadequate a promoter while Gauguin was in Tahiti but who still held the key to the symbolist literary critics whom Gauguin deemed essential to the success of his publicity. He also resumed his atten-dance at Mallarmé's "Tuesdays," where he could not only regain the sup-port of the master but impress the members of the group who had joined since Gauguin's departure.[35]

Gauguin also went out of his way to mend his relationship with Schuffenecker, who had broken off with him two years before. Schuffenecker had had enough of Gauguin's impositions, and in a touching letter ("you were made for dominance and I for independence"), he extracted himself from Gauguin's web as best he could.[36] With Monfreid's intercession, however, Gauguin won Schuffenecker back that fall and once again had free access to his works in Schuffenecker's studio and the group of important friends that clustered around the popular art instructor. Because Schuffenecker was also close to Gauguin's wife and had been shipping works for her to sell in Copenhagen, Gauguin may also have wanted to gain more control over that relationship and those transactions. Mette wryly noted her husband's success in courting their mutual friend when she wrote to Schuffenecker in January: "I am happy to know that Paul has been friendly with you; with me he writes only about how poor he is and how much he owes."[37]

Gauguin quickly saw that Schuffenecker would be an important ally in what was shaping up to be a lengthy battle with his former friend Emile Bernard. Bernard, who had long questioned Gauguin's character but had always benefited from the friendship too much to break it off, had confronted Gauguin at his auction in 1891 and accused him of stealing the credit for the new style.[38] At the time, the defection of both Bernard and Schuffenecker was a significant blow to the Gauguin entourage. In an exquisitely timed follow-up blow, an article, "Notes sur le peintre Emile Bernard," appeared in the small journal *La Plume* on September 15, just as Gauguin was resettling in Paris. Written by the critic Francis Jourdain, it was meant to establish once and for all that Bernard had been the innovator and Gauguin the follower in those seminal days in Brittany.[39] An unsigned reply to Bernard's claim appeared soon afterward in an article titled "Gauguin et l'école de Pont-Aven," which reasserted Gauguin's position as head of the synthetist school.[40] Gauguin saw that it would benefit him to win back as many of his old followers as he could, like the influential Schuffenecker, to keep the tide of opinion from flowing against him.

He was no doubt also alarmed to discover that what he thought had been an exclusive exhibition in Copenhagen in the spring of 1893 had, in fact, been shared with that madman Vincent van Gogh. Vincent had been the subject of a recent exhibition in Paris and several articles, many either written by or proposed by Emile Bernard. In death, Vincent was becoming more of a serious rival to Gauguin than he had been while alive.[41] Gauguin could not control the vindictive Bernard's campaign to promote Vincent, but again, he could make sure that others in their old group were not so active on Vincent's behalf and that his own role as teacher to Vincent was well publicized.[42] Although he did his best to take credit for Vincent's style, he made sure that he capitalized on the growing value of Vincent's pictures. Gauguin remembered that Vincent had wanted to trade some pictures with him and took this old promise to Theo's widow, who honored it by sending Gauguin some of Vincent's paintings in return for two of his own.[43]

As Gauguin reestablished connections with the intellectual circles in Paris, he took advantage of the intense curiosity that Parisians felt about exotic locales like the South Seas and their eagerness to believe his erotic stories of life among the Tahitians. The full impact of the paintings would have to wait until the dramatic unveiling of the exhibition in November, but until then, he frequently regaled his friends with his Tahitian tales. Work on *Noa Noa* was well under way by October,[44] and although it was not completed in time to coincide with the exhibition, Gauguin often gave dramatic readings from the manuscript to his friends that fall and winter.

Writing the book was the beginning of Gauguin's writing of an erotic life for himself, a life he created for public consumption to substitute for the reality of an increasingly prosaic and often desolate life; he was, after all, a man approaching fifty without the comfort of family or community respect. The erotic persona he created in *Noa Noa* was not simply that of a man successful with women but that of a man whose sexual passions and experiences were unusual—involving pleasure and pain with young men and women of other races. This distinctive persona set him apart and allowed him to claim original creativity because of it.[45] By writing *Noa Noa*, Gauguin, more than any other artist of his generation, shaped the concept of the modern artist: original art is that which has been created by an original person.[46]

The book and Gauguin's theatrical presentation of it were part of his campaign to make the Durand-Ruel exhibition—upon which his future rested—a success. The opening, initially scheduled for November 4, took place on November 10. Forty paintings and two sculptures were tastefully arranged in Durand-Ruel's large gallery on the rue Lafitte. The many reviews of the show, including a glowing one by Gauguin's champion in 1891, Octave Mirbeau, made the important connection with Pierre Loti: "We search in vain [in Loti's book] for the soul of this curious race, its mysterious and terrible past, the strange voluptuousness of its sun, nor do we find the thrill of its exceptional and unique character [as we do in Gauguin's exhibition.]"[47] In spite of the rather high prices placed on the works (1,000 to 4,000 francs), eleven paintings were sold.[48] The total income from this exhibition rivaled that from his auction in 1891, and although he had incurred expenses that had to be deducted from his receipts—and claimed to be disappointed—he must have come away with a respectable sum: close to 10,000 francs.[49] This, along with the inheritance from his uncle, gave him a net wealth that he hadn't possessed since his last windfall on the stock market in 1879.[50]

Within a month after the close of his exhibition, he moved into the first real apartment he had had in Paris since becoming an artist. This two-room apartment on the rue Vercingétorix was on the edge of the Montparnasse district of studios, theaters, and artists' lodgings, which he had begun frequenting in 1889. He painted the rooms olive green with yellow trim, decorated them with a piano and imported furniture, and began to hold a weekly salon.[51] Gauguin displayed the souvenirs from his trip—costumes, masks, and weapons—and supplemented his own with other Oceanic ethnographic items that he picked up in Paris and claimed came from an uncle.[52] He apparently dressed in these costumes and sang and danced in a Polynesian manner for his guests. Purposefully or not, he had created an exotic interior very similar to Pierre Loti's own prized Oriental decor in his home in Rochefort, on the west coast of France.[53]

To enhance the impact of the art and the stories and create the appearance (and if possible, the reality) of an erotic life, he took in a dark-skinned young woman who was believed to be "half Indian, half-Malayan," known only as Annah the Javanese (fig. 61).[54] Though still in her teens, she apparently participated in artistic life as a model and companion. The dealer Ambroise Vollard claimed to have introduced her to Gauguin. She had a flamboyant theatricality of dress and manner similar to Gauguin's, and the two made a startling couple when they attended art events and openings together. Her youth and Polynesian-type complexion were suggestive of Gauguin's vahine from Tahiti, and her presence at his readings helped to make his Tahitian stories more vivid.

About the same time, in January of 1894, Gauguin set himself up as a teacher in his own Académie Vitti (Fiji), which was under the aegis of a school started by a former teacher at the Académie Colarossi, Raphael Collin. This new academy, which stressed art principles of the Far East, attracted only a few pupils — mostly Scandinavians — but gave Gauguin the kind of status as a teacher that he had always wanted. His pupils wrote home about him in glowing terms: "He has never been 'taught': he has struggled all by himself to find his way. His teaching is such that I have never heard anyone speak so well."[55] They also socialized with him at the artists' café, the *crèmerie* run by Madame Caron, and were invited to his home: "He had a great exhibition here, from which he sold more than twenty paintings, remarkably enough. I did not have a chance to see the exhibition but I saw more than ten of his paintings in his atelier. He has also sculpted in wood, depicting the most fantastic ideas. Most of his works have been executed in Japan. Everything is painted in truly pure colours: all have burning yellow frames, so that unaccustomed eyes are dazzled."[56] The facts aren't all correct, but the hero worship is evident.

This period of teaching lasted only a few months, but it was a memorable time for both the students and for Gauguin. His 1903 memoir contains many references to art students he observed in the studio and at the café, most having to do with the faults of women students and their cold, clinical study of the male nude and sexual organ.[57] On the whole, however, Gauguin enjoyed his identity as a teacher and derived special pleasure from never having needed teachers or academies to become a great artist himself.

Naturally he attracted new handsome young men as disciples now that he was not only charismatic but also reasonably wealthy. His favorite admirer at this time was the fledgling poet Julien Leclerq, who became his traveling companion and spokesman in early 1894. The art students called him Gauguin's "impresario" because he actively sought to have Gauguin represented in exhibitions and the modern art press.[58] The two traveled to Belgium together in late February, when Gauguin's art was once again included in the annual exhibition of the group formerly called Les XX, now called La Libre esthétique.

This trip to Belgium and Gauguin's relationship with Leclerq point out two significant lacunae in what was otherwise a period of great success. The first and most obvious gap was the total absence of any thought of including Copenhagen on the itinerary. In the past, Gauguin had talked of it every time he exhibited in Brussels, and in 1891, he actually went to Copenhagen. In 1894, however, relations with his wife had deteriorated to

such a degree that he was not even remotely inclined to visit. The second, less obvious, but perhaps even more profound gap was the absence in his professional life of Durand-Ruel or any other major modern art dealer in Paris; one would normally have carried out the kind of promotion that Gauguin enlisted Leclerq to do. Given that Gauguin's exhibition at Durand-Ruel's gallery was a success both in sales and publicity, it is puzzling that Durand-Ruel did not capitalize on the artist who had offered such proof of salability.

According to Monfreid, Gauguin's exhibition was followed by "un insuccès pécuniaire" (financial failure), which arose from a quarrel between him and Durand-Ruel; of the details Monfreid was ignorant.[59] In Paul's letters to Mette, which are vague at best, there seems to be a downward spiral after his first reports ("many bidders went as far as 1,500 francs . . . my exhibition has had a very great artistic success").[60] In a later letter he made a disingenuous apology to his daughter: "You ask me if I have sold many pictures; unfortunately no, otherwise I should take great delight in sending you some pretty things for your Christmas tree."[61] Although Gauguin's motives were always suspect when he reported his financial successes and failures to his wife, other friends, such as Monfreid and Morice, also came away with the strong impression that he had suffered a major failure despite evidence to the contrary. Charles Morice later described the opening of the exhibition as the moment at which Gauguin recognized that he would suffer universal repudiation, and illustrated his noble stoicism in the following heart-wrenching scene. "Near the end of this ill-fated day, going to the door with M. Degas, who spoke to him of his admiration, he did not respond to him; but as the illustrious old master was leaving: 'Monsieur Degas, you are forgetting your cane," said Gauguin, indeed handing him a cane, but a cane he had sculpted himself that was on display there, and that he had just taken off the wall.'"[62]

But whether the failure took place during or after the exhibition, it was a tragedy for Gauguin's career. In some way he lost his chance to be represented by Paul Durand-Ruel, the most influential modern art dealer in Paris, who had also recently opened a branch in New York and could be said to have brought Impressionism to the vast American market. Gauguin's career would have been markedly different if he had had the same resources and connections working for him as for Degas, Monet, and Renoir. Gauguin's fellow newcomer to the Impressionist group in 1879, Mary Cassatt, for instance, had herself been recently taken on by Durand-Ruel. Her first major exhibition was held immediately following Gauguin's in December 1893. In the next few years not only did she sell enough to buy a château in the country, but her art blossomed in the security of such a dealer's care.[63] But Gauguin apparently could not come to terms with Durand-Ruel, and his art suffered accordingly. In the next year he apparently decided to serve as his own dealer with the help of admirers like Leclerq. The following fall he held his own exhibition in his studio. It was another seven years before he once again attracted an influential dealer, Ambroise Vollard, in 1900.

Whatever happened, even though Gauguin had an enviable cushion of money through sales and inheritance, he knew he had lost his chance for the kind of steady income and promotion that only an established dealer like Durand-Ruel could provide. Even more, he had lost his bid for the respectability that Degas, Monet, Renoir, Pissarro, and Cassatt now enjoyed. With his Tahiti pictures and the initial response to them, he thought he had earned a place among the most influential artists of the modern movement. Instead he found himself classified as a "writer's painter" whose followers were the precious Nabis, like Sérusier and Vuillard, and branded as "difficult" for not coming to terms with Durand-Ruel, as selfish in his treatment of his family, and as flamboyantly bohemian in costume and behavior.[64]

By April of 1894, when he headed out to Brittany for the summer, Gauguin had quarreled with so many people that he began striking back in the press. He had Leclerq write a piece in his defense for the journal *Mercure de France,* which served as the arena for many artistic battles. The article started with the provocative statement "People who repudiate Gauguin have three grievances against him: his ignorance, his extravagance, and his barbarity" and proceeded to counter all these charges.[65] Gauguin's feeling of repudiation was well founded; the Parisian art world had no sympathy for an artist who squandered his chances so recklessly.

Gauguin's pugnaciousness spilled over into other aspects of his life. At the end of May a short trip to the seaside town of Concarneau ended in a brawl during which Gauguin's leg was broken. He sued two of his assailants for 10,000 francs; the court eventually found in his favor but awarded him only 600 francs.[66] He was soon in a Breton court again to sue Marie Henry, the concierge of the inn in Le Pouldu where he had stayed so happily five years before with Meyer de Haan and Filiger.[67] When he returned to Paris in 1890, he had left behind a number of canvases as security against his unpaid bills. When Henry didn't return the works, he took her to court. This time the court ruled against him, and he received nothing.

He spent time trying to wrest other works that he believed to be his property from their owners. In addition to his petition to Jo van Gogh–Bonger to retrieve the works by Vincent that he claimed ownership of, he wrote insulting letters to Mette's brother-in-law, Edvard Brandès, in an attempt to buy back for a low price his old collection of Cézannes and other Impressionist paintings.[68] In the same spirit of accounting for what was once his, his letters to Mette took on a threatening tone as he repeatedly demanded that she list the works of his that she had sold. Outraged by the insinuation that she had cheated him and at last impervious to his demands, she refused to answer.[69] Her silence inflamed him. In July he wrote to Schuffenecker to express his frustration, knowing that Schuffenecker was sympathetic to his wife. "In the last five months I have written 3 letters to my wife, very friendly letters *but* asking her the names of the works sold in Denmark. *No response* and for my *birthday* [June 7] not a word from her or the children. You see, my dear Schuff, that with all the goodwill in the world, I can *excuse nothing* from that quarter. The fissure grows deeper and deeper."[70]

In the next sentence, while complaining of the rainy weather in Brittany, he gives the first indication that he is thinking fondly of Tahiti: "Where are you, sweet land of Oceania?" In the letters that followed, he developed this theme to Schuffenecker. On July 26 he spoke of the futility of his pursuit of fame and his longing to retire to the islands, far from petty concerns. He went on to blame his wife for forcing him into such a flight: "In the past few months the conduct of my family is all the excuse I need."[71]

By September, only a year after setting foot in France, his plans to return to Tahiti had become firm. He could not live with the consequences of his shameful treatment of his family, nor could he accept his failure to engage an important dealer. He did not want to abide by the standards of behavior required by European society, nor could he bear rejection when he had had success so tantalizingly within his grasp. In his experience, Tahiti was a more tolerant society; the people winked at his irregularities and treated him with consistent good humor. Why should he take the hard road

for my friend J. Conor
one man of Samoa.
P Gauguin 1894

when the easy one would do? Once again he returned from Brittany to Paris focused on doing everything he could to launch himself back onto the high seas.

Without a dealer or the prospect of an exhibition, Gauguin's summer had been relatively aimless. Since January he had been working on illustrations for *Noa Noa,* which he executed in an experimental woodcut technique. Then, in the summer, he branched out into watercolors of similar scenes. The few oils he painted were primarily portraits of his friends or of himself. When he decided to put everything up for sale once again to finance his return to Tahiti, he had few new major works to put on sale. Instead, he turned his apartment in Paris into an art gallery for a week in December and plastered the walls with the woodcuts, drawings, and watercolors that acted as a reference to the body of large oils he had brought back from Tahiti.[72] This exhibition yielded few sales but did serve as a prelude to the auction at the Hôtel Drouot that he arranged for February. There he put on the block all the major canvases he had left in his possession.

Gauguin's behavior during the summer in Brittany and during the winter of 1894–95 in Paris was largely a matter of theater, as had become his custom. His unusual dress, the fawning retinue, and the pose of noble primitive were now familiar to the writers and painters in modernist circles. But Gauguin's failure to gain a financial foothold in Paris to replace the prestigious position he had once held with Theo van Gogh and the well-known split with his wife gave his behavior a new edge of abandon and bitterness.

Gauguin's companions in Brittany were all new friends—young artists or art students flattered by the attentions of this famous man. His old friends—Schuffenecker, Monfreid, Bernard, even Sérusier—had summer plans that did not include Gauguin. Gauguin did look up Filiger, who was living near Le Pouldu with a teenaged local boy as a companion. He tried to establish himself in Le Pouldu once again and stayed briefly in a villa rented by the Polish artists Wladyslaw Slewinski and his wife, whom he had met in Paris the winter before. But he couldn't find lodgings of his own in Le Pouldu—the one innkeeper who had been willing to give him credit, Marie Henry, had closed her hotel, and he was suing her.

He returned to Pont-Aven, where he could get an inexpensive, if not free, room at Marie Gloanec's new hotel, Ajoncs d'Or. After the brawl in Concarneau on May 25, Gauguin was more or less confined to his room there for the next month, but he stayed on until mid-November. Perhaps he chose the noisy, crowded artists' colony of Pont-Aven (from which he had formerly kept a distance during the summer) because he wanted to be visible to the largest number of curious artists as possible, but this is mere speculation. One account of the crazy scene at Pont-Aven during the summer makes note of the rampant drunkenness that seemed essential to the creative process of the various schools of "Stripists," "Dottists," and "Spottists." Of the group most likely to have been Gauguin's, the observer wrote, "The Primitives afforded joy. Their distinctive mark was a walking-stick, carved by a New Zealand Maori, which they carried about with them. It gave them inspiration. So powerful was the influence of these sticks that even the head of a Breton peasant assumed the rugged aspect of the primitive carvings in their paintings."[73]

Gauguin held court in his bedroom, where many visitors watched him work on his prints or drawings while they conversed. These minor works on paper made ideal souvenirs for Gauguin's awestruck guests, many of whom treasured the signed and dedicated works for years (fig. 62). Two young men became particular favorites of Gauguin's that summer: the Irish painter Roderic O'Conor and the French painter and printmaker Armand Séguin. These two had been working together on a large series of etchings at Le Pouldu the summer before, and their footloose lifestyle must have impressed Gauguin. Once he decided to return to Tahiti, he discussed the trip at length with them and believed that he had persuaded them to go with him.[74]

Gauguin felt completely at ease with them, and through O'Conor, we get a glimpse of the type of conversation he favored with his friends. Gauguin and O'Conor corresponded after Gauguin returned to Paris (O'Conor remained in Brittany until 1904), and a letter to O'Conor was described by a later owner as "too scatological for publication—details of the ideal position in sexual intercourse."[75] Gauguin ultimately proved to be too offensive for the bohemian but well-bred Irishman, who, when asked about Gau-

63 Paul Gauguin, *Self-Portrait* (verso), 1893–94. Oil on canvas, 18 x 15 in. (46 x 38 cm). Musée d'Orsay, Paris.

64 Paul Gauguin, *Portrait of William Molard* (recto), 1893–94. Oil on canvas, 18 x 15 in. (46 x 38 cm). Musée d'Orsay, Paris.

guin's invitation to Tahiti, responded with indignation: "No, but do you see me going to the South Seas with that character!"[76] Another visitor to the Hôtel Ajoncs d'Or, who was perhaps closer to Gauguin in his aesthetics of offensiveness, was the writer Alfred Jarry, who wrote three poems based on Gauguin's paintings while there.[77]

Gauguin's fascination with the details of physical sexuality, with which he must have shocked many unsuspecting visitors, was made even more piquant by the continuing presence of Annah in Gauguin's retinue. Although there is no hint of a love attachment between them (as there had been with Juliette Huet and Tehamana) nor, thankfully, a pregnancy, Gauguin encouraged people to believe that the two had a sexual relationship. Highly suggestive of this would have been the display of his nude portrait of Annah (see fig. 61). One imagines Gauguin in front of this painting telling his stories of androgynous love in the South Seas or discussing positions of sexual intercourse while the clothed Annah silently serves tea to the spellbound visitors. Her age and color heighten what is already a highly charged and illicit conversation.

Little is known about Annah's reaction to her role in the drama, but the fact that she left Gauguin at the end of the summer and continued her career as artist's model and companion with Alphonse Mucha indicates that she neither sank into hopeless degradation after her experience with Gauguin nor retreated from the artistic world into a safer sphere.[78] Her own sense of theatricality seems to have been engaged by such games; on the other hand, if the report is true that she stole whatever she could from Gauguin's apartment in Paris, it is difficult not to believe that she deserved whatever she took as compensation for her long run as prop in the Gauguin mythmaking production.[79] Gauguin was undoubtedly as niggling in his payments to her as he was with all the other women who took care of him in one way or another.

Gauguin's obsession with adolescent girls, which he had apparently been allowed to act on in Tahiti, was another questionable feature of his behavior during his two years back in France. Annah was the most visible and shocking manifestation of this predilection, and her presence is noted in virtually every account or reminiscence of Gauguin in 1894. But her race, like that of Tehamana, actually deflected the attention of Gauguin's European friends away from her age. A more delicate matter was Gauguin's flirtatiousness with the young daughters of his friends, which never exceeded the boundaries of European behavior to the extent that he had to be chastised but which must have been disturbing nevertheless. Some of these daughters never forgot the experience of this famous man coming to them for affection and wrote about it at length later on.

The most famous of these was Judith Gérard, the daughter of Ida Ericson, a Swedish sculptor who rented the apartment below Gauguin's in Paris. Ericson had married a French-Norwegian composer, William Molard, who treated Judith as his own child (figs. 63–64). Judith was thirteen when Gauguin moved in above them, and she, like her parents, was drawn into his mesmerizing orbit. Ida sculpted a bust of Gauguin, who was to paint portraits of William and Judith. Ida was progressive enough to give Judith a great deal of adult independence and privilege; she herself had led an independent life when young. Consequently, Judith was allowed to attend Gauguin's "Thursdays" and was allowed to pose for her portrait without a chaperone.[80]

According to later recollections, however, when Ida discovered that Gauguin was painting her as a full-length frontal nude, she soon put a stop to the sessions.[81] Gauguin must have convinced Ida that his attentions were merely paternal, for Judith continued to spend time with him alone, ostensibly taking painting lessons. But Judith's most vivid memories were of his sexual advances: "I walk quietly to Gauguin, his arm steals around my waist, and he puts his hand like a shell on my budding breast. His husky voice, barely audible repeats, 'These are mine . . .' Of course they are his, his tenderness, my young feelings which have not yet been aroused, my whole soul. Standing on my tiptoes, I search for his cheek. It is his mouth that I meet. My whole soul is on my lips, he can take it away."[82]

The full-length nude that was completed shows Annah instead of Judith (see fig. 61), but the scandalous Tahitian title of the work, *Aita Tamari Vahine Judith te Parari* (The Child-Woman Judith Is Not Yet Breached), made it clear that both girls were to be imagined in similar states of undress.

Gauguin also paid attention to Jeanne Schuffenecker, the pretty child whom Gauguin had depicted in a ceramic in 1888, who was now twelve or thirteen. Jeanne treasured a photograph of herself taken by her father's old friend in 1894–95, about the same time he was painting Judith/Annah, which may have been in preparation for a portrait of her.[83] Charles Morice's stepdaughter, who later wrote under the pen name Marie Jade, also recalled the affection that Gauguin lavished on her at that time, when she was about ten. Gauguin conversed with her and caressed her and arranged for his new disciple Séguin to paint her portrait while he watched.[84]

Looking back, Marie Jade assumed that his affection stemmed from his separation from his own daughter, whom he often talked about while gazing at her.[85] Like Ida Ericson, her mother had also been a progressive woman whose second husband was a younger man. Madame Morice liked Gauguin and encouraged him to talk about his wife and family. The pathos with which Gauguin portrayed his wife's cruelty, especially in separating him from his children, aroused her sympathy and caused her to see his affection for her daughter as purely paternal. She undoubtedly threw them together at every opportunity and brought her daughter to Gauguin's soirées, as did Ida Ericson. With Annah, Judith, Marie, and possibly Jeanne Schuffenecker in attendance, Gauguin's Thursdays must have had a strong component of adolescent sensuality for the forty-seven-year-old artist and his male friends.

Although no scandal along these lines ensued, Gauguin's lifestyle took on the unsavory reputation that can be found in most accounts of his days on the rue Vercingétorix. Those few old friends who still stood by him did their best to counter the tales of drunkenness and abandon that circulated freely during Gauguin's lifetime and were put into print after his death. In a commemorative article in 1903, Daniel de Monfreid quoted one of the most extravagant accounts:

> Returning from Brittany to Paris, he was comfortably installed in a studio where the faithful were welcomed every night in exchange for regaling him with the grossest, most copious, and interminable flattery. While the demigod on a sofa, which was perched on a stage, pulled at his pipe, the poet Julien Leclerq crouched at the back of the stage, on the ground, strummed his mandolin, and, with two low bows, with clownlike animation, improvised couplets [of praise] for the occasion. Scattered about in attitudes of mute adoration, the audience, among whom bottles and glasses circulated, inhaled fine, green, or hot grog; and from time to time, at a signal from the acolyte with curly hair [Leclerq], hailed at the top of their voices the savior of painting, who, with a smile and a wave quieted them.[86]

On the contrary, claimed Monfreid, Gauguin smoked cigarettes, not a pipe; Leclerq was always very discreet in his homage to Gauguin; and Gauguin served green tea, not grog. One heard only classical music in Gauguin's studio, as befitted the friend of the composers Molard and Delius. Furthermore, Monfreid asserted, "In this setting Gauguin lost all his ferocious arrogance, became a good boy, simple and welcoming. In a word, he unbent among those who were sympathetic to him."[87]

In assessing these two vastly differing accounts of Gauguin, one can readily imagine that both were indeed true. Gauguin had the ability to temper his behavior among those whose cooperation he needed and behave like the well-bred Parisian he was. But his greater enjoyment came from theatrical scenes where he held center stage and where restraint of any kind was unnecessary. When he lost his place among the more respectable members of the Paris art world, he succumbed whenever possible to this self-indulgence.

The effect this had on his career can be seen in the way his auction of February 1895 was conducted as compared to his triumphant auction of 1891. In 1891 he was still able to marshal the forces of the French literary and artistic worlds on his behalf. Both Mallarmé and Mirbeau had worked enthusiastically to make the sale a success; Degas, Pissarro, and Monet had all had a hand in it. But in 1895, after making a last-ditch effort to avert an auction by offering Durand-Ruel a group of thirty-five canvases at 600 francs each, Gauguin found himself without support from any part of the Paris modern art establishment.[88] This time he resorted to August Strindberg for a spokesman, a bold and unusual choice; Strindberg's play *The Father* had had a *succès de scandale* at its opening on December 13.[89] Although the association with Strindberg placed Gauguin with a newer wave of the avant-garde, Strindberg did not bring with him a stable of collectors and patrons, which Gauguin sorely needed to have a successful auction.

Strindberg himself had a checkered reputation in Paris. His own fascination with taboo sexual subjects in his writing paralleled Gauguin's, as did his behavior in real life. Strindberg's ambivalence toward women in general and his three wives in particular was often echoed in the misogynist undertones of such plays as *The Father*. Furthermore, he was drawn to homosexuality as a theme, as in *The Defense of a Madman* (1887), in which he expresses revulsion for the lesbianism of the wife of the hero—a sentiment repeated in his accusations against his own first wife. Strindberg's own homosexual impulses were indulged by going to gay bars and meeting places from time to time.[90]

Gauguin and Strindberg spent the evening together on January 31 and discussed, among other things, the introduction to Gauguin's auction catalogue, which Gauguin planned to use for publicity. The next day Strindberg wrote a lengthy piece that was ostensibly a letter of refusal, but it served well as the desired introduction and must be seen as written for that purpose. He started the letter by admitting that he did not understand or like Gauguin's art, but went on to dissect Gauguin the man: "What is he, then? He is Gauguin, the savage who hates the restraints of civilization, who has something of the Titan who, jealous of the Creator, makes his own little creation in his spare time, the child who takes his toys apart to make others; the one who renounces and defies, preferring to see the sky red, rather than blue with the crowd."[91] In discussing the man, Strindberg suddenly finds that he understands the art and now appreciates it. This compelling argument—that art first and foremost should be original and unique, rather than beautiful or familiar, and thus must be the product of an original and unique *artist*—was no doubt arrived at in his discussions with Gauguin. The process that had started with Gauguin creating an exceptional, erotic life for himself in *Noa Noa* had ripened into Strindberg's portrayal of him as the godlike creator of new worlds.[92]

Strindberg's 1895 vision of Gauguin as an uncompromising, unique individual contrasts starkly with Mirbeau's 1891 essay on Gauguin as a Parisian of good family whose trip to Tahiti was primarily motivated by a search for his familial roots. The two disparate accounts, just four years apart, reveal how far Gauguin had slipped outside the net of social and artistic connections that had once served him well. Gauguin made a virtue of his isolation once he saw it was inevitable, but it was not the outcome he had desired when he gambled on Tahiti the first time. In fact, his isolation in Paris had become so bitter that he had no choice but to try to regain his place in the more accepting society of Tahiti.

With the letter from Strindberg and a reply from Gauguin as the major publicity for the sale,[93] the auction on February 18 was, not surprisingly, sparsely attended. Bargain hunters tried to pick up Gauguin's high-priced canvases for much less, but Gauguin fiercely defended his prices by buying in works that did not reach the minimum bid.[94] With his healthy bank account, he was not desperate enough to unload paintings for whatever they would bring. Consequently he sold only nine paintings out of the forty-seven items on the block; but he sold at least six of the drawings to Degas. How much money he made at this auction is difficult to calculate. Paul claimed to Mette that he *lost* 464.80 francs, but it is more likely he netted about 3,000 francs.[95] Whereas his profits were considerably downplayed in his letter to Mette and in the press,[96] a possible sign of the actual monetary success of the auction was that he could afford to stay in Paris another four months rather than leave immediately for Tahiti.[97]

In March, April, and May of 1895, Gauguin made himself as visible as he could in order to imprint himself upon the memory of the Paris art world while he was gone, or perhaps in order to make one last attempt to gain a dealer and make flight unnecessary after all. His hopes may have centered on the young, energetic Ambroise Vollard, who had opened a gallery in late 1893 and showed Gauguin's works in March 1895. Although Vollard had begun promoting Cézanne and the Nabis, he and Gauguin, predictably, did not come to terms.[98]

At the same time, Gauguin was drawing attention to a large ceramic sculpture that he titled *Oviri* (Savage; fig. 65), which he had fired during the winter and submitted to the salon of the Société Nationale des Beaux-Arts, opening in late April. This puzzling female nude with demonic eyes holds a bushy-tailed fox, a creature he had used before in *Soyez amoureuses* (1889) and *The Loss of Virginity* (1891), which thus ties it to his previous scenes of uncomfortable sexuality. It is hard to determine exactly what Gauguin intended, particularly in regard to the furry animal draped down the thigh of the female figure. In an 1889 letter to Bernard, Gauguin had referred to the fox in *Soyez amoureuses* as the "Indian symbol of perversity," but such an interpretation of fox symbolism cannot be substantiated today in mythology from either India or South America.[99] There is, however, a long tradition of the fox in Asian lore having magic powers to change into a woman, particularly in order to seduce a man and drain him of his potency during intercourse.[100] Because Gauguin had made it clear — by proclaiming that he planned to place the ceramic on his grave — that this female savage was his alter ego, it is likely that he thought the furry creature was as changeable in gender as he was, and symbolic of dangerous sexuality. He and his disciples made much of the fact that the jury had originally rejected the ugly figure with its obscure symbolism but that Gauguin's old mentor, Chaplet himself, had insisted on its inclusion in the exhibition.

In a flurry of publicity, Gauguin wrote an outraged letter on modern ceramics to the editor of *Le Soir* two days before the salon opened and an editorial protesting the selection of artists for an exhibition in Berlin.[101] On May 13 he arranged for an interview to be published in *L'Echo de Paris* in which he reiterated his artistic theories of freedom from convention and representation. The author of the article, Eugène Tardieu, introduces him as follows: "He is the wildest of all the innovators, and of all the 'misunderstood' artists the one least inclined to compromise. A number of his *discoverers* have forsaken him. To the great majority of people he is just a humbug. Yet he calmly goes on painting his orange rivers and red dogs, and for every day that passes adheres more and more to this personal *manner*."[102] In the interview Gauguin disavows claims that he is a revolutionary or that his theories are new, but he defends his red dogs as "absolutely deliberate." An artist should have total freedom to decide what colors he uses in depicting nature, he says, as long as "his work is harmonious and thought-provoking."[103]

The eloquence of these arguments, which had been long part of avant-garde theory, had in the past lured many an artist and art lover into Gauguin's camp. It is a measure of how isolated and vulnerable Gauguin had become in Paris that he immediately encountered criticism within his own avant-garde circles. The next issue of *Mercure de France* ran not one but two attacks on Gauguin. The first was the coincidental publishing of a letter from Emile Bernard that had been sent in February from Bernard's new

location in Cairo; in it Bernard once again claimed his place as the innovator of "Gauguin's style."[104]

The second was the monthly column by the regular art critic for the
journal, Camille Mauclair, in which the Gauguin interview by Tardieu
was directly ridiculed. Dismissing Gauguin as a simplistic theorist, Mauclair
questioned why, if he dismissed reality as a basis for his art, Gauguin
needed to go to Tahiti at all. "Why must he leave his Breton digs and exile
himself to Tahiti to execute this painting, which could, as Gauguin himself
said, be done without leaving his own room?"[105] Although Mauclair's
opposition to Gauguin's symbolist theory shows the critic's allegiance to the
older Impressionist school, he does make a valid point about Gauguin's
true motivation in returning to Tahiti. It was not what Gauguin saw that drew
him back to the island but the sensuality he felt when he was there. That,
more than any visible aspect of Tahiti, inspired his paintings.

Gauguin had Morice publish a retort to Mauclair in *Le Soir* on June
28, the day of his departure.[106] Still, Gauguin left Paris with Mauclair's
attack ringing in his ears. It capped an almost two-year period during which
Gauguin made a great deal of money but lost the respect he had once
held among writers, critics, and artists. When he had departed in 1891, he
had had the backing not only of his personal disciples but of the great
names of modern French culture—Degas, Mallarmé, Mirbeau, and the dealers Boussod and Valadon. This time he had only Morice, Monfreid, and
an obscure dealer named Lévy, who had taken on some of his works. He
felt that he had engendered enough interest to continue selling in Paris, but
he no longer had any hope of being thrust into a lasting position of prominence. He knew he would not return.

As for his wife and family, whose affection he had rekindled before his
first trip, there was certainly now no hope of reconciliation. Husband
and wife had not managed to resolve the issues of abuse and betrayal that
had dogged them over the years. Mette had broken free of her crippling
expectations of him and now accepted her life in Copenhagen. "I am happier
here in a different way than in Paris," she wrote to Emile Schuffenecker
in May of 1895.[107] She no longer kept up with her husband's doings—he didn't
write, and she didn't ask for news of him from artist-friends who traveled
to Paris. When she needed to get in touch with him, she went through
Schuff: "Dear friend, read the enclosed letter, and add the address. I have
forgotten the number of the house: I write him so rarely and I think of
him even more rarely; but I consider that when I learn he has money, it is my
duty to remind him that he has five children and that the work I do is not
enough to maintain them all. . . . But it is unjust to complain. . . . It is just that
my children will one day blush for their father, and that is hard for them."[108]
Although Mette's letter had no effect on her husband's generosity, it was
another bitter pill for Paul. Not only had he betrayed his family, but Emile
Schuffenecker and others were unmistakably aware of it. Someone had even
called him a criminal. When he wrote to Monfreid that fall, he referred
to the accusation: "My family will get out of its scrapes by itself, so far as I
am concerned! . . . Ah yes, I am a great criminal."[109] This bitterness helped
make his second experience in Tahiti very different from his first.

# 13 Tahitian Resident

1895–1901

Of all the picturesque spots that artists retired to in the 1890s—one thinks of Homer at Prout's Neck and Monet at Giverny—Gauguin chose by far the most spectacular. Regardless of the circumstances under which he left Paris, it would be difficult not to see his desire to end his days in the South Seas as anything other than luxurious. With enough money in the bank to live on for several years without selling any art, he could indulge his most pleasurable inclinations. He could forget his recent family and professional struggles and devote himself to the utterly hedonistic. The brilliant, sensual paintings he brought back from his first trip could have blossomed into even more extraordinary studies in color and mood. The erotic liaisons he so lovingly described in *Noa Noa* could have become a permanent reality.

What happened instead? The aging, syphilitic artist spent the lion's share of his time venting his anger against his enemies (his wife, the short-sighted art world of Paris, and his upright Tahitian neighbors) rather than making love or art. This makes us think that the extraordinary opportunity was wasted on him, but the propagandistic image of both Gauguin and Tahiti notwithstanding, neither the man nor the island was sensual enough to support a long-term erotic experience. Gauguin could not escape the habits of a lifetime that propelled him into attention-getting public conduct that often, to his delight, bordered on the scandalous. Conversely, the small, insular community of Tahiti, as cosmopolitan as it was, tolerated much less of this kind of behavior in a permanent resident than it did in a tourist. Gauguin's penchant for erotica involving very young partners, with its accompanying androgynous and often violent overtones, soon tried the patience of the normally broad-minded Tahitians. If Gauguin had chosen to live and work in a remote part of the island, as he had during his first trip, the results might have been different. But he lived near and at times in Papeete for six years and wore out his welcome. When he left for the Marquesas in 1901, he left few friends behind.

Even the art of these years is oddly uneven and often unsatisfying. Although he produced some of his most self-conscious masterpieces, such as the large *Where Do We Come From? What Are We? Where Are We Going?* (see fig. 70), there is a labored quality to the dark colors and reworked subject matter. As time went on, he lost touch with the vital Paris avant-garde, although, ironically, his new, more subdued paintings found a broader audience, which brought him the lasting acceptance he had always craved. The livelier, more colorful works that he executed during those years were for his audience in Tahiti, but because his themes were often violent and outright pornographic, few of these have survived.

Another paradoxical aspect of this retreat was his supposed rejection of European culture in favor of the "primitive" society of Polynesia. Although he made the acquaintance of many Tahitians and, later, Marquesans during these years and was generally an advocate for native arts, it is impossible not to recognize that his social world consisted almost exclusively of well-educated Europeans. He complained constantly and bitterly about the European social conventions that held sway on Tahiti and Hiva Oa but never considered doing the obvious—taking up the truly native way of life, as many European beachcombers had done.[1] On the contrary, he was "above all a Frenchman," he declared in a speech decrying lax Tahitian immigration policies.[2]

And yet, despite this declaration and his active correspondence with old friends from intellectual circles in Paris, he never voiced the desire to return to France or participate once again in the elite art world he now kept at arm's length. In fact, he had assumed the ambiguous identity of a settler, or *colon* (colonist), a type found throughout the colonial world, whose allegiances were notoriously shifting and complex.[3]

In the two years that had passed since Gauguin left Tahiti, certain signs of modernity, such as electricity, had appeared; but overall, much that was familiar welcomed him on September 9, 1895, when he disembarked for the second time in Papeete.[4] Except for the departure of Lieutenant Jénot and some other French officers whose tours of duty in Tahiti were over, most of Gauguin's acquaintances from the first trip—the Goupils, the Suhas, the Cardellas—were still at the center of Tahitian society and caught him up on the political gossip.

In spite of this reception, he succumbed to the typical disappointment felt by newcomers to Tahiti. Within days of his arrival, he was telling friends that he intended to settle in the Marquesas;[5] in the same spirit, he took advantage of an opportunity in late September to tour the neighboring islands of Raiatéa, Huahine, and Bora Bora, which to this day offer a more exotic resort-type of experience to the European visitor.[6] Seeing these islands apparently cured Gauguin of his desire for the more picturesque but remote locations, and he was once again lured by the modern conveniences and cosmopolitan society of Tahiti to make it his home.

By November he had rented a plot of land in the district of Punaauia, about ten miles outside Papeete, and was having a large house built.[7] The house symbolized not only his new financial status (a good portion of his inheritance and sales profits remained) but also his willingness to assume a place in Tahitian society as a resident rather than a tourist.[8] Many of the important Tahitian families resided along the western coast of the island as far as Punaauia because the road was good and the commute into Papeete was convenient. Foremost among these was Auguste Goupil, whose large Victorian mansion graced the hillside above Outumaoro (three miles from Gauguin's house) and whose plantations of coconuts extended into the Punaauia district.

Although today it is assumed that Gauguin's house overlooked the brown volcanic beach and sweep of the sea toward Moorea, he does not mention an ocean view in his own descriptions of the site.[9] Instead, his house was built quite close to the road, with the primary view across the road and toward the mountains. Several houses might have already existed between his and the beach (as they do today), blocking his access to the water. His house was in a large cluster of houses, all similarly designed in the Polynesian manner with reeds forming the exterior walls and palm leaves woven into a thatched roof. Gauguin's neighbors were both European and Tahitian. The community was served by a general store, a tavern, two churches, and a public school, all arranged, like Gauguin's house, along the main road.[10]

He lived next to the school and soon had young hopefuls coming to his bed, vying for a permanent position with the wealthy European. He related his good fortune to Monfreid. "Every night some mischievous little rascals come to sleep with me. I had three to attend to yesterday."[11] Even his old vahine, Tehamana, checked back in with him. Now about sixteen (if Gauguin's age for her in *Noa Noa* was correct) and married, she may have thought some arrangement might still be worked out if he were attached to her. "My old sweetheart got married in my absence; so I was obliged to fool her husband, but she can't stay with me, though she did run away to me for a week."[12]

Instead, the lucky winner was the daughter of neighbors in Punaauia, named Pahura (Pau'ura) a Tai.[13] At fourteen she took on the role of Gauguin's housekeeper and bed partner in exchange for the usual room, board, and occasional gift. She stayed with Gauguin the entire time he lived in Punaauia, until 1901, and was pregnant twice. She raised the second child (Emile, b. 1899) herself, and Emile's descendants still live in the area.[14]

Because of Gauguin's affectionate description of Tehamana in *Noa Noa,* it has been assumed that Gauguin had strong personal feelings for the young Tahitian women (Tehamana and Pahura) who shared his home over the years. But the bulk of the evidence points to a more pragmatic type of relationship in both cases and accounts for their remaining little more than ciphers in the overall scheme of Gauguin's life. Tehamana, for instance, apparently thought so little of the relationship that in later years when others were talking to journalists at length about their experiences with Gauguin, she made no effort to identify herself.[15] This might indicate that there was no single Tehamana or that, if there was, the girl saw her encounter with the European artist as nothing special—more of a job than a romantic liaison. Other male tourists describe their own experiences with local women as essentially between employer and employee, primarily a matter of housekeeping services rendered, regardless of how precociously skilled the young women might be in the erotic arts.[16] Even Loti, whose relationship with Rarahu was seemingly based on love, continued to pursue an upper-class woman in Papeete during the entire course of his relationship with her.

The casual and sometimes sarcastic tone Gauguin used in the few references to Pahura in his letters in the more than five years of their association also suggest that she was more of a servant to him than his lover.

Furthermore, Gauguin frequently accused her of stealing and trespassing and tried to take legal action against her, even while she was pregnant. That these accusations were unreasonable can be inferred from the protection that the community, both Western and native, offered her against him.

Until her death in 1944, Pahura was sought out by visitors curious to meet the woman they confused with Tehamana, the young bride in *Noa Noa*. Somerset Maugham, during his visit in 1917, was alarmed to find, instead of the dewy young creature Gauguin described, a strident, mature woman whose memories of Gauguin were less than friendly.

> Before me stood, shy and ill-at-ease, and a little sullen, too, a Tahitian female of slight stature; in years according to my calculations, about thirty-eight, but so very aged before her time, attired in a tattered, faded sack-dress. . . . Her French was poor, and she answered my questions reluctantly, dully.
>
> Yes, yes, she was Pau'ura a Tai, Koké's *vahine* who had given birth to his son. Had we come to bring her some money from Koké's family in Europe? When I told her no, she snapped: "Den why-for you come all-way to Punaauia to see me if you haf no monnee fo' me?"
>
> Pau'ura had no worthwhile memory of Gauguin.[17]

As time went on and Gauguin's fame increased, Pahura's memories changed to meet the expectations of the eager pilgrims. One of the last to meet her was the journalist Eric Ramsden, who, in an article marking her death, recalled their interview several years before: "It was apparent that time had softened the memory of Gauguin. Local tradition had it (and it is invariably correct in such matters in Tahiti) that Koké [Gauguin] and Taurua [Pahura] were not on the best of terms when the former shook the dust of the Punaauia road from his feet and left his young mistress forever. . . . Woman-like, Taurua seemed anxious to protect the memory of the man she called her *tane* [husband]."[18] Unlike some of Gauguin's other acquaintances in Tahiti, who carried their dislike of him to the grave, Pahura seems to have been bullied into giving acceptable answers to the questions of visitors. "The old lady was glad to know that I was not French. The British, as a rule, she commented, did not ask her to describe Koké's love habits."[19]

Perhaps if Gauguin had written a second installment of *Noa Noa*, detailing his life with Pahura, the relationship might now have more of an

erotic glow. Because we have to rely solely on the documentary evidence of his personal relationships, without his sensual descriptions, his second stay on Tahiti falls flat—attesting to the power of his own words in shaping the erotic life he wanted to be known for.

Once he had built his house and taken Pahura as his vahine, Gauguin began his new life as a citizen of Tahiti. Although tourists still went out to the guesthouses of the district chiefs and sat at their feet while the old family histories were recited, Gauguin now used his time to learn about the dynamics of modern Tahiti and establish himself as a distinguished professional artist within the prosperous colonial society. Gauguin no longer spent his days visiting the fern grottoes of Maara or taking hikes into the interior or going along on fishing trips. He set up his studio in his new house and devoted himself to art.

Few other professional artists are known to have been in residence on Tahiti at this time; still, Gauguin was acquainted with many transient artists and amateurs.[20] These included two amateur but accomplished photographers, Henry Lemasson and Jules Agostini. Only a few patrons of the arts, such as Auguste Goupil and Jules Auffray, could be found among the colonists. Otherwise, Gauguin satisfied his need for a professional context by keeping up an active correspondence with artists, critics, dealers, and patrons in Paris. He also subscribed to what was now well established as the foremost journal of modern culture, *Mercure de France,* and no doubt subscribed or otherwise had access to the more general French newspapers and journals that kept the French-speaking population abreast of the European news.

True to his longtime preferences, Gauguin gravitated toward the younger, attractive, unmarried men of the cultured community, impressing them with his eloquent discussions of art theory and his own tragic life. But Gauguin was not able to re-create the theatrical bohemian lifestyle that had had such a grand effect in Pont-Aven and Le Pouldu.

In light of his dramatic portrayal of his life as "native" in style, it is important to keep in mind that it was bourgeois compared to the lives of the many working-class Europeans (sailors, laborers, and others) who stayed on the island, married local women, and lived with their families in the slums of Papeete or in the small country villages. Nor was he a purist like the internationally famous American "nature man," Charles W. Darling, who has occasionally been confused with Gauguin. Arriving in Papeete in 1903, Darling lived with minimal food and clothing in order to "return to nature." His voluminous writings and correspondence made his theories known around the world, and he attracted like-minded purists to the island.[21]

In contrast, Gauguin's life as an artist-colonist was surprisingly conventional. One of his young admirers on Tahiti, the government official and photographer Henry Lemasson, described Gauguin this way:

> I knew the painter Paul Gauguin very well during the last eight years of his life, from 1895 to 1903. Like him, at that time I lived in our Polynesian colony, where I held both the posts of director of postal services for French Oceania and postmaster for the Postal Bureau in Papeete, the capital of the colony. Because of this double title, I had reason to see Gauguin frequently. He lived in the district of Punaauia, about ten kilometers from Papeete, and whenever the monthly postal courier that linked Tahiti and France through America came or went, Gauguin would come to my office to receive or to mail his personal correspondence. . . .
>
> Gauguin, who had just turned fifty in 1898, was twenty-two years older than I. In Punaauia, the artist lived in a wooden hut in the simple style of most of the local European and even native habitations, a hut summarily fitted out with ill-matched furniture and other objects, where, in the words of the poet, a handsome disorder was an artistic effect! . . .
>
> The artist was an imposing figure, blue eyes, somewhat swarthy, ruddy complexion, brown hair and beard that were graying, a sparse goatee. When at home he generally dressed in the manner of the natives, in a simple cotton pullover and a loincloth, or *pareu,* leaving his legs naked. When he came into Papeete, he dressed like a European: a jacket (with a straight collar) and white linen pants, or more often blue, of a type of Vichy cotton, white linen slippers, and a wide-brimmed straw hat.[22]

Paul Gauguin, *Te Tamari no Atua (The Son of God)*, 1896. Oil on canvas, 37 1/2 x 50 in. (96 x 129 cm). Bayerische Staatsgemäldesammlungen, Neue Pinakothek, Munich.

Aside from his few artistic comrades, like Lemasson, Gauguin also cultivated the men in Papeete society, who socialized daily in the local clubs. He owned a horse and carriage, so he was able to make the trip into Papeete every day if he so desired, to transact business and participate in the social life of the capital.[23] If he followed the patterns of the other well-to-do island residents, work was confined to certain hours of the day and certain days of the month. The American journalist Frederick O'Brien described the normal leisurely pace of Tahitian life: "When the monthly mail between America and Australasia was in, few packs of cards were sold, for every one was busied with letters and orders for goods. But only three or four days a month were so disturbed, and for nearly four weeks of the month Papeete lolled at ease, with endless time for games and stimulants."[24]

O'Brien also reported that those men who did not have regular working hours—professional men, planters, ship captains, traders, and probably artists—tended to spend only the morning hours at their labors, leaving the afternoons and evenings free to gather in the several clubs and restaurants in town where drinking, cardplaying, and the telling of colorful tales was the primary occupation. The pearl traders, planters, and sea captains who later claimed to have known Gauguin recalled that his favorite drink was absinthe, which he occasionally ordered in a concoction of lime and pome-granate juice called a Dr. Funk.[25]

When Gauguin started painting again after a hiatus of at least a year, his new circumstances as a Tahiti resident must have influenced the out-come. Several large paintings of reclining nude Polynesian women (such as *Te Arii Vahine* [The Noble Woman], *Nevermore,* and *Te Tamari no Atua* [*The Son of God*]; fig. 66) continue his long-standing series of sexually available women, or Eves. In all of these paintings, Gauguin reaches beyond his personal symbolism to quote from famous paintings and literature, including the Bible, and draw on world culture generally.[26] The paintings from his first trip to Tahiti had been so tantalizingly personal that Gauguin had felt it necessary to write *Noa Noa* to give them a narrative context. In the second Tahitian group, however, he used symbolism and imagery that gave the Western viewer a starting point in interpreting the works. This indi-cates that he had in mind a more general audience than the quirky intellectu-als of the symbolist group with whom he had been associating in Paris—an audience more like his new cultured, but not avant-garde, friends in Papeete.

The painting *Te Tamari no Atua* employs a particularly interesting blend of European and Tahitian references that typify Gauguin's compli-cated allegiances as a colonist. It shows a nativity scene in which Mary, the Christ Child, and the nurse are enacted by Tahitian models in an exotic Polynesian setting. As if that weren't enough of a melding of cultures, the background view of a stable has been taken directly from a Dutch paint-ing that had been owned by Gauguin's old mentor, Gustave Arosa. Having given birth to Jesus, the exhausted Mary stretches out on a bed in the foreground while the child is held by a woman reminiscent of the Tahitian spirit figure in the background of Gauguin's earlier painting *Manao Tupapau.* Because *Te Tamari no Atua* was shipped off to Paris in December of 1896, it must have been intended primarily for a European audience. But Gauguin's intense interaction with colonial society at this time suggests that the over-all meaning was also intended to resonate with the group that Gauguin held in his thrall in the clubs of Papeete.

Gauguin's return to religious subjects would have reminded the knowl-edgeable Parisian viewer of the work he had done in Brittany in 1889 and 1890, when he had consolidated his leadership of the young symbolist artists. After his two years in France, Gauguin knew that religious symbol-ism had gained a secure foothold in avant-garde circles and that groups like the Rose + Croix and the Barc de Boutteville gallery displayed art with a mystical bent. Both his former disciples Filiger and Bernard had attracted the financial support of the flamboyant patron the Comte de La Rochefou-cauld with their religious imagery, and Gauguin was himself eager to court the wealthy count.[27] Gauguin might also have wanted to squelch once and for all Bernard's annoying claims that Gauguin's earlier Pont-Aven innovations in religious symbolism would not have been possible without the collaboration of the younger man.

While the device of re-creating a biblical event, particularly a Madonna and Child, in a modern but "primitive" society was commonly used by painters of peasant life all over Europe in the 1890s, there was also a great deal of interest in using such devices in intellectual circles in Tahiti at that time. Christianity had been so thoroughly embraced by native Tahitians by the 1890s that a conscious effort was now being made to preserve any and all connections with pre-Christian native culture by stressing the universality of religious concepts. Gauguin's use of Tahitian titles for his paintings may be seen as part of the larger insistence on the use of the Tahitian language at all levels of public and governmental activity. His recasting of familiar biblical subjects in Tahitian guise would have been perceived by his colonist friends as appropriate and timely. One of the most popular books in Tahiti was Jules Soury's *Le Jésus historique,* which quoted the work of an English author, Gerald Massey, on the interconnectedness of world religions.[28] With this information at hand, Gauguin also began a long tract on the misguided efforts of the Catholic church; the result was the manuscript "L'Eglise catholique et l'esprit moderne" (1902).

An investigation into the intertwined roots of the great world religions was more than part of the general intellectual climate of the 1890s both in Europe and its colonies; it also had a special meaning in colonial Tahiti because of the structure of the political parties in which Gauguin became embroiled. Historically, religion was the basis of the practical power wielded by government officials and their loyal opposition. The two political parties that vied for control of island affairs were called simply the Protestant and Catholic parties.

The Protestants traced their power to the early history of European control of the island, beginning in 1815, when envoys from the London Missionary Society converted the district chief Pomare II, who in turn conquered the rest of the island and delivered the whole of Tahitian society into the hands of the Protestant church. In the 1840s French Protestant missionaries challenged the authority of the British, fomenting a civil war that decimated the population of the island but resulted in a French victory. In 1880, Tahiti was officially annexed by France and became the capital of French Polynesia. Although government and military rule displaced the power of the missionaries throughout the colonies, the descendants of the British and French missionaries had become so rooted in Tahitian society that Protestantism was still the most influential Christian religion. But since 1880, with the increasing numbers of French civil servants, military, and other professionals on the island, Catholicism had gained considerable ground. In the 1890s virtually all villages, no matter how small, had both a Catholic and a Protestant church, and disputes based on this division were common in Tahitian life.[29]

Gauguin's use of religious subject matter therefore carried a wealth of associations with intellectual and political currents in his two worlds. Like a typical colonist, he tried to balance his allegiance to the traditions of the mother country with the peculiar circumstances of the new hybrid culture in the colony. Given this complex web of demands, it is hard to come to any conclusions about what personal meaning religious subjects might have held for the artist. Aside from the brief period of his first acquaintance with Bernard in the summer of 1888, he seldom voiced any religious beliefs; rather, his daring Breton religious paintings, including those in which he cast himself as Christ, suggest that he had little respect for the teachings of Christianity. It is possible, however, that in his attempt to assimilate into Tahitian society in the early days of being a new permanent resident, he was genuinely inspired to embrace the religious beliefs that were so meaningful to his neighbors.[30]

What might be more in keeping with his previous practices, however, would be to interpret his religious paintings as an attempt to enliven conventional symbolism with a discreet but shocking paradox. In the case of *Te Tamari no Atua*, for instance, the "virgin" Mary lies on her bed, knees apart, covered only by a loosely draped pareu. Although it is unusual enough to see Mary partially nude and in the aftermath of childbirth, it is even more shocking to read the pose simultaneously as the aftermath of sexual intercourse. The unmade bed with its large pillow and the cat at Mary's feet seem to be borrowed from Manet's famous painting of the notorious courtesan, *Olympia*, which Gauguin had copied in Paris in 1891 and of which he kept a photograph hanging prominently on his wall. The spent, reclining woman also recalls Gauguin's earlier Eve, *The Loss of Virginity*—with a fox rather than a cat nestled intimately against the young, androgynous body (see fig. 51). Gauguin's interpretation of Mary in *Te Tamari no Atua*, in light of these oblique references, seems to revolve around the piquant issue of her virginity in sexual terms.

The painting is a humanized version of the religious story, relating the birth of Christ to universal maternal experience; in this vein, Gauguin stresses the sexual experience that leads up to human pregnancy and birth. To make the authenticity of Mary even stronger, Gauguin's audience could assume that his own vahine, Pahura (who was pregnant at the time), was the model and that consequently Gauguin himself would be the violator of the virgin and thus the Holy Father. Seen in these terms, the painting is about the sexuality of Mary, Pahura, and Gauguin all at once—an uncomfortable but intriguing series of images to contemplate. Gauguin may not have put a new version of *Noa Noa* into writing, but his paintings continued to present to the world the erotic life that Gauguin wished to convey in his art and his personality.

Gauguin's reinterpretation of traditional Catholic imagery may have helped him ingratiate himself with the Protestant faction. Gauguin had had perhaps more acquaintance with Protestantism than most Frenchmen because his wife had been a Protestant, and they had been married in a Protestant church in Paris. Although neither husband nor wife had been particularly religious, this experience may have made Gauguin more tolerant, or at least familiar with those espousing Protestant beliefs. A point of contact with the Protestant church in Tahiti was Pahura, who was Protestant.[31] All this may have helped him when he decided to enter Tahitian society on a permanent basis because he was immediately befriended by many of the old, powerful Protestant families.

Foremost among them was that of the Frenchman Auguste Goupil, a lawyer trained in Paris and London who settled on Tahiti in 1869 (fig. 67). Over the years he had gained much power by representing the interests of the French government and the most prominent traders. He had also

acquired land and produced copra, the dried meat of the coconut. He was easily the wealthiest and most powerful man in Tahiti and had erected the
most elaborate mansion on the island. Sociable by nature, he was known to all
residents as well as most tourists of any standing, who were often invited
to his country house. Gauguin was no exception; in fact, during Gauguin's
first year back in Tahiti, Goupil was a major supporter and patron. Although
French, Goupil had studied in London and, after settling on Tahiti, married
a woman from one of the prominent British merchant companies in Papeete,
Sarah Gibson. Madame Goupil was active in the Protestant church and
had also achieved renown among all segments of the Tahitian population
as a dedicated homeopathic healer.[32]

The Goupils' embrace of educated newcomers made them acquainted
with ideas current in intellectual circles abroad. As Gauguin completed
his first major paintings in the studio in Punaauia in the spring of 1896, the
Goupils would have been very interested in his approach to religious art,
which deliberately rejected the rigid conventions of the Catholic church in
portraying subjects like the birth of Christ and picking fruit from the
Tree of Knowledge. For Protestants in Europe and the United States, the re-
enactment of these traditional subjects by ordinary people, particularly devout
peasants (including Tahitians), was a gratifying way of making use of the
spirituality of Catholic art without accepting its dogma.[33] Although Gauguin
saw his primary audience as the Paris art world, it certainly would not
hurt him to engage and please these influential neighbors.

Gauguin's attention to local religious debates paid off when the Goupils
invited him to give art lessons to their three younger daughters, Madeleine,
Sarah, and Vaïte ("Jeanne" in Tahitian). They also commissioned Gauguin

to paint a portrait of Vaïte, who was nine years old in 1896 (fig. 68). They surely issued these invitations knowing the radical nature of Gauguin's style, because they had been acquainted with him since at least 1892 and had had many occasions to see his work and debate artistic issues with him.[34]

For the Goupils to allow the persuasive artist such free access to their adolescent daughters was perhaps a mistake. Given his recent attentions not only to Tehamana, Annah, and Pahura a Tai but also to Judith Molard, Jeanne Schuffenecker, and Marie Jade, we know that Gauguin's portraits and lessons for young girls could be overly affectionate. According to the recollections of Vaïte Goupil, the experience of posing for Gauguin, who greeted her in his studio dressed only in a pareu, was an unpleasant one: "At the time, Gauguin was living like a native, his flowered pareu wrapped round his body. His hut was made of bamboo, and it lacked the most necessary things. I stayed only as long as the sitting demanded and then quickly ran back home where the orderliness, the polished furniture and the large armchairs were a comforting contrast. My father found the finished portrait so unlike me, so ugly, that he at once had it removed to the attic."[35]

The portrait is indeed a startling one of a girl not yet ten years old. The elaborate dress and fan, polished coif, and smooth, masklike face give Vaïte the appearance of a young sophisticate. Her parents' shock at seeing the portrait probably had less to do with the abstract style than with their uneasiness about Gauguin's inappropriate view of their daughter and perhaps other suspicions they may have had about Gauguin's behavior with young girls, even those from good, European families. After this, their relationship cooled, and the hard feelings over the portrait may have been at the root of Gauguin's eventual defection to the Catholic party. Gauguin's later vituperative attacks on the Goupils, so surprising in light of their earlier friendship, have the personal edge characteristic of Gauguin's treatment of those, like his wife, whom he has wronged.

Gauguin had not been on the island for a full year before he felt it necessary to revive his old identity as a martyr. This image had been absent from his painting during his first trip to Tahiti, but now, no longer on an extended holiday, he painted a new Christ-like *Self-Portrait near Golgotha* to hang in his studio to remind his Tahitian friends and neighbors of his importance and his need for their sympathy (fig. 69). As for his European audience, it wasn't long before he slipped back into the familiar self-pitying refrain in his correspondence. He had lost his old sympathizers—his wife and Emile Schuffenecker—who now had no patience for this gambit. As Mette wrote to Schuffenecker in early 1896, "Yes, Paul and his ferocious egoism surpass all human comprehension and what irritates me the most is that he considers himself 'a martyr of art.' Enough!"[36] Instead, he concentrated his efforts on Monfreid and Molard, as well as Charles Morice and the various small dealers with whom he had left work to be sold. But the gist of the letters is virtually the same as it had been ever since he left Copenhagen in 1885: Lack of appreciation, ill health, and extraordinary expenses have combined to rob him of his funds; please send more. It is difficult for the modern reader (as it was for the more skeptical of his contemporaries) to believe his tales of poverty.

On Tahiti, Gauguin's appeals for money were so heartfelt that many initially tried to help him. The small collections of paintings amassed by such friends as the attorney general of Tahiti, Edouard Charlier, and the businessman Germain Coulon were probably the result of their willingness to buy his art or accept his art as a repayment of loans when Gauguin appealed to their charitable feelings. But the local community, particularly the Europeans, eventually tired of what they perceived as Gauguin's duplicity in money matters. One disgruntled merchant recalled years later how Gauguin had asked him to repair a stove but, as usual claimed poverty when it came time to pay, and offered art instead. "If he wanted anything from you, he was servile in manner; if he did not want anything, he was a bully and a braggart —just as it suited him. I did not care for Paul Gauguin."[37]

Although Gauguin's pleas of poverty may not have been sincere, his health complaints were certainly valid. He was hospitalized four times in Papeete with various complaints, but the recurring and most crippling condition was the eruption of sores up and down his legs. At first, Gauguin

associated his problem with the broken ankle he had received in 1894 during the brawl at Concarneau.[38] But as time went on, the pain he experienced in walking was coupled with the continual presence of open sores, suggesting to observers a range of conditions from eczema to leprosy. Today it seems most likely that Gauguin's lesions were symptoms of the secondary phase of syphilis and that his frequent heart attacks beginning in the fall of 1897 and finally causing his death in 1903 were signs of the cardiovascular type of tertiary syphilis.[39] The cost of treatment of the various symptoms, in spite of Gauguin's attempts to leave doctors' and hospital bills unpaid, was a drain on his budget, as were the related costs of keeping a carriage and, eventually, hiring additional help.

Weighing Gauguin's tendency to complain against the real possibility that he spent more than he should, it is wisest to see him as neither impoverished nor hoarding great sums of money but living comfortably on a thin cushion of funds. By playing on people's sympathies, he was able to stimulate his sales both in Paris and on Tahiti when he needed to; he was able to borrow liberally from friends as well as banks; and he was able to get others to pay bills for him. He never again found protectors like Nino and Charles Laval, Theo and Vincent van Gogh, or Meyer de Haan, but with the remnants of his nest egg from Paris and increasingly steady sales, he was no longer so greatly in need of one. By the end of 1896, after almost a year of complaints about money and his health, he let slip to Monfreid one of those rare but important expressions of satisfaction: "My studio is very beautiful and the time goes quickly. I can tell you that from six in the morning until noon I can do a lot of good work. Ah my dear Daniel, if only you knew this Tahitian life, you would not want to live in any other way."[40]

The first half of 1897 continued to be peaceful and productive. In March, Gauguin was able to send eight more major canvases to Paris to add to the first group he had sent the previous summer. He also sent some woodcuts made in the style of the popular French folk prints, "images d'Epinal," but redone to include Polynesian motifs. He gave strict instructions to Monfreid not to allow Schuffenecker to submit any of his works to the annual exhibition of the Indépendants (an exhibition Gauguin still shunned), resting all his hopes on the abilities of his various small dealers to place the paintings with appropriate connoisseurs. He had come to believe that exhibitions attracted only enemies; it was better to sell privately. "The best way to sell is in silence, always working with the dealer. Van Gogh alone was able to create his own clientele; today no one knows how to tempt the amateur."[41] After almost seven years, Gauguin still regretted the loss of Theo van Gogh. He even rebuffed the request of Ambroise Vollard that spring for drawings and wood sculptures, pointing to the many unsold examples gathering dust in friends' closets in Paris.[42]

At home in Tahiti, Gauguin was upset to learn that the land he rented and had built a house on was to be sold. Though regretting the loss of his reed and thatch house, he found a nicer, wooden one nearby that he could buy, along with the ground it was on. He added a studio and stable to the new house and once again settled in. This house, when sold in 1901, was bought by a Swedish merchant, Edward Nordman (1846–1902), who lived in it with his wife and five children. Nordman's son Oscar became one of the most prominent Tahitians of his generation.[43] The Nordmans kept the house for many years and rented it to such notables as the British writers Robert Keable and Alec Waugh, but it has long since been replaced as the neighborhood has grown and changed.

Soon after the move in May of 1897, Gauguin's letters resumed the old self-pitying tone. For most of the summer and fall he complained of numerous physical ailments, adding conjunctivitis and heart trouble to the usual problems with his legs and feet, which were being treated with arsenic. In addition, he grappled with the tragic news of his daughter Aline's death, which had occurred in January and he had heard news of in April. Aline's death at the age of nineteen, from pneumonia she caught after leaving a ball, was naturally a shock to her father; but because he had spent only one week with her in the last twelve years, it must have been somewhat abstract.

His first responses, in letters to Monfreid from April and May, reflect his ambivalence and were seemingly heartfelt. "Your letter arrives at the same time as a short and terrible letter from my wife. She tells me brutally of the death of my oldest daughter, who was carried off in a few days by pernicious pneumonia. The news did not move me particularly, I have grown so used to suffering. Then each day memory comes back, the wound opens more deeply, and just now I'm completely discouraged."[44] As his finances worsened during the summer, he began to use the death of his daughter in an increasingly melodramatic and self-serving way. He finally wrote a rambling and nasty letter to his grieving wife, blaming her for Aline's death and all the other evils she has perpetrated against him: "I will not say, 'God keep you,' but, more realistically, 'May your conscience sleep to keep you from waiting for death as a deliverance.'"[45]

In a letter to William Molard, from whom he expected results from his business dealings, he pulled out all the stops. "Ever since my infancy, misfortune has pursued me. Never any luck, never any joy. Everyone always against me, and I exclaim: God Almighty, if You exist, I charge You with injustice and spitefulness. Yes, on the news of my poor Aline's death I doubted everything, I gave a defiant laugh. What use are virtue, work, courage, intelligence. Crime alone is logical and rational."[46] Years before, he had used his son's accident to stir up the sympathy of the Van Gogh brothers. Now he was not above using his daughter's death to make a similar impact on the kindhearted Molards, especially since they held his power of attorney over any matters pertaining to the publication of *Noa Noa*, which would soon be published in *La Revue blanche*.

When he received a copy of the first installment of *Noa Noa* with "of course, no money," he tried a new tack with Monfreid.[47] "My health goes from bad to worse. . . . I haven't even a piece of bread. I live on water and a few mangos and guavas, which are now in season, then sometimes a few freshwater shrimps, when my vahine is able to catch them."[48] This pitiful account of foraging for food was guaranteed to appeal to the European image of life in Tahiti but bore little resemblance to reality: Gauguin bought almost all of his food from the neighborhood grocery store. It laid the groundwork, however, for Gauguin's startling announcement two months later that he had tried unsuccessfully to commit suicide.

Suicide was the fitting climax to Gauguin's campaign for attention and financial assistance during the summer and fall of 1897.[49] Rewards of his campaign appeared by February of 1898, and within the next five months 2,000 francs had arrived from his various friends and agents in France. He had stimulated the European imagination about his sad circumstances in Tahiti. In addition to the eroticism of his life in Tahiti, he had now added the specter of his own death. The symbolic allusion to death was present in his Eves from *The Wine Harvest* on, but this is the first time it appeared in the ongoing narrative of his artistic life. The drama of the suicide was used in the promotion of an exhibition that Leclercq had organized in Sweden, as well as a new exhibition at Vollard's gallery in Paris at the end of the year.

Gauguin's solemn announcement that he had gone into the mountains and ingested an overdose of his medicinal arsenic would perhaps be more credible if it were not dramatically linked in his letter to the equally solemn

painting *Where Do We Come From? What Are We? Where Are We Going?* (fig.
70).[50] "But before I died," he wrote to Monfreid, "I wished to paint a large
canvas that I had in mind, and I worked day and night that whole month in
an incredible fever."[51] He went on to claim that this was his greatest work:
"I shall never do anything better, or even like it. Before death I put into it all
my energy, a passion so dolorous, amid circumstances so terrible, and so
clear was my vision that the haste of the execution is lost and life surges up. . . .
So I have finished a philosophical work on a theme comparable to that of
the Gospel."[52]

Gauguin's breathtaking comparison of his philosophical theories
as presented in *Where Do We Come From?* to the Gospels reflects his own bold
self-identification with Jesus and, at the same time, is consistent with the
religious context of Tahitian society. Nevertheless, this large and intriguing
painting is thought by many to live up to Gauguin's claims. His poetic

and abstract interpretation—which contrasts age with youth, science with innate happiness, and inferior understanding with intelligence—have been repeated with reverence, during his lifetime and ever since.[53] Like *Te Tamari no Atua,* it is a blend of European and Polynesian artistic and religious motifs associated with the underlying purpose of life. Gauguin has added his original ideas to this mixture of Old and New World traditions to enliven them and make them more personal. For example, the central figure appears to be male, and yet it reaches for an apple from the Tree of Knowledge in the traditional gesture of Eve—the perfect expression of Gauguin's androgynous ideal. The painting has been linked with themes of life and death in contemporary avant-garde theater, a link made even more appropriate by the theatrical manner in which Gauguin announced it to the world.[54] It was followed in due course by eight other monumental paintings, sent off in July and destined for his exhibition in Paris.

Gauguin's pleas of poverty, ill health, and perhaps even suicide were also heard on the island of Tahiti. His friends there were not art dealers but bureaucrats, who quickly arranged for him to obtain a position as a draftsman in the Department of Public Works, which he began in March 1898. As a consequence, he moved into Papeete, where he remained for almost a year. As with other jobs that Gauguin claimed to have held over the years (hanging posters in Paris, 1886; digging the Panama Canal, 1887), this one is difficult to substantiate. In one of only a few slight references he made to the job, he said he was paid only six francs a day, a sum that would hardly have justified moving out of his house and into a rented apartment in town, where he would have had to pay rent on top of his mortgage.[55] The paucity of details from Gauguin and the complete lack of documentation from government records about his employment makes our understanding of Gauguin's job vague at best.[56]

By Gauguin's own admission, he "prostrated himself before the government officials" in order to receive some government relief from his financial difficulties.[57] According to Lemasson, he had his eye on a lucrative position as secretary-treasurer at the Agricultural Bank, which was a government appointment.[58] But what he got instead was a position "copying building designs," which, according to later reminiscences, was in the Department of Public Works for the city of Papeete.[59] Although some believed that his appointment was the idea of the new territorial governor, Gustave Gallet, it is much more likely to have been arranged by Gauguin's friends, such as the amateur photographer Jules Agostini, who was director of the Department of Public Works of Tahiti until January 1898,[60] and the amateur painter and connoisseur Jules Auffray, who was deputy director and then director (May 1898) of the Department of Public Works for the city of Papeete.[61] Auffray reportedly remembered Gauguin as a temperamental employee who arrived late and was easily angered.[62]

That Gauguin was able to ready a shipment of eight major paintings for exhibition and sale in Paris by July suggests that he was somewhat free to attend to his painting schedule while he held the government post. Because he continued living in Papeete even after receiving enough money from France to pay off the mortgage on his house and other debts and kept his somewhat loose government post, Papeete must have had claims on him.[63] The first was no doubt medical care, for he suffered bouts of illness in September and December and had to be hospitalized for almost a month. But the second seems to have been his growing interest in the politics of local government and his intellectual engagement with the more influential and contentious community leaders.

Still, although Gauguin was becoming more deeply involved in non-art issues in Papeete, he was able to finish eight paintings for his first major exhibition in Paris since 1893. Now that Gauguin's ferociousness was turned more toward local politics than to art, both his art and his newly muted personality were apparently more palatable to those in Paris who had to work with him.

The crucial figure in channeling Gauguin's art into a more acceptable position in the Paris art world was the dealer and publisher of fine prints

Ambroise Vollard. Vollard, who turned thirty in 1898, had owned a gallery in Paris since 1895 and was already responsible for the promotion of Cézanne, the Nabis, and other avant-garde artists in the 1890s. Vollard had exhibited pieces by Gauguin and had corresponded with him in Tahiti about taking his drawings and sculpture directly. It is unclear how he arranged to show nine of Gauguin's most recent paintings from Tahiti in November of 1898, because Gauguin had shipped them thinking that they would be shown privately with Durand-Ruel or Bing, the decorative arts dealer, or in the studios of old faithfuls, like Chaudet and Monfreid.[64] But in a sudden coup, Vollard convinced Monfreid to sell him the whole batch for 1,000 francs and then exhibited them so that only Vollard himself would profit from the increased exposure. Gauguin was understandably furious when he found out about this later.[65]

The exhibition drew favorable reviews in *Mercure de France* and *La Revue blanche,* among other radical journals, and the new, calm, and classical mood of Gauguin's most recent paintings was widely admired. Critics were glad to see that Gauguin was no longer using art to threaten or mystify his audience but showed a stronger adherence to natural forms while using colors and designs in a pleasing, decorative manner. Gustave Geffroy called for stained-glass windows and tapestries from Gauguin,[66] and Thadée Natanson wrote that now "one takes greater pleasure in his riches."[67] The review that pleased Gauguin the most was in *Mercure de France,* whose previous art critic, Mauclair, had sent Gauguin off to Tahiti in 1895 with stinging ridicule. This time the *Mercure*'s art critic, André Fontainas, wrote of his grudging respect for the new work. "I don't like the art of M. Paul Gauguin . . . [but] I at least have felt arise and take hold in me a secure and profound esteem for the solemn, contemplative, and sincere work of this artist."[68] Gauguin was so affected that he took the unusual step of writing to Fontainas and corresponded with him at intervals over the next few years.[69]

The calm, decorative works that Gauguin had just produced, including the majestic *Where Do We Come From?,* have to be viewed partly as the outcome of Gauguin's weakening grasp of current artistic issues. The style is more classical, based increasingly on his photo collection of famous works of art rather than on his discovery and posing of interesting models. The content is also less personal and no longer geared to a small in-group of fellow radicals. Instead, Gauguin again takes familiar classical themes, using biblical and other subject matter, such as the fruit picker, in a more abstract, idyllic setting filled with symbols from Polynesian and Asian art. The female figures tend to be more conventionally feminine rather than androgynous and there are no overt references to rape or violence of any kind (fig. 71). This approach is more universal, but it is also more vague, and reflects Gauguin's confession to Monfreid that "I'm no longer a judge of Parisian taste. Perhaps it's a good thing—I don't know."[70]

Although Gauguin was making his monumental paintings for Paris milder and more decorative, he had by no means stopped using his art to threaten and mystify the audience at hand—his Tahitian friends and neighbors. Bengt Danielsson, a Swedish anthropologist and Gauguin researcher on Tahiti, recounts a story of how the Catholic priest of Punaauia attempted

to have Gauguin remove a suggestive sculpture of a nude woman from his grounds. The location of the sculpture was very public, for Gauguin's property was along the road next to a school. Gauguin not only refused but apparently threatened to sue the priest.[71] In another case, Gauguin gave a large painting to a workman, Léonore, who had helped him print his newspaper, *Le Sourire*. "He called it 'Tahitian Love.' It was a woman, completely naked, stretched out on a mat: her man held her by her hair and was beating her! The woman was red and the man was entirely green. . . . For a long time I kept it in my closet, but my wife said it might give me evil ideas. I destroyed it."[72] The same man remembered another sculpture that came up for sale in the auction following Gauguin's death. "It was a nude woman with her head on the ground and her ass in the air! It was destroyed on the spot."[73]

Several years after Gauguin's death, when his reputation as an artist grew to international proportions, it became popular for Tahitians to claim that they had inadvertently lost or destroyed works by Gauguin in their possession and thus had thrown away a fortune.[74] Many also confessed that they had destroyed Gauguin's works either because the art was offensive or because the artist had later turned on them. Both Germain Coulon and Edouard Charlier had burned collections of Gauguin's works when their friendships with Gauguin turned sour. Charlier was still angry when he was interviewed before his death in 1937: "Gauguin was nothing but an ingrate! I welcomed, nurtured, and took care of him. He was a monster! The most disagreeable and tyrannical man who ever lived. . . . I destroyed his paintings when he challenged me to a duel."[75]

The peaceful image of Tahiti projected by the canvases that Gauguin sent back to Paris belied the actual state of affairs for Gauguin after his year in Papeete in 1898. Although he moved back out to his house in Punaauia in February of 1899 and made it beautiful again—he repaired damage caused by the neglect of the previous year and planted a lush garden of flowers with seeds sent from France—his spirit was bitter.[76] His friends from Papeete were political partisans, and, as he entertained them in his home with abundant food, drink, and vahines, they aired their grievances and concocted ways of lashing out at their enemies.

Now that Gauguin had been on the island for more than three years, his arrogance and contentiousness had fully emerged. As in his sharp dealings with opposing artistic groups in France and in his seesaw relationships with his wife and old friends, Gauguin had by now carved up Tahitian society into the small group that was loyal to him and the larger group made up of his enemies. Because Tahitian society was unusually tolerant of outsiders and nonconforming behavior, virtually every one of Gauguin's enemies had at one time been his friend. One senses from the reminiscences of people like Charlier that Gauguin must have gone to extremes if he overcame the Tahitians' natural inclination to accept and like him.

Perhaps Gauguin's need for enemies was stronger than his need for friends. When he left the hospital in Papeete in the summer of 1896 without paying his bill,[77] he was shocked that the next time he went for treatment he was classified as "indigent" and made to pay in advance.[78] Gauguin magnified this supposed insult into a plot against him: "You will easily understand that, although in great pain, I had to refuse to go in with a mixed lot of soldiers and servants. Besides, here, as in France, there is a faction that considers me a rebel, and, like everywhere else, in fact here more than elsewhere, a man in financial straits is ill treated. Of course I am talking only about the Europeans in Papeete, because here in my part of the island the natives are, as always, very good to me and very respectful."[79] The key word for Gauguin was "respect." He had no use for those who questioned his behavior or morals, particularly in matters of money.

Gauguin's year in Papeete brought many seemingly minor disputes to a head. While mixing with Tahitian society in town, he seems to have clarified who his enemies were, as well as his friends. He blamed the low status of his job at the Department of Public Works for the snubs that he began to receive, but it is likely that his arrogance and questionable morals were more than enough to offend those who now saw him every day.[80]

In addition to his interactions with town society, Gauguin was fighting battles in Punaauia. While he was away, Pahura (who was pregnant), her family, and other unidentified neighbors apparently made ample use of his house. He tried to have Pahura arrested and sent to jail for this (even though the house was her home, too), but neither the local law enforcement officers nor the courts would carry out his wishes. He took the dispute to the top of the Tahitian justice system, to his old friend Edouard Charlier, attorney general of Tahiti, who also refused to prosecute Pahura.[81]

Gauguin's touchiness in matters of money and women was elevated to a political principle when he noticed that the individuals who had "snubbed" him were Protestants. With his enemies thus identified, Gauguin found that he could attack them freely under the guise of political debate. By channeling his anger along political lines, he was also assured of a group of loyal supporters — members of the opposition Catholic party led by François Cardella, longtime mayor of Papeete and good friend of Gauguin's.

From 1884 to 1889, Cardella and the merchant Victor Raoulx published a newspaper, *Le Messager de Tahiti,* which voiced opposition to the colonial government, itself represented by the dry, bureaucratic weekly *Le Journal officiel des etablissements français de l'Océanie.* Since 1889, Cardella and Raoulx had wanted to revive an opposition newspaper, and in March 1899 they launched a small monthly that offered stinging political commentary, *Les Guêpes* (The Wasps). It is not clear whether Gauguin had a hand in the founding of the paper, but by June he was a major contributor.

Gauguin's family background in journalism — which included both his grandmother, Flora Tristan, and his father, Clovis Gauguin — was a source of great pride. Furthermore, his occasional forays into publishing in Paris over the years, as well as the publication of *Noa Noa* in 1897, no doubt whetted his appetite. But nothing in Gauguin's past writings approximated the unrestrained, vituperative prose that launched Gauguin's career as a journalist in *Les Guêpes.* Of his four submissions to the June 1899 issue, one was an open letter to Charlier in which Gauguin called him vain, stupid, and incompetent, and the other was a salacious article on "the parasol mushroom of Sumatra," which was signed with Gauguin's new pseudonym, Tit-Oil.

The open letter to Charlier ended by challenging him to a duel and was the cause of Charlier's destruction of Gauguin's paintings and his lasting enmity. The article signed Tit-Oil was intended to offend everyone else. Like the signature PGo, which Gauguin introduced in the center of the ceramist Chaplet's rosary on the bottom of vases, Tit-Oil is sacrilegious and scatological. For English speakers it reads as "oil for tits," but for Tahitian speakers (and everyone who lived in Tahiti) it was an inadequately veiled version of "Titoi," the most loathsome sexual curse in a language full of colorful sexual expressions. "Go fuck yourself" is only a pale approximation of its meaning in Tahitian.[82] Its sexual belligerence suited Gauguin's irrepressible desire to shock and offend.

The exhilaration of Gauguin's new hold on the public imagination led him to go one step further. After publishing again in *Les Guêpes* in July, he introduced his own monthly publication, ironically titled *Le Sourire: Journal sérieux* (The Smile: A Serious Newspaper), later *Journal méchant* (A Wicked Newspaper; fig. 72). As publisher, editor, writer, illustrator, and distributor, Gauguin had the spotlight to himself. For the next nine months Gauguin picked his targets, such as Auguste Goupil's attempt to capitalize an island railroad, wrote the satirical articles, and illustrated the sheets with woodcut mastheads and cartoon caricatures. He wrote out the text in his neat

clerk's handwriting, added the graphics, and printed the whole on an early version of the mimeograph machine. These crude but intriguing sheets were read by all those who enjoyed scandal; but like Gauguin's art in local collections, the issues of *Le Sourire* were too offensive to preserve, and few sets have found their way into public collections.[83]

*Le Sourire* was published alongside *Les Guêpes,* with Gauguin continuing to write for both, until February 1900, when Gauguin was made editor of *Les Guêpes.* Two months later he discontinued *Le Sourire,* and he concentrated on *Les Guêpes* until his departure from Tahiti in the summer of 1901. Although he drew a salary for this position, which no doubt was attractive to him, his desire to lash out in words or images and thus draw much-needed attention to himself was a strong enough motivation to keep him writing and editing this newspaper month after month. He saw his enemies increase during this time and ignored pleas for justice and moderation. After Gauguin viciously attacked Georges Dormoy, a schoolteacher in Faaa, the man wrote an open letter in reply: "You, Monsieur Gauguin, have chosen to spread lies and calumny about innocent people for gain. To exploit the good faith of his fellow men and shamefully abuse the public trust is a strange employment for an artist."[84] Even tourists noticed the hysterical tone of *Les Guêpes.* A British pair wrote, "The only newspaper published, called *Les Guêpes,* comes out but once a month, and chiefly confines itself to scurrilous abuse of the Governor and the Government generally."[85]

Gauguin's abrasive nature had found a fitting outlet in the pages of a political journal, but the intensity of his bitterness ended his ability to live on Tahiti with any comfort. If the censure he encountered in Europe over the treatment of his wife and his inability to adequately promote his career was enough to drive him back to Tahiti, the censure he felt in Tahiti was surely enough to force him into yet another retreat. Gauguin had made so many powerful enemies that "Tahiti had become a little unhealthy for him."[86]

During 1900, Gauguin fought off the growing pressure of his many enemies by clinging to the small circle of friends who were funding the paper and whose financial and political interests were being served by *Les Guêpes* just as much as were Gauguin's personal needs. Gauguin's banquets at Punaauia became more elaborate in those days, with festive native dinners served whose menus were written and decorated in Gauguin's own hand.[87] "Gauguin seemed to be rich, being always well stocked with spirits and every sort of tinned goods. Nearly every Sunday he would invite a few friends to a *tamara'a* [native meal]. The meal was always very carefully prepared and everything would pass off quietly and decently during dinner. After dinner, however, some new guests would arrive and the party would really warm up and usually would go on through the night. Gauguin liked to amuse himself by persuading his guests to make fools of themselves (such as getting the women to undress). Although he drank copiously, he never seemed to get drunk himself, and always kept himself under control."[88] The friends that Gauguin entertained in this manner were not the inexperienced young men who had always formed Gauguin's coteries in France, but powerful, mature men whose dalliances with Gauguin had only the appearance of sincerity. In 1901, when Gauguin began to talk of leaving for a purer, more sympathetic island, there was no outcry, no attempt to keep him. When he was gone, friends like Germain Coulon, whose printing plant published *Les Guêpes,* threw the art and other remembrances of Gauguin into the trash.[89] In the 1940s a journalist interviewing Tahitians who had known Gauguin reported, "Not one person with whom I spoke who had known him (with the solitary exception of his old mistress), had a good word to say concerning the painter."[90]

# 14  Final Retreat

1901–3

The citizens of Atuona, the largest town in the Marquesas island group, must have welcomed Tit-Oil to their community with some trepidation. Though about eight hundred ocean miles northwest of Tahiti, the Marquesas were as linked to the capital city of Papeete as the provinces of France were linked to Paris.[1] The mail boat, like most other vessels coming to the Marquesas, steamed in from Papeete, bringing all official government correspondence and all unofficial gossip. In addition, there was a good deal of traveling back and forth between Tahiti and all the islands of French Polynesia, not only by government officials and traders but by most people, native and European, of any standing. The Marquesas had been gradually losing population to the more cosmopolitan island of Tahiti, which meant that virtually everyone in Atuona now had a relative in Papeete who kept them informed of the latest styles and scandals of the capital.

When Gauguin arrived, he already knew personally or was familiar with most of the key people in Atuona because of their ties to Tahiti. One young pastor, Paul Vernier, had stopped briefly in Tahiti in 1897 after finishing divinity school in France and before proceeding to the Marquesas to head the Protestant mission there. After reading a letter sent by Vernier from his new post in Atuona, which was published in the Protestant evangelical journal, Gauguin lampooned Vernier's earnest tone and Protestant fervor in the July 1900 issue of *Les Guêpes*.[2] The young man of thirty was not Gauguin's main target; rather, he aimed at his father, Frédéric Vernier, the most powerful Protestant minister in Tahiti, former friend of Pomare IV, and founder and president of the official Conseil supérieur des églises tahitiennes.[3]

The Atuonans had good reason to fear the writer of such vicious, often obscene attacks on individuals whom they knew and liked; but compounding this fearsome reputation was the impact of his physical appearance in 1901. By this time the sores on Gauguin's legs were so noxious that he was seldom able to keep them covered for long periods of time. Most people on Tahiti were aware of the extent of his disease, and his new neighbors in Atuona learned of it immediately, too. It had become common on Tahiti for people to avoid having contact with the potentially contagious man, and they were especially careful to keep their children away from him if they could.

The principal dentist in Papeete, William Davis, went to the trouble of traveling to Punaauia for appointments with Gauguin because he refused to have open sores in his office in town. He took great sanitary precautions when treating Gauguin and covered himself with sterile cloths.[4] A man who grew up in Punaauia near Gauguin remembered that his father always sent the children away when Gauguin came to the house. "His legs were covered with sores and the flies pestered him mercilessly."[5] Whether people thought it was syphilis, leprosy, or simple eczema (all three were given as explanations by those who knew him), they could not but find him repulsive. Naturally enough, Gauguin found the most sympathetic reception in Atuona from the principal health-care workers in town, the Vietnamese Nguyen Van Cam and Gauguin's former journalistic victim Paul Vernier.[6]

His repulsiveness notwithstanding, Gauguin arrived in Atuona aiming to please. He had sold his property in Punaauia for a handsome profit and intended to build an even more splendid house from which he could regale the citizens of Atuona with his genius in art and literature. Retired now from political journalism, which had been satisfying but had not engendered the respect he thought he deserved, he planned to return to the occupation and identity of internationally famous artist. During the years that he was directing his venom solely toward Tahitian political targets (1899–1901), the art world in Paris had been able to forget his personal failings and had grown considerably warmer toward him.

Furthermore, as Paris prepared to celebrate the turn of the century with its spectacular International Exposition, the Impressionists and their successors were welcomed into the mainstream. Gauguin's old colleagues, such as those who had participated in the Volpini exhibition of 1889, were anxious to include him in one of the many celebratory reunions of the old radical groups being organized for 1900. In June 1899 he wrote to Maurice Denis an extraordinarily self-pitying letter calculated to make the accommodating Denis work harder on Gauguin's behalf. After taking yet another swipe at Bernard ("everybody knows that I have actually pillaged my master, Emile Bernard"),[7] he declared, "My work is finished. . . . Being very ill and obliged to earn a little bread by doing work that is anything but intellectual, I no longer paint, except Sundays and holidays."[8] This picture of himself as too poor to paint cunningly disregards the truth: he had quit his job in Papeete and was once again living comfortably in his renovated house in Punaauia with only his monthly journalistic efforts taking time away from his art. But it had the impact he desired on Denis and the wealthy group of Nabis, whom he reminded of their privileges and, by implication, their responsibility to him: "Nearly all of you having means, a numerous clientele, and powerful friends, it would be astonishing if each of you could not reap the legitimate fruit of your talent and your discoveries."[9] Having prodded his former followers, Gauguin went on to explain to Monfreid in a concurrent letter that, rather than be relegated to a group exhibition, he wanted his own show at Vollard's during the centennial year and would send from Tahiti "a dozen good canvases" to exhibit with some of his older works.[10]

Gauguin's clear intention of repeating the success he had had at Vollard's in late 1898 was duly communicated to Vollard by Monfreid. At about the same time that Vollard would have received this news (fall 1899), the small dealer who had emerged as Gauguin's principal agent in Paris, Georges

Chaudet, unexpectedly died. Vollard had occasionally bought Gauguin's paintings from Chaudet but now saw that his best course would be to deal directly with the artist and establish an exclusive relationship with him.[11] Vollard had had reasonable success in this way with Gauguin's old colleague and rival Cézanne, whose works he bought in large quantities and, with judicious exhibitions, was beginning to sell regularly. Cézanne, who had competed with Gauguin for Pissarro's attention twenty years before, had now emerged, like Vincent van Gogh, in the position of leadership in modern art circles that Gauguin wanted so badly for himself. Vollard wrote to Gauguin with the first offer that Gauguin had received from a major dealer since the death of Theo van Gogh in 1890: "In short, I am willing to buy everything you do; the only stipulations are that we must come to an understanding in regard to prices, and that the pictures must be painted on good canvas, which I could send you, and with good colors, which I could also have sent to you."[12]

Although at first Gauguin treated Vollard high-handedly ("When I was in Paris, I sold for prices starting at 2,000 down to 500 at the lowest"; "What I am and what I want to go on being is this: a great artist"; "A price of 200 francs is what you pay a beginner, not a man with a well-established reputation"), once he learned of Chaudet's death, he saw how a temporary agreement with Vollard would be useful until he could feel really established in Paris.[13] He agreed to a monthly sum of 300 francs, which Vollard would send him as credit against a regular flow of paintings—eighteen paintings a year—priced at 200 francs each. By the fall of 1900 the money had begun to come in, and Gauguin had begun working systematically. Although Vollard did not mount the desired exhibition in 1900 (nor indeed any exhibitions until after Gauguin's death in 1903), and Gauguin often complained that Vollard was late in his payments, both men were ultimately satisfied with the bargain they had struck.

It has often been said that Vollard's monthly payments freed Gauguin from poverty at long last and allowed him, first, to return to painting full-time and, second, to relocate to the Marquesas, a dream of his. At the very time that Vollard's payments began, however, Gauguin casually mentioned to Monfreid that he had saved up "five or six thousand francs, which [he was] enjoying to the fullest."[14] In light of Gauguin's real financial comfort, we must acknowledge that Vollard's money was no doubt a nice supplement to Gauguin's finances, but hardly a life-saving windfall. Therefore, the impact of Vollard's contract was more symbolic than financial: it affirmed Gauguin's belief in himself as a great artist and was useful in impressing the Polynesian community. It also forced him to produce art in a more regular manner and to think once again of an audience beyond the one he regularly lambasted in his local political articles and cartoons. Whereas most of his artwork in 1900 consisted of drawings and woodcuts related to the caricatural art printed in *Le Sourire,* by 1901 he was painting still lifes and figure paintings that he felt could be shown to good effect in Paris.

Because Gauguin's desire to leave Tahiti for Hiva Oa did not arise until some time after the contract was settled, his departure was probably not a direct result of the financial arrangement. In the fall of 1900, Gauguin was still convinced that he would live the rest of his life on Tahiti.[15] Rather, now that he was faced with the obligation of addressing a sophisticated Parisian audience again, the idea of new, more picturesque subject matter led him to think of pulling up stakes. His intense unpopularity in Tahiti was probably another incentive. In the spring of 1901 he informed correspondents in Paris of his intentions, and in September he sold his property and set sail.

Gauguin's relief at escaping a place that had become hostile to him (a relief he had felt many times in the past) was made even more pleasurable this time because he had confidence that his art was becoming successful in Paris. Whereas Gauguin's previous retreats were launched in the hope of future success, the move to the Marquesas was based on established success. Gauguin got off the boat in Atuona a happy man. With 4,500 francs from the sale of his house in Punaauia and the remains of the 5,000 or 6,000 francs he reported having in 1900, he believed he would be one of the wealthiest and most famous citizens of the Marquesas.[16]

Gauguin's move from Tahiti to Hiva Oa was like his move from Pont-Aven to Le Pouldu. Without sacrificing his connection to the larger, more active Tahiti, he was nevertheless sufficiently removed that he could live without the scrutiny of a cosmopolitan population. Atuona was a small town compared to Papeete, which, with 3,720 people, had a greater population than all of the Marquesas islands combined.[17] And although Atuona was the most important town in the Marquesas and was organized into the same colonial social structure as could be found on all Pacific islands of any size, it did not have such a powerful set of old families nor such an impressive list of important visitors and tourists as Papeete did. Gauguin could be much more prominent in Atuona's modest social system than he had been in the competitive Tahitian one.

He immediately took advantage of his high standing by buying a prime piece of property in the middle of town from the Catholic mission, upon which he built his impressive "native" house. Topped with a thatched roof and decorated with polychromed carvings, the two-story house was like many island homes in that the shady, open-air ground floor served as the main dining and living area and the upper floor was for sleeping.[18] Hiva Oa was hotter and more humid than Tahiti because of its location closer to the equator, so Gauguin used the second floor for his painting studio in an attempt to reduce the effects of the humidity. The landscape of Hiva Oa was denser than Tahiti's, which had offered to its population a convenient large, flat plain around the central core of mountains. The town of Atuona, on the other hand, was situated in a rocky valley that made transportation (particularly by horse and carriage) difficult and, in addition, was overgrown with lush trees and vegetation that gave each of the houses in town a sense of privacy. Gauguin was thrilled with his location: "I am in the center of the village although no one could guess it, my house is so well surrounded by trees."[19]

Gauguin was also fortunate in his neighbors. Nearby was the town's principal store, run by the American merchant and shipowner Benjamin Franklin Varney, who had married a local woman and settled in Atuona in the early 1890s. Through Varney, Gauguin was in touch with the world. He could import the American lumber used to build his house and order French wines and absinthe; and through Varney's branch of the Société commerciale de l'Océanie (a German bank serving all Polynesia), Gauguin received his monthly payments from Vollard. As in Tahiti, Gauguin was quickly received into Atuona's European community of traders and plantation owners, among whom there was an active social life with and without wives. Closest to Gauguin was Emile Frébault, merchant and retailer, who had originally owned the land Gauguin built his house on. Frébault and his English wife, Fanny Keane, were Gauguin's nearest neighbors and most frequent visitors. Gauguin soon reestablished the dinners he had held for his male friends at Punaauia with Frébault and the other wealthy men of the island, including Pierre Guillitoue and Zacharie Touahaafeu, cotton planters from the nearby south coast, and the copra planter Renier.[20]

As might be expected, Gauguin's relations with the official community of Atuona were more checkered. Though not the capital of the Marquesas (which was Taiohae, on the island of Nuku Hiva), Atuona, because of its size, was home to many government and missionary officials, who shared the responsibilities of providing schools, health care, and law enforcement on the islands. The Marquesas had historically been the center of French Catholicism in Polynesia because the British and French Protestants had not gained the foothold there that they had in Tahiti. When the French naval admiral du Petit-Thouars took the Marquesas peaceably (and almost imperceptibly) under French sovereignty in 1842, Catholic missionaries set up their headquarters in Atuona, and had provided the most constant European presence ever since.[21]

When Gauguin arrived, the Vicaire apostalique (Bishop) of the Marquesas was Monseigneur Joseph Martin, a Frenchman about Gauguin's age (early fifties) who had served in Tahiti from 1878 until 1890, when he was appointed to his present post. Though dedicated to the welfare of the native Marquesan population—fifteen books were published in the Marquesan language under his administration—he was troubled by the rejection of missionary influence throughout the islands and the new spirit of political action that came with the twentieth century. The most visible sign of change was the closing of the missionary schools, established earlier with great difficulty. The schools became victims of the act separating church and state throughout the French empire in 1901 and had not yet been replaced by a system of secular public education.[22]

Bishop Martin's knowledge of Gauguin was extensive by the time the artist arrived. He had reason to be wary of the contentious man who had had run-ins with his parish priest in Punaauia and whose nickname Coquain implied a greater sexual licentiousness than does the harmless English translation, "rascal"; the feminine version, "coquaine," means "slut." But Bishop Martin was also aware of Gauguin's allegiance to the Catholic party on Tahiti, and Gauguin's attacks on Martin's Protestant rival, Paul Vernier, indicated that he would be a useful ally. For the same political reasons, Gauguin took special pains with Bishop Martin in his first few weeks in Atuona, and when he discovered that the bishop controlled the prime piece of property he wanted to buy, he redoubled his efforts. He was seen frequently in the town church, which was marked by a monumental Crucifixion with bronze figures and by a white cross, erected out front in 1901.[23] He also evinced an interest in the Marquesan language and other intellectual topics dear to the learned priest's heart.

The uneasy alliance yielded Gauguin his property and the cooperation of the bishop in recommending workmen to build the house, but Gauguin soon encountered mission disapproval of his sexual practices. Within two months, Gauguin was writing to Monfreid, "Except for the annoyance of the priest, it's perfect."[24] In his later memoirs, Gauguin described the falling out like this: "A chicken had come along, and war had begun. When I say *a* chicken I am modest, for all the chickens arrived, and without any invitation. His reverence is a regular goat, while I am a tough old cock and fairly well seasoned. If I said the goat began it, I should be telling the truth. To want to condemn me to a vow of chastity! That's a little too much."[25] As on Tahiti, any new European man in Atuona was quickly surrounded by candidates vying for his favors. The humor of the pursuit of Gauguin by the known "loose women" was captured in verse by Nguyen Van Cam in the lengthy epic "Loves of an Old Painter," which made the rounds of Atuona society with Gauguin's approval.[26]

It is unlikely that such a common occurrence as a liaison between a European man and a local adult female prostitute (according to Nguyen Van Cam, Gauguin's final choice was twenty years old) would have drawn the disapproval of the priest. Rather, it is more likely that Gauguin's taste for adolescent schoolchildren was the issue for the church and for Atuona's family-oriented community. Bishop Martin's efforts to educate the children and keep them from premature sexual relationships encountered enough opposition from traditional Polynesian values that Gauguin's preference for marginal sexuality was an extra annoyance.

As in Punaauia, Gauguin built his house on the main road; he could observe the girls going to the girls' school a block away and the boys going to their school next door to him, only a few yards away. As in Punaauia, Gauguin used his front lawn as a stage for art that would offend his neighbors. He soon carved a caricature of Bishop Martin as a lascivious devil and set it opposite a carving of a nude woman labeled "Thérèse," the name of the bishop's young servant: "It was enough to name her Thérèse for everyone without exception, even the school-children, to see in it an allusion to this celebrated love affair."[27] That he wanted more from the school-children than an audience for his scandalmongering was evident to all, and at least one, the fourteen-year-old Vaeoho (also called Marie-Rose), served as his sexual partner and became pregnant with his child.[28]

The news quickly spread about town that Gauguin's house was full of sexual art with which he entertained his visitors, from the amused local planters to the wide-eyed schoolchildren. Visitors remembered seeing porno-graphic art of all kinds—photographs, Japanese prints, and a "series of paintings of sexual anatomy"—lining the walls.[29] The statues of Bishop Martin and Thérèse and the relief panels surrounding the doorway which proclaimed this the "house of pleasure" were mild compared to the many carvings of penises scattered about as cane handles or objets d'art. A story told around the islands was that Bishop Martin had seen all the phalluses around Gauguin's house and thought they were hammers.[30] Once most people realized what they were looking at, they could not help but have a strong response, much to Gauguin's delight.

Many were offended by Gauguin's use of sexual imagery to provoke and titillate, but as usual, Gauguin found a small group of young men who were charmed by his eloquent arguments to justify such offensiveness in the name of modern art and individual liberty. Surprisingly, one of Gauguin's most fervent admirers was his old Protestant target Pastor Vernier. Vernier's youth and recent education in France made him much more open to Gauguin's modernist philosophy than was Bishop Martin, who was long divorced from the flow of avant-garde ideas in France and was burdened by the more practical issues dogging his mission. Vernier's training in health care may have made him initially more valuable to Gauguin than most officials on the island, but his genuine interest in art and religious reform led to many a lengthy tête-à-tête over absinthe in the artist's studio. Although Vernier never felt that he was Gauguin's friend, their shared antipathy toward the powerful Catholic mission and the strict law enforcement officials made them allies; and in Vernier's later descriptions of Gauguin's isolation and idealistic nature, one senses that Vernier liked to see much of himself in Gauguin.

Vernier was certainly impressed with Gauguin's standing among the great modern writers in Paris, with whom Vernier was already familiar. He described one of his meetings with Gauguin in detail to Gauguin's first biographer, Jean de Rotonchamp, after the painter's death: "I went immediately [at Gauguin's summons] to the artist's home. He suffered horribly in his legs, which were red and swollen and covered with eczema. I recommended the proper medication, offering to rub it on for him if he wished. He thanked me very kindly, saying he could do it himself. We talked. Forgetting his pain, he spoke to me of his art in very admirable terms, portraying himself as an undiscovered genius. . . . He loaned me several of Dolent's and Aurier's books and *L'Après-midi d'une faune,* which he had from Mallarmé himself."[31] Vernier was moved by Gauguin's affection for the Marquesan landscape and population, which matched his own and which he felt Gauguin portrayed sympathetically in his art.

Even the pornographic images that Gauguin surrounded himself with were acceptable to Vernier. Vernier found in them one more point of disagreement with the local officials, both secular and religious, who tried to dictate public morality. When the police official who was conducting the auction of Gauguin's possessions in Atuona after his death destroyed one of the phallic walking sticks, Vernier objected: "You have no right to break this walking stick; you do not know that it is a work of art and not the piece of filth you have just called it."[32] Vernier's passionate defense of Gauguin in the years after his death did much to mitigate the widespread dislike of the man and create the sympathetic image that Gauguin had been unable to create for himself.

Gauguin's relationships with natives of the Marquesas were typical of those in any colonized Polynesian society. As on Tahiti, many of the Europeans married into the upper-class Marquesan families, and social lines between whites and natives were frequently blurred. Gauguin's young vahine, Vaeoho, was the daughter of one of the district chiefs of Hiva Oa, and their child was brought up in the same Europeanized manner that Vaeoho had been, attending boarding school in Atuona and marrying a similarly educated local man. Among Gauguin's friends, Varney, Renier, and Nguyen Van Cam were all married to prominent Marquesan women.

Vernier reported that Gauguin was well liked by the Marquesans because of his easy, democratic manner. This is largely based on Gauguin's friendship with Tioka, Vernier's local deacon, who owned the land next to Gauguin's. Although Tioka was not the district chief of Atuona (this position was held by a man named Mahitete Karoro), he was apparently an influential man in the community. He organized the building of Gauguin's house and offered his two nephews as servants to the ailing artist.[33]

The younger of the two nephews, Timo, was fifteen at the time and later became chief of Atuona.[34] Timo, well educated and cultured, recalled that Gauguin enjoyed teasing Tioka about being a cannibal: "Koké [Gauguin] used to give him tobacco and he often teased him with some question as to whether human flesh tasted good."[35] Tioka, who sported the traditional Marquesan tattoos "from head to toe," played the part for Gauguin: "How Tioka's teeth would glitter! He had extraordinary teeth—so long and white they were! He could have opened a can of tinned fruit with them."[36]

When Gauguin arrived in Atuona, he agreed to exchange names with Tioka, a custom that Marquesan natives eagerly pressed on European visitors, who later learned to be more cautious. Frederick O'Brien had a low opinion of the custom: "One woman pointed to me and said that she wished to take my name and give me her own. This is their custom with one to whom they are attracted, but I affected not to understand. . . . 'Keep your name to yourself, *mon ami*,' said Le Moine. 'They expect much from you if you give them yours. They will give you heaps of useless presents, but you alone have the right to buy rum.'"[37]

Gauguin's liberal consumption and sharing of liquor was certainly one of his most endearing qualities in the minds of some in Atuonan society, but others considered it one of his worst qualities. The issues of liquor and the native population caused Gauguin to be in the center of the maelstrom caused by attempts to regulate its sale and consumption by natives, upon whom it seemed to have an unusually deleterious effect. Gauguin advocated the repeal of all such regulations and did his part personally to circumvent them whenever possible. In the inevitable clashes with the authorities that resulted, Gauguin used many arguments to defend his actions, invoking personal liberty, the sadism of the local police force, and, the colonist's ultimate appeal, economic impact: "Since the very recent ban on drinking, which does away with a trade that had been profitable for the colonists, the native can now think of only one thing—drinking—and therefore he flees the towns and goes to hide somewhere else, which is why it is impossible to find workers."[38]

Aside from Gauguin's desire to relax the local authorities' regulation of children's sexual morality and natives' drinking habits, Gauguin had another interest in the Marquesan population that most Europeans did not have: their use as models in his art. Although he liked to emphasize that he painted from his imagination, he nevertheless needed to absorb some elements of the Marquesan people and landscape that would set these paintings apart from his Tahitian phase and would stir the Parisian imagination about this exotic locale. Before he left Tahiti, he imagined that the Marquesan setting would allow him to produce pictures as different from the Tahiti series as the Tahiti pictures had been from those done in Brittany.[39] He imagined that the less populated, more remote islands with their dramatic history of cannibalism would yield wilder, more primitive motifs.

Yet the Marquesan pictures can be distinguished from the Tahitian pictures only by experts or by clear dates inscribed on the canvases by Gauguin himself, demonstrating that it was harder than Gauguin had thought to find distinctive Marquesan models and symbolism. Some have questioned whether certain works that he sent from Atuona may in fact have been done on Tahiti or painted from photographs and sketches brought with him from Tahiti. Curiously, none of the Marquesan paintings include the most famous sign of Marquesan culture—the body tattoo—which Gauguin had ample opportunity to observe in Atuona.

However, several paintings dated 1902 show Gauguin's attempt to depict two local Marquesan types whose equivalents would not have been found on Tahiti. The first is an androgynous man with long, black hair in *Marquesan Man in a Red Cape* (fig. 73). The red cape is so unusual a garment for the South Seas that the man has been supposed to be a *taua*, or priest, or at the very least a mahu, or homosexual. Attempts to identify the model as a native friend of Gauguin's, Hapuani, have been inconclusive; at any rate, the painting suggests that Gauguin deliberately depicted an exotic local character.[40]

The second model is more easily identified. She is Tohotaua, the red-haired beauty identified by Pastor Vernier when he sent a photograph of her to Monfreid after Gauguin's death (fig. 74). Although red hair was unusual among Polynesians, it was not as rare as Danielsson has suggested, and Gauguin no doubt saw it as a symbol of a distinctive Marquesan ethnic type.[41] The Marquesans are believed to be the most pure and ancient of the island ethnic groups, having arrived from Asia via the Samoan chain about 300 A.D. and subsequently radiated out to other Pacific islands.[42] Taller and stronger in physique and lighter in skin color than other Polynesians, the Marquesans were admired by Western visitors as the most beautiful of them all. Gauguin's choice of this redheaded model for *Woman with Fan* and the mysterious related painting, *Contes barbares* (Primitive Tales), was effective in setting the Marquesan women apart from the uniformly dark-haired Tahitians (figs. 75–76).

Gauguin chose exotic types to impress the Parisian viewer, for whom these were intended, but he also made changes in the appearance of the models to make them seem more sexually available. The most obvious change was to his female model, Tohotaua, who actually posed fully dressed, as can be ascertained by the photograph sent by Vernier. In his painting, however, Gauguin has discreetly slipped her wraparound garment down so that it is tied above her waist, thus revealing her breasts and catering to the wishful notion of European men that Marquesan women normally con-

ducted their lives in a state of undress. Her male counterpart, the man in the red cape, is similarly disrobed, although this would not be immediately obvious to a European viewer. In typical male Marquesan dress, the wrap-around pareu would be worn as a long skirt covering the legs. A shirt, such as the one in the painting, would be worn on top. In Gauguin's rearrang-ing of the man's garments, the pareu is now inexplicably draped over his shoulders as a cape, leaving his legs visible and his shirt just barely covering his genitals. This suggestion of sexual availability is less often found in male figures than in female, but an audience that finds a barely covered male body erotic would appreciate how Gauguin has offered this attractive young man to their gaze. The long hair and the startling discovery of a tiare, the flower of sexual invitation, tucked over his ear and another held out in his hand toward us give a final clue to Gauguin's daring eroticization of the fig-

**74** Anonymous, *Tohotaua in Gauguin's Studio,* 1901.

**75** Paul Gauguin, *Woman with Fan,* 1902. Oil on canvas, 36 1/4 x 28 3/4 in. (92 x 72 cm). Museum Folkwang, Essen.

ure. Echoing his earlier Tahitian painting *Vahine no te Tiare* (see fig. 59), only this time with a male figure, *Marquesan Man in a Red Cape* may have been meant as a kind of self-portrait—his own "welcome to the Marquesas." At any rate, the beautiful, strong legs of the man contrast to Gauguin's diseased ones and may represent the younger, more desirable man he liked to identify with.

In the related painting, *Contes barbares,* Gauguin juxtaposes the red-headed Tohotaua against a revived image of his old Dutch friend the red-headed Meyer de Haan. De Haan, who died in 1895, must be seen here as a ghost, or tupapau, like the head of the old woman in *Manao Tupapau* (Spirit of the Dead Watches) from 1892. He is androgynous, because he now wears a lavender dress, but has the taloned feet of a "cock," as his name in Dutch signifies. De Haan's pose, borrowed from the double portraits that Gauguin painted in the inn at Le Pouldu, is used here to show the Dutchman's contemplation of the "primitive tales" recited by the Marquesan women, just as it had, years before, been used to show his contemplation of the books of Carlyle and Milton, or, one might say, "civilized tales." Gauguin sent these paintings to Vollard without interpretation, as far as can be ascertained, but no doubt he was confident that the models would pique European curiosity about the strange and distinctive people to be found halfway around the world.

Gauguin's thoughts were increasingly directed toward his Parisian audience. Now that he had retired from political journalism in Tahiti, he sought the more prestigious outlet of the French press. The publication of a new book-length version of *Noa Noa* in 1901, before he left Tahiti, inspired him to begin other manuscripts that would also make short books or long articles.[43] He dusted off the old treatise on the Catholic church from 1896–97, when he was a new resident of Tahiti, and added insights gained from his conflicts with Bishop Martin in Atuona.[44] He also put into book form a treatise on critics and art criticism, "Racontars d'un rapin" (Tales of a Dabbler). This he sent to André Fontainas, art critic of *Mercure de France* (which he still read religiously), hoping for early publication.[45] And in early 1903 he gathered all his notes, letters, and former articles around him and, in about a month's time, constructed a patchwork of a memoir, called "Avant et après" (Before and After; fig. 77).

Because there is no overt explanation of the title in the manuscript of "Avant et après," it is likely that Gauguin followed the practice he outlined on the first page: "I should like to write as I paint my pictures—that is to say, following my fancy, following the moon, and finding the title long afterwards." The title, an appropriate one for a memoir and similar to that of his grandmother's unpublished memoir, "Past and Future," allowed him to stress the themes of primitivism ("Before") and modernism ("After") that had brought him to the South Seas in the first place. It also linked this memoir to the painting he considered his great philosophical masterpiece, *Where Do We Come From? Who Are We? Where Are We Going?*, which he had already written about to Monfreid and Morice. In "Avant et après" he recounts a dream in which he encounters primordial human creatures with whom he cannot communicate. An angel appears to him, explaining that change is inevitable. "You must know that these beings are men such as you were once, before God began to create you. Ask this old man [Father Time] to lead you later into Infinity, and you will see what God wishes to do with you and learn that you to-day are far from completion."[46]

In the often maddeningly fragmented and contradictory memoir, the theme that emerges most clearly is that in the face of monumental change and shifting values, the duty of every individual is to forge a personal, if temporary, truth. In the last few pages he boils his philosophy down to two simple ideas: "No one is good; no one is evil; everyone is both, in the same way and in different ways"; and, "It is so small a thing, the life of a man, and yet there is time to do great things, fragments of the common task."[47] In this message it is possible to glimpse, perhaps for the last time, Gauguin's charisma—which was still powerful enough to transform the idealistic Pastor Vernier from an enemy into a lasting defender. Gauguin's exhortations to his reader are inspirational to this day: to liberate oneself from rigid institutional values (religious, moral, or artistic) and accept that it is one's duty to work. "Toil endlessly. Otherwise, what would life be worth?"[48] Even if one can't grasp the full meaning of one's art or occupation, "Still, it is the duty of everyone to try, to practise."[49]

Gauguin's belief that a person must create his or her own life and philosophy, in the same way that a painting is willfully constructed rather than merely derived from reality, suggests that life can have an artistic basis and may even achieve the level of a masterpiece. One must start with what is there ("Learn first what is within you. You have solved the problem, I cannot solve it for you. It is the task of all of us to solve it"). Then one proceeds to develop a philosophy that is not a "deduction from things" but an "image, even as a picture is." This philosophy is more than a neutral operating principle; it is a creation with which one changes the outside world. In Gauguin's aggressive metaphor, it is "a weapon, with which we alone, even as savages, fabricate ourselves."[50]

The philosophy that Gauguin created in his words—that of a man who held freedom above all other human values—may have been a gloss on a real life spent pursuing selfish goals at the expense of all around him; but it was a heady one nevertheless. Fabricated in part to justify actions even he recognized as unworthy, it evolved over time, and he expressed it forcefully in "Avant et après." The effectiveness of Gauguin's philosophy of life was enhanced by its link to developments in modern culture that stressed the rejection of old rules and traditions. As the years passed and the paintings of others, like Cézanne and Van Gogh, seemed more modern in style than Gauguin's, he could always claim that his life at least was more modern than theirs.

Certainly Gauguin felt a certain satisfaction in looking back at his life while sitting in his second-story studio in Atuona in 1903. "Shrewd, far-sighted sailors," he wrote smugly, "avoid dangers to which others succumb, partly, however, thanks to an indefinable something that permits one to live under the same circumstances in which another, acting in the same manner, would die."[51] Proof of this emerged even while Gauguin was writing his memoirs—the great cyclone of January 13, 1903, swept away most of the dwellings in Atuona except for those, like Gauguin's, that were built high, with solid, imported materials; he, the far-sighted sailor, survived being "tossed about by every wind."[52]

The life-threatening cyclone made Gauguin experience the real fear he incorporates into the narrative. "God, whom I have so often offended, has spared me this time; at the moment when I am writing these lines a quite exceptional storm has just been making the most terrible ravages."[53] "Toward ten o'clock a continuous noise, like the crumbling of a stone building, caught my attention. I could endure it no longer and went outside my hut. . . . I was in the midst of nothing more nor less than a torrent which, sweeping the pebbles along with it, was dashing against the wooden pillars of my house. There was nothing for me to do but to await the decision of Providence and resign myself."[54] Although he ends by turning the account into yet another diatribe against the colonial government, this is one of the few times he attempted to communicate his actual experience in the South Seas to his readers in Paris, and it supports his contention that his life has been one of extraordinary experiences.

Aside from these passages of inspirational personal philosophy, the remainder of the manuscript bespeaks Gauguin's lonely process of sitting at his desk by the window, compelled to write but grasping for things to write about. His decision to write a memoir, as he admits at once, goes against the grain. "Memoirs! That means history, dates. Everything in them is interesting except the author."[55] Indeed, once Gauguin picked up his pen, his desire to lash out, to justify himself, and in general take his Parisian audience by the lapels and shake them into appreciating his worth overwhelmed him. "The best thing would be to hold my tongue, but it is a strain to hold one's tongue when one is full of a desire to talk. . . . Life being what it is, one dreams of revenge."[56] As much as he enjoyed Atuona, he craved a measure of the old, Parisian conversation. "What can I say to all these coconut trees? And yet I must chatter; so I write instead of talking."[57]

Over the more than two hundred neat, handwritten pages he presented as the final version, Gauguin flitted from topic to topic—art, literature, travel—often with reference to specific books or reproductions that he obviously had within his reach in his studio. His library was large and included several dictionaries and encyclopedias on various topics that he writes about as he rifles through them. His walls, as we know, were crowded with art of all sorts, including reproductions of works by Degas, Holbein, and Puvis de Chavannes, which he returns to again and again. He also has at his fingertips all the issues of *Mercure de France* since 1895, which had become his bible of modern intellectual thought.[58] In the manuscript he incorporated his responses to certain key articles that inflamed him; and a reader who knows that he sent the manuscript to the art critic of the *Mercure,* André Fontainas, can sometimes sense a "letters to the editor" mode.

Revenge inevitably drives Gauguin's prose. From the first, he intends to defend his morality against all those who have judged him over the years, with special venom reserved for his oldest and newest enemies: his wife and Bishop Martin. He brings up issues of virtue and morality early on, attacking marriage and the family on the one hand and the church on the other. He praises pornography for its ability to drive away the detested "respectable people" and ridicules the recently newsworthy holy relic, the Holy Shroud of Lourdes. "I, myself, know nothing about such matters, and perhaps if I ever have hemorrhoids I shall set about plotting how to get a fragment of this Holy Shroud to poke into myself, convinced that it will cure me."[59]

While it is easy to see why Bishop Martin and the Catholic church were on Gauguin's mind as he watched the schoolchildren pass in front of his house, it is something of a surprise to find his venomous pen reviving the old grudge against his wife. In fact, his wife had been on his mind for the past few years. When he stopped writing to Emile Schuffenecker in 1897, he imagined that he had put all reminders of his family in Denmark behind him. But in 1900 another of his teenage children met an accidental death when Clovis died of blood poisoning after routine surgery. Mette asked Schuffenecker to forward a letter to Paul,[60] and although no response from Paul is known, Schuffenecker probably did as she asked.

Paul Gauguin would have received this news just as he was concluding his negotiations with Vollard, and if his past behavior is any guide, he probably worried that she would find out about the new agreement and try to divert some of his income to the children. When he wrote to Morice in 1901 about a plan to sell *Where Do We Come From?* to a group of subscribers for donation to the Luxembourg Museum, he included Edvard Brandès in Copenhagen in his list of people to contact but underlined "*Write nothing to my wife.*"[61] At this very time (summer 1901), he was dismayed to find that he could not sell his house in Tahiti without his wife's consent, owing to a community-property clause in French colonial law, and rather than write her directly, he had Monfreid write on his behalf.[62] Although he discovered a loophole in the law before she could reply, he still must have been relieved when she wrote the requested release without demanding any part of the proceeds.[63]

In the fall of 1902, after his move to the Marquesas, he was once again reminded of the threat she posed to his income. She had visited Paris that summer and been in touch with Schuffenecker at least, if not the others, like Monfreid, Morice, and perhaps even Vollard, since the art world of Paris was still very much of interest to her.[64] She did not write to him of her visit, but others apparently did, for he wrote belligerently to Monfreid, "And your wife is dying. It makes me think of mine who is *not* dying. . . . What does it matter? Let us leave the dirty bourgeoisie—even if they are our children—in their dirty place, and finish the work we have begun."[65] Monfreid, who had a grudge against his own wife, fed Gauguin's paranoia. In a letter that Gauguin received while he was writing "Avant et après" (February 1903), Monfreid described his own pique that Mette Gauguin had not written a cover letter to him when she sent the requested release for Paul Gauguin to sell his house in Tahiti, "in spite of the fact that I had written her an extremely polite letter."[66] Monfreid speculated callously that while Mette was quiet now, she would surely show up if Paul were to have a widely publicized success. Gauguin's efforts to keep any of his profits from falling into his family's hands included thinking about the future. In "Avant et après" he describes with disgust how an artist's heirs exploit him: "The artist dies; the heirs fall upon his work; everything is divided up: copyrights, auctions, and all the rest of it. There he is, completely stripped. With this in mind, I strip myself beforehand. That is a comfort."[67]

As if to justify his mean-spiritedness, Gauguin, throughout "Avant et après," argues the larger case against wives and, to a certain extent, all women. He starts out with his often-quoted line "I like women when they are fat and vicious; their intelligence annoys me; it's too spiritual for me."[68] In the text that follows Gauguin seldom writes of a woman without accusing her of some "perversion"—foul language, promiscuity, prostitution, adultery, frigidity, or lesbianism. He admires the beauty of the Marquesan woman, with her body shaped like a man's;[69] and it is "to be had for almost nothing."[70] But he reserves his most scathing criticism for his wife, her family, and her fellow Danes.[71]

It excited him to think about these attacks on his wife being published in Paris for all to see. As he wrote to Monfreid, "There are terrible things in my MS for some people, especially about the conduct of my wife, and of the Danes."[72] And to Fontainas: "I will send you the manuscript by the next mail: in reading it you will divine between the lines the personal and malicious pleasure that I should feel in getting the book published."[73] Without having any direct contact with Mette and little with any of her known supporters, Paul Gauguin still felt the need to counter the criticism of his behavior toward her that he knew existed in Paris; it obviously still existed in his own heart.

As for Mette, at fifty-two she was still teaching in Copenhagen and was now headmistress of a prominent girls' school. Her financial burden was considerably lighter since the tragic loss of both Aline and Clovis. Furthermore, Emil had married and left home and was working as an engineer in South America. He was being helped by his aunt Marie Uribe, Paul's sister, with whom Mette was still friendly. Jean-René was also away from home most of the time; he had followed in his father's footsteps and apprenticed himself in commercial shipping. Only the youngest, Pola, nineteen, remained at home. Mette's sister Ingeborg had divorced Edvard Brandès in 1900 and moved to Paris, where Mette visited her as often as she could. Later Ingeborg moved back to Norway, where she lived near their sister Phylle, who had married a prominent Oslo educator, Hans Horst, after the death of her first husband, Hermann Thaulow, in 1890. The three Gad sisters remained close. Mette's friendship with Marie Heegaard Stephensen also continued, and when Marie's mother died, in 1905, Mette received a sizable inheritance.[74] At this point in her life, Mette had little interest in pursuing Paul for whatever money he might be making with his new dealer; but since she still owned several of his works herself and was part of the Danish modernist art world, she maintained a keen interest in the Paris art market and the rise and fall of her husband's reputation. Gauguin was wrong in thinking that she turned people against him, but he was right in thinking that she was still very much a person to be reckoned with.

"Avant et après" contains a number of references to children that show Gauguin's defensiveness on the subject of his own abandoned brood. In one of his short parables of modern European life, he tells the story of a woman who sleeps with a servant just so she can have a child. Even though she refuses to marry the servant, she claims desertion when she has deserted him. Echoing his frequent complaints that Mette kept the children from him, he accuses this woman of wanting "to have her child to herself. The egoism of maternal love."[75] To this Gauguin contrasts the Polynesian practice of raising children communally. Here one finds the embodiment of Rousseau's Emile: "The education of Emile takes place in the broad enlightening sunshine, deliberately adopted by some and accepted by the whole of society. Smiling and free, the young girls can give birth to as many Emiles as they wish."[76] The irony of Gauguin's making such a statement was of course lost on the self-righteous artist, who had obviously forgotten that he had no intention of sharing in the education of his own Emile, his son with Pahura, whom he left behind on Tahiti, or any other of his four known Polynesian children.

Gauguin's remarks about marriage and children in "Avant et après" were, like his opinions about art, artists, and critics, intended for a Parisian reader. Even the sections devoted to the excesses of the Catholic church, he felt, would resonate in the anticlerical climate of turn-of-the-century France. But when Gauguin wrote about corrupt gendarmes, he was addressing a primarily Polynesian audience. The police on Hiva Oa were powerful people in a small society with few other figures of authority. The patrolmen tended to be bullies, and the officials, sent out from the central government in Papeete, had little stake in the local community. Gauguin had an especially hard time with the officials because his natural antisocial behavior combined with his highly developed antipathy for the government in Papeete to make them his enemies. Most of the officials who served in the Marquesas during the years that Gauguin lived there knew Gauguin from his years on Tahiti and were themselves predisposed against him.

The clashes began almost immediately and built to a crescendo while Gauguin was writing "Avant et après." There were three major issues — taxes, school attendance, and liquor — and a host of minor issues concerning which Gauguin accused the officials of incompetence; they accused him of general licentiousness. He wrote numerous letters to the capital of the Marquesas in Taiohae and to officials in Papeete, including the new governor of French Polynesia, Eduoard Pétit, sent copies to his friends in Paris, and, for good measure, reproduced several of them in "Avant et après." This campaign against law enforcement in the Marquesas finally caused Gauguin, already unpopular in Papeete, to be hauled into court and convicted of "libeling a gendarme in the course of his official duties."[77] On March 27, 1903, he was fined 500 francs and sentenced to three months in prison. For the next month, Gauguin renewed his letter-writing cam-

paign to everyone he knew, gaining legal advice from Léonce Brault, the Marquesan legislative representative in Papeete, and 1,500 francs from the wealthy collector Gustave Fayet, in France.

From the forceful language and the strong handwriting in these letters and "Avant et après," there is little indication that Gauguin's health was failing (fig. 78). But Vernier was called three times to Gauguin's bedside in April and early May for emergency medical care. Gauguin was in great pain and unable to walk. Vernier medicated the sores on his legs and lanced an abscess at the base of his spine. Twice he revived Gauguin when he fainted. He provided painkilling laudanum and finally morphine. When Vernier left Gauguin the third time, early in the morning on May 8, 1903, he believed that Gauguin's condition was stable. But at eleven that morning Gauguin's neighbor Tioka found him dead from a heart attack.[78]

Obstinate to the bitter end, Gauguin had kept fighting his enemies in the face of terrible physical deterioration. As Vernier wrote to Roton-champ, "The few times one would run into him in the valley of Atuona he cut a pathetic figure, dragging himself along with difficulty, his legs wrapped in strips of cloth."[79] Unlike in earlier days, when he complained constantly about his health, when he truly began to suffer from the advancing syphilis, he spoke of his physical condition less and less. In "Avant et après" he joked, "Who knows? The syphilitic and the alcoholic will perhaps be the men of the future."[80]

It is both ironic and fitting that a man whose public life had revolved around his physicality should deteriorate in such a visible and loathsome way. If he had died in Europe, the ravages of syphilis would have been politely hidden from public scrutiny; instead, he spent his last years in a climate warm enough to allow full exposure of the symptoms of a sexually transmitted disease. Gauguin's legs thus became the unexpected last vehicle of one of his most frequent themes—the pain that inevitably accompanies the pleasure of sexuality. In addition, the outpouring of words at this time suggests that he foresaw the approaching end of his life and was anxious to shape for posterity the outlines of the larger, more dramatic presence he wanted to have. Understanding that his erotic life transcended mere physical acts and that it was the product of a daring imagination, he continued to give full expression to it in his writing until the very end. His manuscripts, as well as the time he invested in cultivating certain key friends in Atuona, paid off handsomely in the reputation as an artist that he acquired in the next two decades.

The pathos of Gauguin's last days and his sudden death left the Atuonans with a degree of sympathy for him that his Tahitian neighbors never felt. Two important friends at the end of his life were Vernier and Tioka, both of whom had been recent recipients of rare examples of Gauguin's generosity: Vernier had participated in the fascinating discussions of art and literature that Gauguin carried on despite his extreme pain, and Tioka had been given a piece of Gauguin's land so he could build a new house on higher ground. Both men led the Atuonans in retaining a sympathetic memory of Gauguin.

Pastor Vernier had a personal stake in defending Gauguin because he felt the Catholic priests had unfairly taken the body to the Catholic cemetery, and he wanted all to know that Gauguin had nothing but contempt for meddling priests. Vernier was soon able to pass along his impressions of the artist to a young naval physician and writer, Victor Ségalen, who had been advised by friends in Paris to look up the artist during his tour of duty in the South Seas. Ségalen was intrigued by the romantic story and, forming an attachment to Polynesia, was largely responsible for the image of Gauguin as a savior of Polynesian culture.[81]

The governor of the Marquesas, François Picquenot, who had known and sympathized with Gauguin since their time together on Tahiti, handled the official duties relating to the death. Because no one seemed to have any information about Gauguin's wife, he notified Monfreid, who in turn notified Mette and Vollard, as well as Gauguin's old friends in Paris. An inventory was conducted of Gauguin's belongings, and, in the absence of a will, the less valuable objects were auctioned in Atuona and the rest taken to Papeete to be auctioned there. Obviously believing that no heirs were likely to be found and that Gauguin's debts had to be settled quickly, the precious letters, manuscripts, and paintings found in Gauguin's studio were auctioned in Papeete on September 5, 1903, only a few days after Monfreid received word of Gauguin's death (August 23). This quick dispersal of the contents of the studio led to the irretrievable loss of much valuable information about Gauguin's last years. The money realized from the sales (about 4,000 francs) was, however, dutifully conveyed to Mette Gauguin.

In Paris, André Fontainas organized a tribute to Gauguin in the *Mercure de France,* asking several artists and writers to convey their memories of the former Parisian *malin.* For the most part, even those who knew Gauguin fairly well, like Carrière, Dolent, Redon, and Signac, struggled to remember the man they hadn't seen in almost ten years. But thanks to the efforts of the old faithfuls—Monfreid, Morice, and Vollard—Gauguin received the tributes in print and in exhibitions that he had long thought his due. Fontainas did not publish "Avant et après"; instead, it was used as the basis for Morice's long article in *Mercure* in October of 1903 and for a book-length biography by Monfreid's friend Jean de Rotonchamp, which appeared in 1906.

Mette Gauguin was shocked at the news of Paul's death. She had long since stopped corresponding with him but heard occasional news of his welfare from Emile Schuffenecker. She resisted the impulse to rehash the wrongs of the past, instead giving him the tribute that she thought appropriate and probably believed. She began referring to him as "the great artist" and "that extraordinary being who was my husband."[82] She received from Monfreid the proceeds of the auctions in Papeete and Atuona, as well as money from Monfreid's recent sale of paintings to Fayet. Monfreid also turned over to her the paintings by her husband that he was still holding. Because Vollard was up-to-date in his payments to Gauguin, none of the paintings in his possession were still owned by the artist, so none were passed on to Mette. In all, Mette received a small legacy in cash and artwork from the husband who had promised that today's sacrifice would yield tomorrow's fortune.

Mette also found that the men who now wanted to serve as the keepers of her husband's flame had inherited his dismissive attitude toward her. Although she cooperated as much as she could with those writing about her husband, she remained the villain in the story of his life, thanks to the thorough mining of Paul's authoritative-sounding "Avant et après." The original manuscript was passed on to her in 1907, and as soon as the last details of the estate were ironed out (in 1911), she ceased corresponding with the disagreeable group in Paris.[83]

Memorial exhibitions in Paris in 1903 and 1906 showcased Gauguin's art as had never been done during his lifetime, and by 1913, when the Armory Show in New York opened, Gauguin was enshrined in the triumvirate of modernists with his old friends Van Gogh and Cézanne.[84] But it wasn't until 1919, when the end of World War I brought a flood of new literature, that Gauguin's life came to be as interesting to the general public, particularly in the English-speaking world, as his art. The almost simultaneous publication of Somerset Maugham's *The Moon and Sixpence* and the first volume of Gauguin's letters (to Monfreid) in 1918 was followed by the publication of *Noa Noa* (1919) and "Avant et après" (titled *Intimate Journals*, 1921) in English. To those emerging from the bitter years of war in Europe, Gauguin's rejection of the corrupt Old World civilization and his fantastic flight to the South Seas appeared as a model of sane modern behavior. The tenet proposed in the small avant-garde circles of Paris and applied to a discussion of Gauguin for the first time in 1895 in an article by Strindberg —that modern art could be created only by a modern artist—was now universally accepted as a fundamental modernist tenet, and Gauguin, it seemed, offered the purest example of it. Criticizing cultural norms, wearing nonconforming dress, and escaping to remote locations all over the world became the hallmarks of a creator of new art. Modern artists from Matisse to George Biddle found their way to Tahiti in the 1920s.

At least as important as Gauguin's flight from Europe was his flight from his wife, or so it was felt. The wave of misogyny that typically follows a major war, allowing the returning soldiers to reclaim the power in domestic society that women had assumed in their absence, encouraged public agreement with Gauguin's scornful assessment of Mette's failures. In *The Moon and Sixpence*, Somerset Maugham tried to offer a balanced account of an artist of limited human kindness in the treatment of his family, his friends, and his lovers who nevertheless was to be respected for his drive to create great art. When it came to the artist's wife, Maugham created a sweet, sympathetic woman whose major flaw was her dullness.

But art critics, particularly in the United States, decried Maugham's attempt to present an accurate picture of a man who had callously turned his back on his responsibilities, preferring to rely instead on *Noa Noa* and "Avant et après" for the "true" story of a saintly artist victimized by a greedy and hypocritical wife. Frederick O'Brien, whose own book *White Shadows in the South Seas* was published in 1919, took issue with Maugham's Gauguin. "He is charged with trying to portray Gauguin as he was. If he did so try, he failed, for he made a vulgar villain of his hero, and Gauguin was not that."[85] To those, like Maugham, who accused Gauguin of emotional brutality, the American art critic Henry McBride rebutted, "His special type of honesty is a thing the narrow-minded will never understand." The narrow-minded, as far as McBride was concerned, included those who objected to his nonchalant fathering of children: "He seemed to scatter infants about the earth with the careless ease of an Adam and had difficulties with Eves only when they happened to be civilized."[86] Gauguin's unfavorable view of his wife and other women found a ready audience in the postwar period, when many men were having difficulties with their own civilized Eves, who, in the United States at least, had just won the vote.

Since that time, the art and life of Paul Gauguin have been uniquely linked. And, thanks to the early and frequent republications of his writings, he has had a powerful influence over the shaping of his own image. Criticism of his treatment of his wife and family has never been silenced, however, and, if we take his own words at face value—"Pictures and writings are portraits of their authors"[87] and "No one is good; no one is evil"[88]— the ultimate portrait that emerges is more vulnerable than the heroic one he thought he was creating. Rather than a freethinker and a profound artist, we find a diverse, abstract man composed of beautiful as well as despicable elements. Gauguin's life is not, as he would have it, for emulation; but its originality and hypnotic power have earned it a secure place in our imaginations.

The escape of the modern artist—from civilization and family responsibilities—was a cry for freedom of erotic expression. The physical sensation of making art, the emphasis on the nude body as an expressive norm, and the modernist desire to shock and thus temporarily divorce the viewer from unexamined assumptions all revolve around deeply rooted erotic impulses. Whether the artist practices specific sexual behavior is secondary to his or her ability to infuse the art object with an appeal that is erotic or closely akin to erotic. This message was Gauguin's most valuable contribution to the shaping of modern art theory even if it has not been voiced as loudly or as clearly as his philosophy of escape. He had an irresistible urge to imbue his art and his writings with unexpected sexual messages —to surprise the viewer by humanizing and sexualizing biblical figures like Eve and Mary, to make covert references to his own sexuality and that of his wife and friends, and to invoke such sexual taboos as homosexuality and sex with children—and his success in doing so elicits a powerful response and endows his work with genuine originality. It is Gauguin's ability to create an erotic art from his inner life, rather than his life itself, that points the way for future generations.

# Appendix: Mette Gauguin Letters

The following seventeen letters by Mette Gauguin provide fresh insight into the professional and personal relationship of Mette and Paul Gauguin. Although they have been available to scholars at least since the 1940s, only four (I, XII, XIV [the year has been incorrectly transcribed as 1891 instead of 1895], and XVI) have been previously published (Malingue, *Letters*, pp. 64, 247, 249). The originals are held in the Bibliothèque d'art et archeology, Fondation Jacques Doucet, Paris (I) and in the Musée Gauguin, Tahiti (II to XVII). Handwritten in French by the Danish-speaking Mette Gauguin, they are occasionally difficult to decipher; illegible words and passages are indicated by brackets. They are presented here in translation with a close approximation of the original punctuation and format.

I    **Mette Gauguin to Paul Gauguin, 4 June [1888]**

Copenhagen, 4 June

*My dear Paul*

*Although I am not sure that you are still in Pont Aven, it has been so long since I've had news of you, I am writing anyway because I would like you to have this on your birthday. You should know that we are thinking of you here. Finally the summer season and the warm weather have arrived. For me the season has arrived when I have no work and when I earn no money. Fortunately the children have been invited to spend their vacation at the seashore. It is absolutely essential for Clovis and it can't help but benefit the others. As for me, it doesn't matter where or how I spend the summer as long as I don't spend any money. But I have no intention of complaining; you seem to care so little about what happens to us. It has been six weeks at least since I wrote to you and you have not replied. Your last letters have been so unaffectionate that I truly no longer know what to believe. Certainly you do nothing to give me a bit of courage, and it doesn't seem that that would be so very difficult. Oh well, recriminations don't do any good; the purpose of this letter is only to let you know that I am far from forgetting you. You may not care about that at all! Your children are all well, and are sweet and well behaved. Emil is becoming calmer and more reasonable. He spent his Pentecost vacation with his grandmother and was very good. Write me soon. I am terribly worried about you.*

*Your wife, Mette*

II    **Mette Gauguin to Emile Schuffenecker, 22 March 1892**

Vimmelskaftet 47 22–3–92

*My dear Schuffenecker!*

*I received the works yesterday and I thank you immensely—I know how much trouble it is in Paris to send the littlest shipment! Naturally I find the paintings very* beautiful just as they are.—I am going to have them put on stretchers and framed if I find the money, and then exhibit them. What you tell me about Paul's return doesn't surprise me, what [did he think] he was going to do over there? And without precise information on anything? He who doesn't have it in him to live anywhere else except in his own country? And besides, I, better than most people, can understand this! I have also received a letter from him, kind and affectionate, as they have been since his visit to my home here. Perhaps, in the end, he will see that I am worth something and that even the "head cook"—as he said —would not have been able to manage as well as I have.

My children are growing and are so beautiful! Ah, my dear friend, how I wish for my adorable children's sake to have some part of the energy that those monkeys have when they break chairs and beds, not to mention dishes! My Emil is a tall young man—almost 6 feet tall—no less! And very polite! I have every reason to believe that shortly he will be able to help me, if not financially, at least mentally [by lifting my spirits]. Hugs to Mrs. S. And tell Mrs. Reynier that her [illeg. proper name] is quite a lazy fellow who has not [illeg.] let himself be photographed for her!

Goodbye, and thanks again. Write to me and I will answer right away.
Yours,
Mette Gauguin

### III    Mette Gauguin to Emile Schuffenecker, 20 May 1892

Hotel Ste. Marie
83 rue de Rivoli
Thursday, 20-5-92
Dear friend!
I went to your house yesterday, I spoke with your wife and your daughter, very nice both of them, but I must speak with you to ask your help and advice as always! Could you come here and have lunch with me on Sunday—Mme. S. told me that you will be in Paris on that day? I will expect you at 11 o'clock and we could talk without being disturbed while having lunch here at the hotel.

Yours
Mette Gauguin

### IV    Mette Gauguin to Emile Schuffenecker, 25 May 1892

Vimmelskaftet, 25-5-92
Dear friend!
These lines in haste to tell you that one of my young compatriots, a young painter, has left for Paris and that he desires above all to understand and study your art—yours and Paul's. I gave him your address. I hope he won't bother you too much with his bad French and his enthusiasm for the "symbolists"! At the same time, dear S., thank you very much for the paintings—I've already sold some —and I am beginning to believe that there might be some opportunity in Copenhagen. If I can arrange it, I will come back to Paris perhaps next month, but only for a few days, and only if I can get a ticket at a good price.—Greetings to Mme. S and to the children! I have had news from Paul; he is well, but I believe he is bored. I'd like to see him come back;—if he really is to succeed some day, I think that you will reconcile with him;—his immense pride, so difficult to bear,

*will be subdued perhaps with success. The children are well, growing up fast and turning into a bunch of real troupers.*

> *Yours, dear and faithful friend!*
> *Mette Gauguin*

*His name is Johan Rohde.*

### V    Mette Gauguin to Emile Schuffenecker, 9 July 1892

Saturday, 9–7–92

> *Dear friend!*

*I just got your letter, which didn't surprise me, since 8 days ago I got the news direct from Paul, who certainly is without money but who told me that he could perhaps arrange a way to stay another year.—I'll send you that letter—you will see the situation for yourself. At this moment it is completely impossible for me to do anything—I spent everything I had for the trip to Paris, and the 1,000 francs for Aline's board had to be paid to the director of the boarding school, the child is going to go to one of these days. I don't understand how he spent so much so fast! You will see that he is starting to see through M. Morice, who had already upset us, you and I—I hope that he will manage;—he is alone, with no one depending on him, isn't he?*

> *For me, I went [illeg.] but I suffered so much from rheumatism in the right arm, which isn't good for my writing,—so we are all leaving for the country tomorrow and I hope to recover completely there. Hug your wife and children for me—here is [illeg.] for his friend with many thanks. My address until 20 August:*

> *Mme. Gauguin*
> *Faarevejla Rirdkobing*
> *Denmark*

> *Again, thanks and thanks again;—you are really my friend!*
> *Mette Gauguin*

### VI    Mette Gauguin to Emile Schuffenecker, 5 September 1892

Vimmelskaftet 47, 5–9–92

> *My dear friend!*

*This instant I received your letter and I hasten to reply to it, because I see that you are very [sad] and discouraged—and not without reason. If your health worries you; I don't know what I would do if I felt my days wasting away! As I wrote you, I have had terrible rheumatism, but my stay in the country seems to have cured it and I am back in good health with my whole brood doing well. As for Paul, the news seems better too; he complained a little of his heart, but he sold a paint-ing and seemed happier. He talked about leaving Tahiti for another island— he has the devil in him, and cannot stay put like everyone else!*

> *As for M. Morice, he [Paul] is beginning to see him clearly, and I told him what I thought of the man! My paintings are here but I don't think I'll hold the exhibition until spring. Paul promised me some works from Tahiti by then.*

> *And you, dear friend, don't lose courage. You who know that one can find happiness (this pitiful earthly happiness) in sacrificing for others. Don't ever forget that you have 2 children and that these creatures would certainly be worse off without you—and that's all I need say to cheer you. And then your work—*

*[it is the] consolation of the human race! You know that you have in me a friend who understands and who appreciates your true worth! A bientôt—*
    *Mette Gauguin*

**VII**    Mette Gauguin to Emile Schuffenecker, 21 January 1893, on letterhead

Johannes Henriques & Co.
Vexellerere & Banquiers
Amagertorv 24
Kobenhavn

Copenhagen, 21–1–93
    *My very good friend:*
*Enclosed is 700 francs, which I beg you to pass on to Paul as soon as possible. I am not sending it directly because the banking houses in Copenhagen do not have a connection with any in Tahiti. I am happy to be able to do this! I sold some pictures—very cheaply—but he very much needs money; you know, "while the grass grows, the cow dies!" Courage to you, too—and better health.—We are fine, —but I am very tired and growing old. Hugs for everyone!*
    *Mette Gauguin*

**VIII**    Mette Gauguin to Emile Schuffenecker, 11 February 1893

11–2–93
    *Dear Schuffenecker!*
*Thank you for your letter, thank you for taking on such tiresome tasks for Paul, and thank you for your approval! I am going to speak to you again about him, naturally, because I believe that I must agree to let him take part in an exhibition of painting here this spring. I talked to him many times but since he generally does not respond when I ask him something, I had given up the idea until his return, something he no longer talks about.—And yet, I believe that it is something that will be best for him now. M. Philipsen, a Danish artist, and the only friend Paul made here, asked for his paintings, which are with me, for this exhibition, which will be held in the month of March. I can hardly refuse, because he assures me that it will be a great opportunity to sell, and that's why I ask you to tell M. Daniel to send me the works you talked about a few weeks ago. If you want to lend some of your paintings, these men would be very grateful and would assume all the expenses. You can do what you think best. I would like to be able to send something to Paul again, from whom I receive letters that are sad and incoherent —it is very difficult for me to understand what he has done with the funds with which he left;—but anyway—you can see that I am discouraged, but there are limits to everything and I am sad not to be able to understand anything of Paul's path or direction, he who always claims to know exactly what he wants!—*
    *And then, you, dear friend, you also seem in a very sad situation; sick, unhappy. Alas—if I could do something for you, it should be soon, but it's a long way from here to Paris and I am kept in Copenhagen by my heavy responsibilities and my large family; if I didn't have all that, I think that the two of us would comfort each other in discussing our worries and in hoping for better days for our children! At least I have a mother, brothers, and sisters who love me and friends who spoil me—I must not complain of my fate. Whereas you are alone—with that terrible art as your only consolation!*

*My children are big.—Emil is enormous, almost two meters in height and built like my side of the family;—Aline is already taller than me, and is not yet 16 years old;—she is very clever and very much resembles Paul in stateliness.— The three little ones are precious, but very tiring and very expensive.*

*Try, dear and good friend, to reconcile with your wife; you have loved her very much in the past, and your children will suffer too cruelly from your estrangement! Alas—it is easy for me to preach; but I think so often and with such profound chagrin of your sad and broken home!*

*Enough! Write me soon, hug your wife for me; I will try not to bother you with my troubles, I am still strong; I would like to be able to help you to shoulder your burdens.*

*Your faithful friend,*
*Mette Gauguin*

### IX    Mette Gauguin to Emile Schuffenecker, 14 March 1893

Tuesday, 14-3-93

*My dear friend,*
*Yesterday I received and unpacked the crates with Paul's paintings.—Thank you and M. Montfreid for all the trouble you've gone to for us; I hope that it will result in something good for this great man of a husband I have. Everyone finds the canvases superb! Let it be possible to have people here appreciate them enough—and buy some from me! Anyhow, at this moment I am very hopeful! Although we have put rather high prices—a number of works I won't ask for less than 600 francs for—I won't let them go for ridiculously low prices! I don't know Paul's plans any more than you do but I think it would be better for him to come back to Europe.—He can start over there; he is not one of those who can be alone, like me, for example.—The exhibition he is in opens on 25 March.— We have to hurry to frame the works!—I think that this will be a great success for Paul!—*

*As for us, the children and me, we are doing well at this time—winter also is my season of work. I am happy; I work during the day and enjoy myself at night because—I have to say—I am horribly spoiled by my friends.*

*Dear S., will you do me a favor? Let me know the price of a dinner service for 12 of faience cast iron of Moustier design! shipped to Copenhagen?*

*Thanks again to you and to M. Daniel! Please tell him that I would be happy to return the favor at any time. Hug your wife and children for me. Yours,*
*Mette G.*

### X    Mette Gauguin to Emile Schuffenecker, 1 April 1893

Saturday, 1-4-93

*Dear friend!*
*Thank you for the news! I will tell you what must be done when I know what the persons in question want.—I take up the pen this evening to write you first because I am too tired for any serious work / and God knows, however, there's a lot of it to do! / but also because I want to tell you that Paul's works are very success-ful here. I have exhibited—on the advice of a friend, the painter M. Philipsen —several old paintings by Paul, and put reasonable prices on them; and the first*

263

*two days of the exhibition I sold three of them and a pot (the head of Paul for*
*135 frs.; the others for about 100 frs. each)—it's not much but it's always some-*
*thing;—nevertheless I don't think that Paul's art is understood by the public;*
*—most of them are still hanging. The Tahiti pictures I do not want to sell for low*
*prices; I won't sell them unless they bring 6–500 frs.—I sold one—the two*
*women on the yellow cloth—700 frs. to my brother-in-law, the editor Brandès. But*
*I'm afraid I can't keep all the money for Paul;—anyway, I will do what is*
*humanly possible, and I still hope to find a buyer for some works if I have a little*
*patience. The son of M. Pasteur, the secretary to the ambassador here, bought*
*a study of the port of Dieppe that I brought home from my terrible trip to Paris—*
*you remember, back then, way up in Vaugirard, I've forgotten the name of the*
*street. He is charming to me, as is everyone here, who spoil me again and again*
*—if I weren't so tired and if I didn't feel so old, if only I could see Paul in the*
*end!—But that will be a long time still—and I'm 42 years old! It is true that I*
*believe firmly in Paul, and that helps me enormously,—but there is a limit to*
*the strength of a woman, and I begin to believe that I have perhaps been a little*
*overworked. How I regret not having let Paul leave—to paint—ten years sooner,*
*—and yet, who knows what would have happened! One thing is certain, I would*
*not have had 5 beings dependent on me. Paul does not think about their future,*
*but I assure you that it preoccupies me—and harshly!—There, enough "gripes"*
*—because truth be told, the horizon begins to brighten and my children are*
*everything a mother could want or hope for;—my family helps and understands*
*me, my friends love me and I am sure that Paul will appreciate me more than he*
*[ever did?].—*

*Dear friend, I would like to find a word to comfort you, you and your wife,*
*who is also very unhappy, and who could have lived so tranquilly with her chil-*
*dren and her husband. Life is a strange thing! Hug her for me—I feel that I am*
*so old and experienced compared to her—tell her to think of Jeanne and Paul,*
*they did not ask to be brought into the world;—she and you owe them everything;*
*—you have the duty not to sadden their childhood;—and children are terribly*
*clairvoyant! I wish she saw my children leaving for the day, like this morning, with*
*four pieces of bread and butter in their bags and 50 centimes for the train; and*
*returning for dinner with blooming faces and their eyes full of fresh air and spring-*
*time! When one has children one becomes so little, so insignificant.—My great*
*strapping lad Emil comes home tomorrow from school for two days of vacation, and*

*the stately Aline, who is taller than me, which is not a little [illeg.], is out this*
*evening—I am waiting for her because it's after eleven; the three little ones are*
*sleeping after a day in the forest!—Doesn't this picture make you want to escape the*
*pressures of Paris and come live our life—much simpler and healthier! I invite*
*you to spend a month with me—I guarantee the "Danish swill." as Paul says, will*
*not be too unpalatable. I am reading at this time "The Intimate Journal" of F.*
*H. Amiel—it makes me think so often of you, Schuffenecker! Anyway, I think that*
*you have had enough of me. Write me, and I hope your letter will be a little less*
*sad, or rather, [illeg.], I promise that I will be able to make you laugh [illeg.]*

*I am far happier than you in the middle of all afflictions, having always two*
*steps from me some hearts ready to open up—and also ready to laugh with me!*
*How fortunate not to be in the shadow of an artist; and what happiness to be able,*
*at the same time, to understand the soul of an artist. Why is it that you, dear*

*friend, are so far away? I am certain that among us, you would find a bit of con-*
*solation to chat with me, to complain a bit; I think of your divided home with*
*much chagrin and I [illeg.].*

     *Mette Gauguin*

*I haven't had any news from Paul. Have you heard anything. Is he coming*
*home? When?*

<br>

**XI   Mette Gauguin to Emile Schuffenecker, 22 June 1893, on letterhead**

Mette Gauguin

Vimmelskaftet 47

22–6–93

     *Dear Schuffenecker!*

*Enclosed is a portrait that will amuse you, I am sure. You see how my children are*
*becoming gigantic, since the little old lady at the left is your servant, Mme.*
*Gauguin, who is nevertheless quite tall. Aline will soon be taller than me and Emil*
*—well—look. Emil is going to be a "bachelor" [receive his baccalaureate degree]*
*in 15 days. Aline comes home from boarding school in three weeks and we will*
*leave for the country during the first days of July. Do you have any news of Paul?*
*I have had some from Tahiti. He received the 700 frs. and he hoped to depart*
*at the beginning of May. Did he do this? Naturally I am anxious to see him and*
*I understand that he wants to see us all. But I would rather he didn't come to*
*Copenhagen until the month of September, when the painters and others with*
*whom he could chat will have returned to the city. I am spending my vacation at*
*the home of some friends and this is a necessary economy. If he returned, I wouldn't*
*know what to do. Anyway, we will see. I hope everything will work out.—I am*
*fine except I am exceedingly tired. Tell me right away what you know about Paul's*
*return. Kisses to the children and regards to your wife.*

     *Yours,*

     *Mette*

<br>

**XII   Mette Gauguin to Emile Schuffenecker, 15 September 1893**

15–9–93

     *My dear Schuffenecker!*

*I have not responded to your letter of 25–8—in which you told me of Paul's arrival,*
*which in fact happened sooner than we thought, Daniel and I. And so he has*
*returned!—according to his letters—just the same as when he left—steeped in the*
*most brutal selfishness—phenomenal, incomprehensible to me;—no, S., with*
*him one can hope for* nothing! *he never thinks of anyone but himself and his own*
*well-being;—he remains in admiring contemplation of his own magnificence;*
*—that his children should have to receive their bread from his wife's friends—*
*that makes no difference to him—he does not want to know—therefore he does*
*not know! Yes, this time I'm outraged.*

     *You probably know what happened? Eight days after he disembarked,*
*our dear uncle died in Orléans, very handily for Paul, who inherited 15,000 fr. Paul*
*wrote me to know if I could send him some money;—unfortunately the few*
*crowns I had accumulated—I had sold some of the old paintings at the exhibi-*

tion—had been spent for different unforeseen as well as foreseen things—Emil's school bills—clothes for this giant, etc., and I therefore had nothing;—a fact he has been magnanimous enough to pass over in silence, now that he has the little inheritance from his uncle in hand!—We know, you and I, that he left for his little excursion to Tahiti with all the proceeds from the sale—and I said nothing;—this time he does not speak of giving me part of the 15000 fr.—and I give myself permission to point these things out to him because this is too much! In addition, he asked me to find the money for a little trip to Paris!!!—I am more than ever determined to stay—I cannot leave 5 big kids for whom I am solely responsible. If he needs to see us, he knows where to find us—but I am not going to run around the world like a crazy woman!

Perhaps, dear friend, you find me cold, severe, venal, as Paul used to say —but frankly, there is something tiring about all these ways of dealing with things!—I have been very worried about Emil's future—I spoke to Paul about it, who told me that we should not worry—the boy is big enough to fend for himself! Yes, he is big enough, but he will not succeed if we want to see him comfortably situated in society! Fortunately, my friend, the Countess de Moltke thinks differently from his father—she continues to support him after his baccalaureate and tomorrow we will decide where he will go to become a civil engineer. When I see the kindness of others alongside Paul's selfishness, I don't know whether to laugh or cry—I don't do either one, I have too much to do to make these children into useful men;—Aline has returned from the boarding school, she is so charming, and helps me to care for her brothers as best she can;—the children are handsome, healthy, intelligent;—the littlest, Paul, will soon be ten years old.-

Perhaps, Schuff, the hardest part is over, and one day I will reap the rewards of my work other than the satisfaction that comes from performing my duty—which, between us, is not very substantial. But do you understand a father who feels nothing, nothing, nothing! I believe he would watch us die without being moved at all! I am so fortunate to have been able to come here, surrounded and pampered without any worry other than the next day's plans, and this other—very painful, however—the lack of affection from the one who is their father!

Oh well—I have written to you because I needed to unburden my heart;—tell me if you find me unjust;—no, don't say that, because I am afraid that I am of the opposite opinion!—My summer has been good, but I confess that at this moment I am more than furious!

Give Jeanne a hug, regards to Paul. whom you should send to me—I think that it would do him good to breathe in the calm and honesty of this little country, beloved and blessed, where I have found peace;—and my magnificent boys would make good little friends for him!—

Your old friend,
M. Gauguin

Copenhagen, 20–1–94

Dear Schuffenecker!

Thank you for your letter! It is nice to feel that you are thinking of me, and that you understand that at this moment I am very much to be pitied! Yes— I had an enormous disappointment, since I believed—in spite of everything— that Paul was going to succeed with his exposition.—Certainly, I don't want anything for myself,—I know that I would be able to manage anywhere—but the responsibility of the children becomes heavier and heavier. I could raise my children up to now as I wanted, better than I ever could have done in Paris.— But I still have 5–6 years of work for children who cost a lot;—and that's why I feel so discouraged, so sad, so defeated that I would like to throw far from me life's burden, which is much too heavy for the shoulders of a woman! To be forced to ask for help and handouts from others, to no longer be self-sufficient, that's what humiliates me more than anything. And for me to tell this to Paul is like crying out in the desert; he only sees "Himself" and he couldn't care less for me— the bourgeois—the imbecile, who is vain about the children, whom I alone brought into the world.

Ah, if it were not for these creatures so alive, so intelligent, who cluster around me and who have only me, I would leave this evening but it seems to me that this would be [illeg.]. All the same, I am in this moment so tormented for the next day; I so surely—idiot that I am!—counted on a part of this inheritance that I cannot think of anything but money, money, and again money, which I don't have and which I don't know where to find!—

Forgive me for tormenting you with my troubles,—but it is always a type of comfort, a release to cry out when you are suffering too much. And I know that you sympathize with me and that you understand me—you have been unhappy yourself, although in another way! Poor friend! Do you remember our last conversation, when you cried: Were we made to be so miserable?—

You tried to comfort me in assuring me that this state of things could not last.—Maybe that's true, but while the grass grows, the cow dies!—In the middle of all this trouble, I still have the satisfaction of seeing the children love me and care for me. Aline, most of all, is affectionate and good;—she is so willing to help me, and hates to see me cry—the poor thing!—I blame myself for letting her see how sad I am, but it is perhaps good that she knows early on what life is like!—I am happy to know that Paul has been friendly with you;—with me he is not only full of the satisfaction of having fulfilled his duties to the extreme, but also of having made enormous sacrifices;—I confess that I ask myself sometimes how he is made, the nerve of this man! who his whole life has accused me of venality!

Once more—thank you for your friendship, thank you for your good wishes, please remember me to your wife, and hug her for me;—I think often of Jeanne with her big beautiful eyes, and I would like for Paul to see the muscles of my three young ones, who are into woodworking so intensely these days that the house is shaking. Au revoir.

Your devoted

Mette Gauguin

Vimmelskaftet 47

6–5–95

*My dear friend,*

*Forgive me for having let three months pass before responding to your very affec-tionate letter, which I received in the midst of a whirlwind of lessons and work;—which might perhaps excuse me in your eyes;—I had a lot to do this winter, fortunately, and I am a bit tired, but happy to have been able once more to shoul-der the burden that Paul so callously left me with.—Dear friend, read the enclosed letter, and address it to him—I have forgotten the number of his house, I write him so rarely, and I think of him even more rarely;—but I believe that whenever I hear that he has money, it is my duty to remind him that he has five children and that alone I can't support them—ah—if I did not have such devoted friends, where would I be. God in heaven!—But my heart overflows with bitterness at the thought that Paul is so criminally egotistical—and never have I heard of anything equal to this! And yet it is unjust of me to complain. I am far happier here than in Paris, only my children will one day blush for their father and that will be hard for them!*

*Everyone is fine—the enormous Emil is working hard at engineering school. Aline is taller than I am, very pretty and above all very elegant, a young lady terribly* comme il faut. *Clovis works at his factory, coming home in the evenings black as a real blacksmith, washes, eats, and is perfectly happy—because the scamp detests studying and school.—Baby Jean is very like me—outside and inside—he wants to become an officer in the navy and it is on this matter I am asking Paul to help me; which I think is only fair. Pola is pretty, pretty, a little Spaniard, and very intelligent;—they are all happy, but I cannot avoid thinking with a certain apprehension of their future, if something should happen to me—and I am getting older, my hair is almost white, and my energy isn't what it once was.*

*Give your children a hug for me—kindest regards to your wife.—And I'll see you—when?—I confess I am hardly tempted by Paris—I suffered there so much!—But you should come to Copenhagen;—I am not going to the coun-try this summer because of Clovis, who cannot leave his factory. So here is a long letter:—write to me, tell me if I was wrong to approach Paul—it certainly seems that he and I are 200,000 leagues apart, but that doesn't alter the fact that*

*he is the father of these* five *beings whose future means so much to me.*

*Your very devoted,*

*Mette Gauguin*

31–1[?]–96

*Dear friend,*

*Thank you for your letter. Yes, Paul and his ferocious egoism surpass all human comprehension and what irritates me the most is that he considers himself "a martyr to art."—Enough—let him flee.—I am very lucky that you keep me in affectionate enough remembrance that you want to deal with us. If you have some paintings, send them to me; I will try to sell them and I will certainly not* send the money to Paul. This fall I think I will go to live with my mother, who is alone now that my brother Aage has married;—and I would rather that my mother not see me suffer too much from lack of money; I am happy to be with her. The children adore her, but I am naturally afraid that my troubles have made my already difficult temperament even more bitter. Poor Schuffenecker, you too— you do not seem at all happy—and your children, will they thank you one day? As for me, I have only one wish—to leave this difficult life, as soon as I have raised the children—who—God knows—I didn't ask for!

I don't yet have portraits of the two oldest—Emil, the stupid boy, having twisted his knee on the ice; he is a kind of Hercules, [illeg.], and I would like you to see his height alongside that of my daughter, who is a bit taller than I am. Will you ever come to Copenhagen?—the trip is not expensive and I could offer you hospitality as soon as I live with my mother, whom you know and who remembers you and the unfortunate Dalain perfectly well. I have excellent news from my sailor Jean; he is in the Danish Antilles and will not return until the month of March, to go out again this time to Iceland. Myself, I would be fine if money worries didn't obscure the heavens and the earth and all people—ah, what misery to always be living from hand to mouth.

Paul was born in Paris—56 rue Notre Dame de Lorette, 7 June 1848.—

Tell your wife that I would like a portrait of your Paul, whom I hardly know. Is he the same age as mine—12 years old? My little one also wants to be a naval officer. It is a true malady in a country without a future, without a fleet, without an army!—But my children have inherited the willfulness of their father —happily I am here to raise them more suitably than he was raised!

Goodbye, Yours,

Mette Gauguin


### XVI   Mette Gauguin to Emile Schuffenecker, 11 June 1900

Dear friend!

Just a couple of lines to let you know about a cruel blow that has just struck me. My poor Clovis is dead at the age of 21:—you know that 3 years ago he had an accident and, as a result, his hip was frozen—they thought they could fix it with an operation—and 12 days afterward he died from blood poisoning. Tears are all we have to face blows of this kind—and I am crying for the second time over the loss of one of my big children;—alas—I worked and those for whom I worked and hoped are going, leaving in my heart and in my life a hideous void!—I am alone now with the two little ones, Jean and Paul—Emil left for Bogotà the day before yesterday; he did not want to finish his studies—this is another bitter sorrow for me.—but perhaps he will become a man out there—he knows enough to get a job as a civil engineer;—if he really wants to work, I am sure he will find a way.

Dear friend—give me Paul's address, if you have it;—it seems necessary that I write him, although it is painful, because his inhuman selfishness disgusts me every time I think of it! I have borne all the burdens, I have suffered all the sorrows, all the worries alone! Or, would you send him this letter? Do as you think best, and believe me always your devoted

M. Gauguin

**XVII   Mette Gauguin to Emile Schuffenecker, 7 June 1902**

*Dear Schuffenecker,*

*I am going to spend 4 days in Paris next week at the home of my sister Madame Brandàs, 55 rue Laugier. Come and see me there Thursday morning if you are free!*

*Greetings,*

*Mette Gauguin*

7–6–1902

# Notes

### Preface

1    The more typical view of how biography functions in the art historical context is presented by Laurie Schneider Adams: "The meaning of a work . . . is seen as ultimately determined by the artist, with social and economic factors playing a secondary role." *The Methodologies of Art* (New York: HarperCollins, 1996), pp. 101ff.

2    Actually published in November 1899, but with the year 1900 on the title page. See James Strachey, "Editor's Introduction" to Sigmund Freud, *The Interpretation of Dreams* (New York: Avon Books, 1998), p. xii.

3    Of particular interest are Wayne Andersen, *Gauguin's Paradise Lost* (New York: Viking, 1971); Donald Kuspit, "The Pathology and Health of Art: Gauguin's Self-Experience," in *The Signs of Psyche in Modern and Postmodern Art* (New York: Cambridge University Press, 1993), pp. 3–17; Hal Foster, "'Primitive' Scenes," *Critical Inquiry* 20 (Autumn 1993), pp. 69–102; John Gedo, *The Artist and the Emotional World: Creativity and Personality* (New York: Columbia University Press, 1996), pp. 15–16 and passim; Patricia Mathews, *Passionate Discontent: Creativity, Gender, and French Symbolist Art* (Chicago: University of Chicago Press, 1999), pp. 161–77.

4    See particularly Freud's "Three Essays on the Theory of Sexuality" (1905), his "Civilization and Its Discontents" (1930), and Jack J. Spector, *The Aesthetics of Freud: A Study in Psychoanalysis and Art* (New York: Praeger, 1973).

5    David Sweetman's biography, *Paul Gauguin: A Complete Life* (London: Hodder and Stoughton, 1995), is such an example. As most writers do, he proposes that Gauguin creates *in spite of* the sordid aspects of his life.

6    Abigail Solomon-Godeau gives something of this impression in "Going Native: Paul Gauguin and the Invention of Primitivist Modernism," *Art in America* 77 (July 1989), pp. 118–29.

7    For the pros and cons of applying psychoanalytic methods to artists' biographies, see Bradley Collins, *Leonardo, Psychoanalysis and Art History* (Evanston, Ill.: Northwestern University Press, 1997).

8    As Peter Gay puts it, Freud "admitted more than once that he had been anticipated by philosophers or psychologists or, even more, poets and novelists." Gay, introduction to *The Freud Reader* (New York: W. W. Norton, 1989), p. xxi.

9    See Robert Wallerstein, "Epilogue," in *Psychoanalysis and Culture at the Millennium*, ed. Nancy Ginsburg and Ray Ginsburg (New Haven: Yale University Press, 2000), p. 360.

10    Richard Kuhns, "Pimping and Midwifery: Reflections on Art and Psychoanalysis," in *Psychoanalysis and Culture at the Millennium*, p. 278.

11    Ibid., p. 280.

12    See James B. Twitchell, *Dreadful Pleasures: An Anatomy of Modern Horror* (New York: Oxford University Press, 1985), p. 11. This author examines "why we have been drawn to certain images in art and popular culture that we would find repellant in actuality."

13    For example, Jean Teilhet-Fiske, *Paradise Reviewed: An Interpretation of Gauguin's Polynesian Symbolism* (Ann Arbor, Mich.: UMI Press, 1983); or Naomi Maurer, *The Pursuit of Spiritual Wisdom: The Thought and Art of Vincent van Gogh and Paul Gauguin* (Madison, N.J.: Fairleigh Dickinson University Press; London: Associated University Presses, 1998).

14    For example, Stephen Eisenman's attempt to portray Gauguin as a feminist in *Gauguin's Skirt* (New York: Thames and Hudson, 1997).

15 See Kathleen Barry, "The New Historical Synthesis: Women's Biography," *Journal of Women's History* 1, no. 3 (Winter 1990), pp. 75–105. "Feminist-critical biography must assume a self that is knowable through its doing and actions, that is, through intentionality." p. 76

16 Surveying the existing letters is an extremely difficult task because they have not yet been systematically or authoritatively published. The most thorough job has been by Victor Merlhès under the auspices of the Fondation Singer-Polignac, but to date he has published only letters before 1890. Fortunately the remarkable scholar Merete Bodelsen collected copies and transcripts of Gauguin's letters throughout her career and bequeathed her papers to the Royal Library, Copenhagen. I was fortunate to be able to consult these letters and fill in the gaps left by other sources. My project would not have been possible without this resource, and I owe her a tremendous debt of gratitude.

17 Two important studies of the art market in late nineteenth-century Paris are the classic study by Harrison White and Cynthia White, *Canvases and Careers: Institutional Change in the French Painting World* (New York: John Wiley and Sons, 1965); and Robert Jensen, *Marketing Modernism in Fin-de-Siècle Europe* (Princeton, N.J.: Princeton University Press, 1994).

18 See Clifford Geertz, *The Interpretation of Cultures: Selected Essays* (New York: Basic Books, 1973), p. 448.

19 For related methods of analyzing autobiography, see William Lowell Randall, *The Stories We Are* (Toronto: University of Toronto Press, 1955) (on the "poetics of self-creation"); Ruthellen Josselson and Amia Lieblich, eds., *The Narrative Study of Lives* (Newbury Park, Calif: Sage, 1993); and Philippe Lejeune, *On Autobiography* (Minneapolis: University of Minnesota Press, 1988).

20 As posited tongue-in-cheek by Charles Hanly, in "Materialism, Humanism, and Psychoanalysis," in *Psychoanalysis and Culture at the Millennium*, p. 298.

### Introduction

1 See Chapter 11.

### Chapter 1. Ancestry: The Moscosos and the Gauguins

1 Two authors who have grappled with Gauguin's background are Ursula Marks-Vandenbroucke, in "Gauguin—ses origines et sa formation artistique," *Gazette des beaux-arts* (January–April 1956); and David Sweetman.

2 For a summary of Flora Tristan's life, see Doris Beik and Paul Beik, *Flora Tristan: Utopian Feminist* (Bloomington: Indiana University Press, 1993).

3 See Chapter 8.

4 Jean Descola, *Daily Life in Colonial Peru, 1710–1820* (New York: Macmillan, 1968), p. 30.

5 Flora Tristan, *Peregrinations of a Pariah, 1833–1834* (1838; reprint, London: Virago, 1988). For mentions of Tristan in the Sand correspondence, see *Correspondance de George Sand*, ed. Georges Lubin (Paris: Garnier Frères, 1964–1990), letters 2552D, 2702, 2885, 3082.

6 See Mirbeau's mention of Tristan in his 1891 article on Gauguin, discussed below, Chapter 10.

7 Gauguin's wrote his memoirs, "Avant et après," in 1903, just before his death at the age of fifty-four. It was not published until 1918, in Leipzig. The first English version was published in 1921 as *Paul Gauguin's Intimate Journals*, trans. Van Wyck Brooks; preface by Emil Gauguin (New York: Boni and Liveright). This edition was reprinted in 1923 by H. Heineman (London). My references to *Intimate Journals* are to the 1985 reprint by KPI Limited, London, of the 1923 edition.

8 See Beik and Beik, p. xvii.

9 See Marks-Vandenbroucke, "Gauguin—Ses Origines et sa formation artistique," pp. 15–16.

10 In 1838, for example, she published three articles in *L'Artiste:* "De l'Art et de l'artiste dans l'Antiquité et à la Renaissance," "De l'Art depuis la Renaissance," and "Episode de la vie de Ribera dit l'Espagnolet." See Pierre Leprohon, *Flora Tristan* (Paris: Editions Corymbe, 1979), pp. 241–42.

11 On wanderlust and creativity, see, e.g,. Leprohon, pp. 255–56.

12 See Gauguin's diatribe against prohibiting the sale of liquor to the natives, below, Chapter 14.

13 Tristan wrote: "In Nîmes at least

300 to 400 washerwomen are . . . condemned to spend their lives with their bodies in the water up to their waists, and in water that is poisonous since it is filled with soap, with potash, with soda, with bleaching liquid, with grease, and lastly with all sorts of dyes, like indigo, madder, saffron, etc., etc.—There, to earn a living, many women are doomed to uterus disorders, to acute rheumatism, to painful pregnancies, to miscarriages—in a word, to all ills imaginable!" *The Tour of France* (1843–44), quoted in Beik and Beik, p. 167. Gauguin wrote: "My Grandmother was an amusing old lady. . . . She was connected with all sorts of socialist affairs, among them the workers' unions. . . . It is probable that she did not know how to cook. A socialist-anarchist blue-stocking!" *Intimate Journals*, p. 75.

14 Marks-Vandenbroucke, "Gauguin—Ses Origines et sa formation artistique," p. 13; Sweetman, p. 15.

15 Chazal was released in 1856 and died in 1860. Beik and Beik, p. xi. It is not known whether his daughter Aline or his grandchildren had any contact with him during this time.

16 See Chapter 4.

17 See Chapter 12.

18 *Intimate Journals*, p. 77.

19 See Chapter 2.

20 Mette Gauguin to Emile Schuffenecker, 31 Jan.? 1896: "my children have inherited the willfulness of their father—happily I am here to raise them more suitably than he was raised!" in Appendix, letter XV.

21 *Intimate Journals*, pp. 76–77.

22 See Paul Gootenberg, *Between Silver and Guano: Commercial Policy and the State in Postindependence Peru* (Princeton: Princeton University Press, 1989), especially chapter 5.

23 *Intimate Journals*, pp. 76–77.

24 Ibid., pp. 77–78.

25 Beik and Beik, p. 31.

26 Gauguin's sexualized portrayals of his mother (see the discussion of his *Exotic Eve* in Chapter 10) fall neatly into Freud's theory of the Oedipal phase of a boy's life. According to *The Ego and the Id* (1923), if the process of gender identification is complicated by a disturbance (such as Gauguin's loss of his father by this time), it may result in bisexuality. See *Freud Reader*, pp. 640–41.

27 The addresses of the Gauguin family can be traced through the years in the "Liste des adresses" of the annual *Etrennes orléannaises, almanach du Département du Loiret,* Archives Municipales d'Orléans.

28 Louis d'Illiers, *L'Histoire d'Orléans* (Marseilles: Laffitte Reprints, 1977), p. 380.

29 The last time the Gauguin-Juranvilles are listed under "épiciers" is 1838.

30 His exact occupation is unknown. Paul Gauguin referred to his father as "the political correspondent of the *National*" (*Intimate Journals*, p. 75), but nothing has been found published under his name, nor is he recorded as editor.

31 D'Illiers, p. 392.

32 Henri Perruchot, *Gauguin* (Cleveland: World Publishing, 1963), p. 47.

33 The accuracy of the information about how Isidore's will deals with his heirs (1893) shows that he remained in touch with Marie and her family even after they emigrated to Bogotá, Colombia, and with Paul's wife and family in Copenhagen. Will, Isidore Fleury Gauguin, Archives Basseville and Basseville-Bruant, Notaires, Orléans.

34 *Intimate Journals*, p. 134

35 Ibid.

36 Ibid.

37 Ibid., p. 79.

38 Gauguin's belief in the sexuality of children, including himself, might prefigure theories of infantile sexuality that Freud had been developing since the 1890s and would publish in 1905 (*Three Essays on the Theory of Sexuality*). See Gay, *Freud Reader*, p. 239. See also Spector, pp. 18–19: "Several psychoanalytic themes, such as infantile sexuality and the sexual etiology of neurosis, were frequent topics in psychiatric circles of *fin de siècle* Paris."

39 "Ask Pasteur if I did not know him at Orléans? The Zevor boys and Pasteur played with me at St. Mesmin." PG to MG (June–July 1892), in *Paul Gauguin: Letters to His Wife and Friends*, ed. Maurice Malingue, trans. Henry J. Stenning (Cleveland: World Publishing, 1949), no. 128 (redated); hereafter cited as Malingue, *Letters*.

40 Beverly Livingston, "Introduction" to Flora Tristan, *The Workers Union* (Urbana: University of Illinois Press, 1983), p. xxiii.

41 For Gauguin's Peruvian relatives in Paris, see *Intimate Journals*, p. 78.

42  Jean de Rotonchamp [Louis Brouillon], *Paul Gauguin* (Weimar, 1906; reprint, Paris: Les Editions G. Crès, 1925), p. 9.

43  Aline Gauguin, Will, Departmental Archives, Hauts-de-Seine, in National Gallery of Art, *The Art of Paul Gauguin* (Washington, D.C.: National Gallery of Art, 1988), p. 3.

44  Lesley Blanch, *Pierre Loti: The Legendary Romantic* (New York: Harcourt Brace Jovanovich, 1983), p. 51.

45  Herman Melville's decision to sign on to a merchant ship in 1842 was impetuous. See George Woodcock, introduction to Herman Melville, *Typee*, pp. 8–9.

46  See Victor Merlhès, *Correspondance de Paul Gauguin* (Paris: Fondation Singer-Polignac, 1984), p. 322 n. 6.

47  Certificate of enrollment on the *Luzitano*, 1865, reproduced in Marks-Vandenbroucke, figs. 5 and 6.

48  *Intimate Journals*, p. 124.

49  Gauguin's fascination with rivalries and sexual triangles runs through his art and writings. A Freudian interpretation might connect this tendency to the early loss of his father and an unresolved Oedipal impulse. Freud's belief in the central role of the mother-father-child triangle (and its successful resolution) is stressed in a 1920 footnote to his influential "Three Essays on the Theory of Sexuality." Gay, *Freud Reader*, p. 290: "Every new arrival on this planet is faced by the task of mastering the Oedipus Complex; anyone who fails to do so falls victim to neurosis."

50  *Intimate Journals*, pp. 123–24.

51  See Robley Evans, *A Sailor's Log* (New York, 1901), p. 111: "Rio was, comparatively speaking, free from fever at the time of our visit [1867], and we enjoyed it to the utmost. The opera, in which Aimée was the star, was very good. . . . When we had been in port a few days a Russian practice ship came in filled with midshipmen. . . . [That evening] a party of fifteen or twenty midshipmen in Russian uniform took charge of the stage and ran the performance to suit themselves."

52  Perruchot, p. 57.

53  Ibid.

54  According to an undated letter from Gauguin's sister to Charles Morice, he called this experience "the most bitter of his life." Ibid., p. 59.

## Chapter 2. Young Man in Paris

1  The nineteenth-century separation of masculine and feminine spheres put a premium on correct appearance and performance of the two defined roles. Robert Nye sums up the standard of male "bourgeois sociability" at midcentury: "The socially polished man presented to the world a self-creation whose good sense and moderation were indispensable to the civilization of the 'juste milieu.'" Nye, *Masculinity and Male Codes of Honor in Modern France* (New York: Oxford University Press, 1993), p. 129. See also Harry Brod, "Masculinity as Masquerade," in *The Masculine Masquerade: Masculinity and Representation*, ed. Andrew Perchuk and Helaine Posner (Cambridge, Mass.: MIT Press, 1995).

2  Aline Gauguin, Will, Departmental Archives, Hautes de Seine. The childhood home of Paul Gauguin was torn down and rebuilt by the new owners immediately after this sale. Cadastral records, Archives Municipales d'Orléans.

3  *Intimate Journals*, p. 98.

4  Merlhès, *Correspondance*, p. 323.

5  *Intimate Journals*, p. 115.

6  For the painting career of Marguerite Arosa, see Merlhès, *Correspondance*, pp. 323–24 n. 5.

7  For an outline of Schuffenecker's early career, see ibid., pp. 401–2 n. 153.

8  For Gustave Arosa and his family, see Merlhès, *Correspondance*, pp. 319–20 n. 2.

9  *Intimate Journals*, p. 130.

10  See Donn Byrne and Julie A. Osland, "Sexual Fantasy and Erotica/Pornography: Internal and External Imagery," in *Psychological Perspectives of Human Sexuality*, ed. Lenore Szuchman and Frank Muscarella (New York: John Wiley and Sons, 2000), p. 291.

11  Nye, p. 129.

12  It is impossible not to consider Freud's hypothesis that art is a sublimation of sexual desire in regard to Gauguin's self-reported early response to the fine arts. Although his opinions about how unconscious forces of sexuality and aggression affected the creative act vary throughout his writings, in the late *Civilization and Its Discontents* (1930), he concluded, "All that seems certain is its derivation from the field of sexual feeling." Cited in Spector, p. 100. John Gedo sur-

veys more recent theories of creativity and regression to primitive modes of drive organization in *The Artist and the Emotional World* (New York: Columbia University Press, 1996), chapter 1.

13  For Arosa and Bertin, see Merlhès, *Correspondance*, p. 323; Sweetman, pp. 61–65; and Merete Bodelsen, "Gaugin, the Collector," *Burlington Magazine* 112, no. 810 (September 1970), pp. 598–601.

14  William Parker, "The Paris Bourse and French Finance," *Studies in History, Economics and Public Law* 89 (1919), pp. 45–46.

15  The privileged life of the *rentier* resurfaced in Gauguin's later writings. For the growth of the rentier class in France in the mid-nineteenth century, see Charles E. Freedman, "French Securities Market, 1815–1870," in *From the Ancien Régime to the Popular Front,* ed. Charles K. Warner (New York: Columbia University Press, 1969), pp. 77–91 passim.

16  Merlhès, *Correspondance,* pp. 319–20 n. 2.

17  See ibid., pp. 327–29 n. 20; for the marriage of Marie Gauguin and Juan Nepomuceno Uribe-Buenaventura, see certificate no. 29, 28 Dec. 1875, Archives de la Mairie de Saint-Cloud.

18  Merlhès, *Correspondance,* p. 319 n. 1.

19  Most of what we know about the circumstances of Paul Gauguin's social life in 1872–73 comes from the letters written by Marie Heegaard to her family in Copenhagen. A French translation of extracts from them can be found in Merlhès, *Correspondance,* nos. I–XII.

20  Marie Heegaard to her mother, ca. 25 Dec. 1872, Merlhès, *Correspondance,* no. II.

21  PG to Mme. Heegaard, 9 Feb. 1873, Merlhès, *Correspondance,* no. I.

22  Coincidentally, both Mette and Paul had lived in the residence of the head of state of a country: Paul in Lima and Mette in Copenhagen. Mette's relationship with the children of Prime Minister Estrup was extremely important when they became adults. Magdalena Estrup married Count Frederick Moltke (himself the son of a former prime minister) and became the patron of the Gauguin's oldest son, Emil. In addition to assuming the expenses of a Danish boarding school for the boy, Countess Moltke assisted the family in many other ways

when they returned to Copenhagen. See Chapter 4.

23  Otto Rung, *Fra min Klunketid* (Copenhagen, 1942), quoted in Merete Bodelsen, *Gauguin and Van Gogh in Copenhagen in 1893* (Copenhagen: Ordurpgaard, 1984), p. 28.

24  Marie Heegaard to her family, [early January 1873], Merlhès, *Correspondance,* no. III.

25  Marie Heegaard to her family, [late February 1873], Merlhès, *Correspondance,* no. IV.

26  Marie Heegaard to her father, [27 Mar. 1873], Merlhès, *Correspondance,* no. V.

27  Although cross-dressing for costume balls and parties dates to the eighteenth century, it came to have different associations for men and women in the nineteenth century. For women, it was most often associated with social liberation. This seems to be the case with Mette Gauguin: "I remember only one woman from the eighties and nineties who wore her hair short, and yet was everyone's favourite for her plucky femininity wherever she appeared." Rung, p. 28. For men, "feminization" carried a more complicated personal and social meaning. Especially after the Franco-Prussion War, when the Prussian style of masculinity triumphed, wearing women's clothes undercut the man's symbolic masculine power and connoted either a frivolous artistic nature or homosexuality, or both. See Vern L. Bollough and Bonnie Bullough, *Cross Dressing, Sex, and Gender* (Philadelphia: University of Pennsylvania Press, 1993), pp. 125, 169, 180–84.

28  For example, Sweetman, p. 69.

29  *Intimate Journals,* p. 121.

30  When the Gauguins' son Emil decided to broaden his engineering career in the Americas in 1900, the move was arranged via correspondence among the three. MG to ES, 11 June 1900, Musée Gaugin, Tahiti, in Appendix, letter XVI. When Marie Heegaard's mother died in 1906, she left a substantial inheritance to Mette. Maurice Malingue, "Encore du nouveau sur Gauguin," *L'Oeil,* no. 58 (October 1959), p. 68.

31  Marie Heegaard to her sister Louise, ca. mid-July 1873, Merlhès, *Correspondance,* no. VII.

32  He painted Marie Heegaard's portrait and sketched her in the costume of a

fisherwoman, for example. Marie Heegaard to her family, 25 Feb. 1873, Merlhès, *Correspondance*, no. IV; and Marie Heegaard to her family, ca. 1 Aug. 1873, Merlhès, *Correspondance*, no. VIII.

33   Marie Heegaard to her family, [late February 1873], Merlhès, *Correspondance*, no. IV.

34   Marie Heegaard to her family, [late July or early August 1873], Merlhès, *Correspondance*, no. VIII.

35   Or, as Richard Kuhns would call it, an "enactment." To Kuhns an enactment has "four dominant properties: 1) they are events whose presence declares an intention; 2) they are performances requiring space and time; 3) they are effectively charged objects; 4) they are representations that refer to other objects and events, both internal, external, and historical." "Pimping and Midwifery," p. 278.

36   Rotonchamp, p. 18.

37   Merlhès, *Correspondance*, no. VII.

38   Freud would link this moral laxity to the loss of his father and an unresolved Oedipal process. See *The Ego and the Id*, in *Freud Reader*, p. 643. But such issues of morality have also been debated under the heading of "admirable immorality" in philosophical literature, such as Joseph Kupfer, "Gauguin, Again," *Pacific Philosophical Quarterly* 73 (March 1992), pp. 63–72.

39   PG to Mme. Heegaard, 8 July 1874, Merlhès, *Correspondance*, no. 4. "Comme vous le savez je n'ai rien de ce qui fait reconnaître la vertu du vice."

40   It is important to distinguish between morality and honor. Gauguin was an excellent example of the sanctioned use of aggressive behavior for men of honor in late nineteenth-century France. See Nye, pp. 148–71.

41   PG to Mme. Heegaard, 8 July 1874, Merlhès, *Correspondance*, no. 4.

42   Though perhaps also as a token of their friendship with Emile Schuffenecker, who later named his son Paul.

43   Johan Frederik ("Frits") Thaulow (1847–1906) became one of Norway's most influential Impressionist artists. He maintained a frequent presence in Paris while painting and teaching in Norway and Denmark. Among his artistic acquaintances, in addition to Gauguin, were Rodin and Munch. *Norsk Biografisk Leksikon*, ed. Edv. Bull, Anders Krogvig, Gerhard Gran (Kristiania: H. Aschenhoug, 1923–83), pp. 164–70.

44   For instance, he writes to Madame Heegaard, "Please tell M. Heegaard my regrets for my inability to serve him, as there is no business to be done here." PG to Mme. Heegaard, 8 July 1874, Merlhès, *Correspondance*, no. 3; Malingue, *Letters*, no. 2.

45   Merlhès, *Correspondance*, note 19.

46   Merlhès, *Correspondance*, note 153.

47   Merlhès, *Correspondance*, note 5.

48   See Merlhès, *Correspondance*, notes 159, 167, 205.

49   See Chapter 9 for doubts about his direction. In 1894, he wrote to Schuffenecker, "I don't have enough time or pictorial education: hence springs a great obstacle to the realization of my dream." PG to ES, 26 July 1894. Victor Merlhès, *De Bretagne en Polynésie, Paul Gauguin: Pages inédites* (Tahiti: Avant et Après, 1995), p. 82; hereafter Merlhès, *Pages inédites*.

50   Marie Heegaard to her family, [early November 1876], Merlhès, *Correspondance*, no. XII.

51   For Gauguin's employment chronology, see Bodelsen, "Gauguin, the Collector," pp. 598–601; and Sweetman, pp. 86–87 ff.

52   Merlhès, *Correspondance*, note 20.

53   Georges Wildenstein, "Gauguin en Bretagne," *Gazette des beaux-arts* (January–April 1956), p. 86.

54   This reminiscence is unattributed; see Perruchot, p. 75.

55   PG to ES, [1896], Drouot sale, December 1958. Bodelsen, "Gauguin, the Collector," p. 601.

56   Emile Zola, *Money [L'Argent]*, trans. Ernest Vizetelly (1891; reprint, London: Alan Sutton, 1991), p. 105.

57   Ibid. pp. 93–94, 343–44.

58   In 1892, when Gauguin heard from his wife that she had sold one of his early paintings, he reminisced about those days: "What do husbands do and especially stockbrokers? On Sundays they go to the races or to the café or with whores, for men must have a little amusement, otherwise they cannot work, and besides it's only human nature. For my part I worked [painted], and that was my dissipation." PG to MG, [September–October, 1891], Malingue, *Letters*, no. 127.

### Chapter 3. Impressionism

1   For the growth of art speculation and the cult of the artist in the late nineteenth-century art market, see Harrison White and Cynthia White, *Canvases*

and Careers (New York: John Wiley and Sons, 1965), p. 99: "The new dealer-critic system had a built-in motive for encouraging innovative work: tapping the fever for speculation which possessed much of the nineteenth-century French middle class. The financial speculation in art found its cultural counterpart in the speculation in taste. As critics and dealers were wont to say to the 'discerning buyer': 'In twenty years he will be considered a master—and his painting will be worth a fortune.'"

2    See Bodelsen, "Gauguin, the Collector," pp. 598–601.

3    The paintings in question were two good-sized oils, *Paysage en février* (Ny Carlsberg Glyptotek, Copenhagen) and *Les Meules* (location unknown), and a watercolor painting on silk in the shape of a fan, *L'Hiver: Retour de la foire* (location unknown).

4    For Pissarro on Saint Thomas, see Richard Brettell, "Camille Pissarro and St. Thomas: The Story of an Exhibition," in *Camille Pissarro in the Caribbean, 1850–1855: Drawings from the Collection at Olana* (Saint Thomas: Hebrew Congregation of St. Thomas, 1996), pp. 8–17.

5    See Kathleen Adler, *Camille Pissarro: A Biography* (London: B.T. Batsford, 1978), pp. 20, 30.

6    He learned of Henry Murger's real "vie de bohème" through the painter Antoine Chintreuil, who had been a member of Murger's group of poor, starving artists in the 1840s. Pissarro met Chintreuil through Corot and also met Murger's former mistress, Anaïs-Victorine Latrasse, who became a lifelong friend. See Adler, pp. 23–24; and Merlhès, *Correspondance*, note 202. Anaïs Latrasse is later (1889–90) recorded in a Gauguin sketchbook as having bought four of his works. Merlhès, *Correspondance*, note 5.

7    For Julie Vellay Pissarro, see Adler, pp. 31–32.

8    Ibid., pp. 39–41.

9    See Ibid., pp. 44, 53, 71, 103, 114–15, 116. In an example cited by Adler, Julie Pissarro wrote to her son Lucien in 1887 about the family's inability to pay their bills: "I have no money and nobody will give me credit. What are we to do? We are eight at home to be fed every day." P. 114.

10    Ibid., pp. 77–78.

11    The earliest known correspondence between Pissarro and Gauguin, in the spring and summer of 1879, concerns Gauguin's purchases from the dealer Madame Latouche and from Pissarro himself. Merlhès, *Correspondance*, nos. 6, XIII, 7–10.

12    For another outsider's entry into the Impressionist group, see Nancy Mowll Mathews, *Mary Cassatt: A Life* (New Haven: Yale University Press, 1998), pp. 108–18.

13    Ibid., pp. 147–49. Degas paid a highly flattering degree of attention to Cassatt when she entered the Impressionist group in 1878–79 but abruptly dropped her, along with the print project they were working on together (the journal *Le Jour et la nuit*). They were soon reconciled, but Cassatt was more cautious in her dealings with him ever after.

14    For an overview of the fourth Impressionist exhibition (1879), see Ronald Pickvance, "Contemporary Popularity and Posthumous Neglect," in *The New Painting* (San Francisco: Fine Arts Museums of San Francisco, 1986), pp. 243–71.

15    See Merlhès, *Correspondance*, nos. 10, 11.

16    When apart, the Gauguins and Pissarros sent family photos to each other. PG to CP, [late December 1884 or early January 1885], Merlhès, *Correspondance*, no. 61.

17    N. Mathews, *Mary Cassatt*, pp. 122–23.

18    Based on this courtesy in their correspondence, one could make the case for Gauguin's visit to Pontoise to paint with Pissarro as having taken place in August rather than June, as Merlhès has suggested. Whereas Pissarro was already sending greetings to Mette in his letter of July 7, 1879 (Merlhès, *Correspondance*, no. XIII), Gauguin didn't begin to send his greetings to Madame Pissarro until September (Merlhès, *Correspondance*, no. 11).

19    For an overview of the fifth Impressionist exhibition, see Charles Moffett, "Disarray and Disappointment," in *New Painting*, pp. 293–314. For Gauguin's reviews, see p. 304.

20    Armand Silvestre, *La Vie moderne*, 24 Apr. 1880, cited in *New Painting*, p. 304.

21    N. Mathews, *Mary Cassatt*, pp. 135–37.

22    Bodelsen, "Gauguin, the Collector," p. 598.

23    Merlhès, *Correspondance*, note 153.

24 *New Painting*, pp. 305–7.

25 *Intimate Journals*, p. 63.

26 Ibid.

27 Merlhès, *Correspondance*, note 51.

28 Mette Gauguin lent it to the Udstilling exhibition in Copenhagen in 1893 with the title *Valerie Roumi*. National Gallery of Art, *Gauguin*, p. 24.

29 Ibid.

30 Merlhès, *Correspondance*, no. 14. Numbers 13 and 14 in Merlhès are actually excerpts from the same letter to Pissarro, 16 Aug. 1880; see typescript transcription by John Rewald, in Merete Bodelsen Papers, Royal Library, Copenhagen: "The model I had had came back yesterday, I should be able to finish my painting soon."

31 He referred to the picture as "Suzanne," a standard title for nudes posing unaware of their audience, a name drawn from the biblical Susanna and the Elders. His son Pola, in his biography of his father, mistakenly proposed that the sitter was a maid named Justine. Pola Gauguin, *My Father, Paul Gauguin*, trans. Arthur G. Chater (New York: Knopf, 1937), pp. 67–68. Although I cannot give Pola Gauguin the credence that others such as Mary Mathews Gedo and her sources, Charles Stuckey and Ziva Amishai-Maisels, have, I agree with some of their interpretations of the work. See Gedo, "Retreat from an Artistic Breakthrough: Gauguin's *Nude Study (Suzanne Sewing)*," *Zeitschrift für Kunstgeschichte* 58, no. 3 (1995), pp. 407–16.

32 Joris-Karl Huysmans, "The Exhibition of the Indépendants of 1881," reprinted in Huysmans, *L'Art moderne* (1883), translated in *Gauguin: A Retrospective*, ed. Marla Prather and Charles Stuckey (New York: Hugh Lauter Levin, 1987), pp. 40–41.

33 Ibid.

34 Gauguin's violent interpretations of Eve and the loss of virginity are an example; there is even a reference to graphic sexuality in *The Birth of Christ*. See Chapters 9 and 13.

35 *New Painting*, p. 337.

36 For more about Gauguin's collections, see Bodelsen, "Gauguin, the Collector," esp. p. 593; and Merete Bodelsen, "Gauguins Samling," in *Gauguin og Impressionisterne* (Copenhagen: Kunstforeningen, 1968), pp. 73–145.

37 See N. Mathews, *Mary Cassatt*, pp. 159–60; and Ann Dumas, "Degas and His Collection," in Ann Dumas, Colta Ives, Susan Alyson Stein, and Gary Tinterow, *The Private Collection of Edgar Degas* (New York: Metropolitan Museum of Art, 1997), pp. 3–73.

38 Emil Gauguin, preface to *Paul Gauguin's Intimate Journals*, trans. Van Wyck Brooks (New York: Crown, 1936), n.p.

39 Letters from Mette Gauguin to Emile Schuffenecker, 1889–1901, Musée Gauguin, Tahiti.

40 PG to CP, [March 1881], Merlhès, *Correspondance*, no. 15.

41 Ibid.

42 For the seventh Impressionist exhibition, see Joel Isaacson, "The Painters Called Impressionists," in *New Painting*, pp. 373–95.

43 See *New Painting*, p. 399.

### Chapter 4. The Crash

1 Zola, *Money*, p. 378.

2 See John Rewald, *The History of Impressionism* (New York: Museum of Modern Art, 1973), p. 467.

3 Paul Durand-Ruel to George Lafenestre (l'Inspecteur des Beaux-Arts Commissaire générale des Expositions), 18 Sept. 1885, National Archives, Paris.

4 "This year I am completely in the soup from a financial point of view: business being completely dead, I am earning nothing and yet am still forced to meet expenses." PG to CP, [June 1882], Merlhès, *Correspondance*, no. 24.

5 *Still Life with Danish Schnapps Carafe* (location unknown) is not included in the Gauguin catalogue raisonné (Georges Wildenstein, *Gauguin*, vol.1: *Catalogue* [Paris: Les Beaux-Arts, 1964]) but is listed by Merete Bodelsen in her review of the catalogue raisonné as one of the works left out of the book. "The Literature of Art: The Wildenstein-Cogniat Gauguin Catalogue," *Burlington Magazine* 108, no. 754 (January 1966), p. 30, supplement no. 8. She also notes that Marie Heegaard married Bjorn Stephensen in 1879.

6 PG to CP, [June 1882], Merlhès, *Correspondance*, no. 24.

7 Haavard Rostrup, "Gauguin et le Danemark," *Gazette des beaux-arts* (January–April 1956), p. 70 n. 23.

8 Ibid., p. 70.

9 Catalogue numbers refer to the Wildenstein catalogue raisonné; see above, n. 5.

10   Rostrup, p. 63.

11   *Intimate Journals*, pp. 78–79.

12   See Chapter 5.

13   Merlhès, *Correspondance*, note 82.

14   Gauguin gave Bertaux two Pontoise landscapes in November of 1882 to settle a 1,000 franc debt. He later referred to this as a "sale." Bodelsen, "Gauguin the Collector," p. 593.

15   Merlhès, *Correspondance*, no. 24.

16   PG to CP, 8 Dec. 1882, Merlhès, *Correspondance*, no. 30: "I received your letter this morning and I thank you for thinking of me in regard to the 800 francs for the woodcutter that I asked you for."

17   CP to Lucien Pissarro, 18 Jan. 1883, in Janine Bailly-Herzberg, *Correspondance de Camille Pissarro*, vol. 1 (Paris: Presses Universitaires de France, 1980), p. 115 and n. 1.

18   PG to CP, [late October–early November 1882], Merlhès, *Correspondance*, no. 28.

19   PG to CP, [January–February 1883], Merlhès, *Correspondance*, no. 32

20   PG to CP, 9 Feb. 1883, typescript transcription by John Rewald, Merete Bodelsen Papers, Royal Library, Copenhagen [not in Merlhès, *Correspondance*]: "I've just had some annoying things to deal with. My brother-in-law Thaulow is getting divorced, and I had to get involved, and I am still in the middle of all the wrangling."

21   Christiania [Oslo], *Kunstudstillingen*, 1884.

22   PG to ES, [June? 1896], cited in Belinda Thomson, *Gauguin by Himself* (Boston: Little, Brown, 1993), p. 249. Gauguin does not specify the date of this incident, but since he writes of her trip to Denmark and their relocation to Copenhagen soon afterward, it is reasonable to date their quarrel to 1883–84. I would disagree with the often-repeated dating of this incident to 1879, first made by Merete Bodelsen, in "Gauguin, the Collector," p. 601. Although the letter is known only from the fragment published in a Drouot auction catalogue (Paris, 3–4 Dec. 1958, no. 116), the complete fragment, published in Thomson, seems to link the incident more closely in date to Gauguin's move to Copenhagen: "My wife went to Denmark for a few days. . . . On Madame's return, since she didn't want a divorce, we talked everything over; there were tears,

and forgiveness. Men forgive so easily. I went to Denmark, and found everyone against me there."

23   PG to ES, [June? 1896], cited in Thomson, p. 249.

24   Merlhès, *Correspondance*, note 112.

25   Merlhès, *Correspondance*, note 119.

26   PG to CP, [13 Aug. 1883], Merlhès, *Correspondance*, no. 39.

27   PG to CP, [ca. 25–29 July 1883], Merlhès, *Correspondance*, no. 38.

28   PG to CP, [late September or early October 1883], Merlhès, *Correspondance*, no. 40.

29   Ibid.

30   The Monsieur Cellot mentioned in the letter of July 25, 1883, from Camille Pissarro to Lucien Pissarro (Bailly-Herzberg, no. 164) is no doubt the same as the Cellot ("mon cher Cellot") to whom Gauguin writes on Jan. 2, 1885 (Merlhès, *Correspondance*, no. 62), about distributing commercial varnishes while he is in Denmark.

31   CP to Lucien Pissarro, [16 June 1883], Bailly-Herzberg, no. 161.

32   CP to Lucien Pissarro, [31 Oct. 1883], Bailly-Herzberg, no. 185.

33   PG to CP, 11 Oct. 1883, Merlhès, *Correspondance*, no. 41.

34   CP to Eugène Murer, 2 Nov. 1883, Bailly-Herzberg, no. 186. "I had a visit yesterday from Gauguin—he has decided to move to Rouen immediately. . . . He is extremely determined, he will distance himself from Paris to devote himself completely to painting, he is counting on working like a demon to earn a place in the art world."

35   Merlhès, *Correspondance*, note 122.

36   See Merlhès, *Correspondance*, note 124.

37   Frederico Zandomeneghi to CP, [22 Nov. 1883], Merlhès, *Correspondance*, no. XXIV.

38   Wildenstein 131.

39   PG to CP [end September 1884], Merlhès, *Correspondance*, no. 53.

40   National Gallery of Art, p. 37. Although this painting was probably not exhibited, it did find a purchaser in Oslo: Hermann Thaulow, Frits's cousin and the husband of Mette's sister Pauline ("Phylle").

41   "With all the expenses of December, as well as those of moving, my little reserve is almost squandered, and I have at most enough to live on for six months."

PG to CP, [ca. 12–13 Jan. 1884], Merlhès, *Correspondance*, no. 43.

42 Ibid.

43 Merlhès, *Correspondance*, note 153.

44 See Chapter 6.

45 PG to CP [ca. 12–13 Jan. 1884], Merlhès, *Correspondance*, no. 43.

46 Ibid.

47 PG to CP [mid-May 1884], Merlhès, *Correspondance*, no. 48.

48 "When your son comes of age, do you dare advise him to marry any one except a cook?" PG to MG, [June 1888], Merlhès, *Correspondance*, no. 154; Malingue, *Letters*, no. 64.

49 Merlhès, *Correspondance*, no. 43.

50 PG to CP, [ca. 9 Apr. 1884], Merlhès, *Correspondance*, no. 46.

51 Paul Durand-Ruel to CP, 23 Oct. 1884, Bailly-Herzberg, no. 254.

52 PG to CP, [ca. mid-May 1884], Merlhès, *Correspondance*, no. 48; and PG to CP, [end July 1884], Merlhès, *Correspondance*, no. 50.

53 PG to CP, [ca. mid-May 1884], Merlhès, *Correspondance*, no. 48.

54 PG to CP, [ca. end September 1884], Merlhès, *Correspondance*, no. 53.

55 Ibid.

56 Ibid.

57 PG to CP, [October 1884], Merlhès, *Correspondance*, no. 54.

58 "With kisses for both of you, and thank you for having me Monday and for the dress, which Paul couldn't find anything but superb, in spite of the price, which was beyond our budget." MG to Emile and Louise Schuffenecker, 29 Oct. 1884, Merlhès, *Correspondance*, no. XXV.

59 May Alcott Nieriker, *Studying Art Abroad and How to Do It Cheaply* (Boston: Roberts Brothers, 1879), p. 76. The author, Louisa May Alcott's sister, lists couturiers that she would recommend to her American readers, for instance, "Mme. Femary, 42 Rue Boursault. (Price 60 francs; dress materials included.)"

60 "I am selling my life insurance policy, which I've been paying on for 12 years at a 50% loss, and with the 1,500 francs I'll try to go three months." PG to CP, [end July 1884], Merlhès, *Correspondance*, no. 50.

61 Ibid.

62 For the Gauguins in Copenhagen, see Rostrup, pp. 65–66.

63 It is difficult to determine with certainty which translations in *Politken* were Mette Gauguin's, for the translator is not named. But several French novels (by Daudet, Maupassant, Bourget, Richepin, and Zola) inherited by Pola Gauguin had Mette's translation notes in the margins. Unpublished list by Bengt Danielsson and Pola Gauguin, [undated], courtesy of Mette Gauguin (great-granddaughter of Mette and Paul Gauguin), Copenhagen.

64 PG to CP, [late December 1884 or early January 1885], Merlhès, *Correspondance*, no. 61: "I visited the home of the Count de Moltke, an acquaintance of ours here. He has inherited from his father's family a gallery of wonderful Old Masters— Rembrandt, Rubens, Teniers, etc. . . . [but] he has a 40 franc modern cloth covering a table that could be in the Louvre. . . . You see such is the taste of our times among the people who are *noble and very rich.*"

65 Ibid.

66 PG to CP, [November–December 1884], Merlhès, *Correspondance*, no. 57.

67. Merlhès, *Correspondance*, note 194.

68 For examples of his graphology, see PG to CP, [October 1884], Merlhès, *Correspondance*, no. 54; and PG to CP, [late October or early November], Merlhès, *Correspondance*, no. 55.

69 PG to ES, 14 Jan. 1885, Merlhès, *Correspondance*, no. 65.

70 See Robert Herbert, "Seurat in Chicago and New York," *Burlington Magazine* 100, no. 662 (May 1958), p. 151.

71 PG to ES, 14 Jan. 1885, Merlhès, *Correspondance*, no. 65.

72 J. G. Topsoe-Jensen, *Scandinavian Literature from Brandès to Our Day* (New York: W. W. Norton, 1929), p. 18.

73 PG to ES, 14 Jan. 1885, Merlhès, *Correspondance*, no. 65.

74 PG to CP, 30 Jan. 1885, Merlhès, *Correspondance*, no. 68.

75 The letters from Gauguin to Messieurs Dillies and Company (and other related business correspondents) during this time are full of reminders of Gauguin's inability to finance the new venture. For example: "In a few days I shall have to take out of the Customs the material of which you advise me; how am I to settle the bill? All this is a worry and impedes my freedom of action. An acceptable man in whom an important firm has confidence must maintain a certain standard." 13 Jan. 1885, Merlhès, *Correspon-*

dance, no. 64, trans. in Malingue, *Letters*, no. 10.

76  Rostrup, p. 66.

77  Ibid., pp. 67–70.

78  In the 1870s, Thaulow regularly traveled between Norway and France, and in the 1880s, he sent paintings to exhibitions all over Europe. In 1892 he settled permanently in France. *Norsk Biografisk Leksikon*, pp. 166–67.

79  PG to ES, 24 May 1885, Merlhès, *Correspondance*, no. 78.

80  *Intimate Journals*, p. 122.

81  PG to ES, 14 Jan. 1885, Merlhès, *Correspondance*, no. 65.

82  Quand j'avais dix ans à Copenhague . . . je vis mon père d'un coup de poing ensanglanter la figure de ma mère. Emil Gauguin to Georges Crès, 4 June 1926, quoted in Victor Merlhès, *Paul Gauguin et Vincent Van Gogh* (Tahiti: Avant et Après, 1989), pp. 19–20.

### Chapter 5. PGo Emerges

1  Throughout the nineteenth century, the Napoleonic concept of separate spheres was defended in the name of procreation and family. Not only was the "masculine management" of the family the cornerstone of society, but, by guaranteeing an orderly inheritance, it made individual and social prosperity possible in perpetuity. See Nye, pp. 55–57.

2  "Clinicians, especially males, should be very careful not to collude with violent men in their rationalization, minimization, and denial. The early clinical literature on batterers suggests that these excuses were accepted as true, with clinicians using the same terms batterers used, such as 'loss of control,' or blaming victims in the same way that batterers did." Richard A. Stordeur and Richard Stille, *Ending Men's Violence Against Their Partners* (Newbury Park, Calif.: Sage, 1989), p. 43.

3  Studies of violent marriages have shown that abusive husbands prefer to assign responsibility for what happens to outside pressures, mind-altering substances, such as alcohol, or to the wife herself. The wife is then pressured or persuaded to agree that being beaten is her fault. See particularly Margareta Hydén, *Woman Battering as Marital Act* (Oslo: Scandinavian University Press, 1994), p. 118.

4  "Most violent men are not violent

all the time, and one of the reasons a battered woman may stay in a relationship is the hope that this charming, loving side of her partner's personality may 'win out' over the violent, abusive side. Indeed, batterers can have positive, loving, and caring characteristics. However, our clinical experience suggests that this charming side is often one of the methods by which batterers convince women to be involved with them and manipulate them to stay after a violent incident. At times, this charm almost appears to be a parody of true affection, and often reflects a traditional, stereotypic notion of romance, rather than intimacy." Stordeur and Stille, p. 49.

5  Hydén, p. 143.

6  Hydén, p. 138.

7  "Pronounced 'pego' no doubt; a piece of slang, meaning 'prick,' picked up from Gauguin's merchant marine years." Wayne Anderson, introduction to Daniel Guérin, ed., *The Writings of a Savage: Paul Gauguin* (New York: Paragon House, 1990), p. xxiii.

8  "Gauguin was the Master . . . you hung on every word, you repeated his every paradox." P.-L. Maud, "L'Influence de Paul Gauguin, *L'Occident* (October 1903), p. 162.

9  PG to MG, 9 Aug. 1885, Merlhès, *Correspondance*, no. 82.

10  PG to MG, [19 Sept. 1885], Merlhès, *Correspondance*, no. 84.

11  PG to MG, [ca. 20 Dec. 1885], Merlhès, *Correspondance*, no. 91.

12  Charles Kunstler, "Paul Gauguin et la révolution espagnole," *Nouvelles Littéraires* (9 Jan. 1937), p. 7.

13  Jacques-Emile Blanche, *De Gauguin à la revue nègre* (1928), quoted by Françoise Cachin in "Gauguin Portrayed by Himself and by Others," in National Gallery of Art, p. xv.

14  The fortunes of the Uribe family were so badly affected by the crash that in 1886, Juan left for Colombia to begin a new business in Panama City (still a part of Colombia at that time). Marie and the children followed him in 1889, and they made their new home in Bogatá. See Merlhès, *Correspondance*, note 213.

15  PG to MG, [early October 1885], Merlhès, *Correspondance* 26.

16  PG to MG, [ca. 20 Dec. 1885], Merlhès, *Correspondance* 91.

17  PG to MG, 13 Oct. 1885, Merlhès,

*Correspondance* 87, trans. in Malingue, *Letters*, no. 27: "As to Clovis, he goes to school next door, and when I am not here, the concierge, who is a good sort, looks after him; sometimes le Marsouin [Favre] does."

18   PG to MG, 2 Nov. 1885, Merlhès, *Correspondance* 88.

19   PG to MG, [November 1885], Merlhès, *Correspondance* 89.

20   PG to MG, 24 May 1886, Merlhès, *Correspondance* 97.

21   "Really, if you were to come just now (you wanted to see Clovis for an hour or so), I doubt whether I could receive you except spitefully." PG to MG, 26 Dec. 1886, Merlhès *Correspondance*, 115; trans. in Malingue, *Letters*, no. 45.

22   For the eighth Impressionist exhibition, see Martha Ward, "The Rhetoric of Independence and Innovation," in *New Painting*, pp. 421–47.

23   See Henri Dorra, "Le 'Texte Wagner' de Gauguin," *Bulletin de la Société de l'histoire de l'art français* (1984), pp. 281–88.

24   "For a long time, Gauguin carried it [*le papier*] in his pocket and on occasion would show it to his friends." Gustave Kahn, "Paul Gauguin," *L'Art et les artistes* (November 1925), p. 44.

25   For Pissarro's version, see below, n. 64.

26   "When he spoke of Gauguin as he got older, all he would say was: 'He was not easy to get along with.'" Edouard Deverin, "Un Ami de Gauguin: Schuffenecker," *Les Marges* (10 Jan. 1935), p. 15.

27   Schuffenecker, along with Seurat and Signac, was asked to apply to Berthe Morisot for admission to the exhibition. After examining a group of his works, she allowed him to participate. See *New Painting*, p. 440 n. 20.

28   Edouard Deverin's reminiscences give an affectionate view of his teacher Schuffenecker: "Little by little, a group of us gathered around this professor, whose spirit seemed so un-academic. We discussed his lectures, his ideas on art and on society. And, since he was enamored of Oriental and theosophic doctrines, we all went out and read *The Blue Lotus* by Mme. Blavatsky." P. 14.

29   Schuffenecker had male friends who were openly homosexual. Deverin relates meeting a flamboyant character in Schuffenecker's studio: "One day I met an elegant and spiritual young man whose portrait [Schuffenecker] was painting: our old pal from 'philo,' the baron Jacques d'Adelsward. . . . Poet and man of the world, he was fated to play the 'Oscar Wilde,' even down to going to prison." P. 14.

30   See Merlès, *Pages inédites*, p. 44; and *Intimate Journals*, p. 34.

31   PG to MG, [early June 1886], Merlhès, *Correspondance* 99. For Chaplet, see Merlhès, *Correspondance*, p. 427 n. 196; and Merete Bodelsen, "Chaplet's Workshop," in *Gauguin's Ceramics* (London: Faber and Faber, 1964), pp. 209–12.

32   *Sèvres, Le Coteau*, Wildenstein 164, is inscribed "A Mad. Bracquemond, P.G."

33   Judy Le Paul with Charles-Guy Le Paul, *Gauguin and the Impressionists at Pont-Aven* (New York: Abbeville, 1983), p. 237.

34   Ibid., p. 48.

35   Archibald Hartrick, *A Painter's Pilgrimage Through Fifty Years* (1939), quoted in *Retrospective*, p. 63.

36   Ibid.

37   Ibid.

38   *Intimate Journals*, p. 109. Gauguin's aggressive tendencies were fed by the growing popularity of fencing and other martial arts in France after the Franco-Prussian War. In the 1880s fencing clubs sprang up throughout the provinces, and in Paris the Académie d'Armes and the Société de l'Encouragement de l'Escrime held annual competitions that attracted a fashionable crowd in evening dress. See Nye, p. 160.

39   *Intimate Journals*, p. 111.

40   As Anne Campbell puts it in *Men, Women, and Aggression* (New York: Basic Books, 1993), p. 58: "Among men it is understood that there are those who 'look for trouble,' actively seeking aggression in order to demonstrate power. For such men, aggression is not reactive—as proper aggression should be—but rather a way to 'be somebody.'" For Freud, aggression was partly a universal instinct unsuccessfully controlled by "civilized" behavior (*Civilization and Its Discontents*, in *Freud Reader*, p. 753) and partly the result of a raging battle between the id and the superego. Without "proper identification with the father," the instincts are "released in the form of an inclination to aggression and destruction" (*The Ego and the ID*, in *Freud Reader*, pp. 655–56).

41   Wildenstein, *Catalogue*, p. 52.

42 Merlhès, *Correspondance,* note 207.

43 Ibid.

44 Charles Chassé, "De Quand date le synthétisme de Gauguin?" *L'Amour de L'Art* (April 1938), p. 130.

45 Hartrick, p. 64.

46 Hartrick, pp. 64–73.

47 PG to MG, [ca. 25 July 1886], Merlhès, *Correspondance,* no. 107.

48 PG to MG, [July 1886], Merlhès, *Correspondance,* no. 110.

49 PG to MG, [15 Aug. 1886], Merlhès, *Correspondance,* no. 111.

50 PG to MG [ca. 25 July 1886], Merlhès, *Correspondance,* no. 107.

51 PG to MG, 15 Aug. 1886, Merlhès, *Correspondance,* no. 111.

52 PG to MG, [January 1886], Merlhès, *Correspondance,* no. 94. He claimed to have been posting bills, but since he had referred in an earlier letter to having been promised a post as an advertising manager, this may have been a fiction. See PG to MG, [ca. 20 Dec. 1885], Merlhès, *Correspondance,* no. 91.

53 Dorothy Menpes, *Brittany* (London: Adam and Charles Black, 1905), p. 139.

54 Hartrick, p. 62.

55 Ibid.

56 Henry Blackburn, *Breton Folk: An Artistic Tour of Brittany* (London: Sampson Low, Marston, Searle, and Rivington, 1880).

57 Hartrick, p. 73.

58 Gustave Kahn, "Au Temps du pointillisme," *Mercure de France* 171 (1 Apr. 1924), p. 12: "It was Camille Pissarro who discovered Rousseau."

59 See Bruce Altshuler, "The Pranksters of Paris," *Art in America* 85, no. 2 (February 1997), pp. 82–87.

60 CP to Lucien Pissarro, 23 Jan. 1887, John Rewald, *Camille Pissarro: Letters to His Son Lucien* (Santa Barbara: Peregrine Smith, 1981), p. 106.

61 Ibid.

62 See Bodelsen, *Gauguin's Ceramics,* pp. 11–53.

63 For Chaplet's stamp, see ibid., figs. 155, 156, 157.

64 On Dec. 3, 1886, Pissarro wrote to his son, "Lately I have been going with Seurat, Signac and Dubois-Pillet to La Nouvelle-Athènes; entering one evening, we saw Guillaumin, Gauguin, Zandomeneghi. Guillaumin refused to shake hands with Signac; so did Gauguin; there was some explanation; impossible to understand a word of it; it appears that the cause was that affair in Signac's studio, a misunderstanding. Nevertheless Gauguin left abruptly without saying goodbye to me or to Signac." Rewald, *Pissarro,* p. 8. Gauguin may not have been feeling well—he wrote later to his wife that he had gotten a bad enough cold to be hospitalized in the beginning of December. PG to MG, 26 Oct. 1886, Merlhès, *Correspondance,* no. 115.

65 CP to Lucien Pissarro, 22 Jan. 1887, Rewald, *Pissarro,* p. 105.

66 PG to MG, [mid-September 1886], Merlhès, *Correspondance,* no. 112: "I had news of Clovis the other day; it seems that he is liking school more and more and acting like an 'old boy.' I miss him very much, and if I had the money, I would have brought him here. The poor kid did not have a vacation, but you can't always do what you want in this world." PG to MG, [late July 1886], Merlhès, *Correspondance,* no. 110: "Clovis is at a boarding school at Anton (Seine), Pension Lennuyé: you don't need to write, I have news of him from Schuffenecker, who goes to see him; it is on the Sceaux line near his house."

## Chapter 6. The Lost Continent of Atlantis

1 Pola Gauguin reported, "In his long sleepless nights he read books of travel, Pierre Loti, Elisée Reclus, and in particular *Le Journal des Voyages.*" Pola Gauguin, *My Father, Paul Gauguin* (New York: Alfred A. Knopf, 1937), p. 142.

2 PG to MG, 26 Dec. 1886, Merlhès, *Correspondance,* no. 115.

3 PG to MG, [March 1887], Merlhès, *Correspondance,* no. 122: "I'm going to Panama to live 'en sauvage.' I know a place in the sea off Panama, a little island, *Tabogas* [sic], in the Pacific; it is almost uninhabited and very fertile. I'm taking my paints and brushes and I will be reinvigorated in my isolation." One wonders also how much Pissarro's early career might have influenced Gauguin's romantic notion of painting in Central America. Pissarro's companion on his painting trip to Venezuela (1852–54), Fritz Melbye, "was a member of a family of Danish artists who specialized in the transcription of exotic landscapes for Europeans." Brettell, p. 12. Gauguin may have been convinced that there was a significant European market for scenes from this part of the world.

4   "Next month, on the April 10 mail boat, I am sailing for America. . . . Would you make arrangements to bring Clovis home?" PG to MG, [March 1887], Merlhès, *Correspondance*, no. 121.

5   With four children in Copenhagen to support with her French lessons and translations, Mette very likely had to borrow such a sum from members of her family, including Ingeborg's fiancé, Edvard Brandès. This may have been the beginning of the debt to Brandès that Mette paid off over the years in paintings. See Chapter 13.

6   "I have *just* enough to pay my fare and shall arrive in America penniless." PG to MG, [March 1887], Merlhès, *Correspondance*, no. 122.

7   PG to MG, 24 Nov. 1887, Merlhès, *Correspondance*, no. 136: "There are a number of things I can't find here, among them two frames and a snow scene. *Tell me* exactly what you took with you so that I know if anything has been stolen. Send me the Manet, if you haven't sold it in Denmark; I'll try to sell it here."

8   PG to MG, [April 1887], Merlhès, *Correspondance*, no. 123.

9   Ibid.

10   For a reliable overview of the French efforts in Panama, see Maron J. Simon, *The Panama Affair* (New York: Charles Scribner's Sons, 1971).

11   For example, PG to MG, [March 1887], Merlhès, *Correspondance*, no. 121: "Someone wants to commission me to undertake big business in Madagascar." Also PG to MG, [March 1887], Merlhès, *Correspondance*, no. 122: "Some time ago a splendid business proposition was made to me. Knowing my energy and my intelligence (and particularly my integrity), it was suggested that I proceed to Madagascar for one year as a partner to carry on a business established there."

12   See Fin Simensen and Jarle Simensen, *Norwegian Missions in African History* (Oslo: Norwegian University Press, 1986).

13   "My [Madagascar] partners have promised to let me know in Panama when they will be ready. . . . Perhaps this proposition will come off, in any case I will ascertain if Juan would like to have a branch in Madagascar." PG to MG, Merlhès, *Correspondance*, no. 122, trans. in Malingue, *Letters*, no. 48.

14   PG to MG, [May 1887], Merlhès, *Correspondance*, no. 126.

15   For Gauguin and Laval in Panama, see Merlhès, *Correspondance*, pp. 456–61 n. 122.

16   Simon, pp. 66–67.

17   Merlhès, *Correspondance*, p. 58.

18   Gauguin doesn't mention the name of the hotel, but according to the price he was paying for a room, this is the logical one. See Merlhès, *Correspondance*, note 222.

19   Simon, p. 44.

20   *Intimate Journals*, p. 26.

21   Simon, p. 67.

22   Merlhès, *Correspondance*, note 222.

23   PG to MG, [May 1887], Merlhès, *Correspondance*, no. 126.

24   Ibid.

25   Ibid.

26   Simon, p. 72.

27   Hearn describes a "day passed by invitation at one of the old colonial estates": "It is not easy to describe the charm of . . . the cool shadowy court, or the lawn — the delicious welcome of the host — the romance of the unconventional chat, over a cool drink, under the palms and the ceibas . . . overlooking slopes of a hundred greens." Lafcadio Hearn, "La Grande Anse," quoted in Jonathan Cott, *Wandering Ghost: The Odyssey of Lafcadio Hearn* (New York: Alfred A. Knopf, 1991), pp. 224–25.

28   PG to MG, 20 June 1887, Merlhès, *Correspondance*, no. 127.

29   PG to ES, 14 July 1887, Merlhès, *Gauguin et Van Gogh*, p. 39.

30   Ibid.

31   In 1890 another friend of Gauguin and Laval's, Albert Dauprat, visited Martinique and described the neighborhood where Gauguin had stayed three years earlier. "After passing several small houses, used in the days of slavery, you come to a 'little pavilion that the owner rents to inhabitants of Saint-Pierre.'" Merlhès, *Gauguin et Van Gogh*, p. 44.

32   Charles Laval to Ferdinand du Puigaudeau, [July 1887], Merlhès, *Gauguin et Van Gogh*, p. 50

33   PG to MG, [25 Aug. 1887], Merlhès, *Correspondance*, no. 130.

34   PG to ES, 25 Aug. 1887, Merlhès, *Correspondance*, no. 131.

35   PG to MG, [25 Aug. 1887], Merlhès, *Correspondance*, no. 130, trans. in Malingue, *Letters*, no. 55.

36   Ibid.

37   PG to ES, 25 Aug. 1887, Merlhès, *Correspondance*, no. 131.

38   Charles Laval to Ferdinand du Puigaudeau, [July 1887], Merlhès, *Gauguin et Van Gogh*, p. 50.

39   Gauguin repeated Favre's words to Schuffenecker. PG to ES, [October 1887], Merlhès, *Correspondance*, no. 133.

40   PG to Antoine Favre, 25 Aug. 1887, Merlhès, *Correspondance*, no. 132.

41   PG to ES, 25 Aug. 1887, Merlhès, *Correspondance*, no. 131.

42   PG to ES, [mid-October 1887], Merlhès, *Correspondance*, no. 133.

43   He ended the letter by teasing her: "Don't say that I wrote you a nasty letter." PG to MG, 20 June 1887, Merlhès, *Correspondance*, no. 127. He told the story much more simply to Schuffenecker: "To end my letter with something to make you blush— Every day we leave a bundle of our clothes in the hands of a colored Putiphar [*sic*], and there are some who are devilishly pretty. But we are virtuous." PG to ES, 14 July 1887, Merlhès, *Gauguin et Van Gogh*, p. 42.

44   Although Gauguin says "guava," it was the mango that was plentiful on Martinique.

45   PG to MG, 20 June 1887, Merlhès, *Correspondance*, no. 127, trans. in Malingue, *Letters*, no. 53.

46   Cott, *Wandering Ghost*, p. 207.

47   Hearn had his own mango story to tell. After giving a *porteuse* money for cigarettes, she returned "about an hour and a half later . . . to present me with the finest and largest mango I had ever seen, a monster mango. She said she wanted to see me eat it, and sat down on the ground to look on. While eating it, I learned that she had walked a whole mile out of her way under that sky of fire, just to bring her little gift of gratitude." Lafcadio Hearn, "Les Porteuses," in *Two Years in the French West Indies* (New York: Harper Brothers, 1890; reprint, Upper Saddle River, N.J.: Literature House, 1970), p. 113.

48   As Maturin Ballou cautioned in his contemporary travelogue, *Equatorial America* (Boston: Houghton, Mifflin, 1892), p. 46: "Avoid a certain poisonous snake, a malignant reptile, with fatal fangs, which is the dread of the inhabitants. . . . It is singular that this island, and that of St. Lucia, directly south of it, should be cursed by the presence of these poisonous creatures, which do not exist in any other of the West Indian islands, and, indeed, so far as we know, are not to be found anywhere else."

49   See Chapter 9.

50   Hearn expressed such a jaundiced view of the Martinique male, "who is depicted as unable to adjust to emancipation from slavery." Paul Murray, *A Fantastic Journey: The Life and Literature of Lafcadio Hearn* (Folkestone, Kent: Japan Library, 1993), p. 101.

51   Hearn, "Les Porteuses," pp. 101–2.

52   Ibid., p. 105.

53   Ibid., p. 101.

54   Ibid., p. 102.

55   Ballou, pp. 34–35.

**Chapter 7. The Sun God**

1   See Bodelsen, *Gauguin's Ceramics*, p. 103.

2   See PG to MG, 6 Dec. 1887, Merlhès, *Correspondance*, no. 137: "In a month's time I hope to have work in ceramics." And, "I have sold a pot to a sculptor for 150 francs."

3   Ibid.

4   He had been promising to send money since he left Copenhagen in 1885: "I might receive 600 francs in a few days from the sale of a Pissarro and a Renoir; as soon as I have it, I will send you 200." PG to MG, [early October 1885], Merlhès, *Correspondance*, no. 26. But as time went on and he still hadn't sent any, he began to find other ways to deflect the blame: "To tell the truth, when I left Copenhagen, I had reason to believe that you would be helped. Your brother claimed that I was not needed and that they could handle everything. Louise Heegaard [Marie's mother] also said that you would never be in need as long as she was there. All that goes to show that words are a far cry from actions." PG to MG, 6 Dec. 1887, Merlhès, *Correspondance*, no. 137.

5   For a brief history of the Goupil Gallery, see Merlhès, *Correspondance*, pp. 372–75 n. 90. In 1863 the owners, Adolphe Goupil and François Boussod, formed a partnership with the uncle of Theo and Vincent van Gogh and brought his gallery in The Hague under the umbrella of Goupil and Boussod. After spending four years in the galleries in The Hague and London, Vincent van Gogh worked in the Paris gallery for a few weeks in 1874 and again in 1875–76, until

he was fired and left the business alto-gether. Theo was transferred to the Paris gallery in 1878 after four years at The Hague. The firm changed its name to Boussod and Valadon in 1884.

6   Vincent van Gogh started the practice of being called by his first name to avoid confusion with his brother, who was usually called Van Gogh, and to help French speakers, who had difficulty spelling and pronouncing the Dutch name. Art historians have perpetuated the practice for the former reason and have come to refer to his brother, Theo, by his first name as well.

7   *Intimate Journals*, p. 24.

8   See, for example, the portraits by H. M. Livens (1886) and Toulouse-Lautrec (1887), in Jan Hulsker, *Vincent and Theo van Gogh: A Dual Biography* (Ann Arbor, Mich.: Fuller, 1985), pp. 217, 233; as well as the portraits by A. S. Hartrick and John Russell, in Vincent van Gogh, *Complete Letters* (Greenwich, Conn.: New York Graphic Society, 1959), nos. 522, 548.

9   See Chapter 9.

10   "The duty of an artist is to work in order to become strong; this duty I have fulfilled, and all I have brought back from the tropics arouses nothing but admira-tion." PG to MG, 24 Nov. 1887, Merlhès, *Correspondance,* no. 136, trans. in Malingue, *Letters,* no. 58.

11   Vincent chose a small Martinique scene, which Gauguin had framed for him. PG to VvG, [December 1887], Merlhès, *Gauguin et Van Gogh,* p. 56. For an excel-lent recent chronology of Van Gogh, see Detroit Institute of Arts, *Van Gogh Face to Face: The Portraits* (New York: Thames and Hudson, 2000), p. 85 and passim.

12   For Gauguin's works on view in a group show in December 1887, see John Rewald, "Theo van Gogh, Goupil, and the Impressionists," *Gazette des beaux-arts* (January–February 1973), p. 16. He sold *Baigneuses* (Rewald, fig. 8) for 450 francs, out of which Gauguin received 300.

13   Félix Fénéon, "Calendrier de décembre 1887." *La Revue indépendante* (January 1888), in *Félix Fénéon: Oeuvres plus que complètes,* ed. Joan Halperin (Geneva: Librairie Droz, 1970), pp. 90–91.

14   See Rewald, "Theo van Gogh," p. 17.

15   See Norma Broude, "Degas's Misogyny," *Art Bulletin* 59, no. 1 (March 1977), pp. 95–107.

16   He bought it in 1887 and did not sell it until 1889; see Rewald, "Theo van Gogh," pp. 9, 11.

17   "As you know, I have the greatest confidence in Degas's judgment— besides, it is an excellent starting point commercially. All Degas's friends have confidence in him. Van Gogh hopes to sell all my pictures." PG to Emile Bernard, [9–12 Nov. 1988], Merlhès, *Cor-respondance,* no. 178, trans. in Malingue, *Letters,* no. 68. See also Rewald, "Theo van Gogh," pp. 11–12; Jean Sutherland Boggs, *Degas* (New York: Metropolitan Museum of Art, 1988), p. 387.

18   Their similarities have been often described. For a more metaphysical view, see Naomi Margolis Maurer, *The Pursuit of Spiritual Wisdom: The Thought and Art of Vincent van Gogh and Paul Gauguin* (Madison, N.J.: Fairleigh Dickinson Uni-versity Press; London: Associated Univer-sity Presses, 1998), pp. 2–5.

19   See Liesbeth Heenk, "Van Gogh and the Art Market," *Apollo* 145, no. 420 (February 1997), pp. 32–36.

20   For instance, "I am concentrating on making my pictures have some market value. You know that I have only one means of arriving at this end—and that is, by painting them. But I tell myself that if I can manage to do fifty studies at 200 francs this year, in a way I shall not have been very dishonest in having eaten and drunk as though I had a right to it. Now this is pretty steep, because though I have at the moment about thirty painted stud-ies, I do not value them all at that price. All the same, some of them must be worth it." VvG to TvG, [8 July 1888], Van Gogh, *Complete Letters,* 505.

21   "I am inclined to agree with Vincent; the future is to the painters of the tropics, which have not yet been painted. (Novelty is essential to stimulate the stupid buying public.)" PG to Emile Bernard, [November 1888], Malingue, *Letters,* no. 68.

22   For Van Gogh as a teacher in Eind-hoven in 1884, see Hulsker, pp. 187–89.

23   Hulsker, pp. 155–57.

24   VvG to EB, [late May 1888], *Vincent van Gogh Letters to Emile Bernard,* ed. Dou-glas Lord [Douglas Cooper] (New York: Museum of Modern Art, 1938), no. V.

25   Merlhès, *Gauguin et Van Gogh,* pp. 51, 54.

26  For the portrait vases, see Bodelsen, *Gauguin's Ceramics*, pp. 63–73.

27  "Catalogue of Ceramics," in Bodelsen, *Gauguin's Ceramics*, pp. 231–32.

28  For Louise Schuffenecker's opinion of her husband and his friends, see Merlhès, *Pages inédites*, p. 44.

29  *Intimate Journals*, pp. 29–30.

30  Emile Bernard and Louis Anquetin were exploring themes of prostitution in the fall of 1887 and 1888. See Mary Anne Stevens, "Emile Bernard and His Artistic and Literary Context," in *Emile Bernard, 1868–1941: A Pioneer of Modern Art* (Zwolle, Netherlands: Waanders Verlag, 1990), p. 19.

31  VvG to TvG, [1 May 1988], Van Gogh, *Complete Letters*, 480.

32  PG to MG, [early January 1888], Merlhès, *Correspondance*, no. 60.

33  It is difficult to make a reliable total of his earnings from Theo van Gogh because the Boussod and Valadon records don't reflect all of Van Gogh's transactions. The sum of 1,400 francs may be an optimistic accounting, but the amount was at least 900 francs. See Rewald, "Theo van Gogh," pp. 18–19 and n. 34.

34  This suggestion is implied in Paul's response. PG to MG, [January–February 1888], Merlhès, *Correspondance*, no. 139.

35  Ibid.

36  Ibid.

37  "You do not like art; what then do you like? Money? And when the artist is earning, you are with him." Ibid.

38  PG to MG, [February 1888], Merlhès, *Correspondance*, no. 140.

39  "Although I am not sure that you are still at Pont-Aven, so long is it since I heard from you, I write you all the same, for I want you to receive this on your birthday." MG to PG, 4 June 1888, in Appendix, letter I.

40  Vincent addressed a draft of a letter to "Mon cher copain Gauguin," [late May 1888], Merlhès, *Correspondance*, no. XXXVIII; Van Gogh, *Complete Letters*, 494a.

41  "I would like to write to your brother, but I know that you see him every day and I'm afraid of bothering him, busy as he is with work from morning till night." PG to VvG, [end February 1888], Merlhès, *Correspondance*, no. 142.

42  Félix Fénéon, "Aux Vitrines dans la rue," *La Revue Indépendante* (May 1888), in *Félix Fénéon: Oeuvres plus que complètes*, p. 111.

43  PG to ES, [late April or early May 1888], Merlhès, *Gauguin et Van Gogh*, p. 64.

44  "The Cézanne you ask of me is a pearl of great price, for which I have already refused 300 francs; I guard it as the apple of my eye, and short of absolute necessity, I will part with it only after my last shirt; besides, who is the fool who would pay that; you give no clue as to his identity." PG to ES, [early June 1888], Merlhès, *Correspondance*, no. 147, trans. in Malingue, *Letters*, no. 65.

45  PG to TvG, 22 May 1888, Merlhès, *Correspondance*, no. 146.

46  VvG to TvG, [early June 1888], Van Gogh, *Complete Letters*, 494a.

47  "[Gauguin] speaks of some hopes he has of finding a capital of 600,000 francs to set up as a dealer in impressionist pictures, and that he will explain his plan and would like you to head the enterprise." VvG to TvG, [12 June 1888], Van Gogh, *Complete Letters*, 496.

48  Ibid.

49  "But Gauguin must be loyal, and now that I see that his friend Laval's arrival has temporarily opened a new resource to him, I think that he is hesitating between Laval and us." VvG to TvG, [ca. 12 Sept. 1888], Van Gogh, *Complete Letters*, 535.

50  MG to PG, 4 June 1888, in Appendix, letter I. This is the only known letter from Mette Gauguin to Paul Gauguin. It was returned to her (enclosed in a letter from him) and saved with the rest of his letters.

51  "Someone who saw one of your letters recently (I can show them around without discretion because they are like business letters) said in seeing how they end [that they are like ice]. PG to MG, [late June 1888], Merlhès, *Correspondance*, no. 154.

52  Ibid.

53  VvG to TvG, [ca. 21 June 1888], Van Gogh, *Complete Letters*, 501.

54  His use of this term has often been wrongly equated with his later use of the term "savage." "Indian" in this context means "stoic, completely without emotion," while "savage" tends to mean to him a state of unrestrained, primitive emotions. PG to MG, [late January or early February 1888], Merlhès, *Correspon-*

*dance,* no. 139: "You have to remember that I have two sides, the Indian and the sensitive man. The sensitive man has disappeared, which allows the Indian to forge ahead firmly and without deviating."

55  As John La Farge wrote to James Hunecker in 1908, "People thought moral ill of a lover of jap art." Quoted in Lawrence Chisholm, *Fenellosa: The Far East and American Culture* (New Haven: Yale University Press, 1963), p. 42.

56  PG to ES, 8 July 1888, Merlhès, *Correspondance,* no. 156.

### Chapter 8. Theo and Vincent: Flying Too Close to the Sun

1  PG to VvG, [24 or 25 July 1888], Merlhès, *Correspondance,* no. 158: "My friend Laval has returned from Martinique; he brought back some very curious watercolors."

2  "Your letter brings great news, namely that Gauguin agrees to our plan." VvG to TvG, [ca. 29 June 1888], Van Gogh, *Complete Letters,* 507.

3  "I think it would make a tremendous difference to me if Gauguin were here, for now the days go by without my speaking a word to anyone. Oh well. In any case his letter gave me tremendous pleasure." VvG to TvG, [ca. 26 July 1888], Van Gogh, *Complete Letters,* 515.

4  For an overview of the whole group, see Judy Le Paul, *Gauguin and the Impressionists at Pont-Aven* (New York: Abbeville, 1987); and Ronald Pickvance, *Gauguin and the School of Pont-Aven* (1994). [Künzelsau]: Museum Würth; Sigmaringen: Thorbecke, 1997.

5  Roland Dorn, "Emile Bernard and Vincent van Gogh" in Mary Anne Stevens, *Emile Bernard, 1868–1941: A Pioneer of Modern Art* (Zwolle: Waanders, 1990), pp. 30–48. See also Emile Bernard, "Le Symbolisme pictural, 1886–1936," *Mercure de France* (15 June 1936), pp. 514–30.

6  "'The starting point' was not a naturalistic conception but 'a symbolic conception of art.'" Dorn, p. 36.

7  "Notes sur l'école dit de Pont-Aven," *Mercure de France* 48 (1903), p. 678, cited in Dorn, p. 6 n. 20.

8  Vojtěch Jirat-Wasiutyński, "Emile Bernard and Paul Gauguin: The Avant-Garde and Tradition," in Dorn, p. 49: "The fact that, according to van Gogh, Bernard picked quarrels with Gauguin

that winter suggests that his combativeness prevailed even though he shared Gauguin's dislike of the 'petit point.'"

9  Writing before the season had begun in Pont-Aven, Van Gogh thought Gauguin could use the company. "Gauguin, too, is bored at Pont-Aven and complains like you of his isolation. Why not go and see him?" But by the time Bernard arrived in town, Gauguin was surrounded by a crowd of admirers. VvG to EB, [15–19 June 1888], Merlhès, *Correspondance,* 150.

10  VvG to EB, [late September 1888], *Van Gogh Letters to Bernard,* no. XVIII. The artists mentioned were Laval, Henry Moret, and Ernest de Chamaillard. P. 86 n. 4. For a summary of the paintings involved in the exchange, see Vojtěch Jirat-Wasiutyński and H. Travers Newton, *Vincent van Gogh's Self-Portrait Dedicated to Paul Gauguin* (Cambridge: Center for Conservation and Technical Studies, Harvard University Art Museums, 1984), p. 8.

11  VvG to TvG, [ca. 18 Aug. 1888], Van Gogh, *Complete Letters,* 523.

12  PG to ES, 14 Aug. 1888, Merlhès, *Correspondance,* no. 159.

13  Ibid.

14  See Gabriel P. Weisberg, "Vestiges of the Past: The Brittany 'Pardons' of Late Nineteenth-Century French Painters," *Arts Magazine* 55, no. 3 (November 1980), pp. 134–38; and Mathew Herban III, "The Origin of Paul Gauguin's *Vision After the Sermon: Jacob Wrestling with the Angel,*" *Art Bulletin* 59 (1977), pp. 415–20.

15  For a summary of the various recent spiritual interpretations, see National Gallery of Art, pp. 102–3.

16  The first time the painting was put on public view, in the sixth exhibition of the Belgian artists' group Les XX, its mocking tone was recognized. But it was defended then, as now, for its daring stylistic experimentation. See National Gallery of Art, p. 105.

17  Emile Bernard, *Lettres de Paul Gauguin à Emile Bernard* (1911), quoted in *Retrospective,* p. 81.

18  Blanche Willis Howard, *Guenn, a Wave on the Breton Coast,* 15th ed. (Boston: Ticknor, 1883), p. 164.

19  For Bernard's and Gauguin's efforts to claim credit for inventing this style, see Jirat-Wasiutyński, "Emile Bernard and Paul Gauguin," pp. 48–67.

20   Emile Bernard, "Lettres de Paul Gauguin à Emile Bernard" (1911), quoted in *Retrospective*, p. 81.

21   VvG to TvG, [ca. 14 Aug. 1888], Van Gogh, *Complete Letters*, 524.

22   This offer is not recorded in any of the surviving correspondence, but the fact that Gauguin shipped his best paintings from the last nine months to Theo when he left Pont-Aven indicates that such an arrangement had been made. Theo apparently had not requested to see any of Gauguin's work since he had left for Pont-Aven in January. The painting he put in his window in April was a Martinique subject he already had in stock.

23   "They are talking of nothing else at the moment in Pont-Aven, which means that Paris will be talking too. . . . Well, what will be, will be. Only I say now, to prevent further discussions, if it catches on so that Laval and Bernard really come, Gauguin and not I will be the head of the studio." VvG to TvG, [3 Oct. 1888], Van Gogh, *Complete Letters*, 543. See also Åke Meyerson, "Van Gogh and the School of Pont-Aven," *Konsthistorishe Tidskrift* (December 1946), pp. 134–52.

24   Ibid.

25   See particularly Carl Nordenfalk, "Van Gogh and Literature," *Journal of the Warburg and Courtauld Institutes* 10 (1947), pp. 132–47.

26   For Boch, see Anne Pingeot and Robert Hoozee, *Paris-Bruxelles, Bruxelles-Paris* (Anvers: Editions de la Réunion des Musées Nationaux, 1997), pp. 517–18.

27   VvG to TvG, [ca. 5 June 1888], Van Gogh, *Complete Letters*, 498. It's not clear who Van Gogh is referring to, but his tone is petulant: "If Gauguin and his Jewish bankers came tomorrow and asked me for no more than 10 pictures for a society of dealers . . . I do not know if I'd have confidence in it."

28   Ibid.: "If the artists did this [gave ten pictures each], this Jew Society would pocket a good 100 pictures 'to begin with.' Pretty dear, this protection by a society which doesn't even exist!"

29   VvG to TvG, [4 Sept. 1888], Van Gogh, *Complete Letters*, 532.

30   VvG to TvG, [ca. 11 Sept. 1888], Van Gogh, *Complete Letters*, 536.

31   VvG to TvG [ca. 17 Sept. 1888], Van Gogh, *Complete Letters*, 538.

32   "Do you remember in . . . Mau-passant the gentleman who hunted . . . so hard for ten years, and was so exhausted by running after the game that when he wanted to get married he found he was impotent, which caused the greatest embarrassment and consternation. Without being in the same situation as this gentleman as far as its being either my duty or my desire to get married, I begin to resemble him physically." VvG to TvG, [9 July 1888], Van Gogh, *Complete Letters*, 506.

33   "As for me—I feel I am losing the desire for marriage and children, and now and then it saddens me that I should be feeling like that at thirty-five. . . . It was Richepin who said somewhere: 'The love of art makes one lose real love.'" VvG to TvG, [Summer 1887], Van Gogh, *Complete Letters*, 462.

34   VvG to TvG, [ca. 26 Sept. 1888], Van Gogh, *Complete Letters*, 541a.

35   VvG to TvG, [ca. 11 Aug. 1888], Van Gogh, *Complete Letters*, 520.

36   See Elisabeth Walter, "*Madeleine au Bois d'Amour par Emile Bernard*," *La Revue du Louvre* 28 (1978), pp. 286–91.

37   PG to Madeleine Bernard, [mid-October 1888], Merlhès, *Correspondance*, 173.

38   *Still Life: Fete Gloanec*, 1888 (Wildenstein 290). Bernard later claimed that this was a tribute to his sister, but Madame Gloanec thought of it more as a practical joke. Walter, p. 287.

39   This engagement is difficult to document because it appears in only one undated letter from Madeleine to her brother. Walter, p. 290 n. 16. Laval died in 1894, and Madeleine in 1895, still unmarried. Ibid., p. 290 n. 11.

40   See especially Ron Johnson, "Vincent van Gogh and the Vernacular: The Poet's Garden," *Arts Magazine* (February 1979), pp. 98–104; and Evert van Uitert, "Vincent van Gogh in Anticipation of Paul Gauguin," *Simiolus* (1978–79), pp. 182–99.

41   VvG to PG, [3 Oct. 1888], Van Gogh, *Complete Letters*, 544a.

42   VvG to TvG, [9 Sept. 1888], Van Gogh, *Complete Letters*, 534.

43   Vincent wrote to Bernard: "I am rather surprised to hear you say 'Do Gauguin's portrait? Why, that's impossible!' Why is it impossible? That's all nonsense." VvG to EB, [mid-September 1888], *Van Gogh Letters to Emile Bernard* XVI. To

Theo: "[Bernard] says he *dares not* do Gauguin as I asked him, because he feels afraid in front of Gauguin." VvG to TvG, [ca. 17 Sept. 1888], Van Gogh, *Complete Letters*, 539.

44  Despite Vincent's surprise at Bernard's reluctance to paint Gauguin, he himself did no better. Only one small sketch of Gauguin's face in profile survives. See Martin Bailey, "Van Gogh's *Portrait of Gauguin*," *Apollo* 144 (July 1996), pp. 51–54.

45  PG to VvG, [1 Oct. 1888], Merlhès, *Correspondance*, no. 166.

46  As Van Gogh explained to Bernard, "Others seem to have more feeling for abstract studies than I do . . . I exaggerate, sometimes I make changes in the subject; but still I don't invent the whole picture." VvG to EB, [early October 1888], *Van Gogh Letters to Emile Bernard*, XIX.

47  PG to ES, [8 Oct. 1888], Merlhès, *Correspondance*, no. 168.

48  It was the subject of a heated interchange between Vincent and his pious parents as early as 1880. Vincent defended Jean Valjean against their condemnation of him as a criminal. See Hulsker, pp. 85–86.

49  VvG to TvG, [3 Oct. 1888], Van Gogh, *Complete Letters*, 544.

50  VvG to TvG, [4 Oct. 1888], Van Gogh, *Complete Letters*, 545.

51  Ibid.

52  A very helpful source for the meaning of the painting as derived from its technical aspects is Jirat-Wasiutyński and Newton, pp. 3–27. For the derivation of Vincent's Buddhist-monk imagery, see Merlhès, *Gauguin et Van Gogh*, p. 117.

53  It was a letter from Bernard to Vincent that Vincent refers to in his own reply of late September 1888. *Van Gogh Letters to Emile Bernard*, no. XVII and p. 86 n. 15.

54  Ibid.

55  VvG and PG to EB, [early November 1888], Merlhès, *Correspondance*, no. 177.

56  He sent her money for the second time since their separation while living with Vincent. See Chapter 9.

57  VvG to TvG, [24 Oct. 1888], Van Gogh, *Complete Letters*, 557.

58  VvG to TvG, [28 Oct. 1888], Van Gogh, *Complete Letters*, 558b.

59  VvG to TvG, [ca. November 1888], Van Gogh, *Complete Letters*, 563.

60  PG to EB, [end November 1888], Merlhès, *Correspondance*, no. 182.

61  *Intimate Journals*, pp. 9–10.

62  VvG to TvG, [28 Oct. 1888], Van Gogh, *Complete Letters*, 558.

63  PG to ES, 16 Oct. 1888, Merlhès, *Correspondance*, 172.

64  "On several nights I surprised him in the act of getting up and coming over to my bed. To what can I attribute my awakening just at that moment?" *Intimate Journals*, p. 12.

65  PG to ES, [ca. 23 Nov. 1888], Merlhès, *Correspondance*, p. 184.

66  VvG to TvG, [ca. 4 Dec. 1888], Van Gogh, *Complete Letters*, 560.

67  Ibid.

68  See especially Henri Dorra, "Gauguin's Dramatic Arles Themes," *Art Journal* 38 (Fall 1978), pp. 12–17.

69  See Wayne Andersen, "Gauguin and a Peruvian Mummy," *Burlington Magazine* 109, no. 769 (April 1967), pp. 238–42.

70  PG to TvG, [ca. 22 Nov. 1888], Merlhès, *Correspondance*, no. 183.

71  PG to TvG, [mid-December 1888], Merlhès, *Correspondance*, no. 192.

72  VvG to TvG, [ca. 18–19 Dec. 1888], Van Gogh, *Complete Letters*, 564.

73  The amount of violence involved in the episode varied in Gauguin's accounts. For the different versions of the story, see Hulsker, pp. 322–24, 329.

74  *Intimate Journals*, pp. 13–14.

75  Hulsker concludes that Gauguin left Arles before Theo arrived. P. 330.

76  VvG to TvG, [4 Jan. 1889], Van Gogh, *Complete Letters*, 566.

77  VvG to PG, [4 Jan. 1889], on back of Van Gogh, *Complete Letters*, 566 in pencil.

78  EB to Albert Aurier, 1 Jan. 1889, Hulsker, p. 323.

79  VvG to TvG, [17 Jan. 1889], Van Gogh, *Complete Letters*, 571.

80  Ibid.

81  Ibid.

82  Ibid.

83  Ibid.

84  VvG to TvG, [19 Jan. 1889], Van Gogh, *Complete Letters*, 572.

85  VvG to Albert Aurier, [February 1890], Van Gogh, *Complete Letters*, 626a.

86  *Intimate Journals*, p. 12.

87  PG to ES, [ca. 17 Dec. 1888], Merlhès, *Gauguin et Van Gogh*, p. 239.

### Chapter 9. The Martyr

1  Charles Morice, *Gauguin* (1920), in National Gallery of Art, p. xx. This meeting may actually have taken place at

the end of 1890. See National Gallery of Art, p. 49.

2   For an overview of this and various other interpretations, see National Gallery of Art, pp. 125–27.

3   Rewald, "Theo van Gogh," pp. 32–33.

4   National Gallery of Art, pp. 130–32.

5   Most of the attention has focused on the relationships of Emile Schuffenecker and Gauguin to Louise Schuffenecker, who was being painted by both. See National Gallery of Art, pp. 120–22.

6   Paul was so out of touch with his family that he had to ask Mette, "Do you have any news of my sister?" PG to MG, [ca. 20 Jan. 1889], Malingue, Letters, no. 115 (redated).

7   See Bodelsen, Gauguin and Van Gogh in Copenhagen, pp. 24–28.

8   Derek Lionel Paul, "Willumsen and Gauguin in the 1890s," Apollo III, no. 215 (January 1980), pp. 36–45, 37.

9   Rostrup, "Gauguin et le Danemark," pp. 75–76.

10   PG to MG, [mid-December 1888], Merlhès, Correspondance, no. 190.

11   "Emile has written me a letter in worse French than he spoke when he talked to me in Denmark." PG to MG, [ca. 20 Jan. 1889], trans. in Malingue, Letters, no. 115 (redated).

12   "In your letter you make use of an extraordinary word: affectionate. I confess that I do not understand, having learned from long experience that this is a fiction. I believe that affection has some connection with gold." PG to MG, [January 1889], trans. in Malingue, Letters, no. 114 (redated).

13   PG to MG, [ca. 20 Jan. 1889], trans. in Malingue, Letters, no. 115 (redated).

14   See Madeleine Octave Maus, Trente Années de lutte pour l'art: Les XX, la libre esthétique, 1884–1914 (Brussels: Editions Lebeer Hossmann, 1980).

15   Ibid., p. 15.

16   Ibid., p. 51.

17   Actually Ingeborg and Frits had been divorced in 1886, but they kept in close touch because of their two daughters.

18   Conversation, Bretagne, Wildenstein 250, was subsequently bequeathed to the Musées Royaux des beaux-arts de Belgique, Brussels.

19   VvG to TvG, [ca. 27 Sept. 1888], Van Gogh, Complete Letters, 541. See also

VvG to TvG, [ca. 29 Sept. 1888], Van Gogh, Complete Letters, 543: "The one thing I do hope is that by working hard, I shall have enough pictures at the end of a year to have a show if I want to, or, if you wish it, at the time of the exhibition."

20   PG to ES, [end March 1889], Malingue, Letters, no. 77 (redated).

21   John Rewald, Post-Impressionism from Van Gogh to Gauguin (New York: Museum of Modern Art, 1962), pp. 278–82.

22   Gauguin scholars have long felt that the Eve motif was central to Gauguin's art. A few important texts are Henri Dorra, "The first Eves in Gauguin's Eden," Gazette des beaux-arts (March 1953), pp. 189–202); Merete Bodelsen, Gauguin's Ceramics, (1964); Ziva Amishai-Maisels, "Gauguin's 'Philosophical Eve,'" Burlington Magazine 115, no. 843 (June 1973), pp. 373–82; Wayne Andersen, Gauguin's Paradise Lost (New York: Viking, 1974); Edward Henning, "Woman in the Waves by Paul Gauguin," Cleveland Museum Bulletin 71 (1984), pp. 281–89; and Linnea S. Dietrich, "Gauguin: The Eve of My Choice," Art Criticism 4, no. 2 (1988), pp. 47–61. Although their interpretations differ, all the authors accept Gauguin's construction of his martyrdom at the hands of society in general and his wife in particular.

23   Henri Dorra argues that the snake is withdrawing after causing Eve's downfall. Dorra, "Review of The Pursuit of Spiritual Wisdom: The Thought and Art of Vincent van Gogh and Paul Gauguin," Burlington Magazine 141, no. 1158 (September 1999), p. 551. Although this was possibly Gauguin's intent, both the title and the gesture of the woman stress listening to the snake's lies rather than holding her head in anguish after the fact. In either case, the woman's terror is plain to see.

24   For modernized versions of religious themes, see Nancy Mowll Mathews, "Mary Cassatt and the 'Modern Madonna' of the Nineteenth Century," Ph.D. diss., New York University Institute of Fine Arts, 1980.

25   Lafcadio Hearn published a book of Creole sayings from six dialects, Gombo Zhèbes (New York: Will H. Coleman, 1885).

26   Jules Antoine, "Impressionists and Synthetists," Art et Critique (9 Nov. 1889), quoted in Retrospective, p. 130.

27   Bought by the gallery on June 18,

sold to Lerolle on June 21, 1889. Wildenstein, *Catalogue*, p. 84.

28 See Merlhès, *Correspondance*, note 229.

29 PG to EB, [October 1889], Malingue, *Letters*, no. 89 (redated).

30 Paul Gauguin, "Notes sur l'art à l'Exposition universelle," *Le Moderniste* (4 July 1889), pp. 84–86; (13 July 1889), pp. 90–91; Emile Bernard, "Note sur la peinture," *Le Moderniste* (27 July 1889), pp. 109–10.

31 See Fernand Dauchot, "Meyer de Haan en Bretagne," *Gazette des beaux-arts* (December 1952), pp. 355–74.

32 André Gide, *If It Die* (New York: Random House, 1935), p. 216.

33 Letter from Henri Mothéré to Charles Chassé (ca. 1921), quoted in *Retrospective*, p. 121.

34 Ibid., p. 122.

35 Ibid.

36 Ibid.

37 PG to EB, [July–August 1889], Malingue, *Letters*, no. 84.

38 Mothéré to Chassé, quoted in *Retrospective*, p. 124.

39 Rewald, "Theo van Gogh," p. 36.

40 As Bernard wrote to Gauguin, "Pont-Aven is full of abominable foreigners." EB to PG, [August/September 1889], typescript, Merete Bodelsen Papers, Royal Library, Copenhagen.

41 For the symbolist context of this painting and the portrayal of mental illness, see Patricia Mathews, "Passionate Discontent: The Creative Process and Gender Difference in the French Symbolist Period," *Allen Memorial Art Museum Bulletin* 43 (Summer 1988), pp. 21–30. For an examination of Gauguin's religious intent, see Wladyslawa Jaworska, "*Christ in the Garden of Olive-Trees* by Gauguin: The Sacred or the Profane?" *Artibus et Historiae* 19, no. 37 (1998), pp. 77–102.

42 Bernard, *Christ in the Garden of Olives* (1889, present location unknown); see National Gallery of Art, p. 162.

43 Ironically, Gauguin's expressions of betrayal tended to be aimed at those who were most active in helping him: "Degas, who, next to Van Gogh, is the chief author of the whole collapse. . . . He divines in us a movement contrary to his." PG to EB, [November 1889], Malingue, *Letters*, no. 92.

44 The traditional translation of this title, "*Be in love* and you will be happy," loses the sexual connotation of the French word "amoureuses."

45 PG to VvG, [ca. 8 Nov. 1889], *Paul Gauguin: 45 Lettres à Vincent, Théo, et Jo van Gogh*, ed. Douglas Cooper (Lausanne: La Bibliothèque des Arts, 1983), no. 37; hereafter cited as Cooper.

46 PG to TvG, [20–21 Nov. 1889], Cooper, no. 22. (Trans. *Retrospective*, p. 108).

47 *Intimate Journals*, pp. 26–27.

48 PG to EB, [20–21 Nov. 1889], Malingue, *Letters*, no. 95.

49 The house belonged to a M. Mauduit, owner of a stationery business in Quimperlé. See Cooper, p. 283 n. 10.

50 Mothéré to Chassé, quoted in *Retrospective*, p. 121.

51 For an examination of Gauguin's possible esoteric references in this work, see Vojtěch Jirat-Wasiutyński, "Paul Gauguin's *Self-Portrait with Halo and Snake*: The Artist as Initiate and Magus," *Art Journal* 46 (Spring 1987), pp. 22–28.

## Chapter 10. Desperate Measures

1 In his own words, "Par un effort désespéré d'un chien aux abois" (by the desperate effort of a cornered dog). PG to ES, 31 Jan. 1891, Merlhès, *Pages inédites*, p. 70.

2 "Since January my sales have totaled 925 francs. At the age of 42, to live on that, buy colours, etc., is enough to daunt the stoutest heart." PG to EB, [November 1889], Malingue, *Letters*, no. 92.

3 PG to MG, [ca. 15 Dec. 1889], Malingue, *Letters*, no. 82 (redated).

4 "It seems there must be a serious accident before I hear [any news], which scarcely disposes me to cheerfulness, although you say all danger is now over." Ibid.

5 PG to VvG, [ca. 10 Jan. 1890], Cooper, no. 38.

6 VvG to his sister Wilhelmina, [January 1890], Van Gogh, *Complete Letters*, W19.

7 PG to EB, [ca. 25 Jan. 1890], Merlhès, *Pages inédites*, p. 1.

8 EB to ES, [ca. 28 Jan. 1890], Merlhès, *Pages inédites*, p. 42.

9 Merlhès, *Pages inédites*, p. 43.

10 Jean de Rotonchamp, *Paul Gauguin*, in *Pages inédites*, p. 14.

11 The Countess of Nimal was going to intercede on Gauguin's behalf with Maurice Rouvier, premier and minister of

finance. "Rouvier should have returned to Paris on the 14th, and the Countess of Nimal should have already spoken to him about my request for Tonkin." PG to ES, 23 Jan. 1890, Merlhès, *Pages inédites*, p. 39.

12  Ibid.

13  "Gauguin wrote me that he had exhibited in Denmark and that this exhibition had been a great success." VvG to TvG, [February 1890], Van Gogh, *Complete Letters*, 626.

14  Gauguin's response to the arrangements his wife tried to make for this trip was characteristically dismissive. "I have to be in Paris on the 20th for the firing of sculptures I have almost sold, so I couldn't be there until the end of April. So let's not discuss it further. Have a good time this summer, and God help you." PG to MG, [late March or early April 1890], Malingue, *Letters*, no. 101 (redated and retranslated).

15  See National Gallery of Art, p. 48.

16  PG to EB, [ca. 25 Jan. 1890], Merlhès, *Page inédites*, p. 41.

17  See Merlhès, *Pages inédites*, p. 5.

18  Albert Aurier, "Les Isolés: Vincent van Gogh," *Mercure de France* 1 (January 1890), pp. 24–29.

19  VvG to TvG, [February 1890], Van Gogh, *Complete Letters*, 626.

20  PG to VvG, [ca. 28 Jan. 1890], Cooper, no. 39.

21  *L'Arlésienne, Portrait of Madame Ginoux*, 1888 (San Francisco, Fine Arts Museum of San Francisco, Achenbach Foundation for Graphic Arts). For Van Gogh's copies of this drawing, see Cornelia Homburg, "Affirming Modernity: Van Gogh's *Arlésienne*," *Simiolus*, 21, no. 3 (1992).

22  VvG to PG, [mid-June 1890], Van Gogh, *Complete Letters*, 643. This letter, found among Vincent's papers, was never finished or sent.

23  Ibid.

24  See Anne Distal and Susan Alyson Stein, *Cézanne to Van Gogh: The Collection of Dr. Gachet* (New York: Metropolitan Museum of Art, 1999).

25  Van Gogh took responsibility for missing Gauguin in Paris. "I stayed in Paris only three days, and the noise, etc., of Paris had such a bad effect on me that I thought it wise for my head's sake to fly to the country; but for that, I should soon have dropped in on you." VvG to PG, [late June 1890], Van Gogh, *Complete Letters*, 643 (unsent draft of a letter).

26  "Your letter made me think that you had gone North, meaning Holland, and I was waiting for your address to answer you." PG to VvG, [ca. 25 May 1890], Cooper, no. 41.

27  "What I want to do is set up a studio in the *Tropics*. With the money I shall have I can buy a hut of the kind you saw at the Universal Exhibition. An affair of wood and clay, thatched, near the town but in the country." PG to EB, [June 1890], Malingue, *Letters*, no. 105.

28  George A. Shaw, *Madagascar and France* (New York: American Tract Society, 1885), p. 24.

29  PG to EB, [June 1890], Malingue, *Letters*, no. 105.

30  Phares M. Mutibwa, *The Malagasy and the Europeans* (London: Longman Group, 1974), pp. 324–26 passim.

31  "After Wednesday or Thursday next, I shall be at Pouldu, where I shall await the upshot of this business and get ready for the journey." PG to EB, [late May 1890], Malingue, *Letters*, no. 102 (redated).

32  PG to EB, [June 1890], Malingue, *Letters*, no. 110.

33  Letter from Paul-Emile Colin to Charles Chassé, in *Gauguin et le groupe de Pont-Aven* (1921), quoted in *Retrospective*, p. 128.

34  From the reminiscences of Maxime Maufra, unpublished manuscript (1914–16), excerpted in "Comment Je Connus Paul Gauguin," *Bulletin des amis des Musées de Rennes* (Summer 1978), pp. 20–21.

35  Colin to Chassé, in *Gauguin et le groupe de Pont-Aven*, quoted in *Retrospective*, p. 28.

36  See Rayner Heppenstall's introduction to Honoré de Balzac, *A Harlot High and Low* (New York: Penguin Books, 1970), pp. ix–x.

37  For Filiger, see Pickvance, *Gauguin and the School of Pont-Aven*, pp. 98–102; and Will H. L. Ogrinc, "Neither to Laugh nor to Cry: A Failure in the End: Charles Filiger (1863–1928)," *Paidika: Journal of Paedophilia*, no. 4 (Autumn 1988), pp. 32–49.

38  PG to Octave Maus, [early 1891], in Octave Maus, *Trente années de luttes pour l'art* (Brussels, 1926), p. 119: "Please permit me, dear sir, to speak to you of a friend of mine, Monsieur Filliger [*sic*], who is somewhat of a student of mine." See also Merlhès, *Pages inédites*, pp. 66–73.

39  Ogrinc, particularly pp. 33, 36.

40 "On 23 July, M. Filiger made his entry into this little circle, where his influence soon became considerable." Mothéré to Chassé, quoted in *Retrospective*, p. 126.

41 PG to EB, [June, 1890], Malingue, *Letters*, no. 110.

42 See, for example, Robert Welsh, "Gauguin et l'auberge de Marie Henry au Pouldu," *Revue de l'art* (1986), p. 42.

43 EB to Albert Aurier, [summer 1890], typescript, Merete Bodelsen Papers, Royal Library, Copenhagen: "Gauguin asked me to remind you not with the purpose of acclaim or of glorification, but in the interest of calling the public's attention to our communal project, to have you remember your previous idea of writing articles about him. . . . You have done Vincent, Pissarro, Raffaelli. I don't know if those artists are the only 'isolés'; but Gauguin, the most isolated, of all of them, it seems to me, should not be left out."

44 "Naturally I thought the Madagascar project almost impossible to put into practice; I would rather see him leaving for Tonkin. If he went to Madagascar, however, I should be capable of following him there." VvG to TvG, [17 June 1890], Van Gogh, *Complete Letters*, 642.

45 VvG to PG, [late June 1890], Van Gogh, *Complete Letters*, 643 (unsent draft of a letter).

46 "It is very likely that—if you will allow me—I shall go there to join you for a month, to do a marine or two, but especially to see you again and make De Haan's acquaintance." VvG to PG, [late June 1890], Van Gogh, *Complete Letters*, 643 (unsent draft of a letter).

47 "Your idea of coming to Brittany, to Pouldu, seems excellent if it were possible. Yet we are, de Haan and I, in a little hole-in-the-wall far from the city, without any transportation aside from a hired carriage. And for an invalid who needs a doctor sometimes, it would be dangerous. . . .That is the situation in all frankness: Even though God knows how much pleasure it would give me to see our friend Vincent here." PG to VvG, [ca. 24 June 1890], Cooper, no. 42.

48 VvG to TvG [23 July 1890], Van Gogh, *Complete Letters*, 651.

49 For example, "Distressing as this death is, I cannot grieve overmuch, as I foresaw it, and knew how the poor fellow suffered in struggling with his madness.

To die at this moment is a piece of good fortune for him." PG to EB, [ca. 10 Aug. 1890], Malingue, *Letters*, no. 111 (redated).

50 He had sold paintings for up to 500 francs, but he put the price of 1,500 francs on his two panels *Soyez mystérieuses* and *Soyez amoureuses;* see Rewald, "Theo van Gogh," p. 49.

51 PG to ES, [August 1890], Musée Gauguin, Tahiti: "You must have been surprised to get my message. I received the gouges the next day."

52 "Find me an amateur who is interested in being a benefactor." PG to TvG, [mid-September 1890], Cooper, no. 27.

53 He was having severe urinary problems, perhaps as a result of syphilis. "He hadn't urinated for over a week; on top of that were worries, grief, and a violent argument with his bosses over a painting by Decamps. . . . He then became violent. He who loved his wife and his child so much, threatened to kill them." CP to Lucien Pissarro, 18 Oct. 1890, in Merlhès, *Pages inédites*, p. 52.

54 In Arsène Alexandre, *Paul Gauguin, sa vie et le sens de son oeuvre* (Paris, 1930), p. 108. According to Alexandre, this telegram was repeated in a letter from Gauguin to Schuffenecker.

55 PG to ES, 25 Oct. 1890, Merlhès, *Pages inédites*, p. 3: "You have seen de Haan; he was a well-intentioned boy. But always unlucky; he is in hot water up to his neck and it may be because of me."

56 PG to ES, 25 Oct. 1890, Merlhès, *Pages inédites*, p. 53.

57 National Gallery of Art, p. 49.

58 Maurice Joyant to Octave Maus, 17 Oct. 1890, typescript, Merete Bodelsen Papers, Royal Library, Copenhagen.

59 PG to ES, 30 Oct. 1890, Merlhès, *Pages inédites*, p. 58.

60 Although he listed himself as Daniel in the catalogue of the Volpini exhibition and was called that by Gauguin, he is today universally referred to as Monfreid or de Monfreid.

61 Jean Loize, *Les Amitiés du peintre Georges-Daniel de Monfreid et ses reliques de Gauguin* (Paris, 1951), p. 14.

62 P.-L. Maud, "L'Influence de Paul Gauguin," *L'Occident* (October 1903), p. 162.

63 *Retrospective*, p. 133.

64 PG to EB, [June 1890], Malingue, *Letters*, no. 109 (redated): "It is true that

Tahiti is a paradise for Europeans. But the journey costs much more, as it is situated in Oceania. Madagascar, however, offers more attractions by way of types, mysticism and symbolism."

65  "Loti saw things as a writer, and he had his own boat and plenty of money. . . . Despite this I recognize that Tahiti is certainly favoured and that you can live there in fact (almost without money) as we have dreamed." PG to EB, [June 1890], Malingue, *Letters,* no. 107 (redated).

66  Blanch, *Pierre Loti,* pp. 205–6.

67  For the collaboration, see Nicholas Wadley, *Noa Noa: Gauguin's Tahiti* (Salem, N.H.: Salem House, 1985), pp. 7–9.

68  For Pissarro's distaste for Gauguin at this time, see Belinda Thomson, "Camille Pissarro and Symbolism: Some Thoughts Prompted by the Recent Discovery of an Annotated Article," *Burlington Magazine* 124, no. 946 (January 1982), p. 17.

69  Octave Mirbeau to Claude Monet, [late January 1891], in Octave Mirbeau, "Lettres à Claude Monet," *Cahiers d'aujourd'hui,* no. 9 (1923), p. 172.

70  Octave Mirbeau published two articles: The first, "Paul Gauguin," *L'Echo de Paris* (16 Feb. 1890), p. 1, was also used as the preface to the catalogue of Gauguin's auction, *Catalogue d'une vente de 30 tableaux de Paul Gauguin* (Paris, 1891), pp. 3–12. The second, "Paul Gauguin," was published in *Le Figaro* (18 Feb. 1891), p. 2.

71  Octave Mirbeau, "Paul Gauguin," *L'Echo de Paris* (16 Feb. 1890), quoted in *Retrospective,* p. 145.

72  Ibid., p. 146.

73  Ibid., p. 147.

74  This photograph was actually of a painting of Aline Gauguin (ca. 1848–49) by Jules Laure. See Dina Sonntag, "Prelude to Tahiti: Gauguin in Paris, Brittany and Martinique," in *Paul Gauguin: Tahiti,* ed. Christoph Becker (Stuttgart: Verlag Gerd Hatje, 1998), pp. 102, 104 n. 48.

75  This is not to dismiss the psychological implications of such a daring representation—nor the place Gauguin's *Exotic Eve* holds in his series of Eves from 1888 on. See particularly Andersen, *Gauguin's Paradise Lost,* pp. 16–17.

76  See National Gallery of Art, pp. 192–93.

77  Rotonchamp (1907), p. 72, in National Gallery of Art, p. 196.

78  Ibid.

79  Chassé, XXX; see also Sweetman, p. 543.

80  The unnamed woman is presumed to have been Huet. Letter from Willumsen to Rewald, 1949, in Rewald, *Post-Impressionism,* p. 467.

81  PG to DM, 7 Nov. 1891, *The Letters of Paul Gauguin to Georges Daniel de Monfreid,* trans. Ruth Pielkovo (London: William Heinemann, 1923), reprinted as *Gauguin's Letters from the South Seas* (New York: Dover, 1992), no. II.

82  PG to DM, 2 Apr. 1891, *Letters to Monfreid,* I.

83  PG to MG, [November 1890], Malingue, *Letters,* no. 100 (redated). "I thought I'd never get your address or news of the children, when your friend [Ballin] came to see me."

84  See Sweetman, p. 543.

85  PG to MG, [February 1890], Malingue, *Letters,* no. 119.

86  Ibid.

87  PG to MG, [ca. 19 Feb. 1891], Malingue, *Letters,* no. 120.

88  Most scholars have assumed that Gauguin was referring to Vincent, but Gauguin always referred to Theo as Van Gogh. Furthermore, Vincent's insanity and death did not have nearly the devastating effect on Gauguin's career that Theo's did.

89  PG to DM, [June 1892], *Letters to Monfreid,* IV.

90  Or he may have left transactions for a sale in Morice's hands, which he counted in his own mind as "his money."

91  26 Mar. 1891, Ministry of Public Education and Fine Arts document, National Archives, Paris, in National Gallery of Art, p. 50.

92  "During his wanderings he never quite lost touch with us. At irregular intervals he would write to us, demanding our news and sending us affectionate greetings." Emil Gauguin's introduction to *Intimate Journals* (1921), n.p. (I).

93  "Do you remember 3 years ago when you said you would be my wife? I sometimes smile at the recollection of your simplicity." PG to Aline Gauguin [December 1893], Malingue, *Letters,* no. 146.

94  *Intimate Journals,* p. 122.

95  See letter from PG to Phillipsen, [March 1891], Royal Library, Copenhagen,

4983.4, inviting him to tea on Saturday, March 14, 1891, at 47 Vimmelskaftet.

96   PG to MG, 24 Mar. 1891, Malingue, *Letters,* no. 123.

97   MG to ES, 22 Mar. 1892, in Appendix, letter II.

98   PG to MG, 24 Mar. 1891, Malingue, *Letters,* no. 123.

### Chapter 11. Tahitian Tourist

1   Bengt Danielsson, *Gauguin in the South Seas* (Garden City, N.Y.: Doubleday, 1966), p. 60.

2   Nicholas Wadley, *Noa Noa: Gauguin's Tahiti* (Salem, N.H.: Salem House, 1985), p. 12. This translation is from the earliest known manuscript of *Noa Noa* ("Draft Manuscript" 1893), which is believed to be entirely by Gauguin's own hand. For the three major drafts, see Wadley, p. 7; and for the history of the published versions, see National Gallery of Art, pp. 514–15.

3   Tahitian tours today seldom provide for more than one night on the island of Tahiti.

4   Although the indigenous political system was dismantled by the French, the local chiefs were absorbed into the French hierarchy and maintained by election. See Victoria S. Lockwood, *Tahitian Transformation: Gender and Capitalist Development in a Rural Society* (Boulder, Colo.: Lynne Rienner, 1993), pp. 26–27.

5   Although on Tahiti and Mooréa land could be owned by nonnatives, there, as on the other islands of French Polynesia, it tended to remain under the control of Tahitian families. This is not to say that Europeans did not dominate commercial expansion at the end of the century. Lower-class Tahitians practiced primarily rural occupations. Lockwood, pp. 31–32.

6   "While on the other side of the globe, men and women cannot meet their needs except through unremitting labor, while they struggle amidst the convulsions of cold and hunger, prey to poverty and all privations, the Tahitians, on the contrary, happy inhabitants of the unknown paradise of Oceania, know nothing in life but sweetness. For them, to live is to sing and to make love." *Les Colonies et protectorats de l'Océan Pacifique,* in Merlhès, *Pages inédites,* p. 46.

7   PG to MG, [November 1890], Malingue, *Letters,* no. 100 (redated): "There, in Tahiti, in the silence of the lovely tropical

night. . . . Free at last, with no money troubles, and able to love, to sing and to die."

8   PG to ES, 7 Aug. 1890, Merlhès, *Pages inédites,* p. 46.

9   PG to Jens Ferdinand Willumsen, [fall 1890], *Les Marges* 14 (15 Mar. 1918), pp. 165–70.

10   The 1793 drawing by Pierre-Paul Prud'hon was reproduced by Gustave Arosa in a book on Prud'hon (1872) that Gauguin presumably had with him in Tahiti. See National Gallery of Art, p. 261; and David Cateforis, "Joseph and Potiphar's Wife in a Drawing by Prud'hon," *Stanford Museum* (1986–87), pp. 12–13.

11   PG to MG, [ca. 11 June 1891], Malingue, *Letters,* no. 125 (redated): "Thanks to the *Figaro* article and to some letters of recommendation, I am known already [three days after his arrival]."

12   An important resource for biographical information about Tahitian residents is the encyclopedic *Tahitiens: Répertoire biographique de la Polynésie française* by Patrick O'Reilly (Paris: Publications de la Société des océanistes, No. 36, 1975).

13   See Robert Aldrich, *The French Presence in the South Pacific, 1842–1940* (Honolulu: University of Hawaii Press, 1990), pp. 152–53.

14   Ibid., pp. 157–58.

15   Most of the information we have about Gauguin's early days on Tahiti come from P. Jénot, a young sous-lieutenant of the Second Regiment, assigned to duty in Tahiti from 1890 to 1893. He was very friendly with Gauguin during the latter's stay on the island and later visited him in Paris when they both returned to France. Jénot's reminiscences of Gauguin in Tahiti serve as the only firsthand account of Gauguin's activities and thus are extremely important. Because they were written many years afterward and not published until 1956, one must take into account the vagaries of memory and the influence of later publications on Gauguin, particularly Gauguin's own account of the trip, *Noa Noa.* Jénot, "Le Premier Séjour de Gauguin à Tahiti," *Gazette des beaux-arts* (January–April 1956), pp. 115–26.

16   Jénot, "Le Premier Séjour," p. 120.

17   Paul Gauguin, *Noa Noa (La Plume* edition, 1901; translated into English by O. F. Theis, 1919; reprint, New York: Dover, 1985), p. 1. This version includes changes and additions from the Draft

Manuscript of 1893 made by Gauguin and Morice between 1893 and 1897 and was published under both their names.

18  On their first day in Papeete, Jénot helped Gauguin and Captain Swaton navigate the official steps that needed to be taken by newcomers, and then "we ended this very full day at the Cercle Militaire, where they completed their tour of the military station and were crowned with flowers by the local women." Jénot, "Le Premier Séjour," p. 118. "There are two clubs in Papeete, the Cercle Bougainville and the Cercle Militaire, and the hospitality of both is extended to the stranger with an earnestness that would shame the ancient patriarchs. Kindnesses, civil speeches, invitations flow in from all sides. Within twenty-four hours of your landing you have been apparently introduced to half the island." Edwin Pallander, *The Log of an Island Wanderer* (London: C. Arthur Pearson, 1901), p. 301.

19  PG to MG, [ca. 11 June 1891], Malingue, *Letters*, no. 125.

20  He may also have brought photographs of works that he considered important, such as some of his ceramics, his two panels *Soyez amoureuses* and *Soyez mystérieuses,* and perhaps some paintings.

21  For the Goupils' reception of their daughter's portrait, see Chapter 13.

22  Jénot, "Le Premier Séjour," p. 117.

23  "Coming and going to baths here, whites throw off easily the fear of being thought immodest, and women and men alike go to and fro in loin-cloths, pajamas, or towels. I wore the pareu, the red strip of calico, bearing designs by William Morris, which the native buys instead of his original one of *tapa,* the beaten cloth made from tree bark or pith." Frederick O'Brien, *Mystic Isles of the South Seas* (New York: Century Co., 1921), pp. 52–53.

24  Jénot, "Le Premier Séjour," p. 120.

25  "The French administration hoped to abolish the kin-based system of joint land ownership still in place in Tahitian communities and to replace it with one of individual ownership. To this end, the French worked to codify the traditional system and to survey parcels." Lockwood, p. 28.

26  John La Farge, *Reminiscences of the South Seas* (New York: Doubleday, Page, 1912), pp. 344–45.

27  Ibid., p. 345.

28  "When the director of public works asked my advice about arranging the apartment artistically, I signed to him to look at the queen as, with the fine instinct of the Maoris, she gracefully adorned and turned everything she touched into a work of art. 'Leave it to them,' I replied." Wadley, *Noa Noa,* p. 12.

29  Wadley, *Noa Noa,* p. 13.

30  Jénot mentions a trip Gauguin took to Paea, the district next to Papara, but this cannot be substantiated. Possibly Jénot's memory failed him and he actually meant Papara. Jénot, "Le Premier Séjour," p. 125.

31  For a trip to Papara, see Clement L. Wragge, *The Romance of the South Seas* (London: Chatto and Windus, 1906), pp. 255–56: "A quaint little trap is the Tahitian coach, roofed with an awning, and capable of holding six passengers with ordinary gear. It is drawn by two mules, with tinkling sleigh-bells. Poroi receives us with bland smiles. He's a capital and corpulent fellow, and not only follows the profession of the stable, but is President of the Tahitian Philharmonic Society, revels in Chopin and worships Handel."

32  PG to MG, [August 1891], Bibliothèque d'Art et Architecture, Paris, microfilm 5433 (not in Malingue, *Letters*): "I received a letter from France for the first time. . . . Yes, I am a little lonely especially now that I am 45 kilometers from town." Since he left France in early April, he expected to get his first mail in Tahiti in July, but did not—and thus would have received it in August.

33  See O'Reilly, *Tahitiens,* p. 556.

34  Ibid.

35  "I should like to have your memory to learn the language quickly, for very few here speak French. I often say if Mette were here, she would not take long to speak Tahitian, which besides, is very easy." PG to MG, July [1891], Malingue, *Letters,* no. 126.

36  Marshall D. Sahlins, *Social Stratification in Polynesia* (Seattle: University of Washington Press, 1971), p. 39.

37  Ibid., p. 40.

38  Wragge, p. 274.

39  "The Duke of Abruzzi's photograph and one of the Italian war-ship Liguria, were on a wall in the drawing-room, with others of notable people whom the chief had entertained." O'Brien, *Mystic Isles,* p. 337. According to the biographical dictionary *Tahitiens,* O'Brien's visit took

place in 1913, but Tetuanui retired from his position as chief of Mataiea in 1912.

40  O'Brien, *Mystic Isles*, pp. 338–39.

41  He actually chose a house that was already occupied by someone he called Anani [orange grower], who graciously moved out and built another one. Wadley, *Noa Noa*, p. 16.

42  Wilmon Menard, "An Author in Search of an Artist," *Apollo* 114 (August 1981), p. 116.

43  Wadley, *Noa Noa*, p. 17.

44  O'Brien, *Mystic Isles*, p. 340. Some of the parallels to *Noa Noa* in O'Brien's travelogue make one suspect that he had Gauguin's account in mind. Versions of *Noa Noa* had been published since 1897, although the first English version did not appear until 1919. See National Gallery of Art, p. 515.

45  O'Brien, *Mystic Isles*, pp. 342–43.

46  PG to ES, 6 Dec. 1895, *Pages inédites*, p. 88.

47  The descriptions correspond with one of the first letters that Gauguin wrote to his wife, PG to MG, July [1891], Malingue, *Letters*, no. 126.

48  For example, Wragge advises in *The Romance of the South Seas*, p. 291: "Attend native churches to hear the weird singing. Make a detour, by river and forest, tangle and cliff, to Lake Vaihiria. See Chief Ori down there at Tautira; give him a nip and he'll see you through. Stay at Hittiaa with Madame Tepatua."

49  Wadley, *Noa Noa*, p. 33.

50  Wadley, *Noa Noa*, p. 77 n. 54. This was added in the 1901 version, and, as Wadley points out, "It has become almost a tradition among later writers to repeat this information."

51  At the Tiare Hotel in Papeete, one English visitor described the sexual accommodation of tourists, "By day nothing much happens in the yard—but by night, after ten, it is filled with flitting figures of girls, with wreaths of white flowers, keeping assignations." Rupert Brooke quoted in O'Brien, *Mystic Isles*, p. 67.

52  Hassoldt Davis, *Islands Under the Wind* (London: Longmans, Green, 1933), pp. 108–9.

53  "Romance in the islands is a business relationship and a social convenience. I had lived for a month or so in rather a notable celibacy among the natives, content to work and swim and visit rarely the

clubs of Papeete, when it was bruited to me that the natives were beginning to consider me with distrust. . . . That afternoon Tetua, in her brightest cotton dress and with hibiscus in her hair, came to see me. . . . She would teach me her language, do my marketing, cooking, housekeeping, and sleep with me, for, said she, almost no francs at all." Davis, p. 59.

54  Wadley, *Noa Noa*, p. 33.

55  Titi is the usual nickname for "Jeanne" and not, as Sweetman implies (p. 293), a sexual innuendo like "Titty." Pissarro's daughter Jeanne, for instance, was called Titi.

56  Wragge, p. 190.

57  Douglas Hall and Albert Osborne, *Sunshine and Surf: A Year's Wanderings in the South Seas* (London: Adam and Charles Black, 1901), p. 153.

58  PG to DM, [August–September 1892], *Letters to Monfreid*, IX.

59  The common assumption that the child died (e.g., Sweetman, p. 339) seems a less likely explanation for the child's absence from Gauguin's home than that it was adopted according to Tahitian custom.

60  Wadley, *Noa Noa*, p. 42.

61  O'Brien, *Mystic Isles*, p. 339.

62  He suffered his first attack while still living in Papeete. "It seems that great injury has been done to the heart, which is not in the least surprising. I left the hospital, however, and have not had a relapse. I take digitalis from time to time." PG to MG, [September/October 1891?], Malingue, *Letters*, no. 127 (redated based on Mette's trip to Paris in July/August 1891].

63  O'Brien, *Mystic Isles*, p. 479.

64  Wadley, *Noa Noa*, p. 21: "She told me this Olympia was truly beautiful. . . . She added, all of a sudden, breaking the silence that presides over a thought: 'It's your wife.' 'Yes,' I lied. . . . asked if I might paint her portrait. '*Aita* (no),' she said in a tone almost of rage, and went away."

65  Wadley, *Noa Noa*, p. 23.

66  Ibid., p. 42.

67  Hall and Osborne, p. 33.

68  Now destroyed; see Chapter 13.

69  PG to MG, 8 Dec. [1892], Malingue, *Letters*, no. 134 (retranslated).

70  Ibid.

71  Wadley, *Noa Noa*, p. 38.

72  *Noa Noa* (*La Plume* edition), p. 33.

73  This painting and its relation to

Polynesian myths and beliefs has occupied many a scholar (see National Gallery of Art, pp. 279–82). Without disagreeing that the local religious aspects contribute an important part of the overall meaning of the painting, I would argue that Gauguin's sexual predilections should not be disregarded in understanding the intention or the interpretation of the work. Sweetman arrived at many of the same conclusions as I have (pp. 324–30).

74  Gauguin tells of his wife's fright after reading Poe's "The Black Cat" (1843). *Intimate Journals*, p. 70.

75  See Maria Grazia Messina, "Gauguin et les sources littéraires," *Gazette des beaux-arts*, no. 1465 (February 1991), pp. 101–12.

76  "In the nineteenth century and earlier, [the term] 'horror' described the sudden tremors . . . at that moment of transition between the sensation of a boiling fever and the chill that follows." Twitchell, p. 9.

77  Wadley, *Noa Noa*, p. 25.

78  See O'Brien, *Mystic Isles*, p. 215; Davis, p. 35; and Robert I. Levy, *Tahitians: Mind and Experience in the Society Islands* (Chicago: University of Chicago Press, 1973), pp. 130–33. See also Stephen Eisenman, *Gauguin's Skirt*, pp. 104–9.

79  Jénot, "Le Premier Séjour," p. 117.

80  Wadley, *Noa Noa*, p. 20.

81  *A Tahitian and English Dictionary* (Tahiti: London Missionary Society's Press, 1851).

82  "*Double entendre* is caviar to the average man and woman of Tahiti, who call the unshrouded spade by its aboriginal name. . . . One could not publish the phrases if one could translate them." O'Brien, *Mystic Isles*, pp. 59–60.

83  Wadley, *Noa Noa*, p. 5.

84  Ibid., p. 8.

85  Ibid.

86  Ibid.

87  Ibid.

88  Jénot, "Le Premier Séjour," p. 122: "In searching for interesting woods for him, I led him into the mountains above the vallée de la Reine."

89  Thadée Natanson, *Peints à leur tour* (1948), quoted in *Retrospective*, p. 204.

90  Ibid., p. 205.

91  *Noa Noa* (*La Plume* edition), p. 17.

92  Natanson, in *Retrospective*, p. 204.

93  Jénot, "Le Premier Séjour," p. 118.

94  Pierre Loti, *The Marriage of Loti*, trans. Wright Frierson and Eleanor Frierson (Honolulu: University Press of Hawaii, 1976), p. 107.

95  *Noa Noa* (*La Plume* edition), p. 13.

96  Jénot, "Le Premier Séjour," p. 124.

97  During this time he executed a death portrait of Atiti Suhas, the son of Jénot's neighbors, and several letters are headed "Papeete."

98  "Cardiovascular syphilis" had already been documented in medical literature by this time. See Allan M. Brandt, *No Magic Bullet: A Social History of Venereal Disease in the United States Since 1880* (New York: Oxford University Press, 1985), p. 9. Internal hemorrhaging was also caused by massive doses of mercury given for venereal diseases. Ibid., p. 12.

99  "In Papeete she had a terrible reputation. She had buried several lovers in succession." Wadley, *Noa Noa*, p. 16.

100  "Before engaging her to come with him, he asked, 'You've never been ill?'" Wadley, *Noa Noa*, p. 3.

101  Brandt, *No Magic Bullet*, pp. 20–21.

102  New evidence from recently excavated skulls in England, however, shows that syphilis existed in Europe before 1493. G. Gugliotta, "Syphilis: New World May Not Have Been First," *Washington Post* (28 Aug. 2000), p. A8.

103  "Every month I have been expecting money from Morice, with whom I left it, plus the proceeds of pending picture deals, but I have had neither money nor news from him." PG to MG, [September/October 1891?], Malingue, *Letters*, no. 127 (redated).

104  "I just got your letter, which didn't surprise me, since 8 days ago I got the news direct from Paul, who certainly is without money but who told me that he could perhaps arrange a way to stay another year. I'll send you that letter—you will see for yourself the situation." MG to ES, 9 July 1892, in Appendix, letter V.

105  PG to DM, [April 1892], *Letters to Monfreid*, IV (redated).

106  PG to DM, [August/September 1892], Malingue, *Letters*, no. 132.

107  PG to DM, 5 Nov. 1892, *Letters to Monfreid*, V.

108  PG to MG, [June/July 1892], Malingue, *Letters*, no. 128 (redated).

1 This would include art collectors, critics, fellow artists, and a Parisian literary intelligentsia—all of whom could help him achieve fame and fortune. It, of course, did not include his wife, her family and friends, or a "general" public.

2 The first trip is referred to in a letter in mid-May 1891. PG to MG, Malingue, *Letters,* no. 124. The second took place in May 1892. MG to ES, 20 May 1892, and 25 May 1892, in Appendix, letters III and IV.

3 PG to DM, [September? 1892], *Letters to Monfreid,* IX.

4 MG to ES, 21 Jan. 1893, Musée Gauguin, Tahiti, in Appendix, letter VII. She had hoped to get a draft from her Danish bank to enclose in a letter to Paul, but discovered that a draft on a French bank would be more efficient, and at the last minute had Schuffenecker arrange it in Paris. Paul berated her for this peculiar maneuver, not understanding the wisdom of it: "Careless!" PG to MG, [late March?] 1893, Malingue, *Letters,* no. 136.

5 MG to ES, 25 May 1892, Musée Gauguin, Tahiti, in Appendix, letter IV.

6 MG to ES, 5 Sept. 1892, Musée Gauguin, Tahiti, in Appendix, letter VI.

7 MG to ES, 11 Feb. 1893, Musée Gauguin, Tahiti, in Appendix, letter VIII.

8 "They are going to hold an exclusive exposition there next spring and want me to send canvases from here." PG to DM, [September? 1892], *Letters to Monfreid,* IX.

9 PG to DM, 8 Dec. 1892, *Letters to Monfreid,* VI. A ninth painting, *Vahine no te Tiare,* had been sent earlier and was exhibited at the Boussod and Valadon gallery in Paris in September 1892. See National Gallery of Art, p. 207.

10 MG to ES, 11 Feb. 1893, Musée Gauguin, Tahiti, in Appendix, letter VIII.

11 "He desires above all to meet you and study your art—yours and Paul's. I gave him your address. I hope he won't bother you too much with his bad French and his enthusiasm for the 'symbolists.'" MG to ES, 25 May 1893, Musée Gauguin, Tahiti, in Appendix, letter IV.

12 See Kirsten Olesen, "From Amsterdam to Copenhagen," in Bodelsen, *Gauguin and Van Gogh in Copenhagen in 1893,* pp. 29–30.

13 Bodelsen, "Miracle on the Radhusplads," p. 26.

14 MG to ES, 11 Feb. 1893, Musée Gauguin, Tahiti.

15 MG to ES, 14 Mar. 1893, in Appendix, letter IX.

16 Such as *Woman Sewing* and *Nude Breton Boy;* see figs. 15 and 44.

17 MG to ES, 1 Apr. 1893, in Appendix, letter X.

18 MG to ES, 14 Mar. 1893, in Appendix, letter IX.

19 "Do you have any news of Paul? I have had some from Tahiti. He received the 700 frs. and he hoped to depart at the beginning of May. Did he do this?" MG to ES, 22 June 1893, Musée Gauguin, Tahiti, in Appendix, letter XI.

20 "I have not replied to your letter of August 25, in which you informed me of Paul's arrival, which in fact happened sooner than, we, Daniel and I, thought." Most accounts have mistakenly put his arrival on August 30. MG to ES, 15 Sept. 1893, in Appendix, letter XII.

21 MG to ES, 22 June 1893, Musée Gauguin, Tahiti, in Appendix, letter XI.

22 PG to MG, [23? Aug. 1893], Malingue, *Letters,* no. 137 (redated).

23 PG to DM, [12 Sept. 1893], *Letters to Monfreid,* XIII: "I had a break with Bussod [*sic*] . . . there is nothing more of mine in the place."

24 "I don't dare write you not knowing what to say and what to think about your silence." PG to MG, [early September 1893], Malingue, *Letters,* no. 138 (redated, retranslated). "Decidedly I understand things less and less. You have my address since you sent a telegram. . . . Good God, how difficult it is to act when those on whom you rely leave you completely in the lurch—and especially your wife." PG to MG, [Sept. 1893], Malingue, *Letters,* no. 139.

25 PG to MG, [ca. 13 Sept. 1893], Malingue, *Letters,* no. 141 (redated).

26 "And so he has returned! According to his letter, just as he was when he departed, relying on the most monstrously brutal egoism, which for me is phenomenal and incomprehensible." MG to ES, 15 Sept. 1893, Malingue, *Letters,* p. 247; Musée Gauguin, Tahiti, in Appendix, letter XII.

27 MG to ES, 15 Sept. 1893, Musée Gauguin, Tahiti, in Appendix, letter XII.

28 Ibid.

29 PG to DM, [April 1896], *Letters to Monfreid,* XVII: "Had I sent her 6,000

francs instead of 1,500 from my uncle's 13,000, what would have become of me?"

30  PG to DM, 12 Sept. 1893, *Letters to Monfreid,* XIII: "But anyway I have seen Durand-Ruel, who received me very kindly and who is again dealing with the Impressionists. . . . He has promised to come and see my things when they are ready, and to exhibit them."

31  Although Degas had barely returned to Paris himself and Gauguin does not mention seeing him in any of his letters at this time, Degas was particularly close to Durand-Ruel and served as a witness at the marriage of Durand-Ruel's daughter on September 15. Metropolitan Museum of Art, *Degas* (New York: Metropolitan Museum of Art, 1988), p. 488.

32  For Degas's purchase of Gauguin's works, see Françoise Cachin, "Degas and Gauguin," in *Private Collection of Edgar Degas,* pp. 221–34.

33  PG to MG, [ca. 13 Sept. 1893], Malingue, *Letters,* no. 141 (redated, retranslated).

34  PG to MG, [ca. 8 Sept. 1893], Malingue, *Letters,* no. 138 (redated, retranslated).

35  "Taking my chance I will come Tuesday next to tell you a little about my journey." PG to Stéphane Mallarmé, 3 Nov. 1893, Malingue, *Letters,* no. 144.

36  "Neither as men nor as artists were we made to live side by side. [Crossed out: You were made for domination, I for independence.] I have known that for a long time, and it has just been proved." ES to PG, 7 Feb. 1891, Merlhès, *Pages inédites,* p. 74.

37  MG to ES, 20 Jan. 1893, Musée Gauguin, Tahiti, in Appendix, letter XIII.

38  Bernard's complaint stemmed from the insult he had received at the February 2 banquet in honor of Jean Moréas, where Gauguin alone was hailed as leader of the symbolists. Later that month Bernard put the blame for the insult directly on Gauguin. Mary Anne Stevens, *Emile Bernard,* p. 7.

39  Francis Jourdain, "Notes sur le peintre Emile Bernard," *La Plume* (15 Sept. 1893), pp. 390–97.

40  "Gauguin et l'école de Pont-Aven," *Essais d'art libre* 4–5 (November 1893), pp. 164–68.

41  For a study of the growth of Van Gogh's reputation, see Nathalie Heinich, *The Glory of Van Gogh: An Anthropology of Admiration* (Princeton: Princeton University Press, 1996), particularly appendix A, "Van Gogh and Art Criticism in France, 1888–1901," pp. 153–68.

42  Gauguin published his own poetic tribute to a saintly (and mad) Van Gogh in "Natures Mortes," *Essais d'art libre* 4 (January 1894), pp. 273–75.

43  See Cooper, pp. 331–33.

44  "In addition, I am preparing a book on Tahiti, and that will be very useful in making my work understood. What a job." PG to MG, [ca. 15 Oct. 1893], Malingue, *Letters,* no. 143 (redated, retranslated).

45  This idea is hinted at in the letters from Tahiti: "I am fairly pleased with my last works and feel there is dawning in me an Oceanic character, and I can assert that what I am doing here has not been done by anyone else and nothing like it is known in France. I hope this novelty will turn the scale in my favor." PG to MG, [May? 1892], Malingue, *Letters,* no. 129 (redated). "My artistic center is in my head and not elsewhere, and I am strong because I am never thrown off course by others, and what I do comes from inside me." PG to MG, [September/October 1891], Malingue, *Letters,* no. 127 (redated, retranslated).

46  This is Nietzschean in origin and already part of symbolist theory in the 1880s and 1890s, but few artists or writers carried it out as effectively as Gauguin. For concepts of the modern artist, see White and White, especially pp. 98–99, Sarah Burns, *Inventing the Modern Artist* (New Haven: Yale University Press, 1996), Gene H. Bell-Villada, *Art for Art's Sake and Literary Life* (Lincoln: University of Nebraska Press, 1996).

47  Octave Mirabeau, "Retour de Tahiti," *L'Echo de Paris* (14 Nov. 1893), p. 1.

48  For a priced catalogue, see *Vente de tableaux de Paul Gauguin* (Paris: Durand-Ruel, 1893), Thomas J. Watson Library, Metropolitan Museum of Art.

49  "My show has not in fact given the results that might have been expected." PG to MG, [December 1893], Malingue, *Letters,* no. 145.

50  On his inheritance, see above, n. 29.

51  For a recollection of Gauguin's apartment in 1894 by a friend of August Strindberg's, see Tore Håkansson, "Strindberg and the Arts," *Studio international* 181, no. 930 (February 1971), p. 62.

52   Rotonchamp, p. 123. This may possibly have been a collection formed by his seafaring Uncle Chazal (his mother's brother), but was certainly not the property of his Uncle Isidore from Orléans, whose house was thoroughly inventoried upon his death. Inventaire après le décès de M. Isidore Gauguin, Private Archive, Orléans.

53   See Blanch, *Pierre Loti*, pp. 259–60. Known for his exotic costumes and decor, Loti eventually re-created a mosque in his home.

54   Ambroise Vollard, *Recollections of a Picture Dealer* (Boston: Little, Brown, 1936), p. 173.

55   Vaino Blomstedt to Eero Jarnefelt, 16 Jan. 1894, in Marja Supinen, "Paul Gauguin's Fiji Academy," *Burlington Magazine* (April 1990), p. 270.

56   Ibid.

57   "It is worth noting that to-day, when it is the fashion to send pure young girls to study painting in the ateliers with the men, all these virgins draw the nude male model with the greatest care, Master John with more accuracy than the face. When they leave the atelier, these young virgins, foreigners for the most part and always respectable . . . go to Lesbia to console themselves." *Intimate Journals*, p. 57.

58   V. Blomstedt, "Gauguin," *Konst* (1913), in Supinen, p. 270.

59   "Son exposition fut suivie d'un insuccès pécuniaire, à la suite de je ne sais quel différend survenu entre lui et Durand-Ruel." G. Daniel de Montfreid [*sic*], "Sur Paul Gauguin," *L'Ermitage* 3 (December 1903), p. 272.

60   PG to MG, [early December? 1893], Malingue, *Letters*, no. 145.

61   PG to MG, [mid-December? 1893], Malingue, *Letters*, no. 146 (redated).

62   Morice, *Paul Gauguin*, p. 206.

63   See N. Mathews, *Mary Cassatt*, pp. 215–17.

64   "What artist would be more gifted if exclusively literary friendships did not cloud his judgment and paralyze the instinctive sense of painting that he has?" François Thiébault-Sisson, "Les Petits Salons," *Le Temps* (2 Dec. 1893), quoted in *Retrospective*, p. 218.

65   Julian Leclercq, "On Painting," *Mercure de France* (May 1894), quoted in *Retrospective*, p. 227.

66   PG to William Molard, [September 1894], Malingue, *Letters*, no. 152.

67   National Gallery of Art, p. 211.

68   Bodelsen, "Gauguin, the Collector," pp. 603–5.

69   "I must have exact information, and be advised as to precisely what pictures you are selling. . . . You must understand, and everybody would agree with me in this, that I must be informed without any *trickery*." PG to MG, 30 Dec. 1893, Malingue, *Letters*, no. 147.

70   PG to ES, 11 July 1894, Merlhès, *Pages inédites*, p. 79.

71   PG to ES, 26 July 1894, Merlhès, *Pages inédites*, p. 82.

72   See Julien Leclerq's description of the exhibition in *Mercure de France* 13, no. 61 (January 1895), pp. 121–22.

73   Mortimer Mempes, *Brittany* (London: Adam and Charles Black, 1905), p. 139.

74   PG to William Molard, [September 1894], Malingue, *Letters*, no. 152: "I will set out again for the South Seas, this time taking two comrades with me, Séguin and an Irishman."

75   Denys Sutton, "Roderic O'Conor: Little Known Member of the Pont-Aven Circle," *Studio* 160 (July–December 1960), p. 173.

76   Ibid.

77   Alfred Jarry, *Oeuvres completes* (Paris: Gallimard, 1972).

78   National Gallery of Art, p. 294.

79   Ibid. p. 307.

80   See Sweetman, pp. 373–76.

81   Thomas Millroth, *Molards Salong* (1993), in Sweetman, p. 376.

82   Sweetman, p. 76.

83   Now in the Musée Gauguin, Tahiti.

84   Marie Jade, "Gauguin que j'ai connu," *Le Figaro littéraire* (23 Aug. 1952), p. 9.

85   Ibid.

86   Monfreid, "Sur Paul Gauguin," p. 273.

87   Ibid., p. 274.

88   National Gallery of Art, p. 294.

89   Tore Håkansson, "Strindberg and the Arts," *Studio International* 181, no. 930 (February 1971), pp. 62–67.

90   Ibid.

91   August Strindberg to PG, 1 Feb. 1895, quoted in *Retrospective*, p. 248.

92   "I, too, am starting to feel an immense need to become a savage and to create a new world." Ibid.

93   Auguste Strindberg, "L'Actualité:

Le Misogyne Streinberg [*sic*] contra
Monet," *L'Eclair* (15 Feb. 1895), pp. 1–3,
reprinted in auction catalogue.

94 Auction records as reported in
Wildenstein, *Catalogue,* for pieces sold in
the Vente Gauguin, 1895.

95 PG to MG, [March 1895?],
Malingue, *Letters,* no. 158. Gauguin claimed
the figure for the total sales (including
works he had "bought in," or bought himself) was 23,640 francs. The record of the
auction shows that although he bought in
the majority of the pieces, at least ten
were sold to other buyers. Whereas some
of the buyers may have been acting on
Gauguin's behalf (e.g., his friends Seguin,
Maufra, and Schuffenecker), others with
successful bids over 400 francs would
probably have been genuine sales (Degas,
Halévy, Leclanché, O'Conor, Slewinski,
etc.). These sales, plus the drawings bought
by Degas, would probably have netted Gauguin about 3,000 francs (after expenses).

96 *Journal des artistes* (24 Feb. 1895),
reported the total sale amount to have
been 2,200 francs. Cited in National
Gallery of Art, p. 295.

97 PG to DM, in Jean Loize, *Les Amitiés du peintre Georges-Daniel de Monfreid et
ses reliques de Gauguin* (1951), in National
Gallery of Art, p. 295.

98 For Gauguin and Vollard, see John
Rewald, "The Genius and the Dealer," *Art
News* 58 (May 1958), pp. 30–31, 62–65.

99 PG to EB, [early September 1889],
Malingue, *Letters,* no. 87.

100 *Dictionary of Folklore, Mythology,
and Legend* (New York: Funk and Wag-
nalls, 1984), p. 413.

101 "Un Lettre de Paul Gauguin à pro-
pos de Sèvres et du dernier four," *Le Soir*
(23 Apr. 1895), p. 1; and "Les Peintres
français à Berlin," *Le Soir* (May 1895), p. 2.

102 Eugène Tardieu, "M. Paul
Gauguin," *L'Echo de Paris* (13 May 1895),
quoted in *Retrospective,* p. 250.

103 Ibid., p. 251.

104 Emile Bernard, "Lettre ouverte à
M. Camille Mauclair, *Mercure de France*
(June 1895), pp. 332–39.

105 Camille Mauclair, "Choses d'art"
*Mercure de France* (June 1895), p. 359.

106 Charles Morice, "Le Départ de
Paul Gauguin" *Le Soir* (28 June 1895), p. 2.

107 MG to ES, 6 May 1895, in Appendix, letter XIV. (Malingue erroneously
read the date as 1891.)

108 Ibid.

109 PG to DM, [November 1895], *Letters to Monfreid,* XVI.

## Chapter 13. Tahitian Resident

1 Pallander goes into great detail
about the lives of white men who have
married and "gone native." *Log of an Island
Wanderer,* pp. 313–20.

2 Speech reprinted in *Les Guêpes* (12
Oct. 1900), quoted in *Retrospective,* p. 287.

3 See Aldrich, *French Presence in the
South Pacific,* pp. 153–57. "The colonists . . .
were divided between French and Pacific
allegiances—they exhibited an exaggerated and old-fashioned patriotism and at
the same time liked to see themselves as
pioneers. . . . This schizophrenia, and the
lack of evolution of their re-created European societies, may explain many of the
tensions and conflicts of the colonial
world in the Pacific." Pp. 156–57.

4 "Papeete, the capital of this Eden,
Tahiti, is now lighted by electricity. The
big lawn in front of the old garden of the
King is spoilt by a merry-go-round, 25
centimes for a ride, a phonograph, etc."
PG to William Molard, [mid-September
1895], Malingue, *Letters,* no. 160
(redated, retranslated).

5 Ibid.: "Next month I shall be at La
Dominique, a little island of the Mar-
quisas, a delightful place where one can
live almost for nothing and where I shall
meet no Europeans."

6 This was a diplomatic expedition
to enable Isidore Chessé, the French com-
missioner general for Oceania, to negoti-
ate a new treaty with these islands. The
delegation included not only Chessé but
the current governor, Pierre Papinaud,
and Papeete's mayor, François Cardella,
who probably issued the invitation to
Gauguin. See Danielsson, p. 189.

7 PG to DM, [November 1895], *Letters to Monfreid,* XVI.

8 Having money did not prevent
him from falling back into making his old
cries of poverty to stir his friends in Paris
to action. "Of the 4,000 francs that is
owing to me and which would keep me
for two years I have received nothing, and
at the rate things are going, I am afraid I
shall be penniless." PG to William
Molard, [November 1895], Malingue, *Letters,* no. 161 (redated).

9 This impression no doubt comes

from his letter to William Molard, [October 1895], in Daniel Guérin, *The Writings of a Savage* (New York: Paragon House, 1990), p. 115: "I am sitting quietly in my hut. In front of me is the sea, and Mooréa, which takes on a different aspect every quarter of an hour." This letter was written before Gauguin built his house and moved out to Punaauia, so he must be describing the view from his room in Papeete.

10  Danielsson, p. 195.

11  PG to DM, [November 1895], *Letters to Monfreid*, XVI.

12  Ibid. Danielsson reports that Tehamana stayed on at Mataiea after Gauguin left and then married a young man (Ma'ari) from Papara. Although she returned to Gauguin, she did not stay with him because "he was covered with running sores." Oral information from Ma'ari a Teheiura, reported in Danielsson, p. 195 and n. 157.

13  Danielsson, p. 195 gives her birth date as June 27, 1881.

14  There is some confusion as to what happened to the first child. In a later article about Pahura, "Death of Paul Gauguin's Tahitian Mistress," Eric Ramsden reports that the first child was a girl who died in infancy. *Pacific Islands Monthly* (January 1944), p. 23.

15  Danielsson believed he had identified her as the wife of Ma'ari a Teheiura; see above, n. 12.

16  Wragge reports that a native girl would be an all-around house servant for one Chilean dollar (less than one franc) a day. P. 200.

17  Menard, "Author in Search of an Artist," p. 116.

18  Ramsden, "Death of Paul Gauguin's Tahitian Mistress," p. 22.

19  Ibid.

20  One artist was John Maehaa Bambridge (1859–98), a painter and fine furniture maker. Although no connection has been established between them, Gauguin did paint one of his few commissioned portraits of Bambridge's sister, Suzanne Bambridge (Musée des Beaux-Arts, Brussels).

21  O'Brien met some of Darling's followers living outside Papeete in 1913 after the Nature Man himself had returned to the United States. *Mystic Isles*, pp. 258–60.

22  Henry Lemasson, "Paul Gauguin

as Seen by One of His Contemporaries in Tahiti," *Encyclopédie de la France et d'Outre-Mer* (February 1950), quoted in *Retrospective*, pp. 276–79 and passim.

23  Danielsson, p. 197: "He is known to have spent about 300 francs on a horse and trap to make him independent of coaches."

24  O'Brien, *Mystic Isles*, p. 90.

25  Ibid., p. 99.

26  For more on the sources and symbolism of these paintings, see National Gallery of Art, pp. 398–99, 409–13; and Jeanne H. Teilhet, "'Te Tamari No Atua': An Interpretation of Paul Gauguin's Tahitian Symbolism," *Arts Magazine* 53, no. 5 (January 1979), pp. 110–11.

27  In his letter to Monfreid, [June 1896], *Letters to Monfreid*, XVIII, he lists possible participants in a group subscription to his paintings. The last is "Le Comte de la Rochefoucault [*sic*]—he gave both Bernard and Filiger an allowance of twelve hundred francs."

28  See Sweetman, *Paul Gauguin*, p. 440.

29  For Gauguin's later involvement with the Catholic party, see Danielsson, pp. 229–35.

30  This would also apply to Gauguin's use of Polynesian symbolism. A sensible view of Gauguin's mastery of Tahitian ethnology can be found in Ingrid Heermann, "Gauguin's Tahiti—Ethnological Considerations," in *Paul Gauguin: Tahiti*, pp. 162–64: "There is no doubt that Gauguin was inspired by the culture of the Maohi—both the contemporary and the past—and that he showed considerable sensitivity in his exploration of issues of interest to ethnologists as well. His claim to have become a savage, an *oviri*, and as such to have adapted himself to native customs, however, does not bear up to scrutiny."

31  Danielsson, p. 203.

32  *Tahitiens*, p. 186.

33  See N. Mathews, "Mary Cassatt and the 'Modern Madonna,'" pp. 118–32.

34  A handwritten receipt for gardening that Gauguin gave Auguste Goupil is dated 1892. It is hard to believe Gauguin actually worked as a common groundsman for the Goupils during his stay on the island, but he may have consulted on the artistic layout of the grounds or their decorative sculpture.

35  Renée Hamon, "The Recluse of

the Pacific: Paul Gauguin's Life in Tahiti and the Marquesas," *Geographical Magazine* (February 1939), p. 268.

36  MG to ES, 31 Jan.? 1896, Musée Gauguin, Tahiti, in Appendix, letter XV.

37  Ramsden, "Death of Paul Gauguin's Tahitian Mistress," p. 23.

38  "But I am laid up with a broken ankle which hurts excruciatingly; big sores have appeared and I cannot get rid of them." PG to Charles Morice, [May 1896], Malingue, *Letters*, no. 162.

39  David Ostrow, Terry Sandholzer, and Yehudi Felman, *Sexually Transmitted Diseases in Homosexual Men* (New York: Plenum Medical Book Co., 1983), pp. 46–47.

40  PG to DM, [November 1896], *Letters to Monfreid*, XXI.

41  PG to DM, 14 Feb. 1897, *Letters to Monfreid*, XXII.

42  "You also [in addition to drawings] want wood sculptures, models for bronze casts, etc. . . . For four years now all those things have been in Paris without any sales. Either they are bad, and then the new ones I might make would be bad also, and thus unsalable, or else they are works of art. In that case, why don't you sell them?" PG to Ambroise Vollard, [April 1897], Rewald, "The Genius and the Dealer," p. 62.

43  *Tahitiens*, p. 413.

44  PG to DM, [April 1897], *Letters to Monfreid*, XXIV.

45  PG to MG, [April? 1897], Malingue, *Letters*, no. 165 (redated, retranslated).

46  PG to William Molard, [August 1897], Malingue, *Letters*, no. 164.

47  PG to DM, [December 1897], *Letters to Monfreid*, XXX.

48  Ibid.

49  Gauguin's history of using personal tragedy to gain dealer attention and sales makes one view even such a tragic announcement with cynicism. This is not to say that he did not genuinely face such a crisis, merely that his communication of it to correspondents in Europe had an element of professional calculation. Brettell also suggests a possible link to Van Gogh's suicide as a publicity gambit: "Perhaps he was intent on linking the making of the painting with his suicide attempt. In view of his later musings about the suicide of Van Gogh, one

wonders about his motivations for forging so strong a link." National Gallery of Art, p. 417.

50  At the very least, this location for the supposed suicide is doubtful because access to the mountains was difficult by foot—and not at all possible by horse and carriage. With Gauguin's painful feet and legs, he would not have been able to hike.

51  PG to DM, [February 1898], *Letters to Monfreid*, XXXI.

52  Ibid.

53  "Explanatory attributes—known symbols would congeal the canvas into a melancholy reality, and the problem indicated would no longer be a poem." PG to Charles Morice, [July 1901], Malingue, *Letters*, no. 174.

54  See particularly Thomas L. Sloan, "Paul Gauguin's 'D'ou venons-nous? Que sommes-nous? Ou allons-nous?': A Symbolist Philosophical Leitmotif," *Arts* (January 1979), pp. 104–9.

55  PG to DM, [April 1898], *Letters to Monfreid*, XXXIII: "Well I screwed up my courage and prostrated myself before the Government officials. And I have gotten some work, the copying of building designs, for the daily wage of six francs." PG to DM, 15 Aug. 1898, *Letters to Monfreid*, XXXV: "I must continue in this modest employment awaiting the moment of deliverance, when I can take up my brushes again." PG to DM, 22 Feb. 1899, *Letters to Monfreid*, XXXIX: "While I had to toil at those public documents I lost a tremendous lot of time." PG to DM, [June 1899], *Letters to Monfreid*, XLIII: "Just think, some of my old acquaintances, seeing me sink lower each day, especially when I had to work as foreman on the roads (oh, these colonial officials), have snubbed me." Although some have gathered from this last reference that Gauguin was supervising a road gang, it is more likely that he refers to the Department of Public Works, which included Ponts et Chaussées (Bridges and Roads).

56  Danielsson reports that a cyclone in 1906 "leveled the offices to the ground and swept the files out to sea." P. 307 n. 177.

57  PG to DM, [April 1898], *Letters to Monfreid*, XXXIII.

58  Danielsson, p. 216 and n. 172.

59  PG to DM, [April 1898], *Letters to Monfreid*, XXXIII.

60  *Tahitiens*, p. 6.

61 Danielsson, p. 219; and *Tahitiens,* p. 25.

62 Danielsson, p. 219 and n. 177.

63 PG to DM, 15 Aug. 1898, *Letters to Monfreid,* XXXV: "I received also 700 francs from Chaudet. So from now on I am free of all debt here. But I must continue in this modest employment awaiting the moment of deliverance, when I can take up my brushes again, and I shall not do it until I have some money in hand."

64 PG to DM, [July 1898], *Letters to Monfreid,* XXXIV.

65 "Excuse the incoherence of this letter, but I am terribly upset. This heavy blow about Vollard! I can't get it out of my head, and I cannot sleep." PG to DM, 22 Feb. 1899, *Letters to Monfreid,* XXXIX.

66 Gustave Geffroy, "Gauguin," *Le Journal* (20 Nov. 1898), quoted in *Retrospective,* p. 285.

67 Natanson, quoted in *Retrospective,* p. 282.

68 André Fontainas, "Art Moderne," *Mercure de France* (January 1899), p. 235.

69 PG to André Fontainas, [March 1899], Malingue, *Letters,* no. 170.

70 PG to DM, [October 1898], *Letters to Monfreid,* XXXVI.

71 Danielsson, p. 203. It is hard to find the source of this story. In Danielsson's note 163 he refers to the priest as Père Michel Béchu and cites *Tahitiens,* but that entry does not record Michel Béchu as ever having been a priest in Punaauia. *Tahitiens,* p. 39.

72 Renée Hamon, "Sur les Traces de Gauguin en Océanie," *Art moderne* (July 1936), p. 248.

73 Ibid.

74 According to Oscar Nordman, "'When Gauguin left for the Marquesas, my father bought his little house at Punaauia. . . . I was nine years old at the time. . . . In that house the doors and the window panes were painted, the beams were sculpted all over. On the verandah there were three trunks full of oil paintings and drawings, all in good condition. . . . Later, as I rested in my bed, I could not help being terrified by the monstrous 'tikis' (idols) that looked so awful in the moonlight, and I could not sleep. . . . I ordered the crew of the *Pyrenees* to carry the idols as well as the contents of the three boxes onto the reef. In a minute it was all over. I had thrown away a million

into the lagoon.'" Hamon, "Recluse of the Pacific," p. 269.

75 Hamon, "Sur les Traces de Gauguin," p. 249.

76 PG to DM, [April 1899], *Letters to Monfreid,* XLI: "I'm enjoying the seeds you sent me. . . .The iris, the dahlias and the gladioli are doing wonderfully. . . . All this, together with the many flowering Tahitian shrubs, will make a veritable Eden of my house."

77 PG to DM, [August 1896], *Letters to Monfreid,* XX.

78 PG to DM, [January 1897], Malingue, *Letters,* no. 163. Malingue mistranscribed the word as "indigène" (indigenous or native) instead of the actual word, "indigent."

79 Ibid., trans. Guérin, p. 125.

80 See above, n. 56.

81 See Danielsson, p. 225.

82 The 1851 *Tahitian and English Dictionary* (1988 reprint), defines *titoi* as "the intercourse of the sexes; to have intercourse, as the sexes; also to enact the vile sin of Onanism."

83 For an overview, see Bengt Danielsson and Peter O'Reilly, *Gauguin: Journaliste à Tahiti* (Paris: Société des Océanistes, 1966).

84 Georges Dormoy, open letter in *Les Guêpes* (August 1901), p. 3.

85 Hall and Osbourne, *Sunshine and Surf,* p. 75.

86 Ramsden, "Death of Paul Gauguin's Tahitian Mistress," p. 23.

87 See Robert Rey, *Onze Menus de Paul Gauguin* (Geneva: Gérald Cramer, 1950).

88 Pierre Levergos, unpublished memoir, via Yves Martin to Bengt Danielsson; see Danielsson, p. 235.

89 Hamon, "Sur les Traces de Gauguin," p. 248.

90 Ramsden, "Death of Paul Gauguin's Tahitian Mistress," p. 23.

### Chapter 14. Final Retreat

1 See O'Brien, *Mystic Isles,* p. 38: "Papeete is the London and Paris of this part of the peaceful ocean, dispensing the styles and comforts, the inventions and luxuries, of civilization, making the laws and enforcing or compromising them, giving justice and injustice to litigants, dispatching all the concomitants of modernity to littler islands."

2 "With boundless abnegation, Paul

Louis Vernier has settled on a small isolated island [Hiva Oa]—three days distant from Tahiti, where his father lives, and eight days from San Francisco—in a splendid new house built of timber imported from America. . . . [He writes] 'I am weak and yet young, but I trust that God will hear my prayers and take note of my sufferings.' Reading this letter I almost wept, and then had a vague vision of Dante leading Virgil to Hell. At this my soul was uplifted." Danielsson, p. 265.

3   *Tahitiens*, p. 589.

4   Ibid., p. 140.

5   Hamon, "Sur les Traces de Gauguin," p. 247.

6   Nguyen Van Cam, educated in Algeria, was a political exile from Vietnam and worked as a traveling nurse; Vernier, in addition to serving as the island's Protestant minister, also dispensed medical care.

7   PG to Maurice Denis, [June 1899], Malingue, *Letters*, no. 171.

8   Ibid.

9   Ibid.

10   PG to DM, [June or September? 1899], *Letters to Monfreid*, XLIII.

11   Rewald, "The Genius and the Dealer," p. 31.

12   Ambroise Vollard to PG, [ca. 1 Nov. 1899], in Rewald, "The Genius and the Dealer," pp. 63–64.

13   PG to Ambroise Vollard, [January 1900], Malingue, *Letters*, no. 173 (mislabeled "to Emmanuael Bibesco" and misdated).

14   PG to DM, [October 1900], *Letters to Monfreid*, XLVIII.

15   "The large ceramic figure that did not find a purchaser . . . I should like to have it here for the decoration of my garden and to put upon my tomb in Tahiti." Ibid.

16   The price offered for the house was 5,000 francs (PG to DM, [June 1901], *Letters to Monfreid*, LII), but Gauguin eventually settled for 4,500 (Danielsson, p. 45).

17   1902 census in *Annuaire de Tahiti pour 1903*, p. 259.

18   For a description of the house, see Danielsson, p. 253.

19   PG to DM, [November 1901], *Letters to Monfreid*, LV.

20   Guillaume Le Bronnec, "La Vie de Gauguin aux Iles Marquises," *Bulletin de la Société des études océaniennes* (March 1954), quoted in *Retrospective*, p. 312.

21   Lockwood, *Tahitian Transformation*, pp. 25–26.

22   *Tahitiens*, pp. 373–74.

23   Frederick O'Brien, *White Shadows in the South Seas* (Garden City, N.Y.: Century, 1919), p. 93.

24   PG to DM, [November 1901], *Letters to Monfreid*, LV.

25   *Intimate Journals*, p 39.

26   See Frederick O'Reilly, "Les Amours d'un vieux peintre aux Marquises: Comédie en trois actes," *Journal de la Société des océanistes* 18 (December 1962), pp. 113–20.

27   Ibid.

28   Danielsson, p. 256.

29   Guillaume Le Bronnec, "La Vie de Gauguin aux Iles Marquises," quoted in *Retrospective*, p. 310.

30   Hamon, "Sur les Traces de Gauguin," p. 250.

31   Paul Vernier to Jean Rotonchamp, 8 Mar. 1904, quoted in *Retrospective*, p. 337.

32   Reminiscence of Timo to Guillaume Le Bronnec, quoted in *Retrospective*, p. 331.

33   *Annuaire de Tahiti pour 1903*, p. 190.

34   Hamon, "Recluse of the Pacific," p. 273.

35   Ibid., p. 274.

36   Ibid.

37   O'Brien, *White Shadows*, p. 179.

38   PG to administrators, [late 1902], Guérin, p. 291.

39   PG to DM, [June 1901], *Letters to Monfreid*, LII.

40   National Gallery of Art, p. 480.

41   Danielsson, p. 256. O'Brien also encountered a beautiful red-haired woman living in Atuona, Titihuti, during his visit there in 1913. O'Brien, *White Shadows*, pp. 48–49.

42   Jean-Louis Saguet, *The Tahiti Handbook* (Tahiti: Editions Avant et Après, 1995), p. 26.

43   *Noa Noa* (*La Plume* edition).

44   See Philippe Verdier, "Un Manuscrit de Gauguin: L'Esprit moderne et le catholicisme," *Wallraf-Richartz Jahrbuch* 46 (1985), pp. 273–328.

45   PG to André Fontainas, [September 1902], Malingue, *Letters*, no. 176. The manuscript was not published until 1951; see National Gallery of Art, p. 515.

46   *Intimate Journals*, p. 47.

47   Ibid., p. 129.

48   Ibid., p. 128.

49   Ibid., p. 138.

50   Ibid, p. 128.

51 Ibid.

52 Ibid.

53 Ibid., p. 41.

54 Ibid., p. 42.

55 Ibid., p. 1.

56 Ibid., p. 2.

57 Ibid., p. 4.

58 Inventory of Paul Gauguin's estate in *Dossier de la succession* (Papeete: Société des études océaniennes, 1957), pp. 26–43.

59 *Intimate Journals*, p. 4.

60 MG to ES, 11 June 1900, Malingue, *Letters*, p. 249.

61 PG to Charles Morice, July 1901, Malingue, *Letters*, no. 174.

62 PG to DM, [June 1901], *Letters to Monfreid*, LII.

63 PG to DM, [August 1901], *Letters to Monfreid*, LIV.

64 MG to ES, 7 June 1902, Musée Gauguin, Tahiti.

65 PG to DM, [October 1902], *Letters to Monfreid*, LX.

66 DM to PG, 15 Dec. 1902, *Dossier de la succession: Paul Gauguin*, p. 14.

67 *Intimate Journals*, pp. 132–33.

68 Ibid., p. 2.

69 Ibid., p. 45.

70 Ibid.

71 Ibid., p. 121.

72 PG to DM, [February 1903], *Letters to Monfreid*, LXI.

73 PG to André Fontainas, [February 1903], Malingue, *Letters*, no. 177.

74 Bodelsen, "Gauguin, the Collector," p. 604.

75 *Intimate Journals*, p. 52.

76 Ibid., p. 132.

77 Danielsson, p. 288.

78 Paul-Louis Vernier to Jean de Rotonchamp, 8 Mar. 1904, quoted in *Retrospective*, p. 336.

79 Ibid.

80 *Intimate Journals*, p. 2.

81 "Gauguin et Victor Ségalen," *L'Amour de l'art* (December 1938), pp. 384–86.

82 She wrote in the same letter: "My poor Paul has died in particularly sad circumstances. During my last journey to Paris, a year ago, my friend Schuffenecker told me that Paul was ill and unhappy, but I had no idea that the end was so near!" MG to DM, 25 Sept. 1903, in Perruchot, p. 352.

83 Victor Ségalen was particularly unsympathetic to her: "She had married a man with noble and honest feelings, and she says she found a vicious, lying savage. . . . One cannot believe that she has understood Gauguin's painting." Perruchot, p. 354.

84 Christian Brinton, "Fashions in Art," *International Studio* (March 1913), p. ix: "The trinity of modern painting is comprised of Cézanne, Gauguin, and Van Gogh. It is they who have initiated the great and far-reaching movement which bids fair to change the complexion of latter-day pictorial expression."

85 Frederick O'Brien, "Gauguin in the South Seas," *Century Magazine* (June 1920), p. 226.

86 Henry McBride, "Gauguin's Rebirth," *The Dial* (October 1920), p. 399.

87 *Intimate Journals*, p. 130.

88 Ibid., p. 129.

# Acknowledgments

I would like to express my gratitude to the many people and institutions that helped me gather, organize, and interpret archival materials. Throughout my years of work on Gauguin, I have been repeatedly struck by the generosity of those who shared information or debated ideas about this artist. A part of each one of them resides in this book.

Of the Gauguin scholars who talked with me over the years, I would particularly like to acknowledge Caroline Boyle-Turner, Richard Brettell, Bengt Danielsson, Stephen Eisenman, John House, Vojtěch Jirat-Wasiutyński, and Bogmilla Welsh. I have relied on the writings of these and many others whose publications are cited in my footnotes, but one Gauguin scholar must be singled out for a special citation: Merete Bodelsen. Not only is her published scholarship invaluable to anyone working on Gauguin, but her papers, which were deposited in the Copenhagen Royal Library after her death in 1986, are indeed a treasure. Other scholars who broadened my thinking about biography, psychoanalysis, and social history include Peter Burchard, Bradley Collins, Peggy Diggs, Marjorie LaRowe, Suzanna Lessard,Gail Levin, Barbara Lynes, Honor Moore, and Carol Ockman.

Of those who aided my quest for archival materials, I must thank many individuals and their institutions, including, at the top of the list, Palle Ringsted and the librarians at the Copenhagen Royal Library and the incomparable Gilles Artur, curator of the Musée Gauguin, Tahiti. The collection of Gauguin letters, photographs, and other documents in the Musée Gauguin are gradually being published by Victor Merlhès and the Fondation Singer-Polignac. I would also like to thank Leo Jansen and Hans Luyten of the Van Gogh Museum and the staffs of the municipal and departmental archives of Loiret, Martinique, Orléans, Saint-Cloud, Tahiti, and Versailles for their help, as well as those at the Musée départemental du Prieuré, Saint-Germain-en-Laye, and the law firm of G. Basseville and M.-F. Basseville-Bruant, Orléans. Special mention must be made of Mette Gauguin (IV), who generously shared key documents pertaining to her great-grandmother.

Translations throughout this book are mine unless otherwise noted. However, I sought the aid of Nicole Desrosiers in deciphering Mette Gauguin's letters, and I am indebted to her for clarifying much of Mette's idiomatic French.

I owe a debt of gratitude to the many students at Williams College, both graduate and undergraduate, who assisted either as researchers or as sounding boards for ideas tossed around in the classroom. Of these I would like to mention Peter Miller, Tiffany Reed, and Josh Silverman, who were willing to debate gender issues for as long as it took. My deepest thanks go to Lydia Hemphill, whose assistance and friendship were crucial to this effort. I must also gratefully acknowledge the librarians of the Williams College Sawyer and Schow Libraries, particularly Jo-Ann Irace and Allison O'Grady, as well as the librarians at the Clark Art Institute.

Many guided this book toward publication. Among them I would like to thank Gail Ross, Diane Reverend, Terry Karten, Judy Metro, Patricia Fidler, Mary Pasti, Mary Mayer, John Long, Katherine Newbegin, and Aileen Novick, who all made important contributions to its final shape. I would also like to thank once again my friend Cathy Hemming, who has helped me navigate the waters of the publishing world for over twenty years. Two others have been long-term guides: my mother and my partner, Ingrid Montecino. It is fair to say that, in different ways, there would be no book without them.

# Index

Page numbers in *italics* refer to illustrations.

Académie Julian, 77, 106, 136, 156
Adams, Henry, 173, 174, 175
*Agony in the Garden* (Gauguin), *139*, 139–40, 145, 219
Agostini, Jules, 215, 228
*Aita Tamari Vahine Judith te Parari* (Gauguin), 205. See also *Annah the Javanese*
*Among the Mangoes at Martinique* (Gauguin), 87, *88*, 135
Androgyny, 1, 99, 113, 114, 161, 183, 204, 211, 219, 227, 229, 246
*Angelus, The* (Gauguin), *202*
Annah the Javanese, 1–2, 198, 204–5, 221
*Annah the Javanese* (Gauguin), *199*, 205
Anquetin, Louis, 94, 106, 135
*Apple Trees* (Gauguin), 38
*Argent, L'* (Zola), 48
Arles, France: Gauguin and Van Gogh in, 3, 103, 118–19, 121–25
*Arlesienne, L'* (Gauguin), 153
Armory Show, New York (*1913*), 256
Arosa, Achille, 20, 33
Arosa, Gustave / Arosa family, 18–21, 26–34 passim, 50, 51, 162, 217
Arosa, Marguerite, 20, 22, 25, 28–29, 47
Arosa, Victorine, 22
Arosa, Zoé-Françoise, 18, 19, 20
Art dealers and galleries, 76, 91, 92, 94, 96, 111, 148–50, 155, 157, 195, 199, 200, 208, 224, 228–29, 236–37. *See also* Durand-Ruel, Paul; Van Gogh, Theo; and specific dealers and galleries
Artists' models, 2, 28, 42–44, 114, 147, 160, 229; African, 97; local, 103, 104, 105, 150, 174, 180–81, 198, 242–44; sexual possession of, 187–88
Art market, 47–49, 96; America, 200; Denmark, 165; Paris, 96, 145; Scandinavia, 49, 53–56, 79, 164
Art style, 3, 21, 30, 37, 53, 72–73, 77, 136, 209–10, 221; abstract, 108, 115; altered to suit buyers, 94; avant-garde, 68, 71, 97, 139, 173; brushwork, 40, 75; caricatures, 75, 90, 95, 109, 117–18, 144, 187, 232, 237, 240; changes, 137–39, 173, 196; decorative, 64–65, 229; distortion of form, 43–44, 64–65, 75–76, 109, 136, 144; Impressionist, 68, 75, 103, 210; motifs, 171, 178, 243; subject matter, 1, 3, 76, 211; symbolist, 96, 115, 134, 139, 157, 158, 178, 210; use of color, 3, 64, 75, 76, 109, 171, 211–12, 229; working methods, 30, 138
Art world, international, 63; Brittany, 163; Brussels, 148; Copenhagen/Denmark, 49, 58–61, 128, 147–48, 165, 191, 193; Netherlands, 136
Art world, Paris, 67, 77, 94; avant-garde, 87, 89, 90, 91, 147; Gauguin in, 111, 126, 236; Gauguin

rejected by, 98, 201, 206, 207, 210, 212; Gauguin's dominance of, 6, 135–40, 145, 162–63, 189
*At the Café* (Gauguin), 96
Auffray, Jules, 215, 228
Aurier, Albert, 124, 148, 153
*"Avant et après"* (Gauguin), 59, 247, 247–56
Avant-garde artists, 68, 69, 70, 71, 75, 76, 97, 106, 110, 112, 147, 172, 209, 229, 256; erotic imagery of, 99; literary, 156, 157, 166; in Paris, 83, 87, 89, 90, 91

Balzac, Honoré de, 151, 183
Barbizon school, 20, 29, 34, 162
Bernard, Emile: friendship with Gauguin, 196, 203, 209–10, 218, 236; as patron/disciple of Gauguin, 106–12, 126, 148, 153; Van Gogh and, 92, 93, 94, 101, 115; works and exhibitions, 94, 99, 108, 110, 114, 135, 136
Bernard, Madeleine, 113–14, *114*
Bertaux, Emile, 32, 45, 50, 52, 55, 92
Bertin, Paul, 26, 28, 30, 40, 66
Bizet, Germaine, 160
Blanche, Jacques-Emile, 66
Boch, Eugène, 112, 113, 127, 131
Boudin, Eugène, 51
Bouillot, Jules, 31, 65
Bourdon, André, 31, 40
Boussod and Valadon (gallery), 91, 92, 94, 155, 163, 193, 210
Boxing, 72
Bracquemond, Félix, 70, 76
Bracquemond, Marie, 41, 70, 72
Brandès, Edvard, 57–58, 59, 193, 201, 250–51
Brandès, Georg, 49, 57, 58, 59, 162
Brandès, Ingeborg. *See* Thaulow, Ingeborg
Brittany. *See* Le Pouldu; Pont-Aven
Brown, John Lewis, 44

Caillebotte, Gustave, 6, 44, 46, 47, 131
Caldecott, Randolph, 75
Calzado, Adolphe, 22, 27, 52
Cardella, François, 173, 212, 232
Cassatt, Mary, 36, 40, 41, 45, 47, 92–93, 128, 147, 200
Catholic church, 218, 219, 221, 239, 241, 250, 252, 254
Ceramics. *See* Pottery
Cézanne, Paul, 37, 46, 52, 59, 101, 201, 208, 229, 237, 248, 256
Chamaillard, Ernest de, 106, 111
Chaplet, Ernst, 70, 76, 77, 91, 208, 232
Charlier, Edouard, 222, 230–31, 232
Charlopin, Charles, 148, 149–50, 153–155, 162
Chassé, Charles, 150, 160

311

Chaudet, Georges, 229, 236–37
Chazal, Aline, 7, 8, 9
Chazal, André, 6, 7, 14, 96–97
Chazal, Antoine, 6, 97
Chazal, Charles Camille, 6
Chazal, Ernest, 7, 14–15
Cochons, Les (Gauguin), 120
Colin, Paul-Emile, 150–51
Collin, Raphael, 198
Contes barbares (Primitive Tales; Gauguin), 243, 246, 246
Copenhagen, Denmark: Gauguin in, 56–62, 77, 164–67, 198
Cormon studios, 71, 77, 92, 93, 101, 106
Corot, Jean-Baptiste, 20, 22, 35
Costume and dress, 1, 10, 13, 24, 25, 27, 28, 76, 90, 97, 197, 198, 200, 202; in works, 243–44
Cottu, Henri, 80, 82
Coulon, Germain, 222, 230, 234
Cross-dressing, 183

Danielsson, Bengt, 229–30, 243
Darling, Charles W., 215
Dauprat, Albert, 135
Decorative arts, 59, 97, 115, 119, 131, 143, 147
Degas, Edgar, 40–49, 92–96, 128, 132, 140, 155, 157, 162, 200; dealers and exhibitions, 94, 95, 147; Gauguin and, 36–37, 66, 70, 71, 200; as influence on Gauguin, 95–96, 133; as patron of Gauguin, 195, 207, 208, 210; personal life, 90, 96
De Haan, Jacob Meyer, 127, 142, 157, 246; as patron/disciple of Gauguin, 137–39, 142–46, 150–52, 154, 155, 201, 224; Portrait of Theo Van Gogh, 93
Delacroix, Eugène, 6, 20
Delavallée, Henri, 70, 72
Denis, Maurice, 236
Dillies and Company, 52, 56, 60, 65, 85
Du Puigaudeau, Ferdinand, 71, 73, 77–79, 93
Durand-Ruel, Paul, 44, 47, 48, 50, 195; as dealer for Gauguin, 52, 55, 76, 91, 197, 199–200, 229

Echenique, Don José Rufino, 9, 10, 11, 14
"Eglise catholique et l'esprit moderne, L'" (Gauguin), 218
Ericson, Ida, 205, 206
Estrup, Jacob B. S., and family, 23, 25, 28, 41, 57
Eve. See Themes in art
Eve (Gauguin), 132, 133–35, 140, 141
Exhibitions, 92, 94, 106, 145; auction following Gauguin's death, 230, 255; Brussels, 2–3, 198; Copenhagen (1893), 192–93, 194, 196; Denmark, 60, 147; Durand-Ruel gallery, 91, 197, 199–200; Grande Brouillon restaurant, Paris, 94, 107, 131; Impressionist, 37–47, 61, 67–70, 76, 92, 96; Indépendants (1890), 148, 152, 224; Les XX, 131, 148, 152, 162, 164; memorial, 237, 255, 256; Oslo, 53–54, 56; Paris, 2–3, 227–29; Paris auctions, 162–63, 195, 202, 207, 208; Paris Salon, 29–30, 33; Sweden, 225; Union Centrale, 91, 98; Vollard gallery, 225, 236; Volpini, 132, 135–37, 140, 145, 152, 176, 236
Exotic Eve (Gauguin), 158
Exposition Universelle (1889), 139, 141, 145, 147, 150, 176

Fatata te Miti (By the Sea) (Gauguin), 171, 171
Favre, Charles ("le Marsouin"), 28, 52, 56, 84
Fayet, Gustave, 253, 255

Fencing, 1, 16, 72, 121, 123
Fénéon, Félix, 94, 135
Filiger, Charles, 162, 203; as disciple of Gauguin, 150, 151, 152, 155, 161, 201
Flowers, Still Life (Gauguin), 45, 46
Folk art, 20, 75, 76, 90
Folklore, 83, 86–87, 177, 182–83
Fontainas, André, 229, 247, 250, 255
Fouignet, Marie, 22, 26
Fouignet, Pauline, 22
Four Breton Women (Gauguin), 74, 75–76
French colonies, 145, 147, 150, 157, 172, 212, 218, 219, 235, 238. See also specific islands by name
Freud, Sigmund, vii–viii
Frie Udstilling (art group), 193

Galerie Georges Petit (Paris), 52, 76
Gauguin, Aline (Gauguin's daughter by Mette), 45, 57, 66, 158–59, 162, 164, 165, 224–25
Gauguin, Aline (née Chazal, Gauguin's mother), 8, 10–14, 18, 22, 31
Gauguin, Clovis (Gauguin's father), 9, 11, 12, 232
Gauguin, Clovis (Gauguin's son by Mette), 37, 53, 57, 67, 77, 78, 250; lives with Gauguin, 62, 66–68
Gauguin, Emil (Gauguin's son by Mette), 27, 28, 45, 55, 57, 61, 62, 66, 109, 129, 162, 164, 165, 193; as artist's subject, 28, 31, 37, 40
Gauguin, Emile (Gauguin's son by Pahura), 213, 214, 252
Gauguin, Isidore, 11–12, 64, 79, 100, 194
Gauguin, Jean-René, 41, 44, 57, 57, 146, 161, 251
Gauguin, Mette (née Gad), 23, 39, 44, 53, 54, 57, 63, 70, 129–30, 130, 161, 250–51; as artist's subject, 28, 31, 38–39, 45, 53; correspondence, 259–70; as dealer for Gauguin, 165, 166, 191–92, 196, 201; death of Gauguin and, 255; emotional abuse of, 8, 63–64, 65, 67, 100, 102, 121, 210; family life in Paris, 22–27, 61–62; financial circumstances, 32, 51–52, 53, 56, 62, 65, 78–79, 84–85, 100, 129, 130, 161–62, 191, 251; friends in intellectual circles, 27–28, 37, 41, 49, 57, 128, 162; personality, 23–25; physical abuse of, 62, 64, 121, 141, 164, 182; reconciliation hopes, 100, 129–31, 166, 190–92; separation from Gauguin, 56, 61–62, 64, 65, 73, 210; supports children, 7, 165–66, 193, 210
Gauguin, Paul, 2, 5–6, 19, 20, 31, 38, 115, 157, 165; as art collector/trader, 33, 34, 40, 44–45, 50, 52, 55, 56, 96, 101, 128, 148; association with the Van Goghs, 92, 94, 96, 98, 100–107, 111–13, 118–28, 135, 142, 147, 149, 203; attitude toward wives and women, 74, 75, 76, 114, 250, 251, 252, 256–57; begs for money, 123, 146, 167, 188, 221–22, 228; biography of, 25, 126; childhood, 9–14, 18; children by, 1, 27, 31, 37, 41, 44, 53, 160, 161, 213, 219, 240, 242, 252, 256; as dealer and publicist for himself, 155, 159, 200; death, 223, 254; death of Van Gogh and, 153; disciples, 93, 97, 98, 99, 106–11, 113, 114, 117, 137–39, 142–44, 150–51, 156, 157, 169, 174, 192, 198, 202, 203, 206, 208, 210; eroticism in life and art, 1–2, 20–21, 75, 98, 99, 178, 190, 197–98, 208, 211, 219, 225, 240–41, 244–46, 254, 257; financial circumstances, 30–31, 32, 48, 51–52, 54–56, 60, 61, 65, 73, 81, 84–86, 100–102, 119, 127, 145–47, 157, 188–89, 199–200, 212, 225; as full-time painter, 30, 37, 49, 52, 147, 148, 237; government subsidies of, 147, 150, 163, 188, 228; health, 84–85, 180, 188, 222–24, 228, 231, 235–36, 253–54; influence of,

72–73; influences on, 89–90, 95–96, 103–4, 133; literary circles and, 156, 159, 160–61; marriage problems, 51–52, 54–56, 61–62, 68, 70–71, 159, 160; as merchant seaman and sailor, 14–18, 21, 80; patrons of, 53, 127–28, 142, 145–47, 153, 173, 210; personal philosophy, 226, 241, 248–49; political involvement, 52, 54, 55, 80, 218, 228, 232, 236, 239, 247; publishes newspapers, 232–34; reconciliation hopes, 79, 83–84, 123, 129–30, 166, 190–92; reputation as artist, 230, 236, 237, 254; as self-taught artist, 29–30, 31, 97, 117, 198; as stockbroker/agent, 6, 18–22, 28, 30–32, 40, 44–45, 48–50, 52, 54, 60, 96, 113; theory of art, 25, 59–60, 67–68, 72, 73, 118, 135, 209, 215, 252, 257; treatment of family, 14, 26, 61, 62, 78–79, 82, 91, 97, 100, 102–3, 105, 164, 194–95, 198–99, 200, 201, 210, 250–52, 256, 257. See also specific locales
—Personality, 1, 5–9, 25, 33, 72, 94, 137, 138, 156, 202–3, 228; abusive behavior toward men and women, 1, 62, 105, 121–23, 166; aggression and belligerence, 20–21, 56, 60, 121, 135; amoral behavior, 119, 190, 231; arrogance, 190, 206, 231; artistic identity, 6, 115–16; competitiveness, 21, 29–30, 33, 71, 98, 105; cruelty/animosity, 5, 49, 61–62, 63, 97–98; disregard for family and social obligations, 14, 26, 62; doubts of his manhood, 20–21, 63, 65, 161; feelings of guilt, 84–85, 102, 121, 166, 194–95; flamboyance, 6, 32, 63, 65, 66, 96, 118–19, 152–53, 200; identity as a teacher, 198; manipulation of useful people, 3, 22, 50, 65, 94, 128, 161, 172–73, 195, 222, 231, 237; as martyr, 1, 126, 128, 149, 190, 221; need for enemies and revenge, 62, 64, 66–67, 231–34, 238, 250, 252, 254; self-image and personas, 3, 5–6, 21, 38, 63, 103, 141, 190, 225; social identity, 24, 26, 63, 65, 67, 73, 98, 99; theatricality, 139, 151, 152, 198, 204, 206, 215, 227; violent aspects, 62–65, 68, 141, 166, 183, 211. See also Homoeroticism
—Physical appearance, 1, 22, 65, 66, 71, 117, 123, 126, 136–37, 151, 165, 202–3; affected by syphilis, 235–36; in Tahiti, 173–74, 215
—Sexual life, 16, 140–41, 151, 203, 240, 257; attraction to children and adolescents, 2, 8, 99, 170, 181, 183, 205–6, 211, 257; early childhood, 13, 14; fantasies, 1, 20–21, 26–27, 170, 181–83, 229, 254; with prostitutes, 15, 24; as sailor, 15–16, 20, 77; sexuality, 204; on Tahiti, 169–70, 171–72, 178–83, 189
—Works (except literary), 61; abstract, 227; Arles paintings, 120, 128; Brittany paintings, 187, 243; catalogue raisonné, 148; criticism and reviews of, 38, 40, 43–44, 47, 55, 68, 197, 209–10, 229; destruction of, 230–31; drawings, 20, 75, 208, 237; erotic and sexual character, 2, 20–21, 44, 75, 87, 88, 98–99, 103, 104, 114, 152–53, 181; figure studies, 86, 237; landscape painting/sketching, 20, 28, 29, 31, 40, 41, 74, 103, 139; Marquesan paintings, 243; Martinique paintings, 86–89, 93–95, 97, 101, 103, 128, 135, 163; mediums for, 31–32, 49, 53, 133, 202; nude boys as subjects, 103–5, 107, 137, 138, 193; nude women and girls as subjects, 140–41, 159, 181, 193, 204, 205, 217; nudes (general), 42–44, 75, 96, 171, 257; phallic imagery, 65, 136, 152; Pont-Aven paintings, 103, 111, 143; portraits (general), 25, 37–38, 45, 49, 53, 58, 72, 77, 82, 98, 128, 173, 187–88, 202, 221; portraits of men, 135, 136, 137, 143–44, 159, 173; sale of, 44, 49, 53, 54, 55, 58, 70, 91, 94, 127, 147, 148, 155, 162–63, 166, 193–94, 208, 223–24; self-portraits, 107, 115–17, 126–27, 139–45, 202, 219, 226; sketches, 25, 58, 86; still lifes, 41, 42,

44, 45, 49, 53, 237; subjects (general), 28, 41–42, 74, 75, 86, 87, 88, 95, 103, 113–14, 120; symbolism in, 243; Tahiti paintings, 167, 170, 171, 177, 178, 187, 189, 190, 192–93, 195, 200, 202, 210, 211, 217, 231, 243; zincographic drawings, 128, 152. See also Artists' models; Art style; Exhibitions; "PGo"; Pottery; Sculpture and three-dimensional creations; Themes in art; and specific works by title
—Writings, 7–8, 171, 247–48, 255, 257; art theory, 67–68; erotic elements in, 2, 98–99; in Les Guêpes, 233–34, 235; memoirs, 3, 10, 13, 59, 61–62, 141, 195, 198, 240, 247, 247–56; religious, 218; and social issues, 7, 59; symbolist, 156, 157; about Tahiti, 178. See also Press; and specific works by title
Gauguin, Paul Rollon (Pola), 53, 57, 62, 251
Gender roles/reversal, 24, 44, 88, 113, 208
Gérard, Judith, 205
Gide, André, 136, 137
Goupil, Auguste, 173, 181, 212, 215, 219–21, 220, 232
Goupil, Vaïte (Jeanne), 173, 220, 220–21
Goupil Galleries, 91, 96, 145, 148
Granchi-Taylor, Achille, 72, 97
Grande Brouillon restaurant exhibition, Paris, 94, 107, 131
Green Christ, The (Gauguin), 139
Guenn, a Wave on the Breton Coast (Howard), 110
Guêpes, Les (newspaper), 233–34, 235
Guidebooks and travelogues, 110, 172, 173, 176, 179
Guillaumin, Armand, 35, 37, 40, 45, 47, 68, 92, 93, 95, 140; exhibition and sale of works, 50, 52, 94, 131

Hartrick, Archibald, 71, 74–75, 93
Hearn, Lafcadio, 83, 87–88, 89
Heegaard, Marie, 22–26, 28, 30, 49, 251
Henry, Marie, 137, 142, 143, 150, 152, 154, 155, 201, 203
Homoeroticism, 2, 69–70, 74, 109, 113, 114, 128, 135, 160, 161. See also Van Gogh, Vincent
Homosexuality, 2, 24, 65, 114, 207, 243, 257; in literature, 151–52; in Tahiti, 183–85
Horst, Pauline (Phylle; née Gad), 251. See also Thaulow, Pauline
Howard, Blanche Willis: Guenn, a Wave on the Breton Coast, 110
Huet, Juliette, 1, 159–61, 164, 180, 204
Hugo, Victor, 115; Les Misérables, 115
Huysmans, Joris-Karl, 43–44, 95

Impressionism, 33, 36, 44, 48, 51, 108, 131, 236; classic, 46
Impressionists, 40; Gauguin rejected by, 63, 65–66, 70, 93, 98; Gauguin's relationship with, 38, 44, 47, 51, 58–59, 63, 83, 112, 157, 162, 200; in Scandinavia, 49, 53–54, 56
Incest, 8
Incoherents, the, 75
Indépendants, Société de, 61, 68, 70, 75, 131, 148, 224
International Exposition (Paris, 1900), 236
In the Waves (Gauguin), 133, 133
Intimate Journals (Gauguin). See Noa Noa
Isaacson, J. J., 136

Jade, Marie, 205–6, 221
Japanese art, 103–4, 106, 107
Jarry, Alfred, 204
Jénot, Lieutenant, 172, 173, 174, 183, 185, 187, 188, 212

Jongkind, Johann, 20, 44
*Jug in the Form of a Head, Self-Portrait* (Gauguin), 126–27, *127*

Kroyer, S. Peder, 29, 58, 60

La Farge, John, 174, *175*
*Landscape at Paia* (Gauguin), *184*
*Landscape with Poplars* (Gauguin), *32*
Laval, Charles, 71, 76, 77, 84, 92, 153; as dealer/patron of Gauguin, 145, 155, 224; as disciple of Gauguin, 93, 98, 102, 103, 104, 106, 109, 111, 112, 119, 126, 135; homoerotic feelings for Gauguin, 114, 135; in Martinique and Panama with Gauguin, 78, 80–86, 93; in Pont-Aven with Gauguin, 130, 135, 136; works and exhibitions, 82, 83, 84, 135
Laval, Nino, 84, 86, 91, 102, 103, 106, 224
Leclerq, Julien, 198, 199, 201, 206, 225
Leda and the swan, 98, *152*
Lemasson, Henry, 215, 216, 228
Le Pouldu, Brittany, 136, 137, 138, 142–43, 146, 147, 150–51, 153, 154, 159, 201, 203, 215
Lesbianism, 207
Les XX (later La Libre esthétique; art group), 76, 112, 131, 148, 152, 155, 162, 164, 198
*Letter to Emile Schuffenecker with Sketch of Boys Wrestling* (Gauguin), *105*
*Little Dreamer, The* (Gauguin), 45, *47*
*Loss of Virginity* (Gauguin), 159, *160*, 161, 208, 219
Loti, Pierre (Julien Viaud), 14, 173, 197, 213; *The Marriage of Loti*, 145, 157, 174, 187
"Loves of an Old Painter" (Nguyen Van Cam), 240

Madagascar, 79, 81, 150, 153, 157
*Madame Mette Gauguin in Evening Dress* (Gauguin), *53, 54*
Mallarmé, Stéphane, 137, 156, 157, 159, 163, 173, 195, 207, 210, 241
*Manao Tupapau (Spirit of the Dead Watching)* (Gauguin), 181, *182*, 183, 193, 217, 246
Manet, Edouard, 40, 49, 51, 147, 162, 180–81; *Olympia*, 159, 181, 219; *Vue de Holland*, 44
*Man with the Ax, The* (Gauguin), *184*
Marau, queen of Tahiti, 173, 174–75, *175*
*Market Gardens of Vaugirard, The* (Gauguin), *38, 39*
*Marquesan Man in a Red Cape* (Gauguin), 243, 244, *246*
Marquesas, 7, 94, 212, 235, 238–54
Marriage, 5; art in competition with, 33; Gauguin's views of, 3, 19–20, 22–23, 59, 62, 102
*Marriage of Loti, The* (Loti), 145, 157, 174, 187
Martin, Monseigneur Joseph, 239–41, 247, 250
Martinique, 79, 83–90, 134, 135; black culture on, 86–87; Gauguin in, 73, 83–90, 91, 93, 100, 147, 156, 158, 167
Mauclair, Camille, 210, 229
Maufra, Maxime, 151
Maugham, Somerset, 177, 214, 256
Maus, Octave, 131, 155
Mauve, Anton, 97, 131
McBride, Henry, 256
Melbye, Anton, 35
Melbye, Fritz, 34–35
*Mercure de France* (journal), 215, 229, 247, 255
*Mette Gad Gauguin* (Gauguin), *23*
Mirbeau, Octave, 156, 157–58, 160–61, 162, 172, 173, 197, 207, 210

*Misérables, Les* (Hugo), 115
Misogyny, 24, 95, 161, 207
Models. *See* Artists' models
Modern art, 159, 190, 193, 200, 207, 256, 257
Molard, Judith, 221
Molard, William, 204, 205, 221, 225
Moltke, Countess Magda, 41, 49, 58, 61
Moltke, Count Frederick, 49, 58
Monet, Claude, 46–47, 49, 51, 76, 92–94, 131, 157, 200, 207
Monfreid, Daniel de, 160, 199, 250–51; as dealer/patron for Gauguin, 163, 192, 210, 229; as disciple of Gauguin, 156, 174, 188–89, 203, 206; as friend of Gauguin, 65, 156, 161, 190, 196, 200, 203, 221, 255; exhibitions, 135
*Moon and Sixpence, The* (Maugham), 177, 256
Moret, Henry, 106, 111
Morice, Charles, 126, 156, 159, 162, 163, 192, 200, 205, 255; as collaborator on *Noa Noa*, 179; as dealer/patron of Gauguin, 195, 210, 221
Morisot, Berthe, 37, 41, 47, 131, 157
Mucha, Alphonse, 204
Murer, Eugène, 52, 53, 55

Nabis, 106, 156, 162, 200, 208, 229
Natanson, Thadée, 185, 187, 229
*Négresses causant* (Gauguin), *135*
Neo-Impressionism, 90, 94, 106; Gauguin's opposition to, 67–68, 76–77, 98, 107–8, 121, 132
Néos. *See* Neo-Impressionism
*Nevermore* (Gauguin), 217
Newspapers. *See* Press; *and specific newspapers by name*
Nguyen Van Cam, 236, 240, 242; "Loves of an Old Painter," 240
*Noa Noa* (Gauguin): autobiographical travelogue, 98–99, 168, 172, 179–84, 186–88, 190, 213–14, 219; illustrations, 202; as narrative context for Tahiti paintings, 217; publication, 179, 185, 225, 232, 247, 256
*Noa Noa (Fragrance)* (Gauguin), *191*
*Nude Breton Boy* (Gauguin), *138*, 179

O'Brien, Frederick, 177, 180, 216, 242, 256
O'Conor, Roderic, 203–4
Oller y Cestero, Francisco, 35
*Olympia* (Manet), 159, 181, 219
*Oviri*, 208, *209*

Pahura (Pau'ura) a Tai, 2, 213–14, 219, 221, 231–32, 252
Panama, 77, 79–83, 93, 100, 167, 169; Canal, 77, 78, 80
Papeete, Tahiti, 212, 216–17, 218, 238
Paris: artistic community, 25, 28–29, 31, 63; financial community, 28; Gauguin in, 25, 46, 63, 76, 91, 126, 155, 159, 190–200; intellectual community, 20; Scandinavian community, 28, 29, 34–35, 36, 49, 162; South American community, 5, 8, 14, 20, 22, 28, 29, 34, 36
Paris Salon, 29, 30, 37, 47, 83, 84, 94, 157
*Peregrinations of a Pariah* (Tristan), 6, 9
"PGo" (Gauguin's signature logo), 65, 76, 91, 97–99, 134, 136, 232
Philipsen, Theodor, 29, 165, 193
Pissarro, Camille, 20, 34–36, *38*, 44, 48, 55, 95, 128, 155, 157, 200, 237; exhibitions and reviews, 40, 44, 47, 51, 55, 70, 76, 92, 147, 149; Gauguin and, 37, 45–46, 47, 50–53, 56, 60, 64, 68, 71, 77,

93, 207; Gauguin studies and paints with, 37–38, 40–41, 51, 70; influences on, 89–90; *Le Scieur de bois*, 50; paintings bought by Gauguin, 34, 52, 128; *Portrait of Gauguin*, *38*; sale of works, 50, 94; style, 49, 67, 68, 75, 92, 95, 128, 132

**Pissarro, Julie (née Vellay)**, 35–36, 55

**Pissarro, Lucien**, 35, 36, 50–51, 67, 93

**Pointillism**, 67, 152

**Pont-Aven, Brittany**, 70–77, 83, 84, 90, 99, 103, 106, 107, 108, 114, 117, 128, 130, 133, 135, 139, 140, 143, 151, 203, 215

**Pornography**, 2, 20, 104, 212, 240–41, 250

**Portier, Alphonse (art dealer)**, 76, 91, 92

*Portrait Bust of Mette Gauguin* **(Gauguin)**, 38–40, *39*

*Portrait of a Young Woman, Vaïte (Jeanne) Goupil* **(Gauguin)**, 222

*Portrait of Clovis* **(Gauguin)**, *67*

*Portrait of Flora Tristan* **(Lavre)**, *7*

*Portrait of Gauguin* **(Pissarro)**, *38*

*Portrait of Ingel Fallstedt* **(Gauguin)**, *29*

*Portrait of Madeleine Bernard* **(Gauguin)**, *114*

*Portrait of Meyer de Haan* **(Gauguin)**, *143*, 143–44

*Portrait of Pissarro* **(Gauguin)**, *38*

*Portrait of Stéphane Mallarmé* **(Gauguin)**, *159*

*Portrait of the Artist's Mother* **(Gauguin)**, *8*, 158

*Portrait of Theo Van Gogh* **(de Haan)**, *93*

*Portrait of Vincent Van Gogh Painting Sunflowers* **(Gauguin)**, *124*

*Portrait of William Molard* **(Gauguin)**, *204*

**Pottery**, 70, 76, 77, 90, 193, 208–9; exhibitions, 91, 149; portrait vases, 98, 126–27, 128, 205. *See also* Sculpture and three-dimensional creations

*Pour faire une bouquet* **(Gauguin)**, *42*

**Press**, 158, 195, 247; articles about Gauguin, 145, 156–62, 165, 166, 172, 173, 198, 200–201, 208–10, 255; articles by Gauguin, 135, 145, 153

**Primitivism**, 134

*Project for a Plate Decoration — Leda* **(Gauguin)**, *129*

**Prostitution and prostitutes**, 7, 99, 113, 119, 128, 179, 240; in Impressionist art, 44; marriage viewed as instance of, 3

**Protestant church**, 218, 219, 232, 235

*Public Garden with Couple and Blue Fir Tree: Poet's Garden III* **(Gauguin)**, *115*

*"Racontars d'un rapin" (Tales of a Dabbler)* **(Gauguin)**, 247

**Ramsden, Eric**, 214

**Redon, Odilon**, 68, 90, 131, 155, 255

**Religion**, 61, 108–10, 134. *See also* Catholic church; Protestant church

**Renoir, Pierre**, 36, 37, 44, 46, 51, 200

**Rochefoucauld, Comte de la**, 162

**Rotonchamp, Jean de**, 241, 254, 255

**Rouen, France**, 53–54, 77

**Roumi, Valérie**, 42, *42*

**Rousseau, Henri ("Douanier")**, 75, 90, 252

**Roy, Louis**, 135, 152

**Russell, John**, 101, 149

**Salmon, Joanna Marau**. *See* Marau

**Salon**. *See* Paris Salon

**Sanjurjo, José (Pepito)**, 22, 28

**Schuffenecker, Emile**, 41, 45, 47, 51, 98, 128, 162, 201, 210, 255; as agent for Gauguin, 85–86, 111, 155; art career and works, 20, 40, 54–55, 68, 69, 92, 132, 135, 146; founds Indépendants, 61,

131–32; friendship with Gauguin, 20, 28, 68–69, 77, 93–94, 191, 195–96, 203, 221; homoerotic feelings for Gauguin, 69–70, 161; organizes Volpini exhibition, 131–33; as patron/supporter of Gauguin, 68–69, 84, 85–86, 100–101, 111, 126, 145–47, 154, 156, 163, 174; personal life, 59, 65, 70

**Schuffenecker, Jeanne**, 98, 205, 206, 221

**Schuffenecker, Louise**, 41, 70, 98, 128, 161

*Scieur de bois, Le* **(Pissarro)**, 50

**Sculpture and three-dimensional creations**, 2, 20, 31–32, 37, 42, 70, 76, 140–41, 202; exhibitions, 38–40, 149; nudes, 230, 240; Tahiti, 185, 188, 189; wood carvings/woodcuts, 153–54, *191*, 198, 202, 224, 237. *See also* Pottery

**Séguin, Armand**, 203, 206

*Self-Portrait (1885;* **Gauguin)**, *58*

*Self-Portrait (1889;* **Gauguin)**, *143*

*Self-Portrait (1893–94;* **Gauguin)**, *204*

*Self-Portrait (1903;* **Gauguin)**, *253*

*Self-Portrait* **(Schuffenecker)**, *69*

*Self-Portrait* **(Van Gogh)**, *117*

*Self-Portrait: "Les Misérables"* **(Gauguin)**, *116*, 126, 155

*Self-Portrait near Golgotha* **(Gauguin)**, 221, *223*

**Sérusier, Paul**, 106, 111, 126, 136, 150, 151, 155, 156, 200, 203

**Seurat, Georges**, 67–69, 70, 75, 76, 92, 98, 131, 132

**Signac, Paul**, 68, 92, 93, 131, 255

*Singer, The (or Portrait of Valérie Roumi)* **(Gauguin)**, 42, *42*

*Skaters in Fredriksburg Park* **(Gauguin)**, *60*

*Sketches After Degas's Nude Bathers, Album Briant* **(Gauguin)**, *95*

*Sleeping Child* **(Gauguin)**, *54*

**Society of the Friends of Art**, 58, 60, 147

*Sorrow* **(Van Gogh)**, 120, *121*, 141

*Sourir, Le: Journal sérieux (later Le Sourir: Journal méchant;* **Gauguin)**, 230, 232–33, *233*, 237

*Soyez amoureuses vous serez heureuses* **(Gauguin)**, *140*, 140–41, 144, 145, 149, 181, 208

*Soyez mystérieuses* **(Gauguin)**, 153–54, *154*

*Still Life with Profile of Laval* **(Gauguin)**, *77*

**Stock market crash (1882)**, 48–49, 66, 78

**Strindberg, August**, 207–8, 256

*Sur une chaise* **(Gauguin)**, *42*

**Swaton, Captain**, 172, 187

**Swordsmanship**, 1, 16, 72, 121, 123

**Symbolism**, 91, 106–9, 120, 157, 208, 219, 243; literary, 163, 195; pictorial, 107

**Symbolist group, Paris**, 217

**Synthetist school**, 196

**Syphilis**, 3, 188, 211, 223, 254

**Taboga island**, 78, 81

**Taboos, sexual**, 2, 134, 179, 207, 257

**Tahiti**, 94, 145, 163–64; as French colony, 168, 169, 218; Gauguin as resident (*1895–1901*), 211–34; Gauguin as tourist (*1891–1893*), 167, 168–89; Gauguin's employment in Papeete, 231, 236; Gauguin's visits to, 73, 94, 156, 157, 158, 208, 210; government and culture, 3, 168–69, 174, 175, 176, 190, 218; religious politics, 218, 226, 228, 232; sexual mores and practices, 178–82, 183, 185–86, 187; socially tolerant climate of, 3, 201, 208, 211–13; society, 212, 214, 219, 231

*Tahitian Love* **(Gauguin)**, 181

**Tapestries**, 52, 229

**Tardieu, Eugène**, 209, 210

**Tavana, Haamoura**, 176, 177, 180

315

Tavana, Tetuanui, 176, 177, 185, 188
*Te Arii Vahine* (The Noble Woman; Gauguin), 217
Tehamana (also Tehura), 2, 179–82, 185, 188, 204, 205, 213, 214, 221
*Te Tamari no Atua (The Son of God)* (Gauguin), 216, 217, 219, 227
Thaulow, Frits, 8, 27, 27–28, 29, 31, 41, 51, 53, 61, 80, 131
Thaulow, Hermann, 41, 65, 251
Thaulow, Ingeborg (née Gad; later Brandès), 8, 27, 27, 28, 31, 41, 51, 57, 65, 251
Thaulow, Nina, 27
Thaulow, Pauline (Phylle; née Gad; later Horst), 41, 251
Themes in art, 139, 143; Eve and the Fall, 1, 87, 134–35, 161; female nude as Eve, 133–35, 158–59, 181, 183, 187, 217, 225; life and death, 227; martyrdom, 139; primitivism, 247; rape/submission and sex/pain, 1, 134, 140–41, 229; religion, 108–10, 134, 139–40, 217–19, 257; rural, 118, 139; snake as phallic symbol, 1, 65, 87–88, 98, 134, 135, 141, 144, 181; sun, 91; violence, 64, 65, 141, 144, 145, 181, 212, 230
Tioka, 242, 254
Titi, 2, 179, 180, 188
Tit-Oil (pseudonym), 232
Tohotaua, 243, 245, 246
Tonkin, 145, 147, 148, 150
Toulouse-Lautrec, Henri, 94, 99, 107, 131
Tourism, 71–72, 103, 106, 111, 151; in Brittany, 139; destinations for French artists, 211; in Tahiti, 168, 173, 175, 177–78, 213, 214, 233, 238
Tristan, Flora (Célestine), 5, 6–7, 7, 10, 19, 20, 28, 97, 158, 232; *Peregrinations of a Pariah*, 6, 9
Tristan Moscoso family, 5, 6, 9, 10, 11, 31
*Two Tahitian Women* (Gauguin), 230

Union Centrale exhibition, 91, 98
Uribe, Juan, 22, 27, 31, 78, 80, 82
Uribe, Marie (née Gauguin), 8, 9, 10, 12, 18, 22, 25–27, 31, 66, 128, 193

Vaeoho (Marie-Rose), 2, 240, 242
*Vahine no te Tiare (Tahitian Woman with a Flower)* (Gauguin), 186, 187–88
*Vahine no te Vi (Woman of the Mango)* (Gauguin), 170, 171, 246
Van Gogh, Theo, 93, 112, 136, 140; as dealer for Gauguin, 91–92, 94–97, 100, 101–2, 111, 120, 127, 139, 142, 145, 148, 154–55, 162, 224; as dealer for Impressionists and radical artists, 94–95, 112; death, 163, 195, 224, 237; mental breakdown, 155, 163
Van Gogh, Vincent, 71, 92, 124, 149, 188, 237; as art dealer, 92, 96, 101, 113, 224; articles about, 148–49, 153; circle of artist-friends, 92–93, 113, 131; death, 153, 154, 155; dream of a community of artists, 101, 111, 153; exhibitions, 92, 94, 131, 148, 193, 256; feelings for Gauguin, 98, 99, 101, 102, 113–17, 119, 123–24, 128, 135, 149, 153, 155 ; Gauguin's family and, 119–20, 129, 130, 146, 149; Gauguin's personality and, 116–18, 123–24, 137; Gauguin's work and, 92–93, 97, 101, 107, 111, 118–19, 128, 148, 153; organizes Grande Brouillon exhibition, 107; as patron of Gauguin, 145, 224; personal life, 97, 112; personality and appearance, 92, 97; portraits and self-portraits, 107, 113, 115, 117, 117; psychotic breakdown, 121–23, 148, 149, 153; as self-taught artist, 92, 97; *Sorrow*, 120,

121, 141; style and motifs, 68, 92, 118, 119, 248; theories of art, 97, 148. *See also* Arles
Van Gogh-Bonger, Jo, 192, 201
Varney, Benjamin Franklin, 238, 242
*Vases et l'eventail, Les* (Gauguin), 58
Vernier, Frédéric, 235
Vernier, Paul, 235, 236, 239, 241, 242, 243, 248, 253–54
Vignon, Victor, 47
Violence. *See* Gauguin, Mette; Themes in art
*Vision After the Sermon, The* (Gauguin), 108, 109, 110, 126, 139
*Voiliers, Les* (Gauguin), 53
Vollard, Ambroise, 156, 198, 224, 255; as dealer for Gauguin, 208, 229, 236–37, 239, 246, 250
Volpini exhibition (1889), 132, 135–36, 137, 140, 145, 152, 176, 236
*Vue de Holland* (Manet), 44
Vuillard, Edouard, 200

*Where Do We Come From? What Are We? Where Are We Going?* (Gauguin), 211, 226–27, 226–27, 229, 248, 250–51
Willumsen, J. F., 128, 130, 160, 164
*Wine Harvest at Arles, The* (Gauguin), 120, 120, 134, 135, 140, 141, 225
*Woman Sewing* (Gauguin), 43, 103
*Woman with Chrysanthemums* (Gauguin), 96
*Woman with Fan* (Gauguin), 243, 245
*Woodcutter of Pia* (Gauguin), 184
Wrestling, 16

*Yellow Christ, The* (Gauguin), 139
*Young Bretons Bathing* (Gauguin), 104

Zandomeneghi, Federico, 53
Zola, Emile, 32–33, 57, 165; *L'Argent*, 48

## Photo Credits